Better Policing
with
Microsoft Office
2007

Better Policing
with
Microsoft Office 2007

CRIME ANALYSIS, INVESTIGATIONS, AND COMMUNITY POLICING

Christopher W. Bruce

Mark A. Stallo, Ph.D.

A.C.T. Now, Inc.
EXCELLENCE IN TRAINING

Southlake, Texas

Analysis, Consulting & Training Now, Inc.
1005 South Hollow
Southlake, Texas 76092
www.actnowinc.org

15 14 13 12 11 10 09 08   1 2 3 4 5 6 7

ISBN 1-4392-5328-5

Library of Congress Control Number 2009908101

Screen shots taken with SPX Instant Screen Capture 5.0 from MOODYSOFT
Documents on Pages 251-254 copyright Sergeant Robert Newton, Dallas Police Department

Printed in the United States of America
By BookSurge
North Charleston, SC

CONTENTS

ACKNOWLEDGEMENTS

To the extent that either of us are experts, or even quasi-experts, in these Microsoft Office applications, it is because of the many people from whom we have learned over the years, including the many colleagues who have asked challenging questions.

Mark would like to thank the many students who have attended his classes at Midwestern State, The University of North Texas, Tiffin University and the seminars that he has taught.

Chris would like to particularly thank Michelle Arneson, Trina Cook, Carol Fitzgerald, Kim Hathaway, Kim McMahon, Debra Piehl, Lorie Velarde, and Andrea Vey. You have all written to me with various, and increasingly complex, Office questions over the years, and although you thought it was me helping you, you were really helping me by forcing me to expand my Office knowledge so I could answer your questions and amaze you. Bryan Hill: you are my superior in Access skill, and I thank you for the knowledge you have imparted over the years.

Both authors thank the Executive Boards (past and present) of the International Association of Crime Analysts (IACA). Mark has had the pleasure of collaborating with this professional group since its inception in 1990, and Chris has worked with them since 1997. We will always be grateful for your volunteerism and willingness to share ideas to enhance the profession of crime analysis all over the world.

To our students, all of you who have attended seminars or college classes under our tutelage: your questions are the reason this book exists. Your perseverance has inspired us to update this work and to continue to fulfill our goal of providing good and timely training to the law enforcement community.

INTRODUCTION

The Capabilities You Didn't Know You Had

L IKE MOST OTHER PROFESSIONS, LAW ENFORCEMENT HAS THE potential to benefit greatly from the Information Age. When resources are scarce (as they usually are), when demand for service is high (as it usually is), and when citizens demand more from their police agencies (which they usually do), the only way for police departments to achieve their growing missions is to *increase efficiency*.

Increasing efficiency means doing more with less. It means cutting down on wasted resources and maximizing the productivity of those remaining. It means never spending an hour doing something that can be done in a minute, and never spending a minute on something that can be done in a second. Finally, it means doing everything you already do *better*. Usually, technology offers the best solutions to meet these goals.

For example, how would you like to:

- Within one minute, get a breakdown of all crimes that have occurred in your jurisdiction, by year, for the last five years. In another minute, determine whether each crime is going up or down.

- In three minutes, get a list of all nighttime robberies that have occurred at convenience stores in the past three years in which there were two suspects wearing masks who displayed a handgun.

- In five minutes, create a line chart showing calls for service for the past 10 years that projects the current rate of growth for another 10 years in the future.

- Design a quick, easy-to-use application for the Community Policing Unit to use to store bicycle registrations for a new grant program.

- Create an annual report as attractive and professional as one produced by a Fortune 500 company.

- Create a form letter alerting residents to a new police service. Within an hour, print 1000 letters, each with a customized address and personal salutation, as well as 1000 mailing labels.

- Print quick reports of all crimes with similar characteristics so that you can assign them all to the same investigator.

- In two hours, design 20 slides for a one-hour presentation—complete with graphs, photographs, and statistics—to the City Council supporting your budget request for the next fiscal year.

- Every day, arrive at work knowing your top priorities and schedule.

- Have at your fingertips a searchable list, with full contact information, of everyone you've ever met or spoken to.

Ready for the good news? All the technology that you need to accomplish these things is in five computer applications. And chances are, you already have them.

 Microsoft Access is a relational database program that allows you to enter, store, manage, query, and report data on anything important to you: crime, calls for service, known offenders, gun permits, restraining orders, traffic accidents, vehicles, bicycle registrations…the list doesn't end.

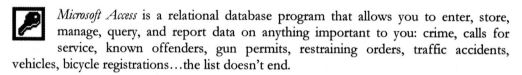 *Microsoft Excel* is a spreadsheet program that allows you to track, sort, aggregate, disaggregate, summarize, and perform advanced calculations on statistical data.

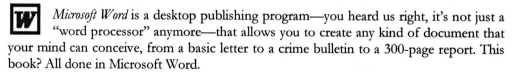 *Microsoft Word* is a desktop publishing program—you heard us right, it's not just a "word processor" anymore—that allows you to create any kind of document that your mind can conceive, from a basic letter to a crime bulletin to a 300-page report. This book? All done in Microsoft Word.

 Microsoft PowerPoint is powerful presentation software that allows you to create slides for an in-person or online show.

 Microsoft Outlook is an all-in-one personal management packages that lets you manage your tasks and priorities, contacts, schedule, and e-mail.

Collectively, these programs (and a few others) are known as *Microsoft Office*. There are several different "versions" of Office that have various combinations of these packages. Most computer companies offer a "default" installation of one of the Office versions. It is rare indeed to find an office computer without Word, Excel, PowerPoint, and Outlook. Access—part of Microsoft Office Professional—is a bit more rare, but we'd bet that at least half of the people picking up this book have the program on their computers, even if they don't know it. If for some reason your computer *doesn't* have Office, chances are your agency or municipality has licenses. And if for some reason they don't, a single-user license of Office Professional currently costs around $400; government agencies can usually get it for less.

Why Microsoft Office? Why not WordPerfect? Why not OpenOffice? There are several reasons we're writing this book about Office instead of one of several other packages that do similar things:

1. *Microsoft has market dominance.* Most people use Office when performing word processing, spreadsheet, and presentation tasks—around 90% in the United States, in both law enforcement and other sectors.

2. *More training, web support, and technical support.* Because Microsoft has market dominance, there is more training and literature available to help you (although, curiously, there haven't been many books focused specifically on law enforcement; that's why we wrote this one).

3. *Easy-to-use and integrated.* In our opinion, Microsoft packages are easier to use that those made by competitors. More important, Microsoft applications are part of the Office "suite"—they all work together. You can easily copy an Excel chart into PowerPoint, export an Access query into Excel, and so on.

4. *Again, you probably already have it.* There's no new software to buy.

Progressive Policing with Crime Analysis

The subtitle to our book mentions crime analysis, and many of the lessons and examples in this book are of benefit primarily to crime analysts. Both of us come from crime analysis backgrounds and have served on the Board of the International Association of Crime Analysts. Crime analysis is very important to us and, for the benefit of readers who may not have a crime analysis program in their agencies, we want to take a moment to explain what it is.

Crime analysis is a police profession dedicated to helping police do their jobs better by providing *information*. By collecting and analyzing data from police reports, other agencies, demographic databases, intelligence files, and numerous other sources, analysts produce information on patterns, trends, and problems that help police solve crimes, develop effective tactics and strategies, find and apprehend offenders, optimize internal operations, allocate resources, and otherwise improve the safety and quality of life of the citizens they serve.

Crime analysis is almost 50 years old, and it was done long before the advent of modern technology. But technology, including Microsoft Office, has made it much, much easier. Today, most of the computer-based work done by crime analysts can be done within Microsoft Office and a Geographic Information System (GIS). We both began in the profession before our agencies had computers, and we can remember creating bulletins with typewriters and drafting tables, tracking patterns in paper matrices, figuring averages and standard deviations with a calculator, giving presentations with handouts and whiteboards, keeping our "to do" list on a pad supplied by the local hardware store, and creating crime maps by sticking pins or colored dots on paper maps hanging on the wall. Would we go back to doing it that way? Not in a million years.

The time that we save with Microsoft Office allows us to put out more products, better products, and in-depth products. The four hours we might have spent shuffling through paper reports to identify a crime pattern is now done in 10 minutes with Microsoft Access. The other three hours, fifty minutes we can devote to *analyzing* the pattern, including many qualitative, problem-oriented techniques that we just didn't have time to consider before. It also means that we can analyze *more* crimes—no more list of six "target crimes" for our agencies; if there's a pattern of noise complaints, skateboarding problems, or "snow rage," we'll find it.

If you want to learn more about crime analysis, we would direct you to *Exploring Crime Analysis: Readings on Essential Skills*, second edition, published by the International Association of Crime Analysts in 2009 and available through our publisher, BookSurge (www.booksurge.com) and other booksellers. We also highly recommend joining the IACA and attending its conferences for training, networking, and certification.

What's New in Office 2007?

In its 2007 edition of Office, Microsoft introduced a number of changes that continue to flummox even experienced users. These are some of the most important. At the beginning of each chapter, after the chapter's introduction, we discuss specific changes to each application.

The Ribbon

Office 2007 radically re-designs the interfaces to which we've become accustomed over the last 15 years. Instead of menus and menu commands, supplemented with toolbars and buttons, Office 2007 combines menus and buttons into a macro interface called the "ribbon." The ribbon is organized in a series of "tabs," specific to each application, on which rest a number of command groups and their associated buttons. Microsoft claims that associated commands are now closer together, allowing for easier access. This is potentially true, but it will take users a while to forget all of the old menu command trees and adapt to the ribbon. And unless you choose the "Minimize the Ribbon" option, it takes up an awful lot of space.

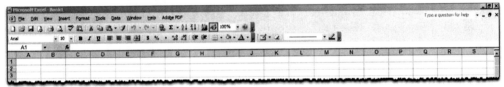

Figure I-1: Excel 2003 menus and toolbars…

Figure I-2: …versus the Excel 2007 ribbon

Contextual Tabs

Office 2007 does a good job of showing commands only when you need them. For instance instead of a "Picture" toolbar, always visible even when you weren't working with a picture, Word 2007 adds a "Picture Tools" tab to the ribbon every time you select a picture in your document. Double-click on the picture, and that ribbon becomes active. Click off the picture, and the tab disappears.

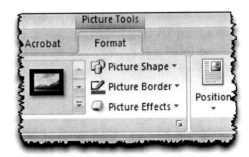

Figure I-2: a contextual tab

The Office Button

 Each Office application features an "Office Button" in the upper left-hand corner. Beneath it are most of the commands that used to appear on the "File" menu, including "Open," "Save," "Save As," "Print," "Close," the list of recently-used files, and the documents properties. The Office Button also holds the "Options" commands that used to be under the "Tools" menu of each application.

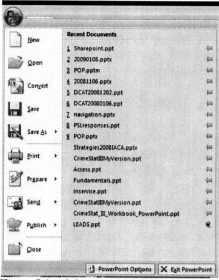

Figure I-3: clicking on the Office Button in PowerPoint

Help

Office's considerable help features are hidden behind a very small button on the far right-hand side of the ribbon: , but the quantity and quality of the content is, in general, greatly improved. Contextual help has been expanded throughout the Office universe. The "Office Assistant" is gone.

One Customizable Toolbar

Each application has a "Quick Access Toolbar" that you can set to appear at the top or bottom of the ribbon. Users can add their most commonly-used commands to this toolbar by simply right-clicking on them.

Figure I-4: our Quick Access toolbar in Excel, at the bottom of the ribbon for easier access

Global Spell-Checker

Changes made to the spell-checker in one program (for instance, by adding proper names) permeate to other Office applications.

The View Bar

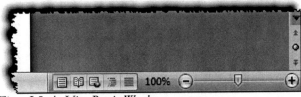

Excel, PowerPoint, and Word all feature a "View Bar" in the lower right-hand corner of the screen. It allows you to switch between the different views for your document and adjust the zoom

Figure I-5: the View Bar in Word

using a slider. As such, it replaces some of the commands previously under the "View" menus. Access does not allow zooming but it does have the other view options.

New File Extensions

Microsoft has replaced its long-used three-letter extensions (.doc, .xls, .ppt, and .mdb) with new Office 2007 extensions: .docx for a Word document, .xlsx for an Excel workbook, .pptx for a PowerPoint presentation, and .accdb for an Access database. The change represents more than just additional letters. Files are automatically compressed, resulting in significant space savings; security features are embedded; and Microsoft claims that the 2007 files are less likely to become corrupt.

Office 2007 will still open documents created in previous versions of Office (in "compatibility mode,") and you can still use these indefinitely, although some features won't be available.

Getting the Most out of the Lessons in this Book

THE HEART OF *BETTER POLICING WITH MICROSOFT OFFICE* 2007 IS A series of lessons that take you through common tasks performed every day in police agencies around the world. Interspersed with these lessons is text that explains the various features, functions, and pitfalls of the various Office applications. These instructions will orient you with the conventions that we use throughout the lessons.

A Note on Versions

The lessons and screen shots in this book were created with Microsoft Office 2007, which is very different from its predecessors in both style and functionality. Users of previous versions of Office simply will not be able to follow along with this book's lessons. If you're using Microsoft Office 2000, 2002, or 2003, we recommend our original *Better Policing with Microsoft Office* until you make the switch.

Working with the Sample Files

For some of the lessons in this book, you will create your own files from scratch. But for many, we instruct you to use a series of files that we have provided at

http://www.actnowinc.org/2007downloads.html

The files are all loaded into a .zip file called **bpoffice.zip**. Download this file to your computer and use WinZip or Windows Explorer to extract it directly to your C: drive. (It should create a folder called "BPOffice.")

If you want to put them in a different folder, you can—but make sure you mentally adjust all of the instructions in this book to point to your chosen folder, instead of C:\BPOffice.

If you have any problems downloading, installing, or using the files, write to

techsupport@actnowinc.org

We will be happy to assist you.

Multiple Ways to Do Anything in Microsoft Office

Before we begin, we should note that there are usually multiple ways to perform any command or task in any of the Microsoft Office applications:

1. A *ribbon button*, found in the ribbons at the top of the screen ("Home," "Insert," "Page Layout," etc., in Word). In the instructions, you will find ribbon commands in **bold Tahoma font**. The syntax is **Contextual Tab | Tab | Group | Command.** (Some commands will not have a contextual tab.) So if we want you to go to the "Position" button in Figure I-6, we'll represent it as **Picture Tools | Format | Arrange | Position.**

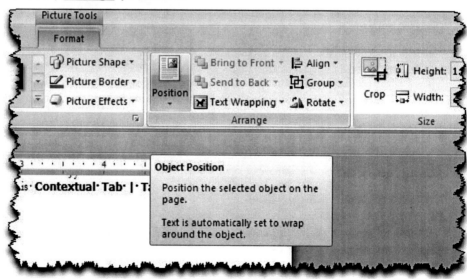

Figure I-6: a ribbon button

2. A *keyboard shortcut*, usually the **CTRL** key and at least one other key. We will annotate these in **bold Tahoma font** with a dash between the keys that you have to hit together. For instance, **CTRL-O** means hold down the "CTRL" key and hit "O" at the same time. **CTRL-SHIFT-K** means to hold down the "CTRL" and "SHIFT" keys and then hit "K" at the same time.

3. A *contextual menu* command, obtained by right-clicking (clicking with the right mouse button) on something, then choosing an option from the "pop-up menu" that appears. When we want you to use a contextual menu, we will spell it out for you: "Right-click on the selected text and choose **Copy**."

4. A *Quick Access toolbar tool*. Each Office Application comes with a "Quick Access Toolbar," which sits at the top of the screen (to the right of the Office Button) by default. You can add commonly-used and hard-to-find commands to this toolbar simply by right-clicking on them and choosing "Add to Quick Access Toolbar." By right-clicking on the Quick Access Toolbar and choosing "Customize," you can arrange your tools and add separators. In general, we will not use the Quick Access toolbar because they're personalized for each user.

For instance, if we want to copy some text to the clipboard in Word (to later paste in another application), we can:

1. Select the text and choose **Home | Clipboard | Copy**.

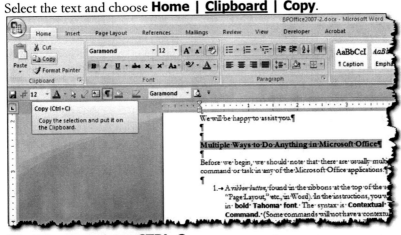

2. Select the text and type **CTRL-C**.
3. Right-click on the selected text and choose "Copy."

In Access there are at least eleven ways to switch from Design View to Datasheet View in a select query:

1. Use **Query Tools | Design | <u>Results</u> | View**
2. Use **Query Tools | Design | <u>Results</u> | Run**
3. Use **Home | <u>Views</u> | View**
4. Double-click on the name of the query in the Navigation Pane
5. Right-click on the name of the query in the Navigation Pane and choose "Open"
6. Right-click on the tab at the top of the query and choose "Datasheet View"
7. Right-click in the blank part of the design grid and choose "Datasheet View"
8. Type **CTRL-.** (period)
9. Type **ALT-H-W-H**
10. Type **ALT-R-W-H**
11. Type **ALT-R-G**

The multiple ways to perform the same task may seem confusing at first, but it's actually a big bonus. Users can adapt their tasks to their own particular styles and preferences. Visually-oriented users may want to depend heavily on the ribbons. Those who can memorize keyboard shortcuts will find their work proceeds much faster. Contextual menus offer the most common functions for each part of the application. Users who have trouble remembering where commands are may want to create custom Quick Access Toolbars.

In the instructions, we will generally use the ribbon commands and occasionally keyboard shortcuts and contextual menus, but feel free to use whatever method works best for you. If we say "choose **Home | <u>Clipboard</u> | Copy**" but you feel like hitting **CTRL-C**, go ahead. You won't break anything.

Navigating Directories

To save space, we do not include screen shots showing you how to open or save a file. Instead, we give directions like "Open the file at **C:\BPOffice\Word\example.docx**" or "Save the file to **C:\BPOffice\Excel\crime.xlsx**."

These paths refer to the directory structure used by Microsoft Windows to store and manage files. **C:\BPOffice\Word** is the "Word" folder in the "BPOffice" folder on the C: drive (the letter used for the primary hard drive of most computers).

Dialog boxes to open and save files look similar. The top of the box has a drop-down list titled "Look in" or "Save in" (depending on whether you're opening or saving). By clicking on this drop-down menu, you can choose the file path of the document you're trying to open or save. To open or save something at **C:\BPOffice\Word**, choose the C:

drive from the drop-down menu, double-click on the folder called "BPOffice" and then double-click on the folder called "Word" (see Figure I-9).

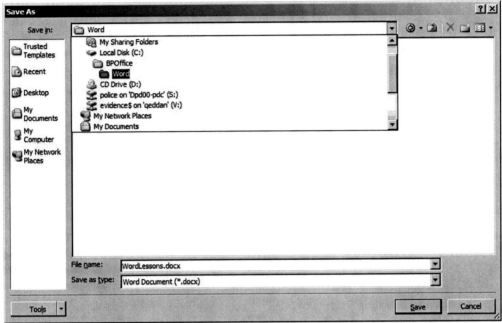

Figure I-9: saving a document as "WordLessons.docx" at **C:\BPOffice\Word**

Toward the bottom of the "Open" or "Save" dialog box is a field titled "File name." Generally, you will not use this field when opening a file, only when saving. It is in this field that you type the name of the document you're saving. The *type* of the file you're saving is set in the bottom box, titled "Save as type" ("Files of type" in the "Open" dialog). By default, the file type will be the one primarily used by the application: a Word file in Microsoft Word; an Excel Workbook in Microsoft Excel, and so on. By changing this file type, you can import or export files in a different format.

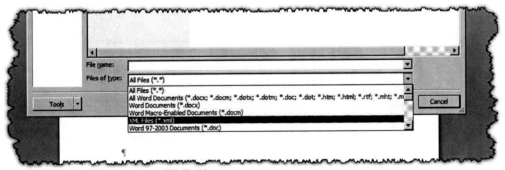

Figure I-10: telling Word to open an XML file

Getting Help

Confused? Here are some ways to get assistance:

- General help is available with the "Help" button on the far right side of the ribbon bar. It looks the same in all Office applications: 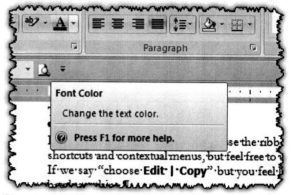. It opens a mini browser that downloads help content from Microsoft online. If you're not online, it accesses help content existing on your computer.

- If you're not sure what a ribbon command does, hover your cursor over it for a couple of seconds, and a pop-up box will open, providing a brief description. The box will also list its keyboard shortcut, if it exists.

Figure I-11: hovering over the "Font Color" command in Word

- If the pop-up box isn't enough, simply type **F1** while hovering over the button. The "Help" window will open to a topic that addresses that particular command.

- You can also try hitting the **F1** key when it a particular field or dialog box. This usually brings up contextual help for that particular option.

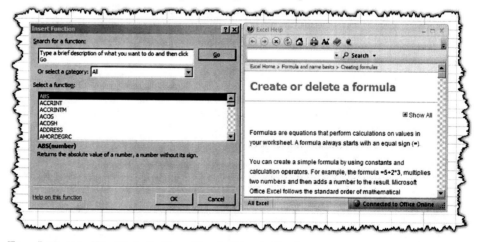

Figure I-12: typing F1 while in the "Insert Function" box in Excel

- Finally, we highly recommend the Microsoft Knowledge Base. This is an online collection of articles on each of Microsoft's applications. We rarely encounter a conundrum that we can't solve through a keyword search of the Knowledge Base. You can search it at **http://www.support.microsoft.com**.

CHAPTER 1

Microsoft Access

MICROSOFT ACCESS IS A POWERFUL RELATIONAL DATABASE development tool. It is the most widely used desktop database application in the world. Now in its eighth version (Access 2007), Access was first released in 1992. Though somewhat limited in its capabilities when compared to recent versions, Access 1.0 revolutionized data management for many businesses and public agencies.

The power of Access derives from its integration of fairly easy-to-use database development *and* application development tools. Any database application, such as your records management or CAD system, requires two components: a database in which to store information and an application with which to enter, query, and search that data. Commercial systems are created with some combination of these two components—for instance, an Oracle database accessed through a C++ application (or "front end"); or a SQL Server database underneath an application written in Visual Basic.

Access is not designed to compete with either these more powerful database servers or these more robust programming languages. It instead offers a more simple solution for the professional who is trained and experienced in neither database server management nor application programming. With Access, the average person can develop a database and create forms, queries, and reports to enter, search, and display information. Many crime analysts use Microsoft Access to track crimes, offenders, and other information; or to create a "front end" for their antiquated, complicated, or otherwise inefficient records management systems.

Access has two primary uses for police agencies:

1. *To track and manage data* about anything that for which the agency does not already have an application, or for which the agency has an inadequate application. If you do not have a full records management system (RMS), you may need an Access database to track arrests, citations, traffic accidents, known criminals, firearms licenses, sex offenders,

Neighborhood Watch members, grants, department inventory, known graffiti tags, and a host of other things. Some agencies even use Access as their primary RMS.

2. *To query and report on large datasets* received from other agencies or systems. Agencies may want to use Access to ask more flexible questions about data in their RMSes, to make sense of a large parole file received from the state's Department of Corrections, to organize data in a warrant file, to translate and merge data from incompatible RMSes or computer-aided dispatch (CAD) systems, and many other things that would take pages to itemize.

Let's look at a couple of examples. Figure A-1 shows an entry form from a database used by the Brookline (MA) Police Department to enter and manage motor vehicle citation records. Figure A-2 looks at a database used by the Lowell (MA) Police Department to track pawn data—both property and pawners. Figure A-3 shows how some California agencies are managing the enormous parolee data dumps received from the Department of Corrections. Figure A-4 is an example of a crosstab query that summarizes tens of thousands of crime data records from the Danvers (MA) Police Department's records management system. Finally, Figure A-5 shows how the Shawnee (KS) Police Department uses an Access report to create a weekly Arrest Report.

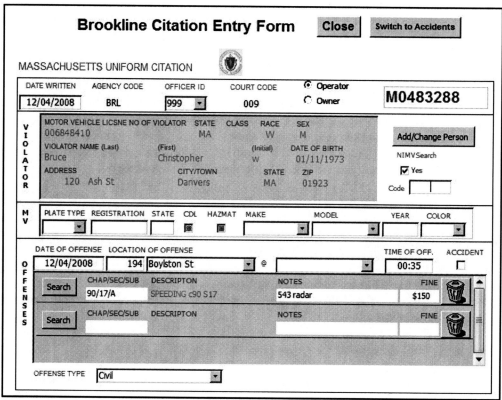

Figure A-1: the Brookline (MA) Citation Database.

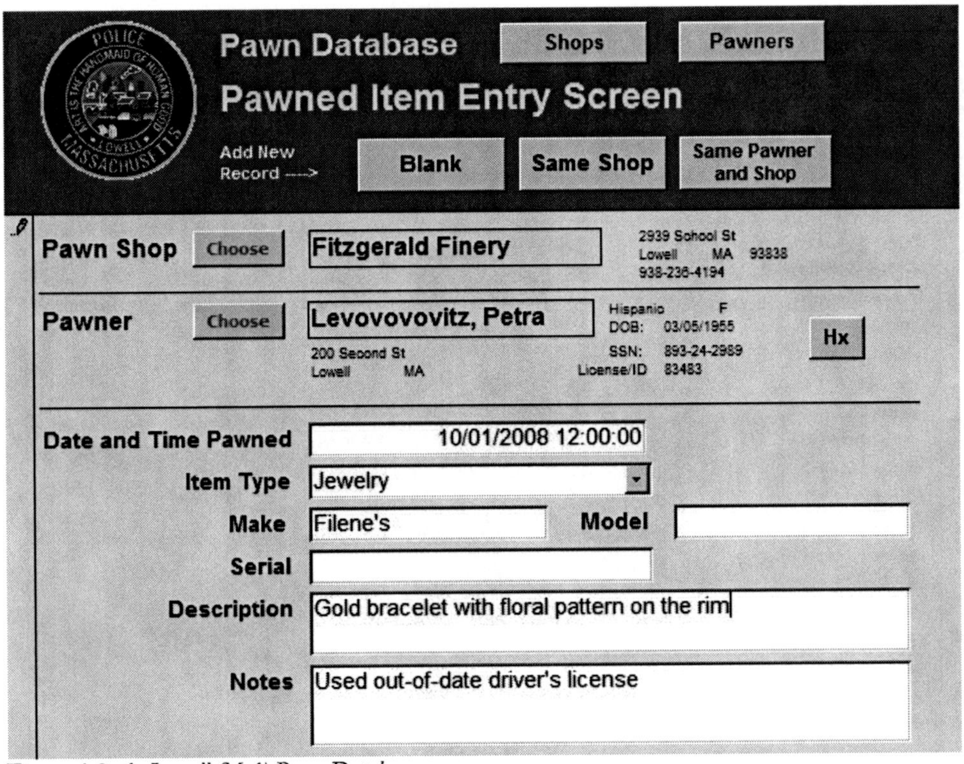

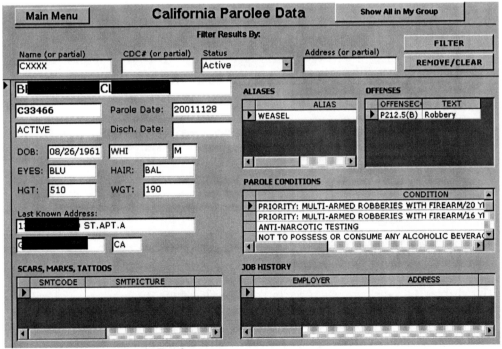

Figure A-2: the Lowell (MA) Pawn Database.

Figure A-3: the California Parolee Database.

IncidentType	2000	2001	2002	2003	2004	2005	2006	2007	2008
Murder		1					1		
Rape		1	1	2		1		1	1
Indecent Assault					1				
Accosting			1			1			
Nonforcible Sex Offens			1	2			1		2
Peeping & Spying				1	1				
Aggravated Assault	23	33	22	18	18	21	23	14	16
Simple Assault	52	59	51	87	75	65	68	66	67
Robbery	2	6		5	3	7	2	3	
Kidnapping				2					
Threats	8	7	12	9	13	5	4	4	4
Bomb Threat							1		
Violation of RO	6	9	13	11	10	5	9	6	5
Housebreak		11	4	5	8	3	2	3	1
Commercial Break	4	3	3	1	9	1	6		1
Larceny from MV	8	7	12	10	8	2	11	15	
Larceny from Building	3	5	3	3	1	4	8	2	
Larceny from Person	1	1		2		3	6	1	
Larceny from Residenc	2	2		1	6	1	7		
Larceny of Bicycle						2	1	1	
Larceny of Services	2	2	1	1	2				

Figure A-4: crimes in Danvers (MA) by year (first half only).

Figure A-5: the Shawnee (KS) weekly arrest report.

This chapter is divided into two parts. In Part 1, we'll create a database to track local gangs and those members associated with them. This will draw upon our abilities to create tables and forms, design macros, and lay out reports. In Part 2, we apply Access's considerable querying capabilities to a large database of crimes that we will import.

What's New in Access 2007?

These are some of the new features, good and bad, in Access 2007:

- As with all of the Office 2007 applications, Microsoft has replaced menus and toolbars with the "ribbon" interface at the top of the screen.

- There's a new "Access 2007" database format: ACCDB. Although Access 2007 supports backwards compatibility with MDB files, some of the new features are only available if you use an ACCDB format.

- The main database window has been replaced with a "navigation pane" on the left-hand side, resulting in two benefits and a drawback. The benefits are that you don't have to constantly minimize windows to switch between different Access objects, and that you can drag items from the task pane on top of open objects, to (for instance) quickly add a sub-form to a form, or quickly add a new data table to a query. The drawback is that if you have a lot of objects in your database, it's more difficult to find them because you have less screen space to list them. A new search bar helps mitigate this.

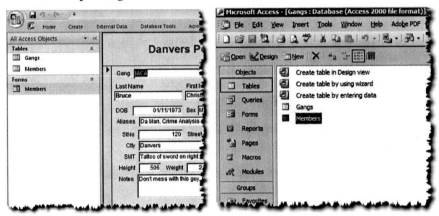

Figure A-6: the new "navigation pane" interface (left) versus the old database window (right)

- Memo fields now support rich text formatting. You can add bolding, text formatting, and other features to your memos.

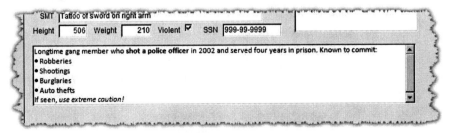

Figure A-7: you can now add rich text formatting to memo fields

- Data Access Pages have disappeared in Access 2007. No one really ever used them in previous versions.

- You can add attachments to data records that go far beyond the old OLE objects in their capabilities, including the ability to add multiple attachments to each record.

- Reports are now interactive. With the Report view, you can filter report results, click on hyperlinks, and do a number of other things previously unavailable in the old Print Preview view.

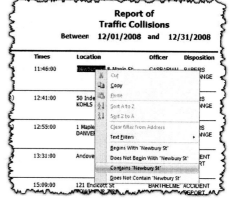

- Forms and reports have a new "Layout View" that's sort-of half-way between Design View and Report/Form View, allowing you to make basic design changes while still seeing your data.

Figure A-8: filtering data in a report

- There are a host of new security features to protect you from malicious coding in databases. You will generally find yourself disabling all of these features so that you can actually get your databases to work.

- There are a host of database templates that can speed up the database development process, if you need that kind of thing.

- Forms and reports automatically created in Access are much more attractive than they were in previous versions.

- Access no longer offers user-level security in .accdb files, although it will still support security in .mdb files.

- There are some changes to macros. A new "Arguments" column allows you to see the arguments associated with each macro action, so you don't have to click on the action and look at the bottom of the screen. Certain actions are hidden by

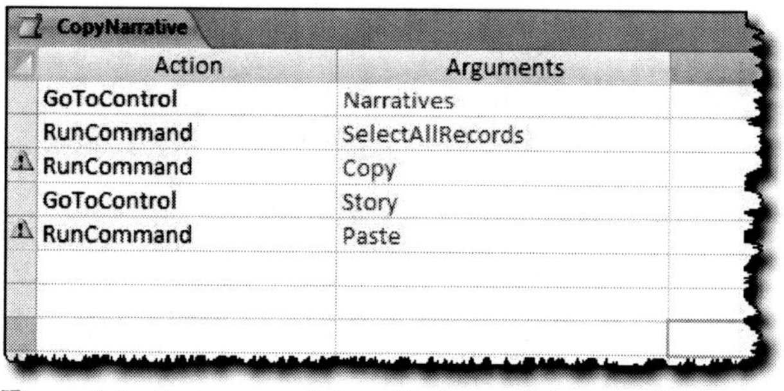

Figure A-9: Access macro design with the new "Arguments" column

default (for security purposes), and you have to choose "Show All Actions" to view them. Finally, Access now supports "embedded macros" that live within forms and reports, making certain macros easier to manage.

Creating a Database and Setting Up for Use

To follow the lessons in this book, take the following steps to set up Access on your computer.

»**Step 1:** Launch Microsoft Access 2007

The launch window has links to a bunch of templates, plus articles and resources from Microsoft Online.

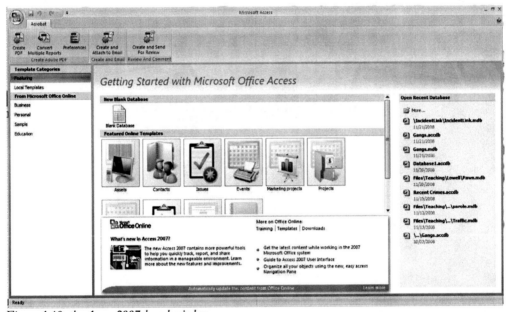

Figure A-10: the Access 2007 launch window

»**Step 2:** Click on "Blank Database" towards the top of the window.

»**Step 3:** In the lower right, click on the 📁 icon to select your folder. Save your database as C:\BPOffice\Access\gangs.accdb

»**Step 4:** Click "Create."

Your new database opens with a new table in Datasheet view. We'll leave that alone for a minute.

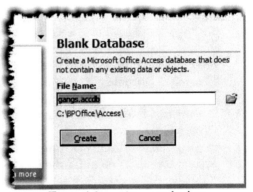

Figure A-9: creating a new database

»**Step 5:** Right-click in the navigation pane to the left and choose "Search Bar." Get in the habit of turning on your search bar for all your databases.

»**Step 6:** Click on the "Office Button" in the upper left 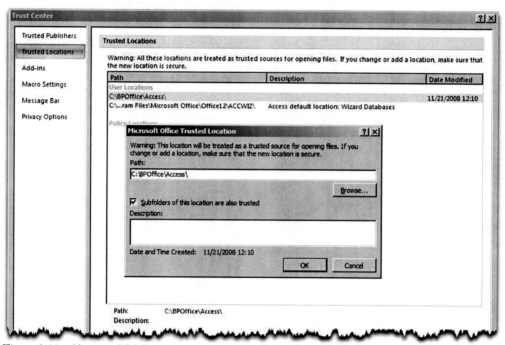and choose "Access options." Click on "Trust Center," "Trust Center Settings," and "Trusted Locations." Click "Add New Location" at the bottom and add **C:\BPOffice** as a trusted location. Check the box that says "Subfolders of this location are also trusted." You may also want to add other locations to which you save Access files you know are safe. Click "OK" when finished.

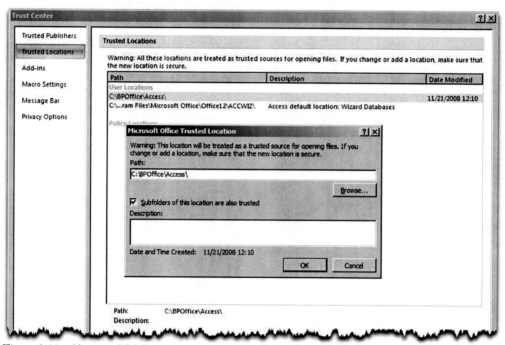

Figure A-11: adding your BPOffice folder as a "trusted location" so that macros work.

»**Step 7:** While you're still in "Access Options," click on "Current Database." Under the "Application options" section, find the "Document Window Options" group and change the selection from "Overlapping Windows" to "Tabbed Documents." Make sure the box that reads "Display Document Tabs" is checked. This will make it easier to navigate among multiple open Access objects. When finished, "OK" out of Access options.

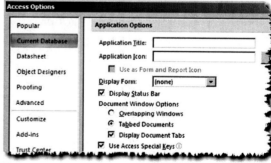

Figure A-12: setting document window options

»**Step 8:** Right-click on the Quick Access Toolbar, above the ribbon and to the right of the "Office" button (yours will have different tools than Figure A-13), and choose "Show Quick Access Toolbar Below the Ribbon." It's easier to access there.

Figure A-13: moving your Quick Access Toolbar.

File Formats

By default, Access 2007 saves databases in Access 2007 file format (ACCDB). This format enables many of the new features of Access 2007, like rich text formatting and file attachments. However, users of earlier versions of Access will not be able to open the database. In Access 2007, you can also save databases in Access 2000 and Access 2002–2003 formats, and Access 2007 has no trouble reading databases in those earlier formats.

You can convert a database from one format to another by going to **Office Button | Convert**. You can change the default file format from Access 2007 to Access 2002–2003 or Access 2000 (or back again) at **Office Button | Access Options | Popular**.

Users of Access 95 and Access 97 cannot share databases with each other or with users of Access 2000, 2002, 2003, or 2007.

The Parts of Access

We will be creating objects of several types during our Access lessons.

- *Tables* are where data is stored. The table is the fundamental unit of a database; it isn't a "database" without at least one.

- *Queries* allow you to ask questions—very complicated questions—about the data stored in your tables. Special types of queries allow you to add, change, and delete data in your tables.

- *Forms* provide an interface for your database. With them, you can display, browse, and enter data, and provide screens for users to choose options and conduct searches.

- *Reports* offer you an effective way to present data in a printed format. Data that is displayed in a report comes from an underlying table our query.

- *Macros* allow you to automate certain tasks by programming a set of one or more actions that produce a certain result. For instance, a button marked "Print Report" on a form might run a macro that prints a report to the default printer

- *Modules* are collections of visual scripts that allow you to add Visual Basic for Applications (VBA) programming directly into your database

In this chapter, we'll perform several lessons with tables, queries, forms, macros, and reports. Modules are advanced features that we'll leave you to explore in books devoted exclusively to VBA programming.

Creating a Table

As we noted before, tables are the most fundamental unit of an Access database. A "database" does not exist without a table. Tables can be created in Access, linked from other databases, or imported from a variety of different file types (we cover importing and linking in the second part of this chapter).

Tables store data in *fields* (represented by columns) and *records* (represented by rows). When you create a table, you specify the fields it contains, as well as the types of data that are stored in those fields, and any parameters or restrictions for that data.

We begin our Gangs database by creating two tables: one to track gangs, the other to track their members.

»**Step 9:** You're already in the Datasheet view of a new table. (If you left after Step 8, reopen your database and choose **Create | Tables | Table.**) Switch to Design view by clicking on **Home | Views | View.**

»**Step 10:** Save the table as "Gangs"

You will be presented with a table design grid with "ID" already entered as the first field. The top part of the grid allows you to specify the fields and field types in your table; the bottom part allows you to specify the properties for each of those fields.

The **Field Name** can be up to 64 characters long, and can include spaces. However, you make it easier on yourself later (when developing expressions in queries and macros) if you keep the name as short as possible (while still being meaningful) and omit spaces (e.g., "GangName" instead of "Name of Gang").

The **Data Type** specifies what you'll be storing in that field. There are 10 data types, as shown in Table A-1.

Data Type	What is Stored?	Examples	Notes
Text	Up to 255 characters—letters, numbers, or both	Last Name Street Name License Plate	See "Memo" and "Number" below
Memo	Up to 63,999 characters—letters, numbers, or both	Narratives Stories Statements	Use Text fields when possible—memo fields balloon the size of a database
Number	Any numbers, including decimals	Address Number Quantity of Property Model Year of Car	Numbers can be stored as text, but always store them as numbers if you intend to calculate or sort by those fields
Date/Time	Dates and times	Date and Time of Report Date of Birth	Available formats (including number of digits in the year) depend on settings in the "Regional and Language Options" control panel
Currency	Currency values	Value of Property Stolen Fine for MV Citation	Currency formats available depend on the Windows "Regional and Language Options" control panel
AutoNumber	An automatically-generated number, sequential or random	Index Number	Used as the Primary Key (see below) when no other option is available
Yes/No	A binary value: yes or no, true or false, on or off, etc.	Domestic Crime? Arrest Made? Person Injured?	Good when there are only two options; usually represented by a check box
OLE Object	A picture or file from another application	Photograph Sound Sample	OLE stands for "Object Linking and Embedding," a Microsoft protocol. Objects can be linked or embedded (stored within the Access database).
Hyperlink	A file path or Internet path, with a maximum of 2048 characters	Web site File location	Has three components: the text to display, the address, and the "tool tip" text
Attachment	Images, documents, charts, and many other supported file types	Wanted posters Criminal histories Crime scene photos	Offers more flexibility in setup than OLE objects

Table A-1: available Access data types

The **Description** field is optional. You can use it to help document your database, in case someone later needs to understand the purpose of a particular field.

»**Step 11:** Continue by filling in your table design view as in Figure A-14. Do not worry about the "Field Properties" (the lower part of the screen) for now.

The last thing to do before we save is to create the **Primary Key**. The Primary Key is the main identifying field for each record. It is the one field that is unique for each record, and it must always have something in it. Which field to choose as the Primary Key depends on the nature of the data in your database. In a table of persons, the "Name" field would not serve as the primary key, because two people might have the same name. The Social Security Number would work, but only if you were sure you would always have it.

Primary Keys—or unique identifiers—abound in modern society. Every vehicle has a VIN (Vehicle Identification Number). Credit cards and driver's licenses have unique numbers. In most towns, every address is unique. On police reports, there is a unique Incident Number or Case Number, and every arrest contains a Booking Number or OBTN. Every court case has a Docket Number. You get the idea.

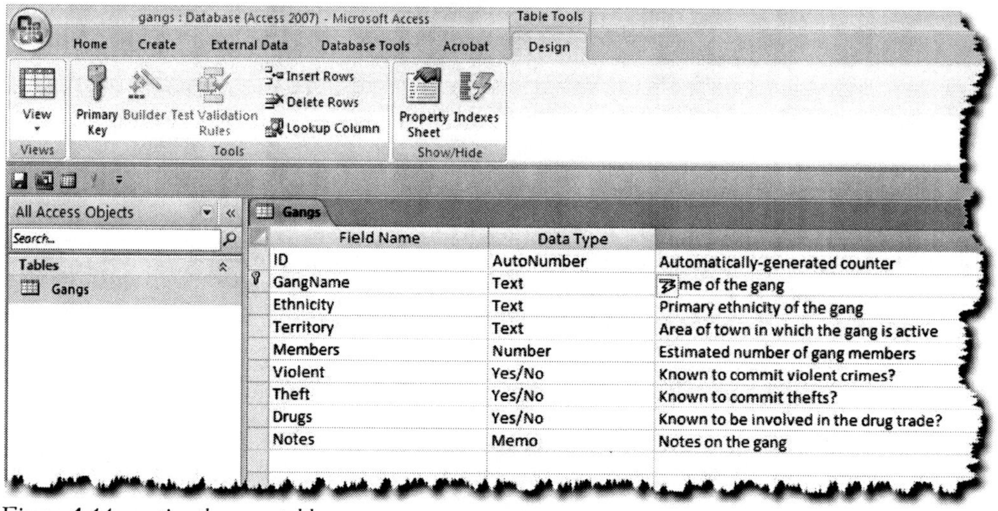

Figure A-14: creating the gangs table

Sometimes, though, there is no obvious field to serve as a primary key for a specific table. Stolen Property is a good example: you cannot be sure of having a unique serial number (or, indeed, any serial number) with every piece of stolen property. In such cases, we might create a table with no primary key, or use an AutoNumber field to generate one. In Access 2007, Access automatically assigns an auto-numbered "ID" field to each tables, as the primary key, by default. You can keep, delete, or change this.

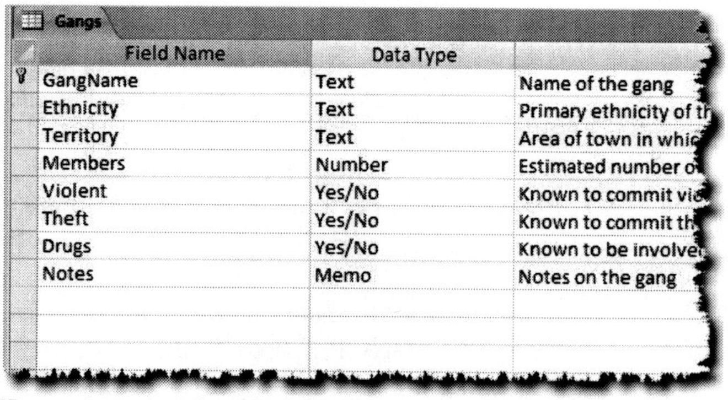

In our "Gangs" table, the Primary Key will be the gang name—no two gangs will share an identical name (at least not in our jurisdiction).

Figure A-15: the "GangName" field is set as the Primary Key

»Step 12: Switch the Primary Key to the gang's name by clicking in the "GangName" field row (anywhere within it—in the "Field Name," "Date Type," or "Description" section) and clicking on **Table Tools | Design | <u>Tools</u> | Primary Key**. Then, select the Access-created "ID" field and use the **Delete** key to get rid of it.

A little "key" icon will appear to the left of the field to indicate that the "GangName" field is the Primary Key (Figure A-15).

Finally, we're ready to save the table and start entering some data.

>**Step 13:** Save the table by hitting **CTRL-S**. You will be prompted to name the table. Name it **Gangs**.

>**Step 14:** Switch to **Datasheet View** by choosing **Home | Views | View**.

Access will switch you to Datasheet View with a blank row, ready for data entry.

This is a good time to point out that Tables, Forms, Queries, and Reports have two main "views": Design View and "display" view. The "display" view for Tables and Queries is called "Datasheet View"; for Forms it's "Form View"; and for Reports it's "Report View." As you might guess, the Design View allows you to change the design of the object, while the "display" view allows you to see the output of your design. (Access 2007 introduced an intermediate view for forms and reports called "Layout View" which serves as a halfway point in between display and design view, allowing you to make some changes to the design while still viewing the data itself.)

You can switch between the different types of views with the **View** button on the **Home** ribbon (also on the various "tools" ribbons), but it can be annoying to have to leave whatever ribbon you're on to go find the **View** button. We recommend adding this button to your Quick Access Toolbar.

>**Step 15:** Find the **View** button on the **Home** ribbon. Right-click on it and choose "Add to Quick Access Toolbar."

The button will change its appearance depending on what view you're already in. When you're in datasheet view, it will look like a carpenter's triangle ![icon], indicating that by clicking on it, you'll go to Design View. When in Design View, it will look like a datasheet ![icon], indicating that by clicking on it, you'll go to datasheet view. Get used to using this button to toggle quickly between the two views. Finally, if you prefer, there is also a "view" section in the lower-right hand corner of your Access window ![icons].

>**Step 16:** Click in the "GangName" field of the blank record and start typing, replicating the two records in Figure A-16 (or making up your own gang data). Use the **TAB** key to move from one field to the next, and use **SHIFT-TAB** if you have to move backwards (e.g., to correct an error).

When you're entering, you can expand the size of columns and rows by clicking and dragging the borders in between them.

While we're entering data, let's talk about **saving in Access**. In Access, the only time that you save something (by **Office Button | Save**, **CTRL-S**, or 💾), is when you want to save the *design* of an object (e.g., a Table design). You do not have to save records or changes to records—Access saves them *automatically* whenever you leave the current record by a) going to another record; b) starting a new record; c) switching to Design View; d) closing the table; or e) quitting Access. This can be perilous: you can't make a bunch of changes to a record and then decide to "quit without saving" because quitting *saves*. If you make changes and don't want to save them, hit the **ESC** key *before* you leave the record. Hitting **ESC** once cancels the last change; hitting it twice cancels all changes to the current record.

ID	GangNam	Ethnici	Territory	Memb	Violen	Theft	Drugs	Notes
1	29 Fevrier Toujours!	French	Little Quebec	30	☐	☑	☑	Little is known about this group of college-aged men except that they host frequent "rave" parties involving Ecstasy, often funded with an extensive check forgery network
2	East Side Hoodlums	Irish	East Side	25	☐	☑	☐	Small, locally-based gang of mostly high school students. Known to commit shoplifting at area merchants. No known enemies. Use red colors and Irish symbology.
*	(New)				☐	☐	☐	

Figure A-16: your first two gang records

You can change the font type, size, color, and background of the data displayed in the table with the various options in **Home | Font**. Except for memo fields set to use Rich Text formatting (more later), font and background changes apply to the entire table. You cannot set different fonts or backgrounds for different fields or records.

Field Properties

Now that we've added a couple of records, let's return to Design View and set some properties for our data.

>**Step 17:** Return to Design View with your Quick Access Toolbar tool 📐 or by going to **Home | Views | View**.

As we saw before, the bottom part of the table design screen shows a list of field **properties**. These properties are specific to each field, and they vary depending on the "Data Type." It's important to understand what each of these properties does. We'll cover them in turn, making changes to our table as we go.

>**Step 18:** Click from field to field and note how the field properties change.

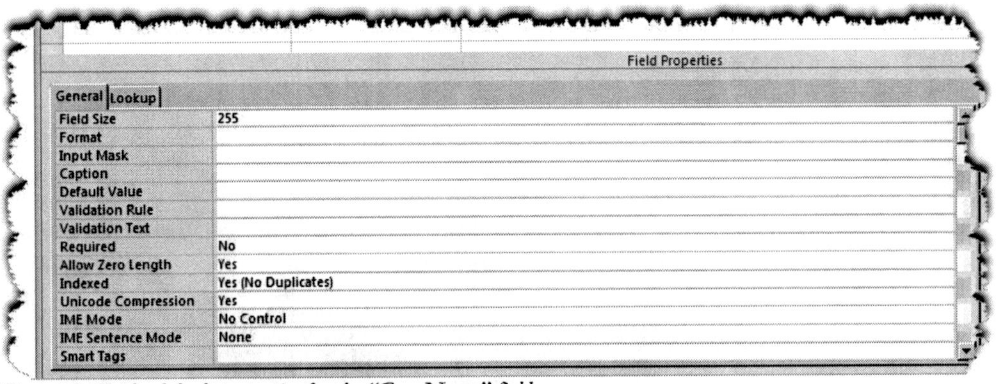

Figure A-17: the default properties for the "GangName" field

Field Size specifies the maximum number of characters (for text fields) or the maximum size of numbers (for number fields). By default, text field sizes are the maximum size: 255 characters. You should set this field size to the shortest possible number that still allows for enough text to be entered—as your database grows, smaller field sizes will keep the file size smaller.

>**Step 19:** Click in the "GangName" field and set the Field Size to 25. Click in the "Ethnicity" field and set the Field Size to 20. Click in the "Territory" field and set the Field Size to 25. Click in the "Members" field and set the Field Size to "Integer."

Note that for number fields, you do not specify a number of digits. Instead, you specify whether the field stores a byte, integer, long integer, single, double, or decimal number. Type **F1** while in the Field Size property to learn about these different sizes.

We'll cover more field properties in the next lesson.

>**Step 20: CTRL-S** (save) your table with the changes that you just made. (Say "Yes" to the warning about field sizes having been changed.) Switch to Datasheet View 🖽 and enter two more records, as show in Figure A-18.

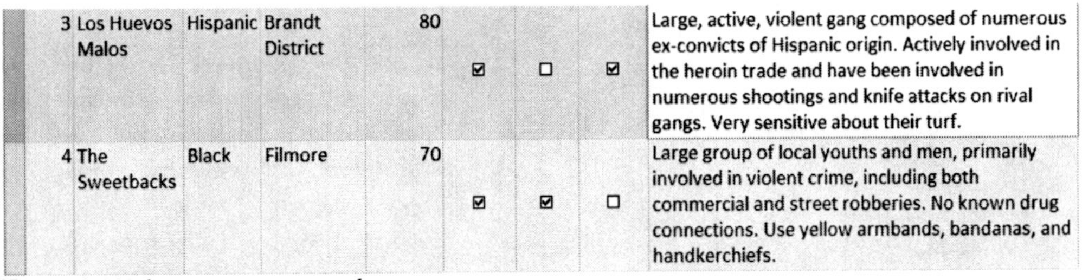

Figure A-18: the next two gang records

>**Step 21:** When you're done entering the data, close ☒ the "Gangs" table.

Now that we have an active table to track gangs, we need something to help us track their members. In this lesson, we'll focus more on the different field properties.

Create a Second Table

We're now going to create a table to track individual gang members. In doing so, we'll learn a lot more about field properties and database design.

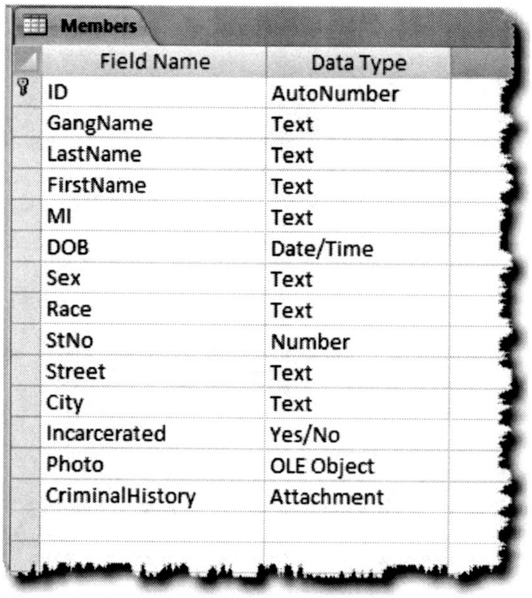

Figure A-19: entering the fields for a gang member table

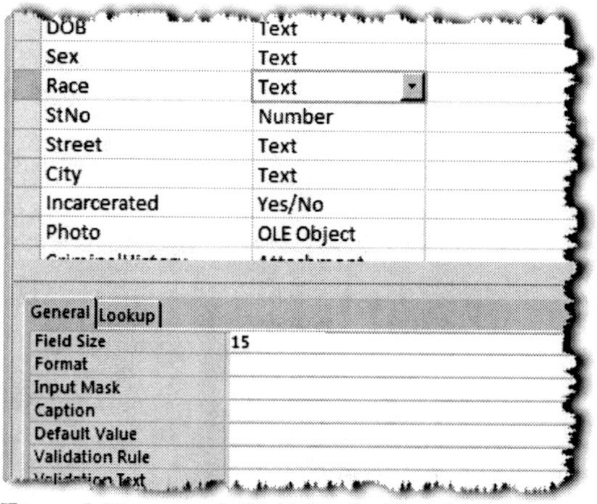

Figure A-20: setting the Field Size for "Race" to 15

»**Step 1:** Click on **Create | Tables | Table**. Immediately switch to Design View. When prompted, save your table as "Members."

»**Step 2:** Enter the fields and data types shown in Figure A-19. You don't need to enter anything in the "Description" segment.

»**Step 3:** Save your table.

Now we set some more advanced General Properties and Lookup Properties for these various fields. We already learned about Field Size.

»**Step 4:** Click in the "GangName" field and set the Field Size property to 25. Set the Field Sizes for both "Last Name" and "First Name" to 20. Set the Field Sizes for "MI" and "Sex" to 1, and for "Race" to 15.

The *Format* property allows us to set a pre-defined format for the field. You can put codes in this field that will affect how your text is displayed (for instance, typing ">" in the Format property causes all your text to appear in UPPERCASE), but for most purposes, you'll only use this field with respect to Date/Time fields.

»**Step 5:** Click in the "DOB" field and then go to the Format property. Click the drop-down menu and choose "Short Date." Note that the other options. "General Date" would be suitable for the date and time of a crime, for instance.

The *Input Mask* property allows you to specify a pattern for data to be entered in a field. For instance, a social security number is always three digits, a dash, two digits, a dash, and four digits: 999-99-9999. An input mask would specify that data would *have* to be entered this way in order to minimize errors and eliminate the need to type the dashes.

»**Step 6:** Click in the "DOB" field and then go to the Input Mask property. Click the ellipse ▣ to the far right. If prompted to save, click "Save."

At this point, one of two things will happen. Either the Input Mask Wizard (Figure A-21) will launch (in which case, go to Step 7), or you will get a message asking you to insert the Microsoft Office CD so that more features can be installed. If the latter happens, it is because Office was not fully installed on your computer—whoever installed it accepted the defaults and did not specify that all features should be installed on the local machine. This may cause problems in other lessons, and you should fix it by having your IT staff perform a full Office installation on your computer. In the meantime, cancel all dialog boxes and type the following in the Input Mask property: **00/00/0000;0;_**

»**Step 7:** Choose "Short Date" and then click "Finish."

Some code will be inserted in the Input Mask property.

The *Default Value* property specifies a value that the field will automatically contain. We can change it for each record if we want. It's best to use this property when *most* of the records you enter will have one value in a particular field, and you'll have to change it only rarely. In our case, we'll assume

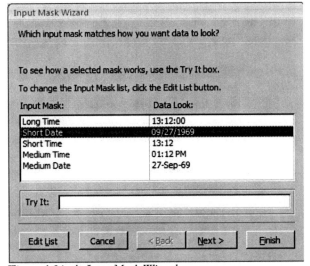

Figure A-21: the Input Mask Wizard

that we work for the City of Metropolis, and that most of our gang members will have addresses in Metropolis.

»**Step 8:** Click in the "City" field, then click in the Default Value property below. Type "Metropolis"—when you leave the field, Access will automatically put quotes around it to signify that it is text.

The *Validation Rule* field specifies constraints on what can be entered in a field. For instance, we have a one-character "Sex" field. Only the letters "M" or "F" should be entered in this field; if anything else is entered, it's an error, and we want Access to reject it. Similarly, since it's unlikely that a gang member will be less than five years old, we probably want Access to reject any "DOB" entries greater than five years ago. We certainly want Access to reject any dates in the future—we shouldn't have a gang member who hasn't been born yet.

The *Validation Text* field indicates what error message will appear when someone entering data violates the validation rule. If we enter nothing in this field, they'll get a confusing Access error message (Figure A-22). We want our error message to be more precise.

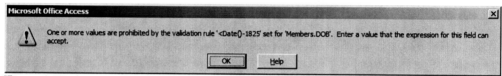

Figure A-22: the error message your users get if you don't add Validation Text

Before we set the Validation Rule for the "DOB" field, you should know a little bit about Access *expressions* and *functions*. *Expressions* are combinations of field values, operators, and functions that produce a result. *Functions* are pre-programmed commands that return a value based on a calculation or other operation. We'll do a lot of work with expressions and functions in Part 2 of this chapter.

For our DOB Validation Rule, we could do one of two things:

1) Tell Access to reject any entry less than five years prior to a specific date. In expressions, Access represents dates with pound signs (#) on either side of the date. If we want to specify that the DOB should be "before June 1, 2004," the expression would be: **<#06/01/2004#**. This works if we're creating our database on June 1, 2009, but we'll have to keep changing this property as the months and years go by.

2) The second option is to use an expression with a function that tells Access to reject anything less than five years ago, based on the *current* date. The function to represent the current date in Access is **Date()**. Calculations are made in days, so five years ago is 365*5=1825. Our expression is thus: **<Date()-1825**.

»**Step 9:** Click in "DOB" field. Enter "<Date()-1825 or Is Null" (without the quotes) in the Validation Rule property. For the Validation Text, enter "Gang members must be more than five years old!" (Figure A-23).

»**Step 10:** Click in the "Sex" field. For the Validation Rule, enter "M or F" and for the Validation Text, type, "You can only enter 'M' or 'F' in this field."

The *Required* property indicates whether the user must enter some value in this field in order to save the record. We won't make any fields required.

There are several other advanced properties under the "General" tab that we'll leave you to explore on your own. You can always click within the property and tap the **F1** key to find out more about what it does.

Before we move on, however, we want to set some "Lookup Properties." Lookup Properties let us specify the default *control* for each field. Examples of controls include

Figure A-23 setting "DOB" Validation Rule and Text

check boxes, text boxes, combo boxes, and list boxes; you will learn more about different controls when we later create forms.

Among other things, the Lookup Properties allow us to specify whether a field should use a "drop-down menu" from which the user can select a value to enter in the field. For certain fields, with a pre-defined list of possible selections, this capability is invaluable.

»**Step 11:** Click in the "Race" field and, at the bottom, click the "Lookup" tab.

At first, we have only a single option: the type of Display Control. A text box is the most basic control type; you've been using it to enter data in the "Gangs" table.

»**Step 12:** Set the Display Control property to "Combo Box."

Suddenly, a host of new options becomes available to us. The three key properties here are the Row Source Type and the Row Source, which together determine what values appear in the "drop-down list," and the Limit to List property, which determines whether the user *has* to pick from the list, or whether he can ignore the list if he wants and enter data freely.

There are three Row Source Types: a table or query, a value list, or a field list. Field lists are used only rarely, and for specific purposes. Basically, we have to choose whether Access should look to an existing table or query for the values in the "drop-down list," or whether we're going to type them in ourselves. Since we have no existing table of races:

»**Step 13:** Set the Row Source Type to "Value List."

We now have to type all of the possible race values in the Row Source box. We do this by typing in each race separated with a semicolon (;).

> **»Step 14:** In the Row Source property, type the following: White;Black;Hispanic;Asian;Native American

»Step 15: Set the Limit to List property to "Yes."

We also want to set Lookup properties for our "GangName" field—we want to make sure that when we enter the data, we choose an existing gang from our "Gangs" table.

»Step 16: Click in the "GangName" field and click the "Lookup" tab in the Properties section.

»Step 17: Set the Display Control property to "Combo Box."

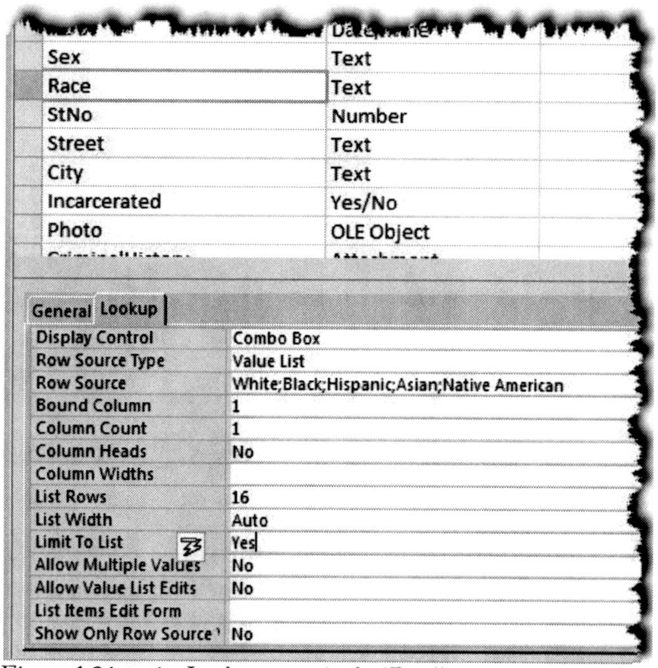

	Data...
Sex	Text
Race	Text
StNo	Number
Street	Text
City	Text
Incarcerated	Yes/No
Photo	OLE Object

General **Lookup**	
Display Control	Combo Box
Row Source Type	Value List
Row Source	White;Black;Hispanic;Asian;Native American
Bound Column	1
Column Count	1
Column Heads	No
Column Widths	
List Rows	16
List Width	Auto
Limit To List	Yes
Allow Multiple Values	No
Allow Value List Edits	No
List Items Edit Form	
Show Only Row Source	No

Figure A-24: setting Lookup properties for "Race"

> **»Step 18:** Leave the Row Source Type set to "Table/Query." Change the Row Source to "Gangs." Finally, set the Limit to List property to "Yes."

Now that we've set all our parameters, we're ready to enter some gang member information.

> **»Step 19:** Save the table and switch to Datasheet View 🖿.

You should now be able to enter some gang members into your table. We're going to start by entering one member per gang. As you enter the records, note the following:

1. If you followed the steps correctly, both the "GangName" field and "Race" field should provide drop-down menus and force you to choose from them (see Figure A-25; if numbers appear in the drop-down instead, it's because you didn't delete the ID field in Step 12 of the previous section).

2. Try initially entering a future date, or one less than five years ago, in the "DOB" field. If you followed the steps correctly, you should get an error message.

3. Try entering something other than "M" or "F" in the "Sex" field. You should get an error message.

4. "Metropolis" should automatically appear as the "City" in blank records, but you can type over it if you need to.

If any of these things do not occur, or do not work properly, hit the **ESC** key twice to cancel the record, return to design view, and follow the instructions above again. (Get used to using the **ESC** key to escape when error messages trap you in a field.)

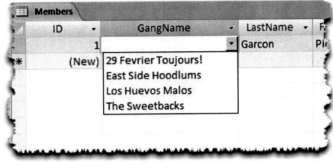

Figure A-25: the "GangName" combo box

»**Step 20:** Enter the gang members in Figure A-26 (ignore the photo and attachment fields for now), or make up your own.

Before we move on to the next lesson, we should talk briefly about the concept of *discrete data*. "Discrete" means separated or compartmentalized. The very act of putting data in records and fields makes it *discrete*. (For instance, the same data about gang members might be contained in a paragraph rather than a database record, but this would make it more difficult to search and almost impossible to aggregate.)

ID	GangName	LastName	FirstName	MI	DOB	Sex	Race	StNo	Street	City	Incarcerate
1	29 Fevrier Toujours!	Garcon	Pierre	L	01/25/1985	M	White	50	Temple S	Metropolis	☑
2	East Side Hoodlums	Malloy	Peter	M	03/17/1982	M	White	17	Erin St	Metropolis	☐
3	Los Huevos Malos	Ramirez	Pedro	D	07/26/1980	M	Hispanic	111	Poplar St	Gotham City	☐
4	The Sweetbacks	Peebles	Puffy	V	09/15/1984	M	Black	315	Main St	Metropolis	☐

Figure A-26: gang members for your table

When designing a table, you can choose how *discrete* you want your data to be. For instance, in the "Members" table, we could have included a single field for "Name," instead of separating it into "LastName," "FirstName," and "MI." This would have been *less* discrete than the method we chose. Similarly, we could have used a combined field for "Address" instead of two discrete fields for "StNo" and "Street."

The problem with making fields less discrete arises when you try to *aggregate* by those fields. To "aggregate" is to summarize data, usually by categories. You'll learn more about aggregation in the second part of this chapter. Assume, for instance, that we wanted to get a list of all the streets our gang members live on, and a count of the number of members on each street. With the "Street" data in a discrete field, this process is simple; in a combined "Address" field, it would be possible, but only with complex and time-consuming expressions.

On the other hand, it is a fairly simple process to combine or *concatenate* discrete fields into a single field later on. If we decide, for the purposes of a query or report, that we want to combine the "StNo" and "Street" fields into a single "Address" field, it's a snap—a lot easier than separating a field that's already combined. For this reason, one rule becomes clear: when creating a database, err towards fields that are *more* discrete.

»**Step 21:** Once you have entered your four gang members, close the table ☒.

Define Relationships

Microsoft Access is a *relational* database program, meaning that it is capable of storing data in multiple tables that can be joined by common fields. This capability to establish relationships is what separates a relational database from a single-table or *flat-file* system.

The advantages of a relational database become quickly apparent when working with any amount of data complexity. A simple table of "Suspects," for instance, functions well in a flat-file format:

SUSPECTS

PersonNo	Name	DOB	Address	Sex
A1329040	Bruce, Christopher W.	02/12/1972	120 Ash St	M
A1329041	Stallo, Mark A.	05/17/1936	157 Baker St	M
A1329042	Piehl, Debra J.	04/05/1978	234 Washington St	F

Table A-2: a single table or "flat file" containing suspects

You could keep it in Microsoft Excel or a Microsoft Word table. But if, along with the suspects, you want to track each criminal incident in which they are involved, duplication becomes an immediate problem:

SUSPECTS AND INCIDENTS

PersonNo	Name	DOB	CaseNo	Date	IncType
A1329040	Bruce, Christopher W.	02/12/1972	2009-03458	02/17/2009	Murder
A1329040	Bruce, Christopher W.	02/12/1972	2009-04789	04/18/2009	Robbery
A1329040	Bruce, Christopher W.	02/12/1972	2009-09777	06/03/2009	Burglary
A1329041	Stallo, Mark A.	05/17/1936	2009-03458	02/17/2009	Murder
A1329041	Stallo, Mark A.	05/17/1936	2009-19400	07/05/2009	Assault
A1329042	Piehl, Debra J.	04/05/1978	2009-09777	06/03/2009	Burglary
A1329042	Piehl, Debra J.	04/05/1978	2009-19400	07/05/2009	Assault

Table A-3: tracking more than one type of data makes "flat files" inadequate

Not only do we have to duplicate person information (and we'd store a lot more than just number, name, and DOB) every time a person is involved in a new incident, we also have to duplicate crime information for every person involved in the offense. This is a terribly inefficient way to store data. Add additional fields for stolen property, vehicles, victims, and so on, and you end up with a flat file nightmare.

A relational database—used by any police records management system—obviates duplication by storing each type of data in its own table and linking those tables through common fields. Because each incident can have multiple suspects, and each suspect can be involved in multiple incidents, we would need three tables—one for incidents, one for suspects, and one to link the two together:

SUSPECTS

PersonNo	Name	DOB	Address	Sex
A1329040	Bruce, Christopher W.	02/12/1972	120 Ash St	M
A1329041	Stallo, Mark A.	05/17/1936	157 Baker St	M
A1329042	Piehl, Debra J.	04/05/1978	234 Washington St	F

SUSPECT-INCIDENTS

PersonNo	CaseNo
A1329040	2005-03458
A1329040	2005-04789
A1329040	2005-09777
A1329041	2005-03458
A1329041	2005-19400
A1329042	2005-09777
A1329042	2005-19400

INCIDENTS

CaseNo	Date	IncType
2005-03458	02/17/2005	Murder
2005-04789	04/18/2005	Robbery
2005-09777	06/03/2005	Burglary
2005-19400	07/05/2005	Assault

Table A-4: a relational database schema

With each type of data now stored in its own table, we minimize data entry and make certain types of querying (particularly *aggregation* queries) possible. This will become clearer when we cover queries later.

Our "Gangs" database already has an appropriate design: gang data in one table, member data in another, with the tables linked by the name of the gang. We now have to tell Microsoft Access how the tables relate.

»**Step 1:** Choose **Database Tools | Show/Hide | Relationships.**

»**Step 2:** The "Show Table" dialog box automatically appears. Add both "Gangs" and "Members" and then close the box.

»Step 3: Click on the "GangName" field in the "Gangs" table, hold down the left mouse button, *drag* the field over to "GangName" field in the "Members" table, and let the left mouse button go.

The "Edit Relationship" window should appear, providing you several options (Figure A-27). Access has already determined the relationship type: "One-to-Many." This means that for every *one* record in the "Gangs" table, there might be *many* related records in the "Members" table. Other relationship types are "One-to-One" and "Many-to-Many"; Access determines the relationship type based on the indexing

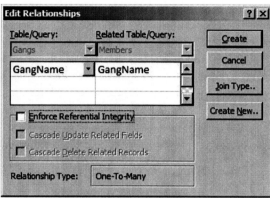

Figure A-27: the "Edit Relationships" box

properties of the linked fields. Primary keys, for instance, must always be "One," whereas fields with no indexing are always "Many."

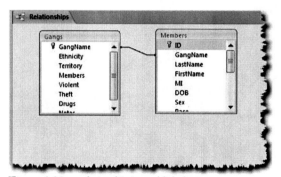

Figure A-28: a relationship is established

"Referential Integrity" and the "cascade" options refer to a system of rules that govern how tables relate to each other. Choosing these options can make it more difficult to make changes to your data, but it can also ensure that careless changes don't cause mismatches between related tables. We won't use these options here.

»Step 4: Click "Create"

A line appears indicating that your relationship has been established (see Figure A-29). This relationship will now help Access create forms and queries based on these tables.

»Step 5: Close the "Relationships" window ⊠. Save your changes.

Before we leave this lesson, let's look at one of the immediate benefits of establishing a relationship.

»Step 6: Open the "Gangs" table by double-clicking on it.

Notice that there is a new left-most column to this table. The column contains a "plus" sign for each record (Figure A-29).

»**Step 7:** Click on the "plus" sign ⊞.

The record will expand to show you the related record from the "Members" table. If there was more than one related record, they would all appear here. This sub-table of related records is known as a *subdatasheet*, and it is an option available to you in both tables and queries. It is automatically available once a one-to-many

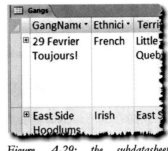

Figure A-29: the subdatasheet column

relationship is established between two tables. You can manually insert a subdatasheet through **Home | Records | More | Subdatasheet**.

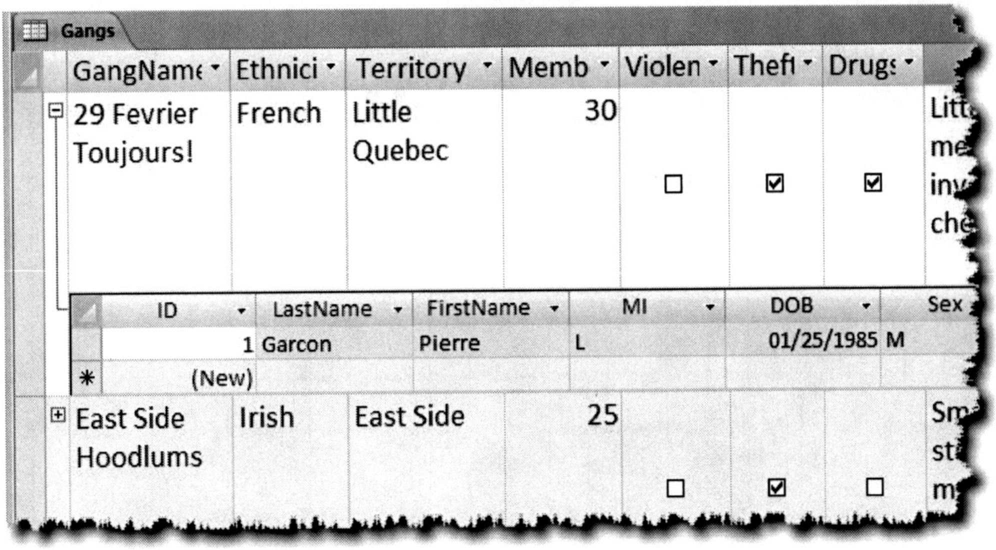

GangName ·	Ethnici ·	Territory ·	Memb ·	Violen ·	Theft ·	Drugs ·	
⊟ 29 Fevrier Toujours!	French	Little Quebec	30	☐	☑	☑	Littl me inv che

	ID ·	LastName ·	FirstName ·	MI ·	DOB ·	Sex
	1	Garcon	Pierre	L	01/25/1985	M
＊	(New)					

| ⊞ East Side Hoodlums | Irish | East Side | 25 | ☐ | ☑ | ☐ | Sm st m |

Figure A-30: the expanded subdatasheet

Create a Form

We've already put some data into our Access database by entering directly into the tables. While there's nothing wrong with entering into tables, it can be a bit clumsy, especially when we have multiple fields and more than one table of related records.

Forms provide, among other things, an attractive interface for entering and browsing records. Most, if not all, of the work done in commercial databases is done through forms. With forms, you can arrange fields and labels, explanatory text, titles, images, and command buttons in an eye-pleasing way.

We can create a form from scratch, but it's easier to let Access do it for us; then we can modify it.

»**Step 1:** Close all open tables.

»**Step 2:** Click on the "Gangs" table to select it.

»**Step 3:** Click **Create | Forms | Form**.

Access provides you with a reasonably-attractive form (Figure A-31). By default, it opens the form in the new (to Access 2007) Layout View, where you can make some basic changes while still seeing your data. Because of the relationship we established earlier, Access has already inserted a sub-form with the gang members.

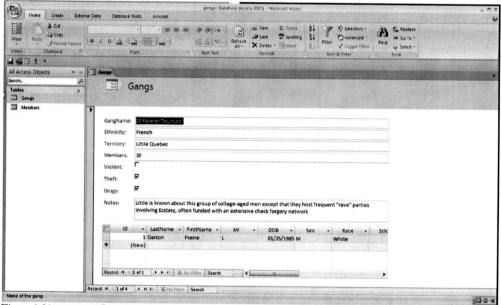

Figure A-31: your new "Gangs" form, in Layout View.

»**Step 4:** Save the form. Accept "Gangs" as the form name.

»**Step 5:** Switch to the regular Form View by choosing **Form Layout Tools | Format | Views | View**.

The most important thing to understand at this point is that the data in the form is linked directly to the data in the table on which the form is based. You're not seeing a "copy" of the table; you're seeing the table itself, just arranged differently. Any changes to the data in the form are automatically saved in the table, and vice versa. The same rules about saving that we covered on Page 26 apply to forms as well.

Navigating the Form

The first thing to learn about a form is how to move around in it. In the bottom left-hand corner of the form, you will see a series of *navigation buttons*. (These were also present when you were looking at tables, but they were less useful there.)

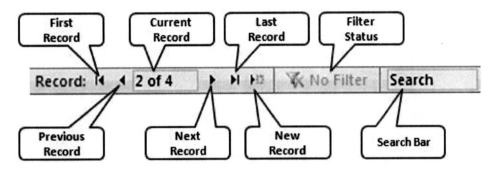

Figure A-32: navigation buttons and their uses

The Search Bar is a new feature in Access 2007 and it allows you to quickly search for specific text anywhere in a record.

Below the navigation buttons is the *status bar*. The status bar provides information about the active control. For instance, click in the "Territory" field, and the status bar reads "Area of Town in which the Gang is Active." By default, the status

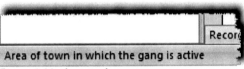

Figure A-33: the status bar

bar text is identical to what we typed in the "Description" field back in table design.

Finally, note that there is a separate navigation bar at the bottom of the sub-form showing your gang members. We'll delete that later.

Form Design, Controls, and Layout

Access has three different view for forms: Form View (see the data), Design View (specify the form's look and feel, fields, and properties), and Layout View (see the data while still performing some design tasks). We are going to do most of our work in Design View rather than Layout View because it preserves all your options.

»**Step 1:** We'll introduce another way to change views here. Right-click on the "Gangs" form in the Navigation Pane and choose "Design View."

Immediately, you should notice that your data has been replaced with the names of the fields. You also have an underlying dotted grid and some new tools at the top ribbon.

Modifying the design of a form involves interacting with a series of objects known collectively as *controls*. These include:

- **Text Boxes**. These are the most common and easiest type of form controls. They allow you to enter text, numbers, dates, times, and so on, with or without an input mask. On our "Gangs" form, "GangName," "Ethnicity," "Territory," "Members," and "Notes" are all text boxes.

- **Combo Boxes**. Combo boxes are distinguished by the little "down arrow" to the far right. Clicking on this arrow gives you a list of values that can be entered in the control field.

- **Check Boxes**: Check boxes are used for Yes/No fields. Checked means "Yes," not checked means "No." Access automatically creates check boxes for use with Yes/No fields, such as "Violent," "Theft," and "Drugs."

- **Toggle Button**: Another type of control bound to a Yes/No field, allows you to push one of two buttons to select the value. Also used with option groups.

- **Option Button:** Yet another Yes/No field control or a field in an option group.

- **Option Group:** A special "area" of a form that can contain multiple check boxes, toggle buttons, or option buttons, allowing the user to choose one of several values. Can be stored in a field or stored for later use in a search form.

- **List Box:** Works like a combo box, but displays all choices at once and highlights the selected one.

- **Command Button:** A button that runs a macro, module, or other procedure.

The default control for each field is based on the "Lookup" properties back in table design. Remember how we changed some of the controls for the "Members" table to combo boxes? When we create a form based on this table, those fields will appear on the form in combo boxes.

Each of these controls, plus a few other objects, can be found at **Form Design Tools | Design | <u>Controls</u>** (Figure A-34). By default, each control comes with a *label*. On our "Gangs" form, these labels are arranged in a column down the left-hand side. Labels may also exist independently of controls, in case you want to add some text to the form. For instance, the "Gangs" title in the form's header is an unbound label.

Figure A-34: Access controls

Let's begin by customizing the header of our database.

»**Step 2:** Click within the "Gangs" title and change it to "Metropolis Police Gang Database."

Now that you've added this title to your form header, you can click on it and drag it to move it to the position you want. You may also use the formatting tools under **Form Design Tools | Design | <u>Font</u>** to change the style of the font (Segoe UI ▾), its size (18 ▾), formatting (**B** *I* <u>U</u>), and color (**A** ▾). If at any point the size of the text exceeds the size of the label box, you can double-click on any of the box's handles (∎)to automatically re-size the box.

»**Step 3:** Adjust the formatting of your box as you see fit. We chose a 22-point Arial font with a dark red color.

Now let's replace the generic "form" image with our police badge.

»**Step 4:** Click **Form Design Tools | Design | <u>Controls</u> | Logo**. Navigate to **C:\BPOffice\Access\policebadge.jpg** and click "OK."

When you are finished, your header should look similar to Figure A-36.

Figure A-31: your form header with a formatted title and a police badge logo.

Now let's turn to the detail section. We have a few thing to accomplish here:

- Although Access has chose a nice, orderly layout for us, the field widths take up far more space than they require. In forms, real estate is at a premium. You want to try to avoid requiring your users to scroll to see all of the items on the form, so there's no room for fields that take up too much space.

- By shorting the widths of the fields, we can also re-arrange them so some of them sit side-by-side rather than directly on top of each other.

- By default, the labels are the same as our field names. We probably want to change a few of them (for instance, we may want to add a space in the "GangName" label).

- While we do want a sub-form for our gang's members, we do not want the tabular format that Access has chosen for us. We'll design a separate sub-form for the members and insert it later, so we can delete the default one.

- Finally, we want to make some formatting and color changes.

When Access automatically creates a form for you, by default it locks the fields to a particular layout style. We have to remove that before we can do anything.

»**Step 5:** Click anywhere within the form. Type **CTRL-A** to select all objects

»**Step 6:** Go to **Form Design Tools | Arrange | <u>Control Layout</u> | Remove**. This removes the automatic layout and will allow you to move and re-size the controls independently of each other.

Before we begin, it's important to understand the difference between the *control* and its associated *label*. The control is where the data appears. The label helps users see what type of data goes in each control. In Form View and Layout View, they're easy to distinguish.

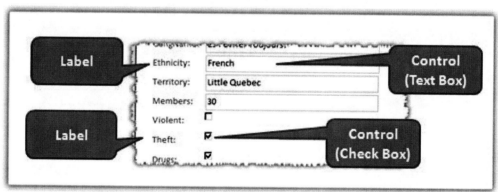

Figure A-32: controls and labels in form view.

But in Design View, they can be a bit tricky, since instead of seeing data in the control, you see the name of the field in the associated table. Since the label is, by default, also the name of the field, you end up with two objects, side-by-side, that seem to have the same name. But the objects are very different. Labels aren't even necessary; you can delete them if you think the field's size and position speaks for itself (not true for any of our fields except maybe the "notes"), and you won't have any effect on the underlying data. You can re-name labels for clarification, and everything will still be fine. But if you change the name of a control, it will screw everything up because the form will be looking for a field name that doesn't exist.

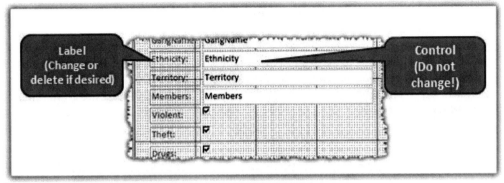

Figure A-33: controls and labels in design view.

As you move each control, its label will move with it, and vice versa. The control with its label is known as a *compound control.* By default, they move as one. You can move them independently of each other by clicking on the one you want to move and then clicking and dragging the handle in the upper-left corner (see Figure A-34).

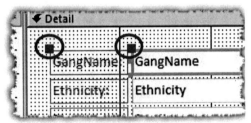

Figure A-34: click and drag on the handle in the upper left corner to move one part of a compound control independently of the other.

If you want to apply formatting changes—font style, size, color, formatting—changes to controls or labels, select the object and use the various tools on the **Form Design Tools | Design | Font** panel. To change the background color of a section, click in a blank part of the section and use the "Fill/Back Color" tool in the **Font** panel.

Perhaps you want to apply the same formatting changes to multiple objects. For instance, you might want to change the font type for all the fields at once. To select multiple objects, you can do any of the following:

- Hold down the **Shift** key and click them one at a time.
- Use **CTRL-A** to select everything.
- Click in a blank part of the form, hold down the left mouse button, and drag a box around multiple controls to select them.

To **re-size** a field, use the little square handles that appear in the corners, top, bottom, and sides of a control when you select it.

Finally, you may occasionally want to add additional labels to your form to clarify different fields and sections. We've done that with "History of:" in Figure A-35. If you want to add additional labels, simply use the **Form Design Tools | Design | Controls | Label**.

»Step 7: Click on and Delete the existing "Table.Members" sub-form at the bottom of the screen.

»Step 8: Move, resize, and apply formatting changes to your form fields and section backgrounds as you see fit, keeping in mind that we'll need to reserve a fairly large rectangular space for our "Members" sub-form. Copy the formatting and layout in Figure A-35 if you desire. Switch to Form View frequently to see how it looks.

»Step 9: Click and drag to adjust the edge of the form at the right and bottom to take up any extra space.

As you lay out your form, you must consider the screen resolution of the computers that will use your database. If you're designing the database on a monitor with a 1280 x 1024 resolution, you should have plenty of space to work with, but if you use all of it, users on monitors with resolutions set to 1024 x 768 or—God help us—800 x 600 will have to do a lot of scrolling. Vertical scrolling is okay, if there are enough fields to warrant it. Horizontal scrolling, just like on web pages, is unforgiveable.

Figure A-35 shows our completed layout. We moved the controls around, putting most of the labels on the tops of the fields. We added a new label for "History of:" above the check-boxes and renamed the "GangName" and "Violent" fields. We gave the header a darker background color and lightened the title, and then gave a light shading to the background of the main section. We bolded all of the labels. Finally, we left a lot of extra space in the lower right for the "members" sub-form that we'll be designing next.

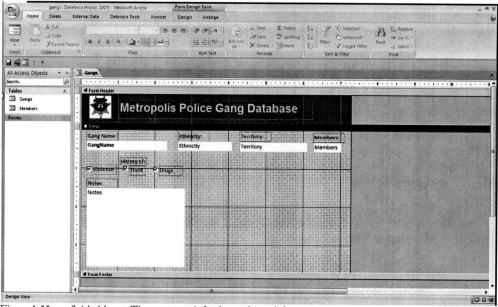

Figure A-35: our finished layout. The extra space is for the members sub-form.

Adding a Subform

Each form must be based on a single table or query, but you can show related data by creating a *subform* that displays data linked to the table or query that makes up the main form. Refer back to Figures A-1 and A-3 for examples of forms with several subforms. Our gangs form originally had a very basic sub-form that showed our members in tabular view, but we deleted it. Tabular view looks great for some data types, but in our case, we want to show photographs with our members.

Before we can insert a subform into our main form, we have to create it. We'll take this opportunity to explore another way to create a form.

>**Step 1:** Click **Create | Forms | Form Design.**

Rather than automatically creating a form the way it did before, Access opens a blank form, with no fields, headers, or other information. We have to add the fields ourselves.

>**Step 2: Click Form Design Tools | Design | Tools | Add Existing Fields**. Access should open a "Field List" dialog that shows all of the tables in the database.

>**Step 3:** Expand the ⊞ **Members** table by clicking the little plus to the left. Then, one by one, double-click each of the fields (including the "Criminal History" group) from this table to add them to the form. When you finish, your screen should look like Figure A-36.

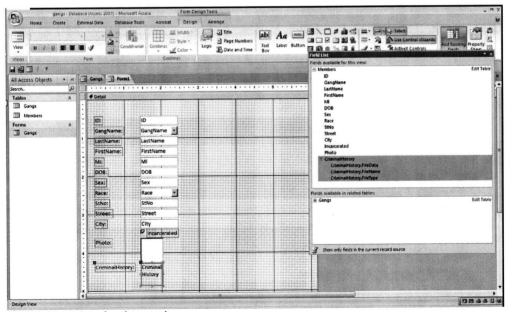

Figure A-36: creating a form from scratch

»Step 4: Close the Field List and save the form, naming it "SubMembers."

»Step 5: Re-arrange, shrink, and edit the fields until it will fit into the empty space you left on the gangs form (Figure A-37). (If you copied the style we used for the gangs form, it will make your members form no more than 4 inches wide.)

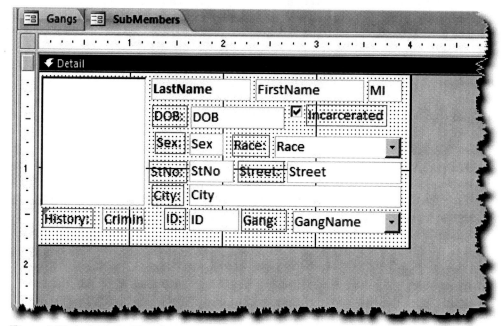

Figure A-37: the finished subform layout

Note that in the interests of conserving screen real estate, we have deleted the labels for some fields (like "Photo" and the various "Name" fields) that are self-explanatory, and we bolded the "LastName" field. The "Criminal History" field is just going to contain a small icon, so we greatly shortened it. Finally, we shortened the labels for "Criminal History" and "Gang Name" to save space.

»Step 6: Save your form and switch to Form View.

In the process of re-arranging our fields, we have thrown the *tab order* into a bit of disarray. Try clicking in the "Last Name" field and tabbing through the form. After the "DOB" field, based on the form's layout, you would expect it to move next to "Incarcerated." Instead, it jumps down to "Sex." That's because the tab order is based on the original layout of the form as created by Access. We have to adjust it.

»Step 7: Return to Design View and choose **Form Design Tools | Arrange | Control Layout | Tab Order**.

The Tab Order dialog box displays a list of the fields on your form, in the order in which you will move from one to the other when pressing the **TAB** key[1]. If you click the "Auto Order" button, Access will rearrange the tab order based on the layout of your form. Sometimes it gets it wrong, though, and it's good to practice manually rearranging your tab order.

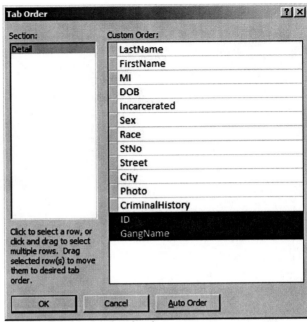

Figure A-38: changing the tab order

»**Step 8:** Click on the "Incarcerated" field once to highlight it. Then click again and hold down the mouse button to drag it up, until it falls between the "DOB" and "Sex" fields. Release the mouse button once you have positioned it there. Use the same process to move "ID" and "GangName" down to the bottom. When finished, click "OK."

Having created the subform, we're now ready to insert it into our main "Gangs" form.

»**Step 9:** Save and close the "SubMembers" form. Return to the "Gangs" form and go to Design View (if not already there).

»**Step 10:** Make sure the [Use Control Wizards] button at **Form Design Tools | Design | Controls** is turned *on*. When it is off, it is a solid color; when on, it is highlighted.

»**Step 11:** Select the "Subform/Subreport" button .

»**Step 12:** Drag a box that fills the blank space on your "Gangs" form. When you let go of the mouse the "SubForm Wizard" dialog box opens.

»**Step 13:** Select "SubMembers" under "Use an Existing Form" and click "Finish" (Figure A-39).

---

[1] Bonus tip that applies to almost all Windows applications: while **TAB** moves you forward through the fields, **SHIFT-TAB** will move you backwards. This makes it easier to go back and correct mistakes, without having to reach for the mouse.

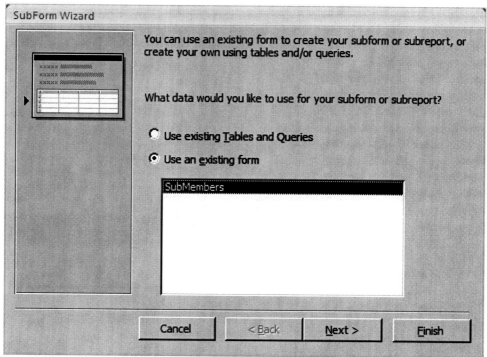

Figure A-39: using the SubForm Wizard to add your "SubMembers" form to the "Gangs" form.

»Step 14: Change the "SubMembers" label to read simply "Members" and modify its color and style to match your other labels. When finished, switch to Form View and check it out (Figures A-40 and A-41).

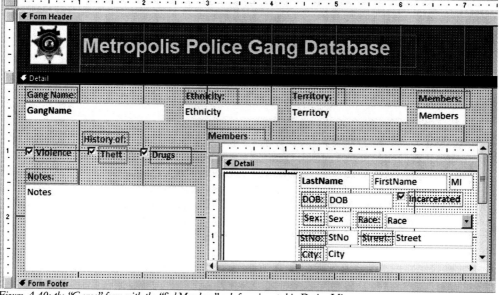

Figure A-40: the "Gangs" form with the "SubMembers" sub-form inserted in Design View...

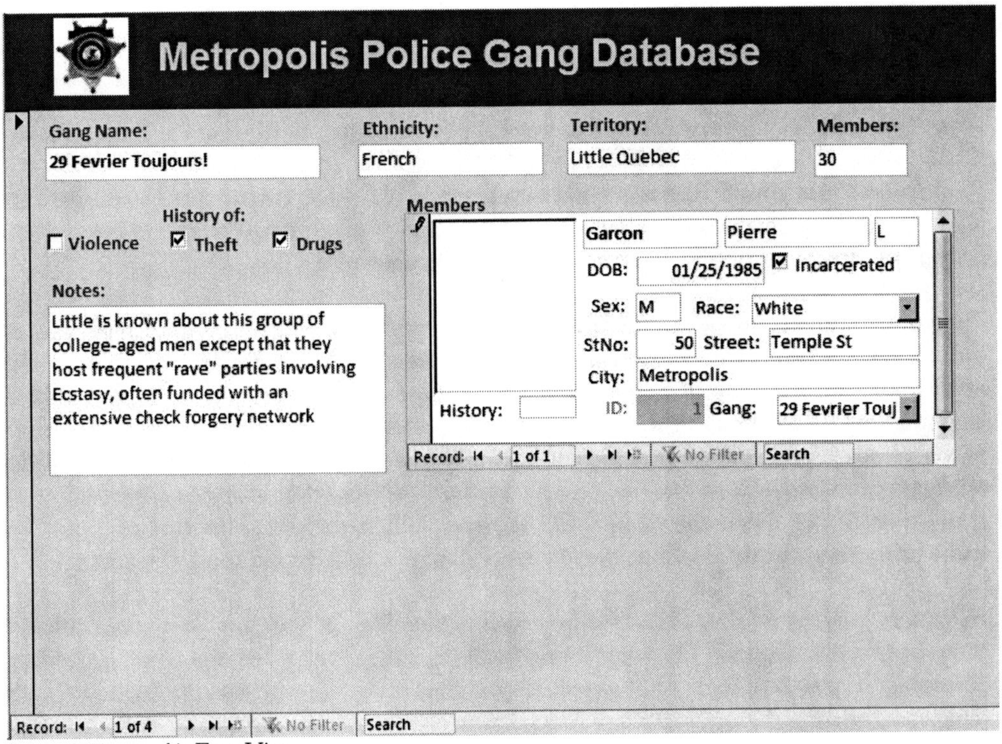

Figure A-41: ...and in Form View

Note that the sub-form has its own navigation buttons. You will use these to move from member to member associated with each gang. To move from gang to gang, use the navigation buttons on the *main* form.

With our form and sub-form created, we will use them to add records to our database.

»**Step 15:** Add one or more new "Member" records to each of the existing gangs using the "New Record" button ▶✳ on the sub-form. Make up names and other data as you desire. Try to tab from field-to-field rather than using the mouse to click. If you set the tab order properly, you should move smoothly through the forms. (Ignore the "Photo" and "Criminal History" fields for now.)

»**Step 16:** Add one or more new records to the "Gangs" table by using the "New Record" button ▶✳ on the main form. Add at least one member to each new gang. Make up the data as you desire.

Adding and Working with Photographs

We added a "Photo" field to our "Members" table and subform, but we have not yet used it. Before we do, we need to understand how Access works with *OLE Objects*.

OLE (Object Linking & Embedding) is a Microsoft protocol that allows files created in one application to be stored, displayed, opened, or even edited in another. As you install software applications on your computer, those that are OLE-compliant will tell Windows about themselves and allow other Windows applications to link to or embed those files.

Photographs and sound files are two examples of OLE objects that can be inserted into all Microsoft Applications. It is because of OLE that you can insert a bitmap into a Word document, then later double-click on it to make changes to it.

As our description suggests, there are two types of OLE objects: *linked* and *embedded*. Linked objects are stored in files on your computer. They are displayed within another application, but not stored there. If you delete the original file, it will no longer open in any application that links to it. But if you make changes to the original file (such as if a newer photograph is substituted for an older one), those changes will appear in the linked application. When you embed an object, on the other hand, it stores a copy within the application. If you delete the original file, the copy still exists within the application. If you make changes to the original file, those changes are not reflected in the application.

In Access, photos work a bit differently from other files. If you link to a sound file and then delete the original file, the sound will no longer play in the Access database. However, if you link to a photograph, Access stores a shot of the photograph in the database. Deleting the original file will not cause the linked photograph to disappear from your database, but you will no longer be able to open or edit it.

There are several different ways that OLE technology works with Microsoft Access. We've already seen one, when we inserted the picture of the badge into our "Gangs" form. Access chose the default method of handling the photo, which was to embed it.

OLE objects can also be stored in database tables, as long as we choose "OLE Object" as the field's data type, as we did when creating the "Members" table. And in forms based on tables with OLE objects, we can again decide whether to link to or embed the files—in our case, the photographs of gang members.

Embedding has obvious advantages: you'll never accidentally sever the link to the original files. If you want to copy the database and move it to a different computer, or take it on the road with your laptop, any embedded photographs copy with it. The downside is *size*; embedded files balloon a database pretty quickly. Access's maximum functional file size is two gigabytes (2GB), but you'll probably find that browsing records, running queries, and opening forms is far too slow well before then.

For any serious efforts to bring files into your database—such as tracking the photograph of each known gang member—linking is the best option. The key is determining a *permanent* location to store the files early on. This location should be a mapped network drive if multiple users in the agency are going to share the database.

»Step 1: Open your "Gangs" form in form view.

»Step 2: Use the navigation buttons to move to the gang called "29 Fevrier Toujours!" Pierre Garcon should be the first member displayed.

»Step 3: Right-click in the photo field and choose "Insert Object" (Figure A-42).

»Step 4: Choose "Create From File" and then click "Browse."

»Step 5: Navigate to **C:\BPOffice\Access\photos**. Choose the **garcon.gif** file and click "OK."

»Step 6: Check the "Link" box, then click "OK."

Pierre Garcon's picture should now display in your database (Figure A-44).

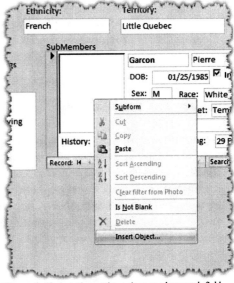

Figure A-42: inserting a picture in your photograph field

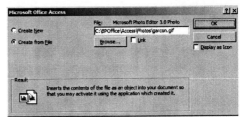

Figure A-43: linking to a photograph

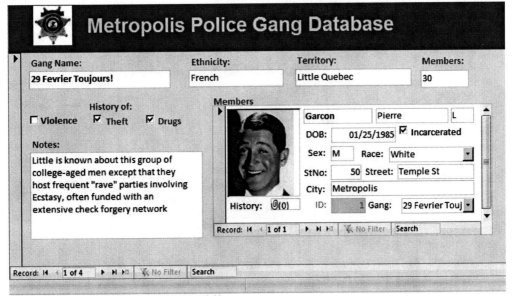

Figure A-44: the photograph inserted in the photo field

»**Step 7:** Scroll through each gang member and repeat Steps 3–6 to add photographs to those members. Each photograph uses the gang member's last name. For the members you added yourself, use the files named **memberX.gif**. Don't worry if you have more members than photos.

Working with Attachments

Attachments are a new data type in Access 2007. They have much of the same functionality as OLE objects, but you can add multiple attachments per record. In a crime database, for instance, you could use attachments to add crime scene photographs, or crime analysis bulletins, to crime records. If we made our "Photos" field an attachment field, we could add multiple photos to gang members. The drawback, at least for photos, is that you cannot display the photo itself in a form or a report—only the file's icon. Hence, it makes sense to use an OLE Object field type for photos and attachments for everything else.

In our case, we're using the attachment field to store police reports and news articles related to each gang member. These files together make up his history with the Metropolis Police Department.

»**Step 1:** Scroll to the East Side Hoodlums gang and to member Peter Malloy. Double-click on the empty "History" field. The "Attachments" dialog opens.

»**Step 2:** Click on the "Add" button and browse to **C:\BPOffice\Access\MalloyShooting20091223.pdf**. Select it and click "Open." The attachment will now appear in your attachments list. You can double-click on it to open it in Adobe Acrobat or Adobe Acrobat Reader (Figure A-45). Click "OK"

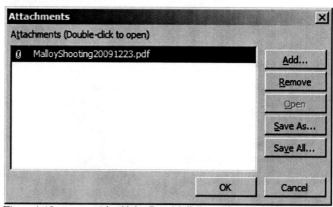

The "History" field now shows a PDF icon in it. The icon is a bit too big for the field, so only part of it shows. We're going to change that in a little bit.

Figure A-45: a news article added to Peter Malloy's record as an attachment

»**Step 3:** Use the same process to add **Incident200900915.pdf** to both Pedro Ramirez's and Puffy Peebles's records, and **PeeblesHistory.pdf** to Peebles's record.

Control and Object Properties

Every control in the form, every label, every object, every section of the form, and the form as a whole all have a series of *properties* associated with them. Such properties include the object's color and style, whether you can see it, whether you can enter data into it, whether something happens when you click on it, and so on. The properties differ based on the type of object: text boxes have different available properties than check boxes, and the form header has different properties than the entire form. Fine-tuning your form often means adjusting these properties, which are contained on a Property Sheet.

So far, we have been changing properties without even knowing it. For instance, when we change the color of a field's font, we are actually changing a property called "Fore Color" associated with the field. Through its various formatting tools and wizards, Access prevents us from actually having to view the Property Sheet as long as possible. However, there are some properties that simply cannot be changed without going to the Property Sheet.

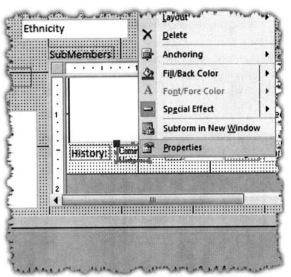

Figure A-46: getting to...

»Step 1: Open the "Gangs" form in Design View. Find the "Criminal History" field in the "SubMembers" subform (not the label, but the field itself). Right-click on it and choose "Properties" (Figure A-46).

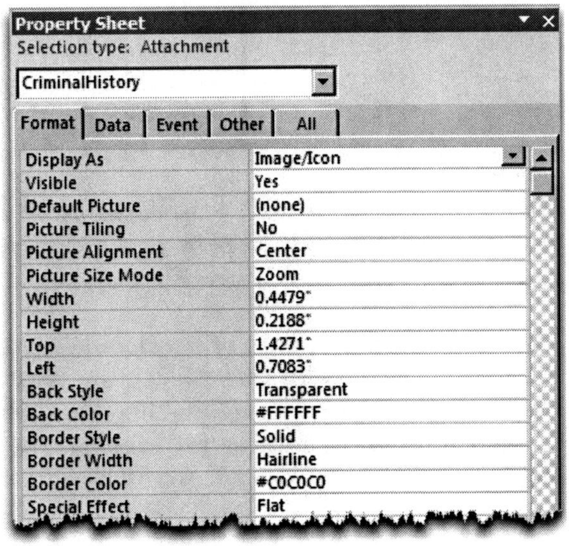

A box appears (Figure A-47), showing the various properties for your image. They are arranged in four tabs: "Format," "Data," "Event," and "Other." You can choose the "All" tab to see them all.

As we indicated, you've already been editing a lot of these properties, including "Font

Figure A-47: ...the Property Sheet

Name," "Font Size," "Font Weight," "Fore Color," "Tab Index," "Height," "Top," and "Left" (the latter two refer to the positioning of the object). For most of these properties, it's easiest just to use the Form Design Tools, but you could edit them all in the Property Sheet. You might want to use the Property Sheet, for instance, to ensure that all fields in a row start at the same "Top" location, so they're exactly aligned. You can't get that precision by dragging the fields.

>>**Step 2:** Without closing the property dialog box, click around the form on different controls, labels, and objects. Click on the "Detail" section and the "Form Header" section. Note how the available properties change depending on the type of object you've selected.

For instance, the first "Format" property for our attachment field is "Display As." If we click on text box, it becomes "Format," and we get a new one just below it called "Decimal Places." Click on a text box, and you lose a lot of options—the first one is "Visible."

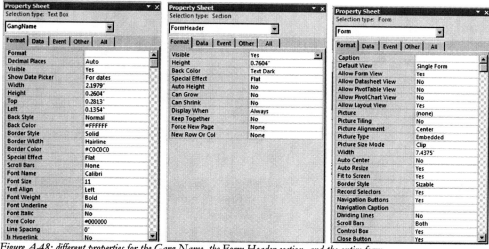

Figure A-48: different properties for the Gang Name, the Form Header section, and the entire form.

It would take an entire book to explore each of the properties available. For now, note that as you click in each property field, the status bar tells you a little about what the property does. You can also press **F1** to get help for a property.

As we said, in addition to all of the objects, the form itself has a series of properties. To select the entire form click on the little grey box to the left of the ruler, just before the form's tab (Figure A-49). The form properties allow you to specify whether the user sees the scroll bars, the record selectors, the navigation buttons, and the "close" box. There are times you want to turn these off, as we will with our switchboard later.

The first properties we'll adjust will fix criminal history attachment icon.

»Step 3: Click on the "Criminal History" field again, if the Property Sheet is still open. If not, repeat Step 1.

»Step 4: On the "Format" tab, find the "Display As" property. Change it to "Paperclip."

»Step 5: Now click on the "ID" field (again, the text box itself, not the label). Since the ID is an AutoNumber, which users cannot manually change, there's no reason for this field to be editable, or even for the cursor to stop there as we tab through the fields. On the "Other" tab, set the "Tab Stop" property to "No," and on the "Data" tab set the "Enabled" property to "No." Then close the Property Sheet.

Now, instead of a PDF image, our field displays a paperclip with the number of files attached. The "ID" field changes to a gray, indicating it's disabled; we cannot click in it (try), and the tab order skips from "City" to "Gang Name."

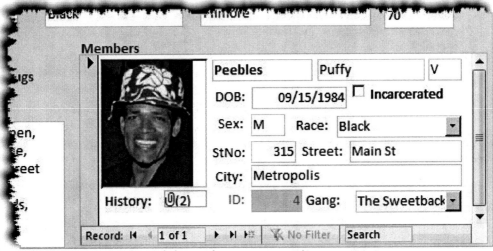

Figure A-49: our gang members sub-form with some new properties

Macros

Forms give you an application interface to your database. *Macros* and *modules* develop this capability further by allowing you to assign buttons, commands, menus, and background procedures to your application.

A macro is a set of one or more actions that perform a particular operation, like opening a form, running a query, or printing a report. Macros help you automate common tasks.

We're going to add three simple macros to the "Gangs" form to help automate operations. The macros will add a new record, close the form, and quit the database. These macros will run when the user clicks on a particular button.

»Step 1: Open the "Gangs" form in design view.

»Step 2: At **Form Design Tools | Design | Controls** turn *off* (unselect) "Use Control Wizards" ⚹ Use Control Wizards . (With some tasks, wizards speed things up. With others, they get in the way. With macros and command buttons, they get in the way.)

»Step 3: Find and click on the "Button" too in your Controls box.

»Step 4: Click in the Form Header. Access will insert a button named "Command##" (Figure A-50).

»Step 5: Doublc-click on these words to select them, and rename the button "New Record."

»Step 6: Repeat Steps 3–5 to add two more buttons. Name them "Close Form" and "Quit."

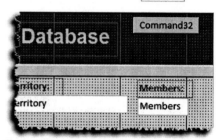

Figure A-50: your new command button

Right now, these buttons—despite the names we have given them—will do nothing. We must assign *event properties* to each one.

Figure A-51: your form with three command buttons added

»Step 7: Right-click the "New Record" button and choose **Properties**.

»Step 8: Click on the "Event" tab.

»Step 9: Find the "On Click" property and click within this field.

»Step 10: Click the ellipse button ⊡ to the right of the field.

»Step 11: Choose the "Macro Builder" and then "OK" (Figure A-52).

At this point, you are in the *macro design* screen. You could have also come to this location by clicking on "Macros" in the main database window and then "New." But this way, the macro we design will automatically associate with the button.

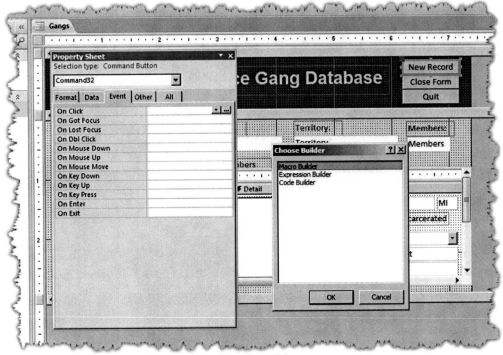

Figure A-52: building a macro to work with the "New Record" button.

In the macro design screen, we enter a series of steps that will occur when the macro runs—that is, when the user clicks the button. We can enter a "Comment" for each of the steps, to document our design for future users, but comments are not necessary. Click on the drop-down menu under the "Action" column, and take a look at all of the different options available to you. Many of these actions have one or more parameters or *action arguments* that you will enter at the bottom of the screen.

»**Step 13:** For the first action, choose "Go to Record."

The different arguments for the "Go to Record" action appear at the bottom of the screen. The "Object Type" and "Object Name" are unnecessary for our purposes—if we leave these blank, Access will automatically use the "active" object. Since we'll be running this macro from within the "Gangs" form, the form will already be the active object.

The "Record" parameter allows us to specify which record to go to. In our case, we want to go to a new record.

»**Step 14:** In the "Record" field, enter "New."

The "Offset" field does not apply to new records, so we do not need to use it.

For the second step, we'll tell Access to automatically go to the "GangName" field after moving to a new record. That will give us a good starting point to enter our new record.

»**Step 15:** For the second action, enter "Go to Control." The single parameter that appears at the bottom is the "Control Name."

»**Step 16:** In the "Control Name" box, type in "GangName." At this point, your macro should look like Figure A-51.

»**Step 17:** Click Macro **Tools | Design | <u>Close</u> | Save As** to save the macro as "NewRecord"; then **Close** and "Yes" to close it and return to your form.

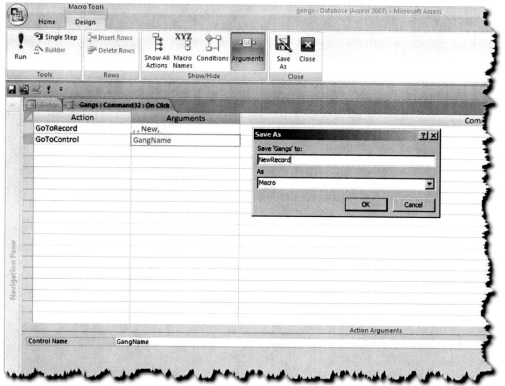

Figure A-51: your completed macro

You should return to the event properties for your command button, only now the name of your macro—"NewRecord"—will appear in the "On Click" property. If you had created your macro from within the main database window, you would select its name from the drop-down menu here.

»**Step 18:** Close the properties dialog box and save the form.

The next step is to repeat this series of steps, starting at Step 7, to create macros for the other two buttons: "Close Form" and "Quit." These macros are easier, as each has only one action and no arguments.

»Step 19: Adapt Steps 7–18 to create the two new macros with the actions shown in Table A-5.

Button	Macro Name	Action
Close Form	CloseForm	Close
Quit	Quit	Quit

Table A-5: actions for your other macros

One you've finished the three macros, save the form, switch to form view, and try them out. After you "Close," you'll have to re-open the form, and once you "Quit" you'll have to re-start Access and re-open the database.

A final note on macros: Access 2007 now supports "embedded macros" that exist only within the form that calls them. In previous versions of Access, your macro screen could get cluttered with macros used only by a single form. With Access 2007, if you simply save, rather than click "Save As" when going through the process above, the macro saves *with* the form, rather than as a separate object. In our case, it might be a good idea to save our "New Record" macro as an embedded macro, since no other forms will use it. "Close" and "Quit," however, are fairly universal commands. We might want to use them for other forms, so we would keep those as separate macro objects.

Reports

Reports exist to present the information in your database in a printed format. Designing them is much like designing forms. The similarities include:

- They both have the same headers, footers, and detail sections.

- They both have the same types of controls (including sub-reports that are analogous to sub-forms).

- They both have the same types of properties.

- You create your report layout by dragging fields around in a manner identical to designing forms.

- They have similar views. Where forms have Form View, Layout View, and Design View, reports have Report View, Layout View, and Design View (as well as Print Preview).

- They both allow you to conduct basic searches and filters (we explore these in the next section).

Consequently, we've already learned much of what we need to know to create a report.

We're going to create a report that prints out information about each of our gang members from the "Members" table. We note here, however, that most of *your* reports will be based on queries. It is rare that you will design a report to print all the information in your tables; rather, you will design reports based on queries that filter or summarize data. Later, as we discover queries, think about how you might lay out a report to present the data you see on the query screen.

As with forms, you can create a report in three ways:

1. Start with a blank surface and add the fields yourself, as we did with the "SubMembers" sub-form.

2. Have Access automatically create the report via **Create | Reports | Report**, then modify the result, as we did with our main "Gangs" form.

3. Use the Report Wizard at **Create | Reports | Report Wizard**.

The problem with Method 2, which is normally quite helpful, is that Access's defaults often present us with a report that takes more time to modify that it would to simply create one from scratch. In our case, Access will create a tabular report, with enormous space between fields, that stretches across two pages in Landscape view. Not helpful. This one time, we'll use the Wizard, but only to start.

»**Step 1:** Click **Create | Reports | Report Wizard**.

»**Step 2:** Select "Table: Members" as the data source, and use the <kbd>></kbd> button to add all available fields *except* for the "Criminal History" attachment fields.

»**Step 3:** Click "Finish."

At this point, a reasonably ugly report will appear before you, in Print Preview, showing each gang member in order of his ID. We have several modifications to make. The first is to add a *grouping level.* Grouping levels allow us to group data on a report under the heading of a common field—in this case, the name of the gang. Rather than have all gang members jumbled together, our report will have the name of each gang in bold letters, followed by a list of each member of that gang.

»**Step 4:** Click **Print Preview | Close Preview | Close Print Preview**. This should take you to Design View.

»**Step 6:** At the bottom, you should see a "Group, Sort, and Total" pane. (If not, click **Report Design Tools | Design | Grouping & Totals | Group & Sort**.) Click on "Add a Group."

»**Step 7:** Select the "Gang Name" field, and a "Gang Name" header should appear (Figure A-52).

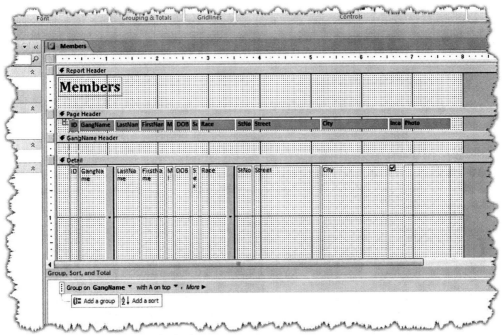

Figure A-52: the form with a grouping level

»Step 8: As we did when creating the form, we have to remove Access's automatic layouts from our fields. Click anywhere within the report, type **CTRL-A** to select all the fields, and choose **Report Design Tools | Arrange | <u>Control Layout</u> | Remove** to free our fields for moving.

»Step 9: Drag the "GangName" control up into the new "GangName Header" section. Now each gang name will appear only once, before the list of its members, rather than with every member. Delete the "GangName" *label* in the page header section. Re-size the field to take away the extra vertical space, but increase the font to 16 points and bold it.

At this point, we can make the rest of the changes to our form. This involves re-sizing and re-arranging the controls in the "Detail" section and their labels in the "Page Header" section. In many ways, it is identical to how we created the forms.

»Step 10: Re-arrange your form. Use Figures A-53 and A-54 as guides, if you want. Switch to Report View (**Report Design Tools | Design | <u>Views</u>**) frequently, to check your progress. Make sure you take up any extra space at the bottom of the "Detail" section by dragging the bottom border.

»Step 11: Change the report title in the Report Header section from "Members" to something better, like "Known Gang Members in Metropolis."

»**Step 12:** Use the "Line" drawing tool 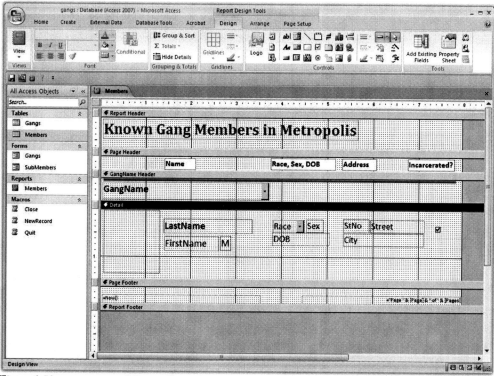 in your Controls section to add a line above the "GangName" field in the "GangName Header" section. You can hold down the **SHIFT** key while drawing it to keep it straight. When finished, use the "Line Thickness" tool to make it thicker.

»**Step 13:** When you're finished, save your report and switch to Report view and admire your work.

Note that we stacked several of the fields on top of each other and deleted and renamed some labels to provide a more eye-pleasing result. We increased the font size on the fields and deleted the "ID" field entirely (as an AutoNumber, it doesn't have much real-world relevance for readers).

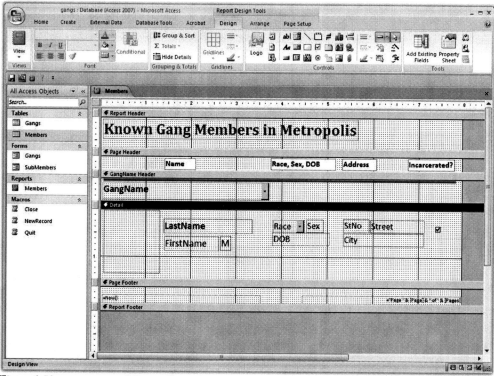

Figure A-53: our new report design…

There are many, many more things that we can do with reports. They can be arranged to present data almost any way you want. They can contain calculated fields, functions, and expressions (all of which we will learn in Section 2). They can include multiple grouping levels and sub-forms. But they take a lot of time and patience to design. After you finish the lessons on queries, begin exploring reports again and see what you can do!

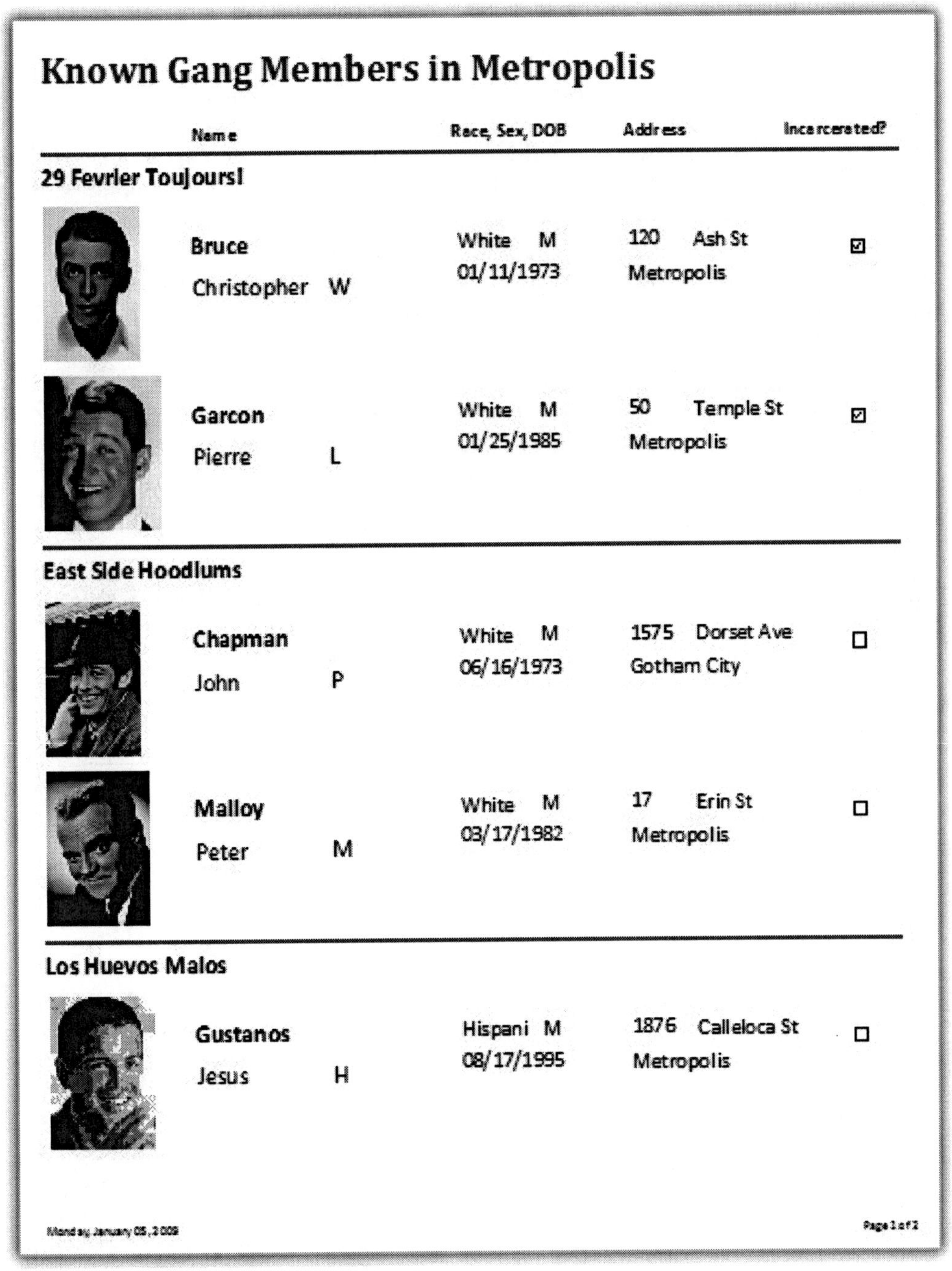

Known Gang Members in Metropolis

	Name		Race, Sex, DOB	Address	Incarcerated?
29 Fevrier Toujours!					
	Bruce Christopher	W	White M 01/11/1973	120 Ash St Metropolis	☑
	Garcon Pierre	L	White M 01/25/1985	50 Temple St Metropolis	☑
East Side Hoodlums					
	Chapman John	P	White M 06/16/1973	1575 Dorset Ave Gotham City	☐
	Malloy Peter	M	White M 03/17/1982	17 Erin St Metropolis	☐
Los Huevos Malos					
	Gustanos Jesus	H	Hispani M 08/17/1995	1876 Calleloca St Metropolis	☐

Monday, January 05, 2009 Page 1 of 2

Figure A-54: ...and the result, in print preview view

Designing a Switchboard

A *switchboard* is a screen that appears when the database is first opened, allowing users to click buttons to go where they want to go. Rather than confront Access novices with the confusing empty database window and Navigation Pane, forcing them to double-click on the form or report they want, a switchboard puts all of the common options on an introductory page.

Access has wizards to help you create a switchboard under **Database Tools | Switchboard Manager**, but as always, we're going to learn it the long way.

The first thing to understand is that a switchboard is just a special type of form, with command buttons that run underlying macros. A switchboard is an *unbound* form, meaning that it doesn't reference or draw upon any data tables. In contrast, our "Gangs" form is a *bound* form; it is bound to the "Gangs" table.

>**Step 1:** Click on **Create | Forms | Form Design**.

A blank form now opens for you, awaiting the creation of your switchboard. This time—unlike with the "SubMembers" sub-form—we will not be adding fields from tables.

>**Step 2:** Save the form as "Switchboard."

Creating a switchboard form is quite easy, since we don't have any fields to drag around and arrange. We simply have to set the background color of the form, add some welcoming text, throw on a few buttons, and save it.

>**Step 3:** Set the background color by clicking in the "Detail" section and using the "Fill/Back Color" tool ![fill color icon] at **Form Design Tools | Design | Font.**

>**Step 4:** Use the label tool on your **Controls** toolbox to add some text reading "Metropolis Police Gang Database" and "What do you want to do?" Adjust the font size, style, and color with the options on the **Font** section.

>**Step 5:** Bring in the badge by choosing **Form Design Tools | Design | Controls | Logo** and navigating to **C:\BPOffice\Access\policebadge.jpg**. Access may automatically open a Form Header and put the logo in there. If so, drag it down to the Detail section and turn off the header at **Form Design Tools | Arrange | Show/Hide | Form Header/Footer** ![header/footer icon].

>**Step 6:** Use the "Command Button" tool on the **Controls** toolbox to add three buttons to your form. Change the label text to read "Enter/Browse Data," "Print Report," and "Quit." Format the text.

»Step 7: Close any existing space on the right and bottom of the form by dragging the borders.

When you're done, your switchboard should resemble Figure A-55. All that remains to complete the form is to write macros that work under each of the buttons.

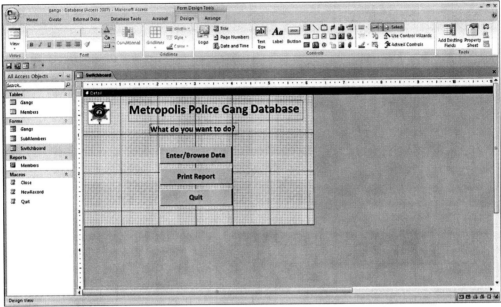

Figure A-55: your designed switchboard

»Step 8: Right-click the "Enter/Browse Data" button and choose **Properties**. Select the "Event" tab and then click in the "On Click" property. Click the ellipse button ⬛ to the right.

»Step 9: Choose "Macro Builder" and click "OK."

»Step 10: Assign one action to your macro: "OpenForm." Down in the "Action Arguments" section, put the "Gangs" form in the "Form Name" box (Figure A-56).

We're going to save this macro as an embedded macro. It will be stored within the form rather than as a separate object.

»Step 11: Close the macro. When prompted, say "Yes" to save the changes and update the property. You will return to the "Properties" box, but now the term "[Embedded Macro]" will be in the "On Click" event property.

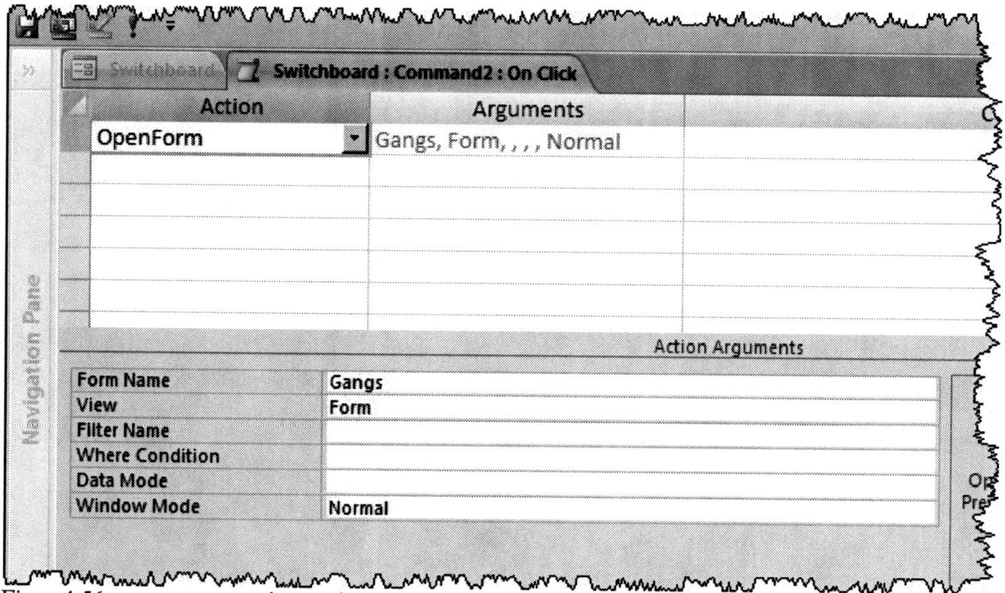

Figure A-56: your macro to open the gangs form.

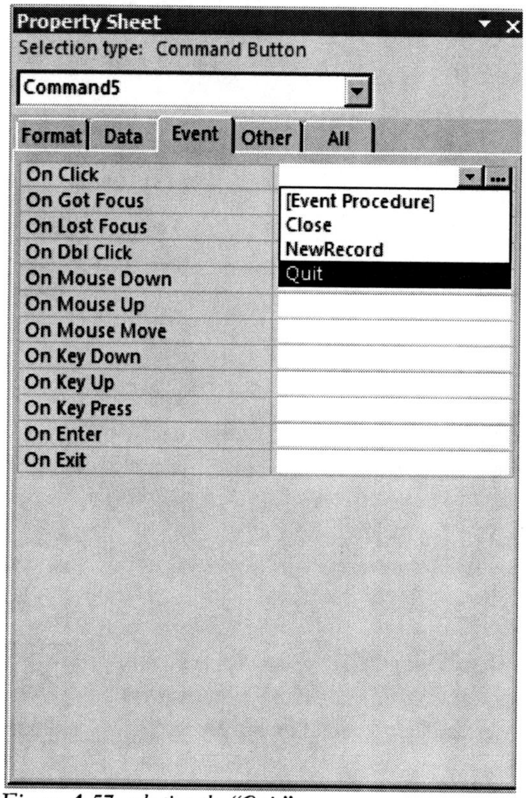

Figure A-57: selecting the "Quit" macro

»Step 12: Modify Steps 7–11 for the "Print Report" button. The macro will have one action: "OpenReport." In the "Arguments" block, put "Members" in the "Report Name" argument. Set the "View" property to "Print Preview."

»Step 13: The final button— "Quit"—is a bit easier, since we already have a macro called "Quit." View the properties for the button, and in the "On Click" property, select the "Quit" macro from the drop-down menu (Figure A-57).

»Step 14: Save your switchboard and switch to Form View.

Your switchboard is finished! Try the various buttons to make sure they work (you will have to restart Access after using the Quit macro). The final step is to tell Access to open the switchboard when the database opens. We do this by creating a macro called "autoexec."

Any macro with this name will run when the database opens. (You can also set a form to load on startup by entering it at **Office Button | Access Options | Current Database | Display Form**.) At the same time, we don't want users messing around with the different objects in the Navigation Pane—perhaps deleting them—so we'll tell Access to collapse that on startup, too.

»**Step 15:** Click **Create | Other | Macro**. This is an alternate way to create a macro we haven't used yet.

»**Step 16:** Set the first action to "RunCommand." The argument for this command is "WindowHide." It will automatically hide the navigation pane when it runs.

»**Step 17:** Set the second action as "OpenForm" and set the "Form Name" argument to "Switchboard."

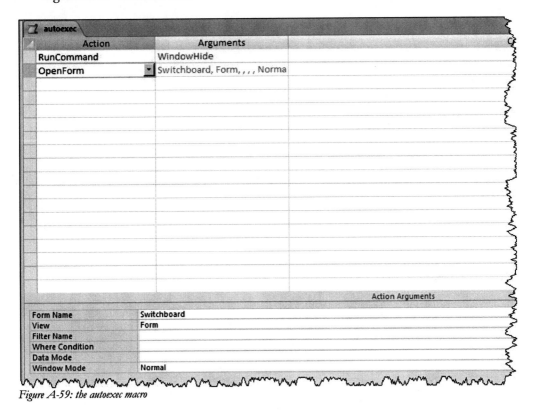

Figure A-59: the autoexec macro

»**Step 18:** Office Button | Save to save the macro as "autoexec" (no quotes). Close it and close the database. Re-open the database and the autoexec macro should run, minimizing the Navigation Pane and opening the switchboard form (Figure A-60).

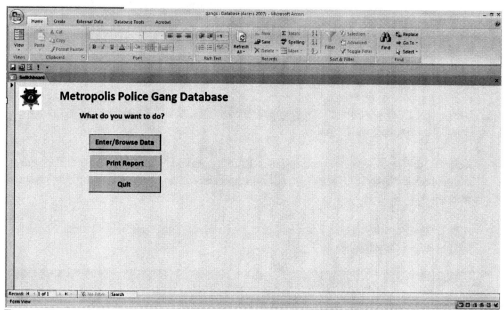

Figure A-60: your switchboard after the autoexec macro has run.

What if *you* (the designer) want to open the database and see the Navigation Pane again? If you ever decide that you want to open the database *without* running the autoexec macro, hold down the **SHIFT** key as you open it. Holding down **SHIFT** disables the "autoexec" macro.

At this point, we have finished with the "Gangs" database. Keep it for future reference if you want.

Using Access to Query Large Datasets

Some police personnel, including many crime analysts, will never use Access to create a full database as we have just done with our gangs. Instead, they will use Access's flexible querying capabilities to make sense of large amounts of data. In this section, we'll use Access to explore a large volume of crime data—filtering, sorting, aggregating, and cross-tabulating it.

ODBC

Access will link to or import data from a wide variety of formats. These include:

- Other Microsoft Access databases

- dbase files

- Microsoft Excel files

- XML files

- Lotus 1-2-3 spreadsheets

- Paradox databases

- Text and HTML files (if organized in a delimited or fixed-width structure)

- ODBC databases

It's the last option—ODBC databases—that really gives you power with Access. ODBC ("Open Database Connectivity") is a technology developed by Microsoft. It uses Microsoft's SQL ("Structured Query Language") to translate data from almost any Database Management System (DBMS).

What this basically means is that almost any application that uses a database (like Access) can connect to almost any kind of database format. ODBC allows you to open information from an Informix database in a Microsoft Excel file. It allows you to connect to a SQL Server database from a GIS program like ArcGIS or MapInfo. And—best of all—it allows you to bypass your old, clumsy, inadequate records management system and link directly to the data with Microsoft Access.

Unfortunately, setting up an ODBC connection is a difficult, multi-stage process, and it often begins with convincing your records management system (RMS) vendor to allow you access to the data in the first place. Some vendors have taken the stance that their database structures are "proprietary," and they consequently refuse to allow open access to the data. This is an obnoxious, harmful stance for vendors to take, and those that refuse open access should be weeded out in the RMS selection process.

Assuming the RMS vendor allows ODBC access, the next step is to install on your computer the appropriate *drivers* for the DBMS that the RMS uses. Some of the most common are SQL Server, Oracle, and Informix. Windows comes with a number of drivers already installed, and certain applications (such as GIS systems) will install additional drivers. If you do not already have the driver for the DBMS that your vendor uses, they should be able to help you obtain it.

With the drivers installed, the next step is to set up the connection to the DBMS in the ODBC control panel. In Windows 2000 and above, this is found by clicking on the "Start" menu, then choosing "Control Panel," "Administrative Tools," and finally "Data Sources (ODBC)." You will need a number of parameters, such as the location and name of the database, and a user name and password to log in. These parameters should, again, be provided by your RMS vendor.

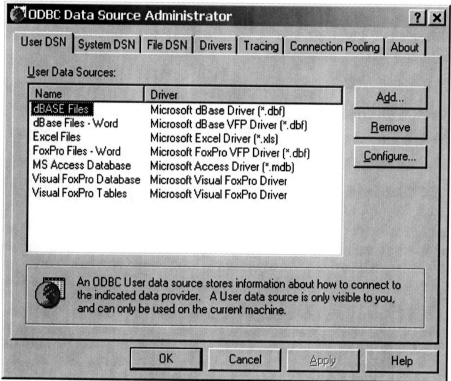

Figure A-61: the ODBC Data Source Administrator control panel in Windows XP.

Once you've set up the data source, you can link to it from almost any application, including Access. You just need to go **External Data | Import | More | ODBC Database.**

Even after you successfully link to the RMS database, however, you many still need to choose from a vast list of tables with confusing names, and within each table you may have to scroll through dozens of fields before you find the ones you want. Depending on the DBMS, you may also have to tell Access how each table is related to the others. It is at this point that a detailed *data dictionary* from your RMS vendor becomes invaluable. But some RMS vendors are unwilling to provide such documentation, and others simply haven't taken the time to create it. The availability of a data dictionary is another question that should be asked during the RMS vendor selection process.

Because of the technical requirements involved, we cannot illustrate direct ODBC access within these hands-on lessons. Instead, we will link to a series of text files that will at least mimic some aspects of direct ODBC connection. These lessons may be particularly valuable for some readers whose RMS vendors do not allow direct ODBC access, but who do allow the system to export data in delimited text format.

Linking to and Importing Data

For these lessons, we have provided a database at **C:\BPOffice\Access\Analysis.accdb.**

»**Step 1:** Open this database, through either Access or Windows Explorer.

To illustrate the various ways of importing and linking to data, we're going to bring in three tables to our "Analysis" database. We will import two of them and link to one of them. These tables will serve as the basis for a number of queries that we shall perform. As we go through these exercises, keep in mind that most of the time, you will access all your tables using a single method; the various ways we're accessing our data are just for illustrative purposes.

It is important to understand the difference between importing and linking to data. When you *import* a table, you make a copy of it. Changes to the original data will not be reflected in your database. When you *link* to data, you are creating a live connection to your source. If the original data changes, the data in your Access database will change. The Access button group at **External Data** called "Import" allows both importing and linking.

Clearly, linking is the best method when you want to be able to work with "live" data, but it has one disadvantage: speed. Imported tables are faster than linked tables, especially when the number of records exceeds a few thousand. Still, the advantages to linking usually outweigh the disadvantages.

While the results of linking and importing are different, the actual process is nearly identical. The steps we follow below would be the same no matter which option we choose.

Our first file is in an existing Microsoft Access database.

»**Step 2:** Choose **External Data | Import | Access.**

The "Files of type" box is already set to "Microsoft Access."

»**Step 3:** Next to the "File name" field, click "Browse." Navigate to **C:\BPOffice\Access\RMS.accdb**, select it, and click "Open."

»**Step 4:** Choose the option button that says "Link to the data source by creating a linked table" and then click "OK."

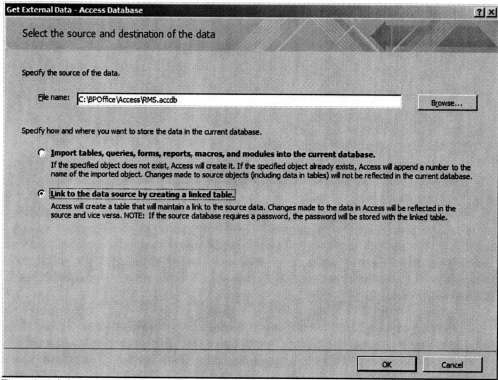

Figure A-62: linking to another Access database

The "Link Tables" box appears. With a real RMS, this box would list many tables—perhaps several hundred, in some systems. In our case, we only have one: "Incidents."

»**Step 5:** Select "Incidents" and click "OK."

The table should appear in your Navigation Pane. The icon next to it ⁺⊞ has an arrow, indicating that it is a linked table.

We will now link to a *delimited text file*. In a delimited text file, data is stored as plain text, with some kind of *delimiter* indicating the separations between each field. Almost any character can be used as a delimiter, but commas, tabs, and pipes (|) are the most common. Our text file is comma-delimited.

»**Step 6:** Choose **External Data | Import | Text File** 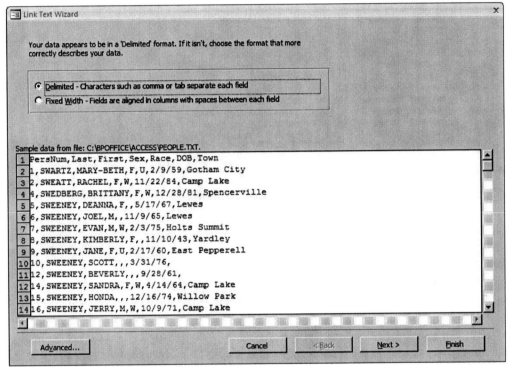.

»**Step 7:** Click "Browse" and navigate to **C:\BPOffice\Access\People.txt**. Select it and click "Open."

»**Step 8:** Choose the option button that says "Link to the data source by creating a linked table" and click "OK."

Access opens the Link Text Wizard (Figure A-63), where we tell it how to treat the file.

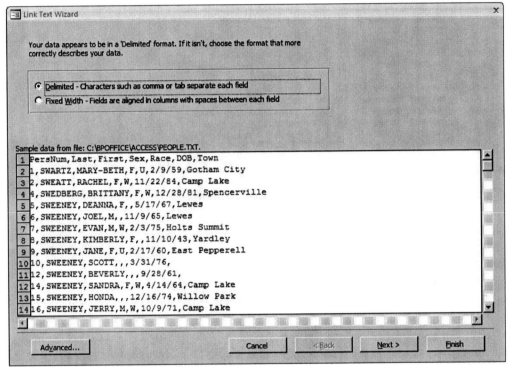

Figure A-63: the "Link Text Wizard"

Access has already (intelligently) figured out that our data is in delimited rather than fixed width format.

»**Step 9:** If Access has already selected "Delimited" then click "Next." Otherwise, select "Delimited" and click "Next."

»**Step 10:** Access now wants to know what our delimiter is. Select "Comma" (Access has probably already selected it).

»**Step 11:** Check the box that reads "First Row Contains Field Names."

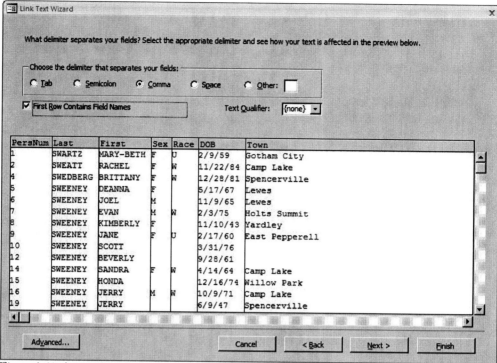

Figure A-64: the second step in the "Link Text Wizard"

In the third step, we can specify our field data types, and in the fourth step, we choose a name for our table. However, Access's defaults are correct on both of these screens, so we do not need to change anything.

>**Step 12:** Click "Next" twice to see what the additional screens look like, then click "Finish."

A new table called "People" should now be available to us. Its icon indicates that it is a linked text file.

In the final stage of this process, we will import a text file in *fixed width format*. Fixed-width files assign a certain number of spaces to each field. The first field starts at space 1, the second perhaps at space 10, the third at space 25, and so on. If the data in the field does not take up all of the spaces allotted to it, blank spaces assume the rest. These files look orderly when viewing them, because everything lines up (Table A-6).

```
Space       1           2           3           4           5           6
12345678901234567890123456789012345678901234567890123456789
INC#          CRIME         DATE        TIME        LOCATION
2004-0006     Larceny       01/01/2004  13:58       200 North St
2004-0007     Robbery       01/02/2004  14:00       100 Fifth St
```

Table A-6: incident data in fixed-width format. "Inc#" begins at space 1, "Crime" at space 14, "Date" at space 28, and so on.

»**Step 13:** Choose **External Data | <u>Import</u> | Text File** 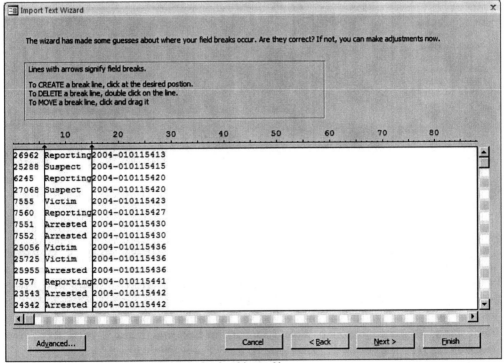 .

»**Step 14:** Click "Browse" and navigate to **C:\BPOffice\Access\ IncidentPeople.txt**. Select it and click "Open."

»**Step 15:** Click the option button that says "Import the source data into a new table in the current database" and click "OK."

Again, Access determines that our data is in fixed width format.

»**Step 16:** If Access has already selected "Fixed Width" then click "Next." Otherwise, select "Fixed Width" and click "Next."

This time, instead of telling Access about delimiters, we have to tell it where one field ends and the next one begins. We do this by drawing lines between the fields. Sometimes Access correctly guesses where a line should go, but other times it does not. In our case, we have to tell Access where the "Role" field ends and the "IncNum" field begins.

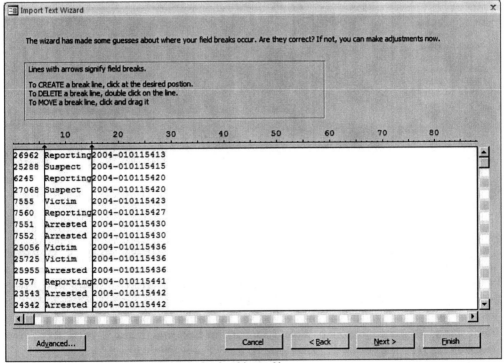

Figure A-65: giving Access instructions on a fixed-width text file

»**Step 17:** Click to add a line at space 15. If you make a mistake, follow the instructions on screen: double-click to delete a line; click to create a new one. When finished, click "Next."

In this case, our file has no header rows. We have to tell Access the names of our fields.

»**Step 18:** Click through the columns and, using the "Field Name" box, change the names from "Field1," "Field2," and "Field3" to "PersNum," "Role," and "IncNum" respectively. See Figure A-66. When finished, click "Next."

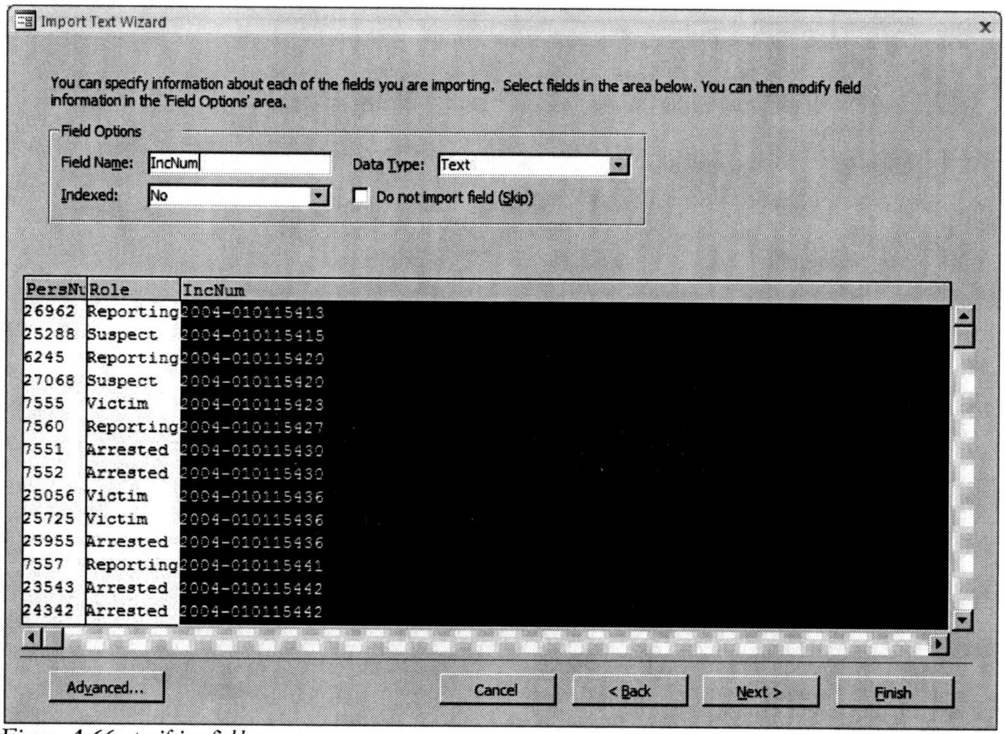

Figure A-66: specifying field names

»**Step 19:** Choose "No primary key" and "Next." Accept the name "IncidentPeople" and click "Finish."

At this point, Access gives you the option to save your import steps. This way, if you need to re-import the file in the future, you won't have to go through all of the options and settings again. (We didn't get this option with the other two tables because we chose to link rather than import them.) If you choose to save them, you even have the option of creating an Outlook task to remind you to re-import periodically! If you choose to save the import steps, you can find them again under **External Data | Import | Saved Imports**. In our case, we don't need to do it, so:

»**Step 20:** Click "Close."

We have now linked to the three tables that we'll be using in these exercises. Your "Analysis" Access database should now resemble Figure A-67.

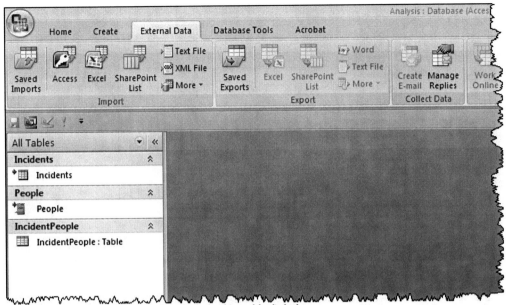

Figure A-67: your "Analysis" database with the three tables linked

Exploring, Sorting, Filtering, and Searching Data

We start our analysis by showing some of the basic exploration functions that can be performed within tables.

> **»Step 1:** Double-click on the "Incidents" table to open it.

> **»Step 2:** Explore the table's columns and rows to get a sense of the data within it.

The "Incidents" table contains all the incidents in the year 2004 in a mid-sized Massachusetts city, plus a few in 2005. There are 54,777 of them. The data has been altered with street names from a different city, and some of the dates have been changed, but it remains a realistic (if not real) synopsis.

The *Find* feature in Access allows you to search for a particular text string or part of a text string within either a particular field or the entire table. We're going to find the first robbery in our data.

> **»Step 3:** Click in the "Incident Type" column and type **CTRL-F** or click the "Find" tool at **Home | Find | Find**.

> **»Step 4:** Type the word "Vandalism" in the "Find What" box. Make sure the "Look In" field is set to "IncidentType."

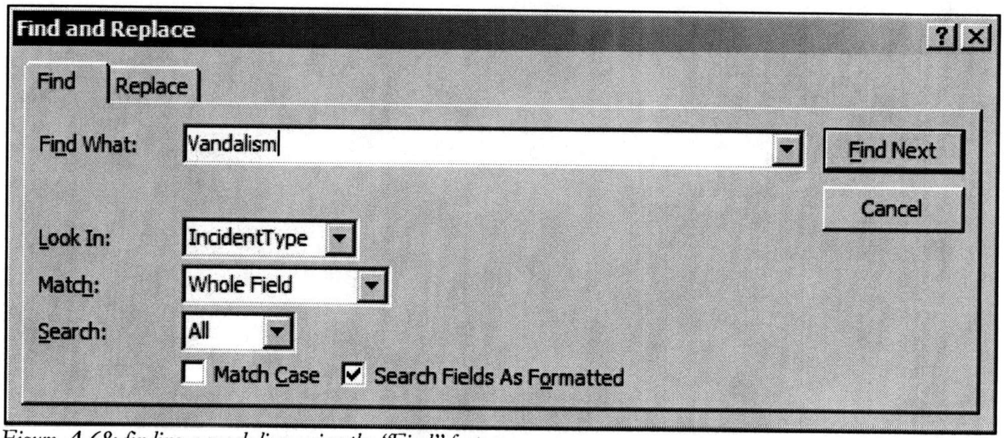

Figure A-68: finding a vandalism using the "Find" feature

»**Step 5:** Click "Find Next." Access will jump to the first vandalism, which is at Record 69. Keep clicking "Find Next" and scroll to a few successive robberies.

This is an example of finding a particular exact text match. There are two other options on the "Match" box: "Start of Field" and "Any Part of Field." Choosing "Start of Field" and searching for "Larc" would find "Larceny from Building," "Larceny from MV," and so on. Choosing "Any Part of Field" and searching for "Break" would produce "Commercial Break" and "Housebreak."

»**Step 6:** Cancel the "Find and Replace" box.

In Access 2007, Microsoft introduced a "Search" box in the Navigation Bar. It works like the "Find" option, except that it finds the text you enter anywhere within the data table—not just in a single field. Sometimes this is helpful, sometimes not.

»**Step 7:** Click the "Search" box on the Navigation Bar and type "Robbery." Note how Access takes you from one record to another as you add letters.

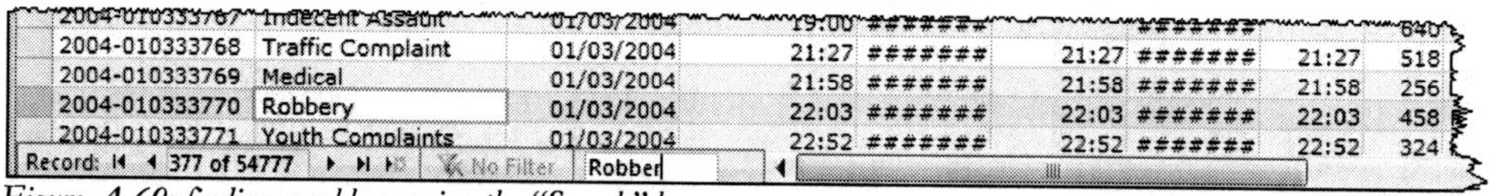

Figure A-69: finding a robbery using the "Search" bar

Now what if we *only* want to see robberies? That involves filtering the data.

»**Step 8:** Right-click on the word "Robbery." A number of possible filters appear at the bottom of the contextual menu. Choose the one that says "Equals Robbery" (Figure A-70).

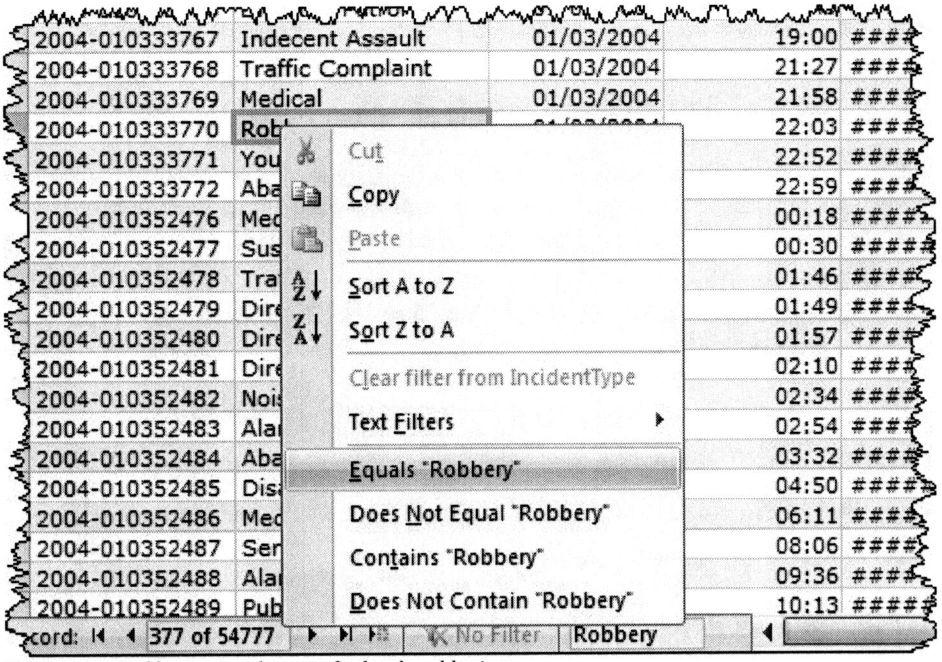

Figure A-70: filtering incidents to find only robberies.

Immediately, 54,777 incidents are filtered down to 35. The navigation bar at the bottom of the screen indicates this new total, as well as the fact that the records are now **▼ Filtered**. The other 54,731 records haven't disappeared; they've just been hidden by our filter.

Assume now that we only want to see robberies that occurred on Main Street, because we think we might have a pattern there.

»Step 9: In the "Street" column, find an incident that happened on "Main St." Right-click on the words "Main St" and choose "Equals Main St."

We now end up with only 11 robberies that occurred on Main Street. But we're not done yet. If you scroll to the right and look at the "Arrest" column, you'll see that two incidents resulted in an arrest. We're not interested in those—we only want the unsolved robberies.

»Step 10: In the "Arrest" column, find an incident in which an arrest was made (i.e., the box is checked). Right-click on the checked box and choose "Is Not Selected."

The two incidents in which an arrest was made now disappear, leaving us with nine. With three quick filters, we have sifted 54,777 records into the nine that most concern us. Read the notes for each of the incidents. Is there something similar to some of the robberies in the earlier part of the year?

»Step 11: Remove the filters, either by clicking the "Filtered" button on the Navigation Bar (▼ **Filtered**), which then changes to "Unfiltered," or by choosing **Home | Sort & Filter | Toggle Filter.**

In addition to filtering and searching, we can also *sort* data in the table. Sorting allows you to organize information in a particular order—for instance, alphabetically by street name, or chronologically by date or time.

»Step 12: Click the "IncidentType" column. Click the "Sort Ascending" tool ᴬ↓ at **Home | Sort & Filter.**

The records automatically sort alphabetically by Incident Type: "911 Errors" first and "Youth Complaints" last.

»Step 13: Click in the "DateOfReport" column. Click the "Sort Descending" tool ᶻ↓. Now the most recent incidents are first.

You can sort by more than one column at the same time. If you wanted to sort by incident type, then by date, for instance, you would select both columns (by clicking on the column header of the first and dragging over to the second), and then click the sort button. Sometimes sorting by more than one column requires you to place them in the proper order; you can re-arrange the order of columns by clicking on the column header once to highlight it, then clicking and dragging it to a desired location.

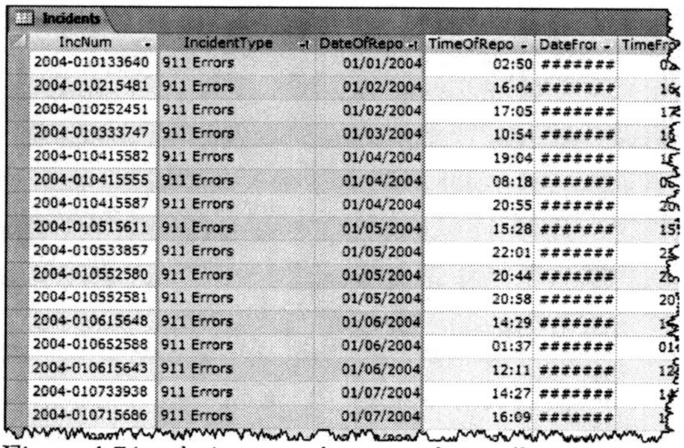

Figure A-71: selecting more than one column allows you to sort by more than one. This selection puts the records in order by incident type first, then by date of report.

Used in concert, finding, filtering, and sorting can be used to quickly organize and understand information.

»Step 14: Click in the "Search" bar and type "Larceny from MV," or use the "Find" tool to find one.

»Step 15: Right-click on the words "Larceny from MV" and choose "Equals Larceny from MV." You should end up with 802 filtered records.

»Step 16: Scroll over to the "PremisesType" column. Thefts at restaurants and bars seem to be an occasional problem. Right-click on the words "Restaurant/Bar" in any record and choose "Equals Restaurant/Bar." You end up with 82 records.

»Step 17: Blanchard Street is over by the college and is a special problem. We'll save thefts there for another day. Right click on the words "Blanchard St" in any record and choose "Does Not Equal Blanchard St." Now we're down to 36 thefts that occurred at restaurants and bars not on Blanchard Street.

»Step 18: What time of day are these incidents most likely to occur? Click in the "TimeFrom" field and click the "Sort Ascending" tool 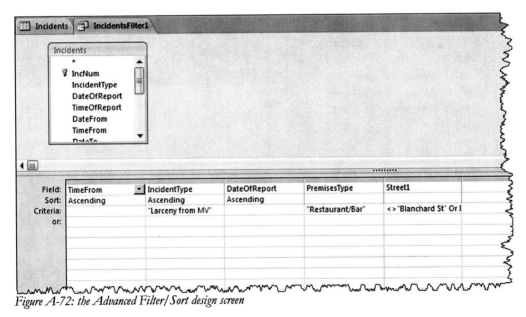. Do you see any patterns in the times of the offenses?

Before we leave this lesson, we should take a quick look at advanced filtering.

»Step 19: Without un-doing your filter, choose **Home | Sort & Filter | Advanced | Advanced Filter/Sort**.

A design grid appears (Figure A-72), and here you can see how Access has written all of the actions we've made in Steps 14–18. We can make additional, more advanced modifications here, but at this point, we're essentially writing a query. In fact, the query design grid looks almost exactly like the screen in front of us. For this reason, we'll leave the lesson here and move on to queries.

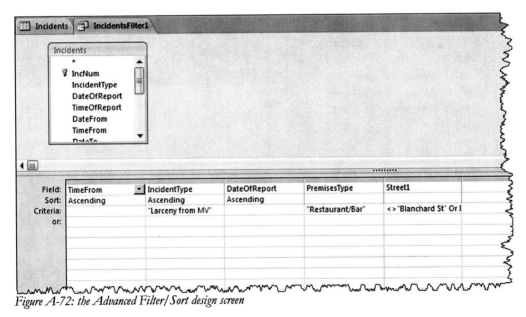

Figure A-72: the Advanced Filter/Sort design screen

»Step 20: Close the filter ☒ and the table. Do not save design changes.

Introduction to Queries

Queries are the power of Microsoft Access. They allow you to join, search, display, and update your data in innumerable flexible and meaningful ways. With queries you can:

1. *Filter Data.* You can use queries to see only the records and fields that you want to see. This functionality is vital for pattern analysis. Have a current report of a convenience store robbery in which a handgun was used? Use Access's filtering tools to find all convenience store robberies in the past year, or all robberies involving a handgun, or all handgun incidents in the same police beat, or any number of other permutations.

2. *Aggregate Data.* With queries, you can summarize data into logical categories to show, for instance, crime statistics for the past year, or the "Top 10" hottest reporting areas for a housebreak.

3. *Cross-tabulate Data.* A logical extension of aggregation, cross-tabulation allows you to compare two categories against each other. How do calls for service break down by shift and beat? How many of each crime have we had each year for the past seven years?

4. *Clean Data.* Special types of Access queries allow you to search for errors and to change, delete, and copy data from one table to another.

The most common type of query is the *select query* which filters data. We'll begin by creating a simple select query and exploring it.

»**Step 1:** Click on **Create | Other | Query Design.** The "Show Table" dialog (Figure A-73) appears, prompting you to add tables to your query.

»**Step 2:** Select the "Incidents" table, click "Add" and then "Close."

You are now taken to the query design grid, and it's worth spending a little time explaining the various parts of this screen, with which you will become intimately familiar. First, though:

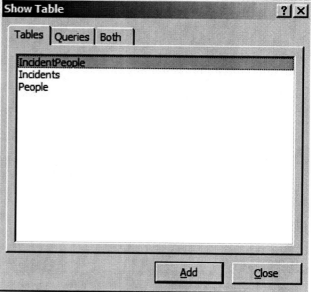

Figure A-73: the "Show Table" dialog box prompts you to add tables to your query

»**Step 3:** In the "Incidents" field list at the top of the screen, double-click on the following fields (you may have to scroll down to reach some of them): "IncNum," "IncidentType," "DateOfReport," "StNo," "Street1," and "PremisesType." When you're finished, your screen should look like Figure A-74.

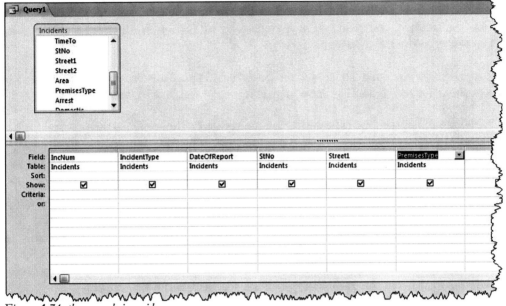

Figure A-74: the query design grid

The query design grid is arranged intuitively. In each column, you specify what fields you want to draw and display from your table. The first two rows allow you to select the field and the table it comes from, but if you double-click on the fields in the field list (as we did), Access fills in those values automatically.

The third row, labeled "Sort" allows us to specify the sort order for the table. There are two options: "Ascending" and "Descending." They work similarly to the "Sort Ascending" and "Sort Descending" tools that we used when exploring tables, but in the design grid, you have the option of combining ascending and descending sorts.

The fourth row, "Show," indicates whether that field is displayed when you view the results of the query. There may be times when you want to specify criteria for a field but not display the field in the final product.

The fifth and subsequent rows are the *criteria* rows, and they hold the power to filtering data in a query. We'll learn a lot about criteria in the next section.

»**Step 4:** Switch to Datasheet View by clicking on **Query Tools | Design | Results | View** to check out the results.

(In a select query, you can also view results by clicking the "Run" button. "Run" and "Datasheet View" are the same thing with select queries. With append, delete, and update queries they are different.)

Note that all of the records from the table are here. We haven't limited the number of records, only the number of fields displayed. Here in the query, you are drawing live data from the table—if you change it in the query, it will change in the table, and vice versa. You can even enter and delete records.

Note also that the query's Datasheet View is indistinguishable from that of a table. You have the same Navigation Bar. You have all the same search, sort, and filter options.

>**Step 5:** Explore the table and its search, sort, and filter options, then return to the query's Design View. (Get used to using this button to switch between Design View and Datasheet View.)

Query Criteria

Learning how to use the criteria rows is essential in creating meaningful select queries. In these fields, you specify which records you want to see by entering exact parameters or parameter ranges. We have text, date, and number fields in our query, and criteria entries look slightly different for each data type. We'll start with some simple ones.

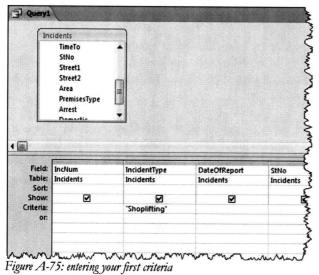

Figure A-75: entering your first criteria

>**Step 1:** In the first "Criteria" field under the "IncidentType" column, enter the word **Shoplifting** (Figure A-75)[2].

When you leave the field, Access will put quotes around any text you enter, signifying that it is *text* you're searching for. You may sometimes have to type the quotes yourself, as Access might get confused if any of the criteria you enter look like functions.

>**Step 2:** Switch to Datasheet View. You should end up with a list of 784 shoplifting incidents. Return to Design View when you're ready.

---

[2] Access criteria are not case-sensitive. You could enter "shoplifting" or "SHOPLIFTING" and get the same results.

What we just entered is an example of an *exact match* criteria: we looked for all records where the "IncidentType" matched the word "Shoplifting" exactly. But there are other types of criteria.

»Step 3: In the first "Criteria" field under "DateOfReport," enter: **>=07/01/2004** (Figure A-76).

When you leave this field, Access will put number signs (#) on either side of the date. This is Access's way of indicating that you are searching for a date or time, rather than text or a number. Again, there may be cases where you have to type the number signs.

»Step 4: Return to Datasheet View.

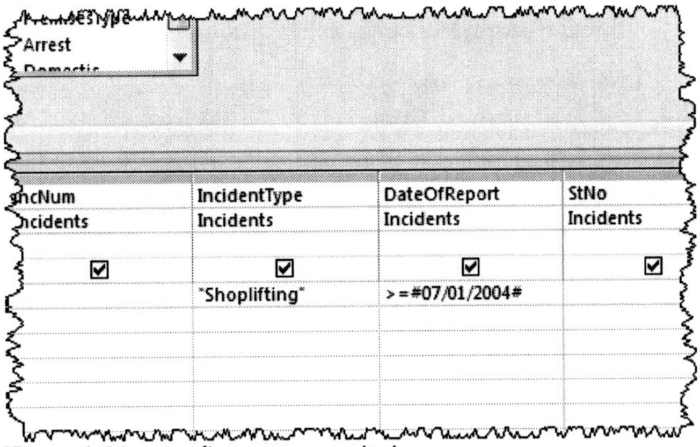

Figure A-76: expanding your query criteria

Now you see 379 shoplifting incidents that occurred on or after July 1, 2004. The "greater than" (>), "less than" (<), "greater than or equal to" (>=), and "less that or equal to" (<=) symbols allow us to search for ranges of data. They are particularly valuable when searching date, time, and number fields, but they also work with text (applying to alphabetical order).

Now assume that we're particularly interested in shopliftings that occurred at different types of department stores, retail stores, and jewelry stores in our area—basically anything that ends with the word "store."

»Step 5: Return to Design View and enter the following in the first "Criteria" row under the "PremisesType" column: **Like "*Store"** (Figure A-77).

This type of criteria is known as a *wild card*. You place an asterisk before the word "store" to search for anything that ends with that string of text. The word "Like" is an Access operator that alerts it that a wild card is coming.

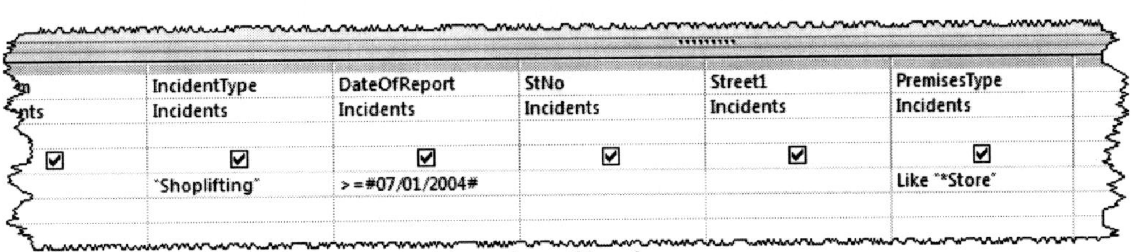

Figure A-77: the query continues to grow, with our first wild card entry

Switching to Datasheet View now will show you 346 records.

Wait!, we decide. We want to see *all* larcenies that have occurred at our various stores during the second half of the year, not just shopliftings. But there are multiple types of larcenies: larcenies from buildings, larcenies from persons, and so on.

>>**Step 6:** For the "IncidentType" criteria, replace the word "Shoplifting" with: **Shoplifting or Like "Larc*"** (Figure A-78).

IncidentType	DateOfReport	StNo	Street1	PremisesType
Incidents	Incidents	Incidents	Incidents	Incidents
☑	☑	☑	☑	☑
"Shoplifting" Or Like "Larc*"	>=#07/01/2004#			Like "*Store"

Figure A-78: combining exact text criteria and wild card criteria in the same field

Now we'll be finding any "shoplifting" but also any crime that begins with the letters "Larc." As you probably guess from this example, you can put the wild card asterisk on either side, or both sides, of the text you're looking for. This is particularly helpful in memo fields, where you might want to find a particular word in a large amount of text.

A trip to Datasheet View shows that we now have 543 records. Time to narrow it down some more, and get more difficult. We're particularly interested in thefts that occurred at the Metropolis Mall, which has addresses between 250 and 380 Main Street, and between 200 and 370 Blanchard Street. We're going to have to add some criteria to the "StNo" and "Street1" fields.

But in doing so, we have to expand to two criteria rows. Understanding why is important. If we were okay with all addresses on either Main Street or Blanchard Street, we could simply enter "Main St or Blanchard St" under the "Street1" field and be done with it. But instead we're looking for specific ranges on each street. Any time you have mutually exclusive combinations two or more fields, you have to expand to multiple criteria rows.

>>**Step 7:** Adjust your query design grid to match Figure A-79.

IncidentType	DateOfReport	StNo	Street1	PremisesType
Incidents	Incidents	Incidents	Incidents	Incidents
☑	☑	☑	☑	☑
"Shoplifting" Or Like "Larc*"	>=#07/01/2004#	Between 250 And 380	"Main St"	Like "*Store"
"Shoplifting" Or Like "Larc*"	>=#07/01/2004#	Between 200 And 370	"Blanchard St"	Like "*Store"

Figure A-79: using two criteria rows

We had to replicate the criteria under "IncidentType," "DateOfReport," and "PremisesType" because we wanted them to apply to both address ranges. Now a jaunt over to Datasheet view shows us 330 records that match these increasingly complicated criteria.

Curses!, we realize. Many of the offenses listed are larcenies from motor vehicles. We're only interested in incidents that occurred *in* the stores.

»**Step 8:** Modify the criteria under the "IncidentType" field on *both* rows to read: **Shoplifting or Like "Larc*" and not "Larceny from MV"** (Figure A-80).

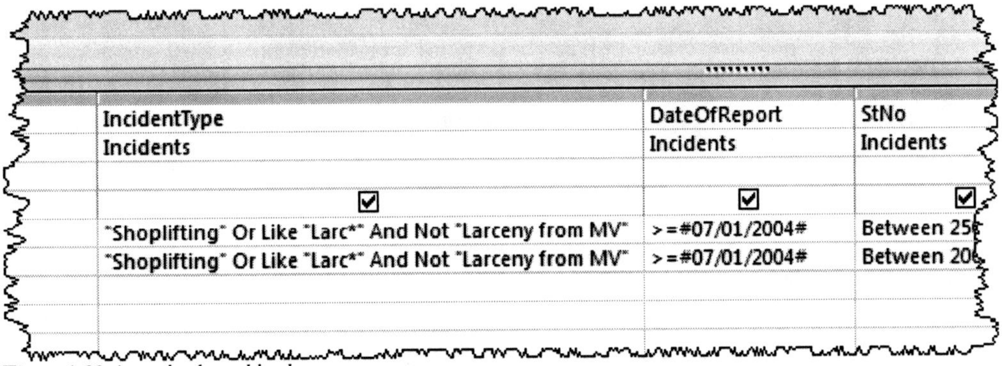

IncidentType	DateOfReport	StNo
Incidents	Incidents	Incidents
☑	☑	☑
"Shoplifting" Or Like "Larc*" And Not "Larceny from MV"	> = #07/01/2004#	Between 25
"Shoplifting" Or Like "Larc*" And Not "Larceny from MV"	> = #07/01/2004#	Between 20

Figure A-80: it gets harder and harder

This modification introduces two new concepts to our criteria. First is the word *and*, which can be used to search for multiple restrictions within the same field. Don't confuse it with *or.* "Shoplifting or Robbery" will find either crime; "Shoplifting and Robbery" will find no crimes, because no incident is going to have two incident types in the same field.

Second is the word *not* which can be used in front of any other criteria to create its opposite. "Robbery" finds robberies, but "Not Robbery" finds anything that isn't a robbery. Similar "Not >=07/01/2005" would find everything in the first half of the year.

Pop over to Datasheet view and you'll see 261 records.

Why are we running this query? Because we have a current spate of larcenies at this shopping mall, and we want to search for any incidents in the past in which an arrest has been made. Perhaps the people we've arrested in the past can be matched to the offenders in the current incident. To perform the final part of the query, we need to add an additional field to the query design grid.

»**Step 9:** In the "Incidents" field list, double-click on "Arrest" to add it to the design grid.

The "Arrest" field is a Yes/No field, which means it can have only two values: yes or no. Therefore, we have only two options for our search criteria.

»Step 10: In the first two "Criteria" rows under the "Arrest" column, enter the word **Yes** (A-81).

Access will *not* put quotes around the word "Yes" because it recognizes the word as a Boolean value (only two options, yes or no). You could also enter "True" or "On" or "-1" in this field to get the same result.

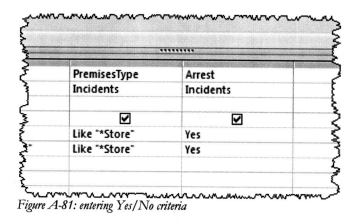

Figure A-81: entering Yes/No criteria

»Step 11: Switch to Datasheet View a final time and see the results of all your querying work: 85 records of larceny arrests at this mall during the second half of 2004.

»Step 12: CTRL-S to save the query as "Larceny Arrests at the Metropolis Mall" and close it ⊠.

The examples in Table A-7 summarize the query criteria and operators we have used so far. You can practice them if you want. The resulting number of records, using the "Incidents" table, is given after each image.

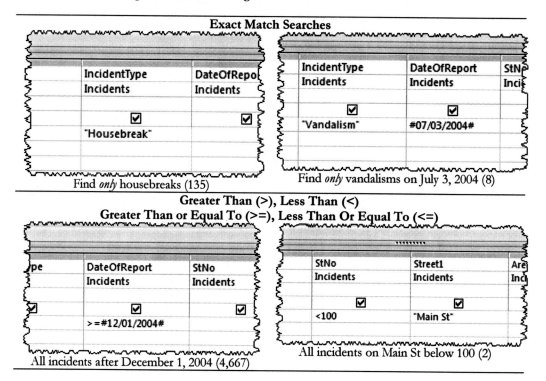

Exact Match Searches

Find *only* housebreaks (135)

Find *only* vandalisms on July 3, 2004 (8)

Greater Than (>), Less Than (<)
Greater Than or Equal To (>=), Less Than Or Equal To (<=)

All incidents after December 1, 2004 (4,667)

All incidents on Main St below 100 (2)

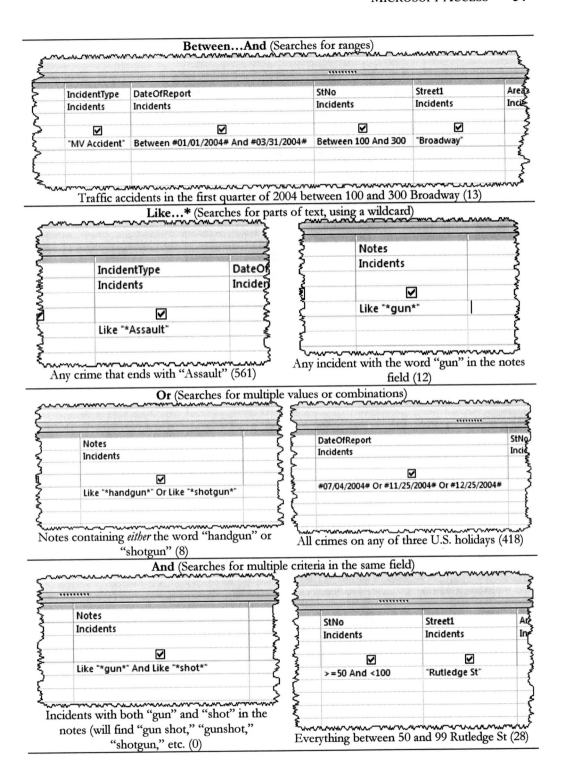

Between…And (Searches for ranges)

IncidentType	DateOfReport		StNo	Street1	Area
Incidents	Incidents		Incidents	Incidents	Inci
☑	☑		☑	☑	
"MV Accident"	Between #01/01/2004# And #03/31/2004#		Between 100 And 300	"Broadway"	

Traffic accidents in the first quarter of 2004 between 100 and 300 Broadway (13)

Like…* (Searches for parts of text, using a wildcard)

IncidentType	DateOf
Incidents	Inciden
☑	
Like "*Assault"	

Any crime that ends with "Assault" (561)

Notes
Incidents
☑
Like "*gun*"

Any incident with the word "gun" in the notes field (12)

Or (Searches for multiple values or combinations)

Notes
Incidents
☑
Like "*handgun*" Or Like "*shotgun*"

Notes containing *either* the word "handgun" or "shotgun" (8)

DateOfReport	StNo
Incidents	Inci
☑	
#07/04/2004# Or #11/25/2004# Or #12/25/2004#	

All crimes on any of three U.S. holidays (418)

And (Searches for multiple criteria in the same field)

Notes
Incidents
☑
Like "*gun*" And Like "*shot*"

Incidents with both "gun" and "shot" in the notes (will find "gun shot," "gunshot," "shotgun," etc. (0)

StNo	Street1	Ar
Incidents	Incidents	In
☑	☑	
>=50 And <100	"Rutledge St"	

Everything between 50 and 99 Rutledge St (28)

Not (Negates other criteria)

IncidentType	DateOfReport		StNo	Street1	Pr
Incidents	Incidents		Incidents	Incidents	In
☑	☑		☑	☑	
Not "MV Accident"	Between #07/01/2004# And #07/31/2004# And Not #07/04/2004#		Not Between 100 And 200	"Blanchard St"	

Everything in the month of July 2004 on Blanchard Street that was *not* a motor vehicle accident, and that did *not* occur on July 4 and was *not* between address range 100 and 200 (314)

Is Null and **Is Not Null** (Searches for blank values or non-blank values)

eport	StNo	Street1
	Incidents	Incidents
☑	☑	
	Is Null		

Notes
Incidents
☑
Is Not Null

Incidents with no street number entered (1,325)

Incidents with something entered in the "Notes" field (47)

Table A-7: different kinds of select query criteria and operators

Aggregation with the Total Row

So far, you've seen how we can use criteria in select queries to filter data. The other major use of queries in crime analysis is to *aggregate* data—to summarize it into categories. Let's see how that works.

»**Step 1:** Click **Create | Other | Query Design.**

»**Step 2:** Add the "Incidents" table and close the "Show Table" box

»**Step 3:** In the field list, double-click on "IncidentType.".

»**Step 4:** Switch to Datasheet View .

So far, nothing new. You have a list of the incident types of all 54,777 records in the database.

»**Step 5:** Return to Design View. Choose **Query Tools | Design | Show/Hide | Totals**. A new row, labeled "Totals," appears in the design grid. The default value is "Group By."

»**Step 6:** Change nothing and return to Datasheet View.

Big difference! Instead of 54,777 records, you now have only 84. No incident type appears more than once. This is because the "Group By" operation has told Access to group the entries in the "Crime" field so that each value appears only one time.

>**Step 7:** Return to DesignVview. Double-click on the "IncNum" field in the field list. In the "Total" row, change the entry under "IncNum" to "Count" (Figure A-82).

>**Step 8:** Switch to Datasheet View.

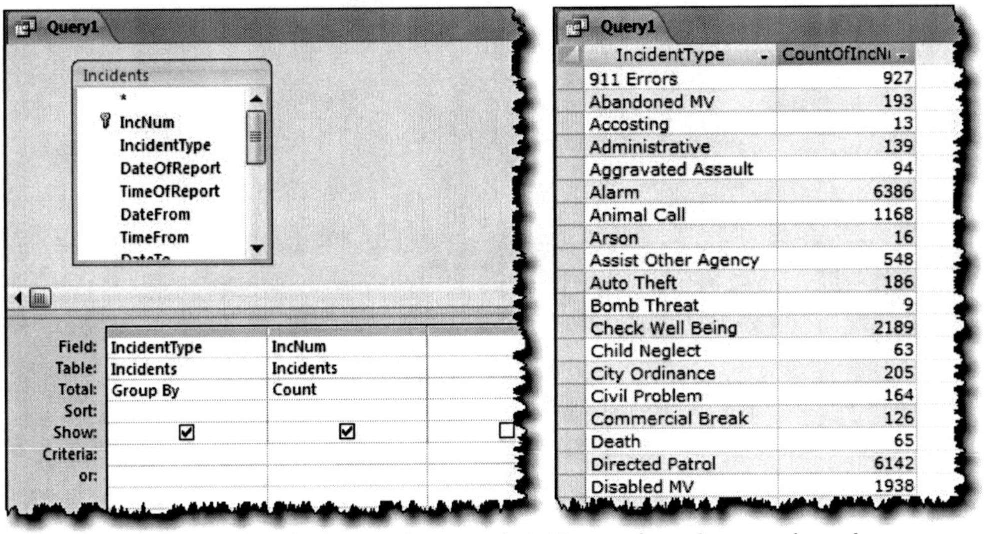

Figure A-82: the design and result of a query that groups by incident number and counts each record

Now we see the power of aggregation! Access has grouped each record in our table by incident type, then counted how many records have those incident types.

>**Step 9:** Sort the count field in descending order ⌄. What are the top incident types that occupy Metropolis police officers' time?

>**Step 10:** Return to Design View.

Note the other options available on our "Total" row: "Sum," "Avg," "Min," "Max" and so on. None of these other aggregation options apply to the data in our table, but they are very useful for numeric data, such as property value. A quick query can give you the maximum, minimum, average, and total of property value stolen for each type of crime, or in each area of the city, or over each month.

When we're simply counting records, it doesn't much matter which field we choose to "Count" as long as it always has a value in it. For this reason, it's usually best to use the table's primary key, as we have done here.

You can combine aggregation with criteria. For instance, assume we're only interested in getting a count of each incident type that occurred during the month of December.

>**Step 11:** Double-click on the "DateOfReport" field to add it to the design grid. Change the "Total" row value to "Where" and enter the following criteria in the criteria row: **Between 12/01/2004 and 12/31/2004** (Figure A-83).

Figure A-83: combining aggregation with criteria searching

Entering "Where" in the "Total" row tells Access that we want to filter by that field, but not group by it, count it, or display it in the query's results. Access first filters out all records that don't match the criteria, then groups by and counts the ones that do.

>**Step 12:** In the "Sort" row under "IncNum," enter "Descending."

>**Step 13:** Switch to Datasheet View.

Now you see (Figure A-84) the top incident types in December 2004.

>**Step 14:** Save the query 💾 as "December 2004 Incident Type Count" and close it.

IncidentType	CountOfIncN
Alarm	577
Directed Patrol	450
MV Accident	446
Medical	429
Disabled MV	230
Check Well Being	221
Suspicious Activity	183
Traffic Complaint	154
MV Offenses	130
Dispute	130
Public Service	109
Service of Papers	88
Road Conditions	84
Larceny from MV	73
Noise Complaints	69
Town Problem	68

Figure A-84: top incidents in December 2004

Multiple Tables in a Query

Part of the value of Access queries is the ability to combine data from multiple tables through related fields. To illustrate this and combine it with the lessons we've already learned, we're going to return to a query we've already created.

»**Step 1:** Right-click on your "Larceny Arrests at the Metropolis Mall" query and choose "Design View" to open it in design view.

(At this point, you may notice that Access, on its own, made some modifications to your criteria rows. It sometimes does this if you have combinations of *ors* and *ands* in the same criteria field. You'll probably see that you now have four criteria rows. This is okay; the query still works the same way.)

This query draws data from only one table: "Incidents." But to be of true value in helping to identify potential suspects in the recent wave of mall larcenies, we need information about the people arrested there in the past.

»**Step 2:** Click on your "IncidentPeople" table in the Navigation Pane, hold down the left mouse button, drag the table into your query design grid, and let it go. Do the same for your "People" table.

(The long way to do this is to choose **Query Tools | Design | Query Setup | Show Table**, select the tables, and click "Add." The ability to drag and drop tables from the Navigation Pane was added in Access 2007.)

When Access adds more than one table to a query design, it tries to figure out how the tables are related. You *must* establish some kind of relationship, because otherwise Access relates every record in one table to every record in the other tables, and utter chaos (often accompanied by the crashing of your computer) ensues.

If you have established relationships between tables in the **Database Tools | Show/Hide | Relationships** window, Access will use these relationships to determine how to join tables in a query. In our case, we didn't set these up. Consequently, Access figures out (correctly) how "Incidents" is related to "IncidentPeople," but not how "IncidentPeople" is related to "People."

»**Step 4:** Click on the "PersNum" field in the "IncidentPeople" field list. Drag and drop it onto the "PersNum" field in the "People" field list.

At this point, you should have three tables in your query design grid with lines connecting "Incidents" to "IncidentPeople" and "IncidentPeople" to "People" (Figure A-85).

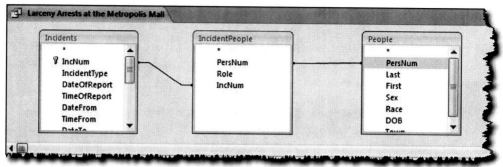

Figure A-85: establishing relationships between tables in a query

>**Step 5:** Double-click on the "Role" field in the "IncidentPeople" field list and the "Town" field from the "People" field list to add them to the design grid.

>**Step 6:** Switch to Datasheet View.

If you'll recall, before we added the "IncidentPeople" and "People" tables to the query, we only had 85 records. Now we have 197. What happened?

There are multiple people associated with each incident. When you join tables in a query, the total number of records reflects the total in the most numerous table. Information from the table with fewer records (in our case, "Incidents") is duplicated for as many records are in the associated table. This is an important factor to understand: there are not 197 *incidents* of larceny arrest at the mall; there are 197 *people* associated with larceny arrests at the mall. Since we're interested in data about people, that's fine. But if we were looking to analyze incident information (such as location and time), we would not want to include the related tables.

>**Step 7:** Return to Design View. Under the "Role" field, enter the word "Arrested" for all of the rows that have other criteria (either two or four, depending on whether Access messed with your query).

Now we're limiting our query to include not just incidents that resulted in an arrest, but also to include person data only for people who were themselves arrested—no witnesses, victims, and so on.

If you run the query now, you'll see 104 records. There are still some

remisesType	Arrest	Role	Town
cidents	Incidents	IncidentPeople	People
☑	☑	☑	☑
ike "*Store"	Yes	"Arrested"	
ike "*Store"	Yes	"Arrested"	
ke "*Store"	Yes	"Arrested"	
ike "*Store"	Yes	"Arrested"	

Figure A-86: limiting the query to those arrested

duplications of incidents because often more than one person is arrested in a single incident. Now let's find out some aggregated information about the people we've arrested for larceny at our mall.

»**Step 8:** Return to Design View. Choose **Query Tools | Design | Show/Hide | Totals**.

»**Step 9:** In the "Total" row, enter "Where" for all fields that currently have criteria (i.e., every field except "Town" and "IncNum"). "Group By" the "Town" and "Count" the "IncNum" field. In the "Sort" row under "IncNum," enter "Descending" (see Figure A-87).

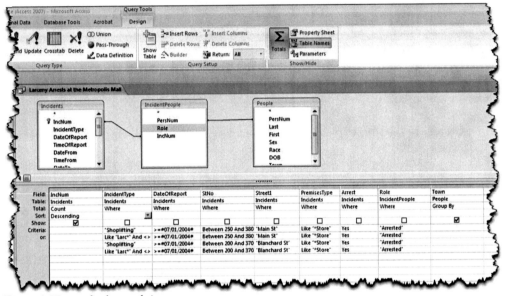

Figure A-87: your final query design

»**Step 10:** Switch to Datasheet View to see the result (Figure A-88). Looks like we need to make a petition to Batman, doesn't it?

»**Step 11:** Save the query and close it.

Creative combinations of criteria (filtering) and aggregation can provide you with the answers to almost any question that you might ask of your data. We encourage you to experiment with more queries to understand the nature of crime and disorder in Metropolis, or your town.

CountOfIncN	Town
17	Gotham City
12	Yardley
9	Camp Lake
8	Metropolis
7	Holts Summit
6	Spencerville
5	Saltville
4	Woodland Beac
4	Lewes
3	Ellsworth

Larceny Arrests at the Metropolis Mall

Figure A-88: top providers of mall thieves to Metropolis

Expressions, Functions, and Calculations

As we learned when we were setting table validation rules back at the beginning of this chapter, *expressions* are combinations of field values, operators, and functions that produce a result. *Functions* are pre-programmed commands that return a value based on a calculation or other operation.

Expressions and functions greatly enhance your ability to manipulate data. We are going to look at a wide variety in this section.

> **»Step 1:** Create a new query (**Create | Other |Query Design**). Add the "Incidents" table and close the "Show Table" box.

Expressions, functions, and calculations are typed in the "Field" row of the design grid, as an alternative to double-clicking on a field and adding it. The simplest expressions do nothing more than re-name an existing field. For instance, the field named "DateOfReport," while descriptive, is fairly clunky. The readers of our reports may want something simpler.

> **»Step 2:** In the blank "Field" row of the first column, type: **Date: DateOfReport** (Figure A-89).

If you switch to Datasheet View, you will see that the column that normally would have a "DateOfReport" heading now simply reads "Date."

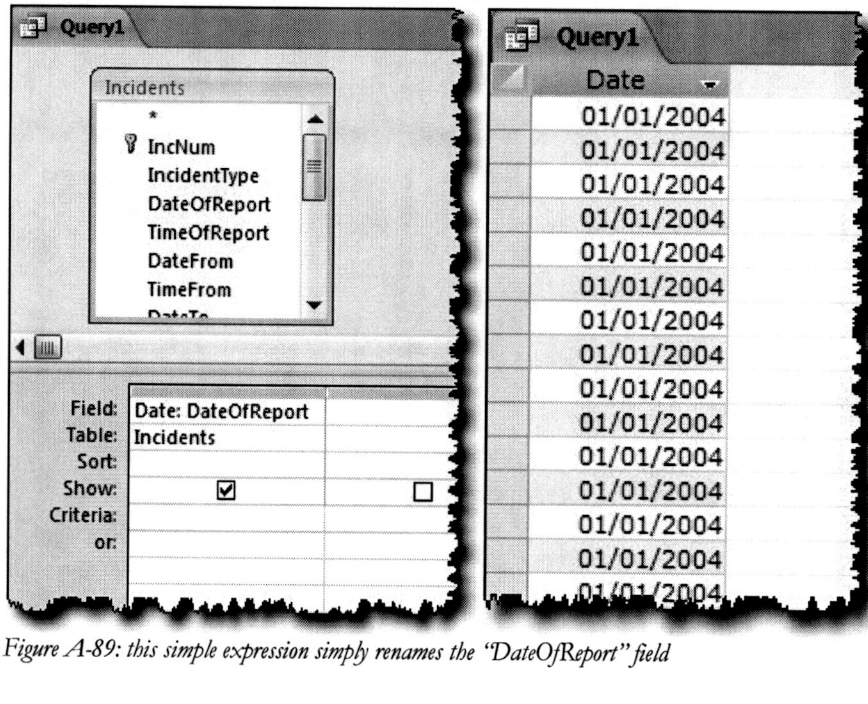

Figure A-89: this simple expression simply renames the "DateOfReport" field

All expressions are preceded with the name of the resulting field and a colon. We will see more examples.

More advanced expressions *concatenate* or combine multiple fields.

»**Step 3:** In the blank "Field" row of the second column, type: **Address: [StNo] & " " & [Street1]** (Figure A-90). Make sure you put a space in between those quotation marks.

This expression sticks the address number and street name in a single field called "Address," with a space between them. The brackets indicate field names—if you don't type them, Access will insert them itself. The ampersands (&) are *operators* that tell Access to concatenate: take the "StNo" field *and* a space (in quotes) *and* the "Street1" field.

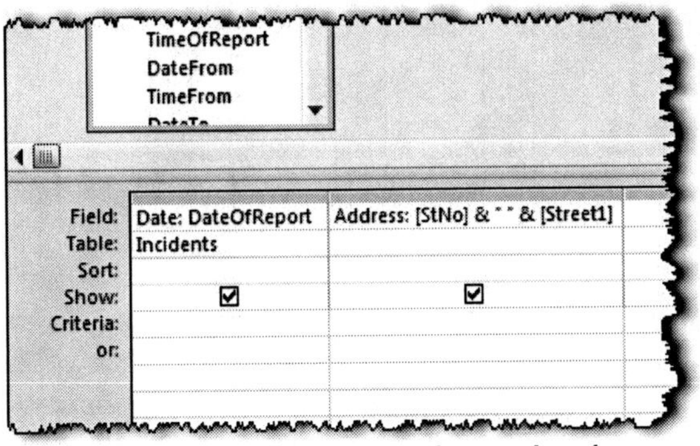

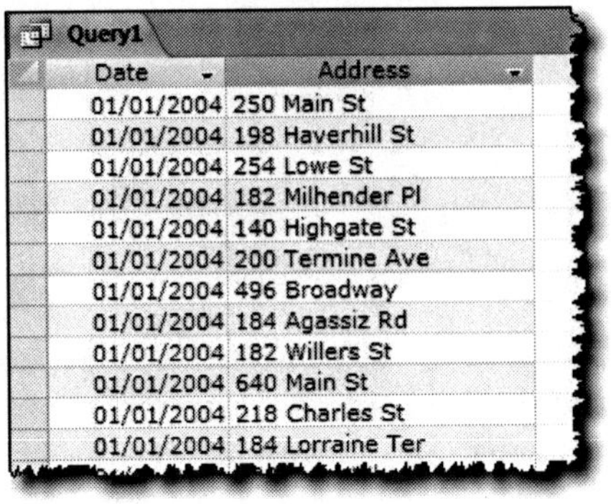

Figure A-90: concatenation expression design and result

Now it's time for some functions, which manipulate existing data in new ways. There are numerous functions available in Access; many are listed in Table A-8. Some of the most valuable extract parts of dates.

»**Step 4:** In successive blank "Field" rows, enter the following functions:
  Year: Year([DateOfReport])
  Month: Format([DateOfReport],"mmm")
  Year-Month: Format([DateOfReport],"yyyy-mm")

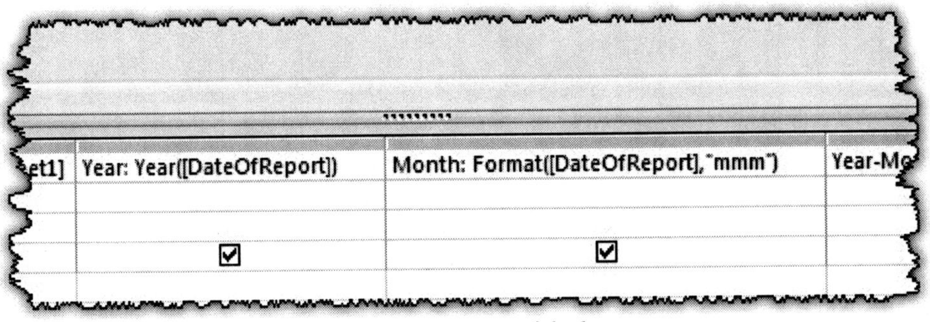

Figure A-91: three functions that re-arrange or extract parts of the date…

Date	Address	Year	Month	Year-Month
01/01/2004	250 Main St	2004	Jan	2004-01
01/01/2004	198 Haverhill St	2004	Jan	2004-01
01/01/2004	254 Lowe St	2004	Jan	2004-01
01/01/2004	182 Milhender Pl	2004	Jan	2004-01
01/01/2004	140 Highgate St	2004	Jan	2004-01
01/01/2004	200 Termine Ave	2004	Jan	2004-01
01/01/2004	496 Broadway	2004	Jan	2004-01
01/01/2004	184 Agassiz Rd	2004	Jan	2004-01
01/01/2004	182 Willers St	2004	Jan	2004-01
01/01/2004	640 Main St	2004	Jan	2004-01
01/01/2004	218 Charles St	2004	Jan	2004-01
01/01/2004	184 Lorraine Ter	2004	Jan	2004-01
01/01/2004	186 India Wharf	2004	Jan	2004-01
01/01/2004	420 Mallon Rd	2004	Jan	2004-01
01/01/2004	280 Hillsboro Rd	2004	Jan	2004-01
01/01/2004	446 Addison St	2004	Jan	2004-01
01/01/2004	730 Main St	2004	Jan	2004-01
01/01/2004	580 Westcott St	2004	Jan	2004-01
01/01/2004	384 Blanchard St	2004	Jan	2004-01
01/01/2004	214 Service Rd	2004	Jan	2004-01

Figure A-92: …and the results

The YEAR and FORMAT functions illustrate function syntax. Functions are always followed immediately by a set of parentheses. Inside the parentheses is the name of the field that the function applies to. If there are any arguments required for the function, these follow the field name after a comma. Some functions, like YEAR, have no arguments—just the field name that contains the date from which the year is to be extracted. Others, like FORMAT, have one argument—the nature of the format. Some functions have multiple arguments (see Table A-8).

A small number of functions, like NOW (calculates the current date and time) and DATE (calculates the current date) have nothing inside the parentheses—you just open and close them: DATE(). The parentheses are still necessary to tell Access that you're using a function instead of, for instance, a field name called "Date."

We will do more with date functions during the next lesson on cross-tabulation. For now, we'll move on to another function and calculation.

>>**Step 5:** Close this query. Save it if you want to refer back to it later.

>>**Step 6:** Select your "Larceny Arrests at the Metropolis Mall" query and open it in Design View.

We already used filtering and aggregation to determine the most likely towns of residence for our mall thieves. Now let's take a look at their ages. There is no "Age" field, but we can calculate the individual's age, at the date of offense, based on his or her date of birth.

»Step 7: Select the "Town" field by clicking on the thin gray selector bar above it. Hit the **DELETE** key to remove it from the query.

»Step 8: In the nearest blank column to the right, type the following in the "Field" row:

Age: INT((([DateOfReport]-[DOB])/365.25)

(Look at the expression carefully to make sure you see the difference between parentheses and brackets. Parentheses follow functions and enclose their arguments; brackets surround field names.)

This expression is two calculations within a function. Let's break it down.

[DateOfReport]-[DOB] subtracts the person's date of birth from the date of the report. This provides the person's age in days.

([DateOfReport]-[DOB])/365.25 takes this age in days and divides it by 365.25 to give us the age in years (the .25 accounts for leap years). The parentheses are necessary to tell Access to perform the subtraction first; otherwise, by normal order of operations, it would perform the division first.

We could go with this calculation alone, but the result would be a ridiculously precise age, down to the nanosecond (e.g., 32.78493910). The INT function strips away the decimals and gives us a straight integer. (We wouldn't want to use a ROUND function, because someone who is 36.99999 is still considered 36 until he reaches his 37th birthday.) So we enclose the entire calculation within the opened-and-closed parentheses of the INT function to achieve our result.

»Step 9: Switch to Datasheet view and see the result. Re-arrange the order of the columns so that the age comes first, and sort ascending ⍖ by this column.

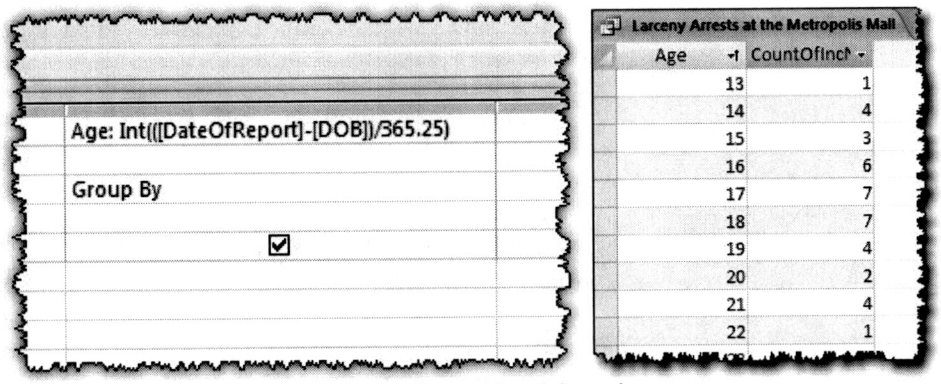

Figure A-93: the "Age" calculation within our design grid, and the result

Table A-8: Common Functions in Microsoft Access

For the purposes of these examples, assume that we have a table containing an incident number, a date, a time, a crime, a street number ("STNO") and a street. Assume that the current date is 05/29/2009. The records that we'll use for most of the examples looks like this:

INUM	DATE	TIME	CRIME	STNO	STREET
I0902150	02/15/2009	19:24	ROBBERY	120	Ash St
I0907151	06/24/2009	09:30	BURGLARY	500	Main St

Function	Use/Parameters	Examples...	...Returns
DATE	Returns the current date	DATE()	05/29/2009
DATEVALUE	Forces access to recognize a field or expression as a date. Use this when you want to build another query that does calculations or performs functions on the date field.	DATEVALUE("01/01/2009")	01/01/2009
DAY	Returns the numeric day from a date field	DAY([Date])	15 24
FORMAT	Re-formats the a date/time (or part of it) to whatever you desire. Requires a parameter (after the comma) that specifies what you want	FORMAT([Date],"mmm")	Feb Jun
		FORMAT([Date],"mmmm")	February June
		FORMAT([Date],"ddd")	Sun Wed
		FORMAT([Date],"dddd")	Sunday Wednesday
		FORMAT([Date],"yyyy")	2009 2009
		FORMAT([Date],"yyyymmdd")	20090215 20090624
		FORMAT([Date],"ddmmmyy")	15FEB09 24JUN09
HOUR	Extracts the hour of day from the time.	HOUR([Time])	19 9
IIF	Allows you to create a series of values based on criteria in your fields	IIF([Time]>=#07:00:00# and [Time]<#19:00:00#,"Day","Night")	Night Day
INT	Chops off decimal places from a number	INT(23.693940)	23
LCASE	Converts a text field to lower case	LCASE([Crime])	robbery burglary
LEFT	Takes the specified left number of characters from a field	LEFT([CRIME],3)	ROB BUR

Function	Use/Parameters	Examples...	...Returns
LEN	Shows you the number of characters in a text field	LEN([Street])	6 7
MID	Returns the specified number of characters from a specified point in a text string.	MID([Crime],2,4)	OBBE URGL
		MID([Street],3,2)	h in
MINUTE	Extracts the minute from the time	MINUTE([Time])	24 30
MONTH	Returns the numeric month from a date field	MONTH([Date])	2 6
NOW	Returns the current date and time. Useful for calculations. When used in calculations, calculates by day.	NOW()	05/29/2009 18:39
		NOW()-[Date]	103.78 -25.22
RIGHT	Takes the specified left number of characters from a field	RIGHT([Crime],3)	ERY ARY
ROUND	Rounds a field or calculation to a specified number of digits.	ROUND(NOW()-[Date],0)	104 -25
		ROUND(NOW()-[Date],1)	103.8 -25.2
TRIM	Removes spaces from the beginning and end of a text string. Useful for cleaning addresses for geocoding.	TRIM(" 150 Main St ")	150 Main St
UCASE	Turns lower case into upper case text	UCASE([Street])	ASH ST MAIN ST
WEEKDAY	Gives the numeric weekday based on a parameter. For 1=Sunday, the parameter is 1. For 1=Monday, the parameter is 2.	WEEKDAY([Date],1)	1 4
		WEEKDAY([Date],2)	7 3
YEAR	Returns the year from a date field	YEAR([Date])	2009 2009

Access has never documented its functions very well, but Access 2007 has better documentation than previous versions. One way to determine the uses and syntax of a function is to use Access's otherwise fairly useless Expression Builder. Right-click on an empty Field row in a query, choose "Build," double-click on "Functions" and then "Built-In Functions." On the right-hand side, select a function you're curious about and click the "Help" button. A small browser window will open with information about that function.

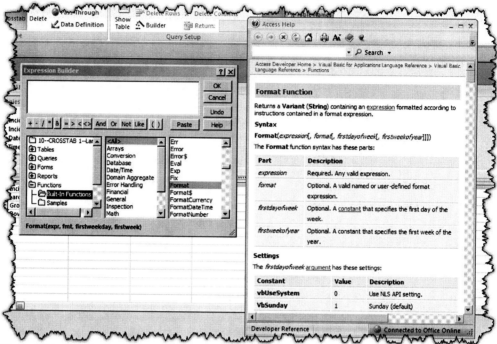

Figure A-94: using the Expression Builder to learn more about functions

You can use functions and expressions in reports as well, by creating a text box and entering the expression where you would normally enter the field name. The one difference in syntax is that instead of beginning the expression with the name of the resulting field and a colon, you begin with an equals sign (=).

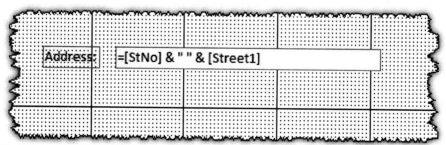

Figure A-95: using an expression in a report

Cross-Tabulations

Cross-tabulation queries build upon aggregation by allowing you to compare two category groupings. We're going to build a cross-tabulation that shows how many incidents we had by type and by month.

>**Step 1:** Start a new query. Add the "Incidents" table and close the "Show table" box.

>**Step 2:** Double-click on "IncidentType" and "IncNum" in the field list to add them to your query design grid.

>**Step 3:** In the third column, in the blank "Field" row, type:
>   **Month: Month([DateOfReport])**

This function, MONTH, extracts the numeric month from a date (e.g., 1 for January, 2 for February, and so on).

>**Step 4:** Click on **Query Tools | Design | Query Type | Crosstab**.

These options under the "Query" menu are how you change from a select query to one of the other Access query types. When you choose "Crosstab Query," you are given two new rows: the "Total" row, which we've seen before, and the "Crosstab" row, which determines each field's role in the cross-tabulation.

A cross-tabulation requires at least three elements: a row heading (the categories that appear along the left side), a column heading (the categories that appear along the top), and a value (what appears in the middle). You GROUP BY row headings and column headings, and COUNT, SUM, or perform some other aggregation on values.

>**Step 5:** Make "IncidentType" the "Row Heading," "Month" the "Column Heading," and "IncNum" the "Value." For "IncNum," change the "Total" row to read "Count." When you are finished, your design should look like Figure A-94.

>**Step 6:** Switch to the query's Datasheet View.

This particular cross-tabulation allows us to see seasonal patterns. Note how animal calls logically increase during the summer months, how robberies seem to be weighted towards the first few months of the year, and how OUI (drunk driving) seems to shoot up for the December holidays.

Cross-tabulations often beg to be graphed. Fortunately, Access allows easy export of *any* query to Excel for that purpose. Choose **External Data | Export | Excel** to convert the query to Excel. A checkbox allows you to immediately open the Excel file.

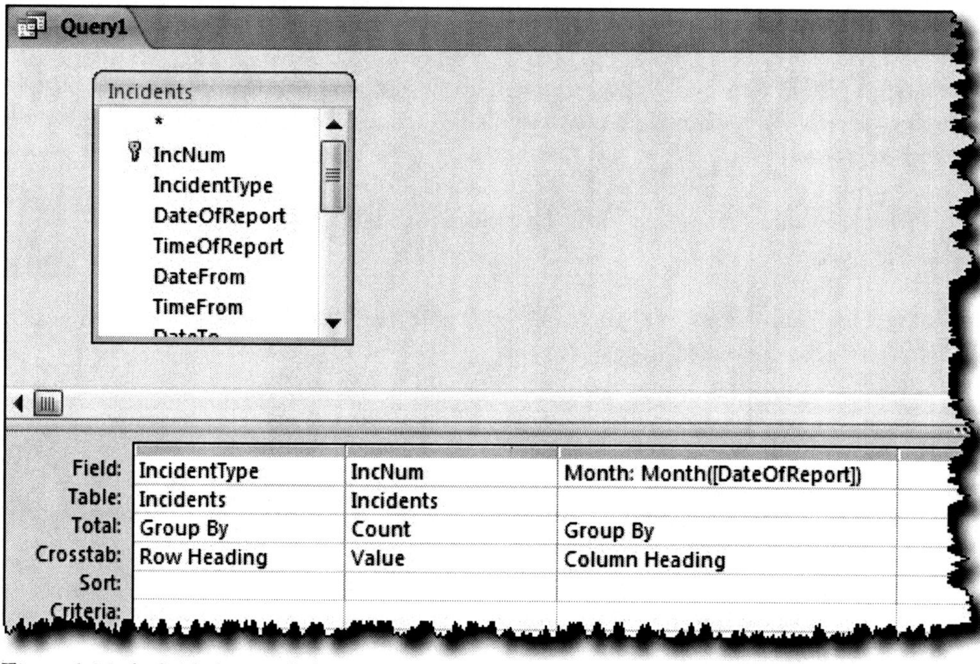

Figure A-96: the finished cross-tabulation query design...

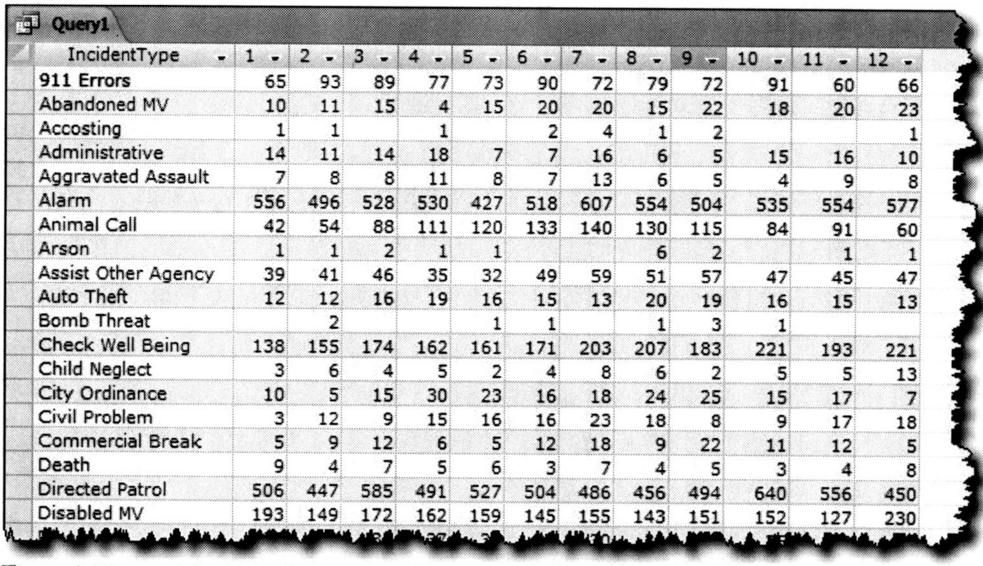

IncidentType	1	2	3	4	5	6	7	8	9	10	11	12
911 Errors	65	93	89	77	73	90	72	79	72	91	60	66
Abandoned MV	10	11	15	4	15	20	20	15	22	18	20	23
Accosting	1	1		1		2	4	1	2			1
Administrative	14	11	14	18	7	7	16	6	5	15	16	10
Aggravated Assault	7	8	8	11	8	7	13	6	5	4	9	8
Alarm	556	496	528	530	427	518	607	554	504	535	554	577
Animal Call	42	54	88	111	120	133	140	130	115	84	91	60
Arson	1	1	2	1	1			6	2		1	1
Assist Other Agency	39	41	46	35	32	49	59	51	57	47	45	47
Auto Theft	12	12	16	19	16	15	13	20	19	16	15	13
Bomb Threat		2		1	1		1	3	1			
Check Well Being	138	155	174	162	161	171	203	207	183	221	193	221
Child Neglect	3	6	4	5	2	4	8	6	2	5	5	13
City Ordinance	10	5	15	30	23	16	18	24	25	15	17	7
Civil Problem	3	12	9	15	16	16	23	18	8	9	17	18
Commercial Break	5	9	12	6	5	12	18	9	22	11	12	5
Death	9	4	7	5	6	3	7	4	5	3	4	8
Directed Patrol	506	447	585	491	527	504	486	456	494	640	556	450
Disabled MV	193	149	172	162	159	145	155	143	151	152	127	230

Figure A-97: ...and the result

You can use filters in a crosstab just like in other aggregation queries. Simply put "Where" in the Total row (as before) and enter nothing in the Crosstab row. For instance, Figure A-98 shows a query design that crosstabulates incident types by month, but only for incidents that occurred at schools.

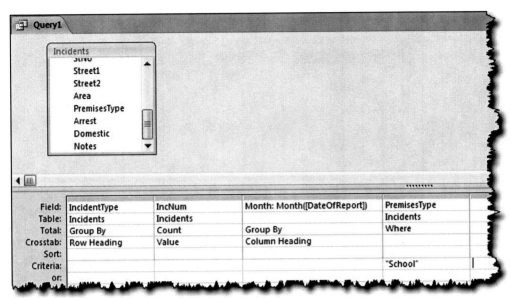

Figure A-98: expanding the crosstab to include criteria fields

Using Parameters in Queries

You may design queries that you would like to run frequently, with the criteria changing each time you run them. For instance, you might want to create a standard "crime matrix" that includes your most valuable fields, but which changes crimes and dates depending on the context. *Parameters*, which replace specific criteria, can accomplish this for you.

To use parameters, we replace specific criteria with prompts, enclosed in brackets. When you run the query, a small pop-up box gives you the prompt, and you enter the criteria that you want to use for that session of the query. We will design a quick example.

»**Step 1:** Start a new query. Add the "Incidents" table and close the "Show table" box.

»**Step 2:** Add the following fields to the query: IncNum, IncidentType, DateOfReport, TimeFrom, TimeTo, StNo, Street1, and PremisesType.

»**Step 3:** Enter the following criteria under the "IncidentType" column: [ENTER INCIDENT TYPE]

»**Step 4:** Add the following criteria under the "DateOfReport" column: Between [ENTER FIRST DATE] and [ENTER LAST DATE]

Refer to Figure A-99 for the specific query design.

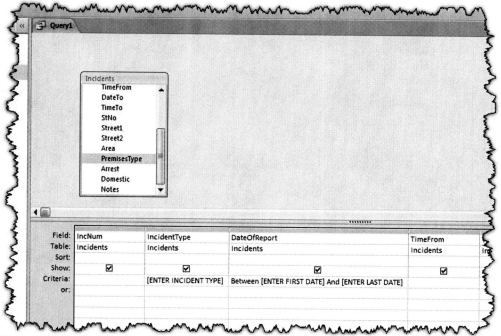

Figure A-99: using parameters in a query

»Step 5: Save the query as "CrimeMatrix" and then run it or switch to Datasheet View. Pop-up boxes should appear with the prompts that you specified in the brackets. Enter "Robbery" when prompted for the incident type, "01/01/2004" when prompted for the first date, and "12/31/2004" when prompted for the end date (without the quote; see Figure A-100).

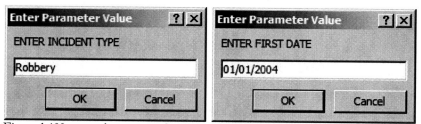

Figure A-100: pop-up boxes prompt for criteria when using parameters

»Step 6: A list of 35 robberies should appear. Close and re-run the query, this time searching for shoplifting between 11/01/2004 and 12/31/2004. You should get 141 records.

You can use parameters in place of specific criteria in any type of query. Always enter the prompt inside square brackets, and when prompted, always enter the criteria exactly as you would enter it in the query design if you weren't using parameters.

Access can get confused with parameters in aggregation and crosstabulation queries, and it may give you an error when you try to use them. To avoid confusion and errors, you must use the "Query Parameters" box at **Query Tools | Design | Show/Hide | Parameters** when in Design View. The "Query Parameters" dialog (Figure A-101) allows you to tell Access what parameters to expect in the query and what type of data those parameters will contain. Although they are not strictly necessary for select queries, it never hurts to use them. Just remember that you must type your parameters in this box *exactly* how you have typed them in the query criteria.

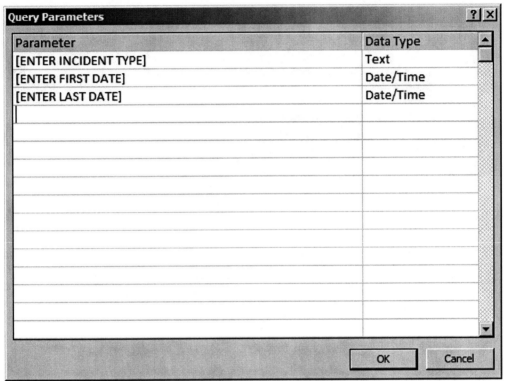

Figure A-101: the Query Parameters dialog, necessary for using parameters in aggregation and crosstabulation

Finally, you should be aware that instead of parameters that *prompt* for the criteria, you can enter parameters that look to a form (usually an unbound form) for those criteria. The syntax for such parameters is [Forms]![*FormName*]![*FieldName*]. For instance, in Figure A-102, you see an example of a screen used by a police Records Unit to generate an automated report of towed vehicles for a particular time period, for purposes of billing the towing companies.

This form is called "Welcome," the first tow date is called "TowDate1" and the second tow date is called "TowDate2." Figure A-103 shows the specific query criteria used to refer to this form and these fields. Clicking the "Tows" button runs a report that looks to this query for its data.

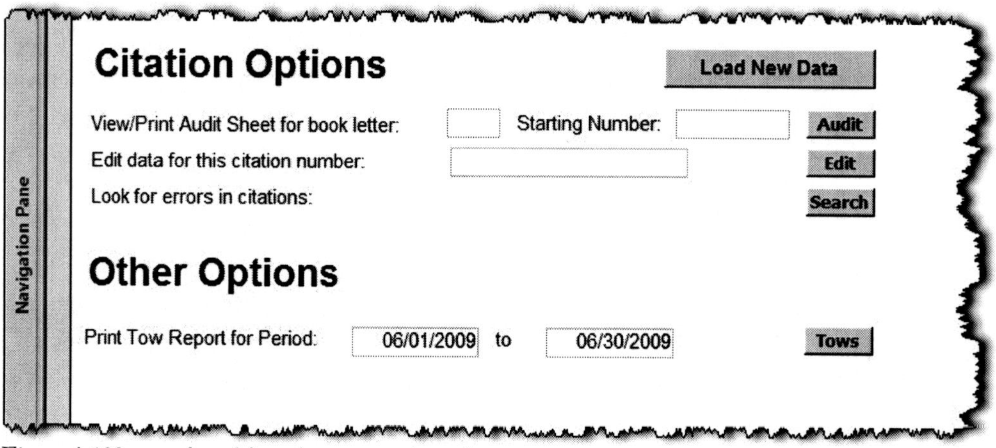

Figure A-102: an unbound form that runs queries and reports

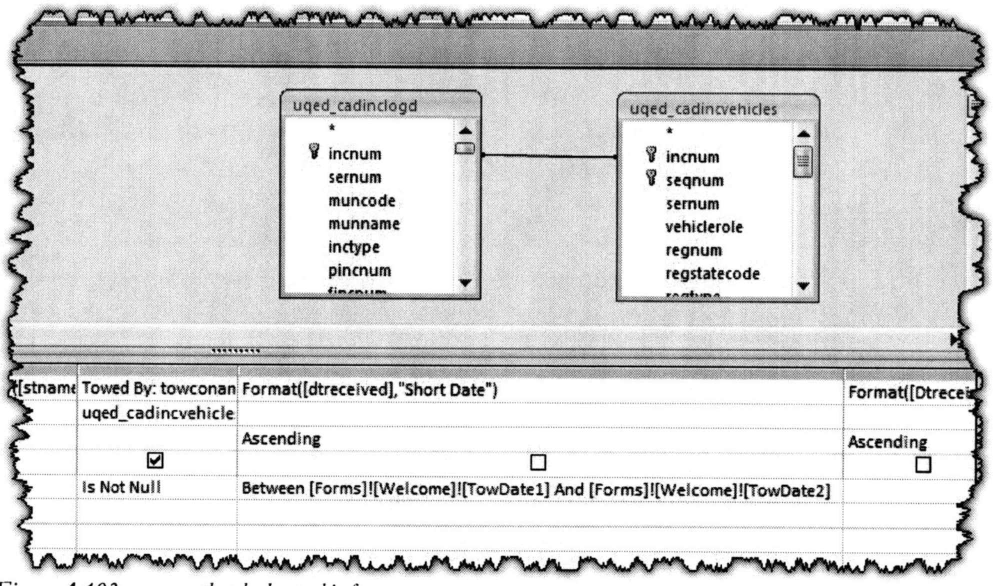

Figure A-103: a query that looks to this form

We have finished our querying lessons, but your exploration of queries does not have to stop here. We have included with the sample files a database called **samples.accdb** which uses these same data tables to illustrate numerous queries and functions. Browse them at your leisure and incorporate the examples into your daily analysis tasks.

Compacting and Repairing Your Database

When you create a new form, macro, table, query, or report, it may add a megabyte or so to the size of your database. If you delete an object, however, the database size doesn't shrink. It just keeps getting bigger until it's bloated and inefficient.

Compacting and Repairing the database will pack the database back down to a lean and fit size. It also removes miscellaneous bugs and corruptions that creep in from time to time.

To compact and repair, open your database and choose **Office Button | Manage | Compact and Repair Database**. Access will run through the routine. On large databases, and on databases stored on network drives, this process may take a while.

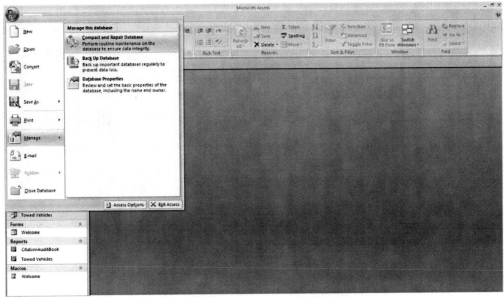

Figure A-104: compacting and repairing a database

We recommend compacting and repairing every three months on an infrequently used database, every month on a moderately-used database, and every week on a database that sees heavy use. Always compact and repair before copying a database to disk, zipping it, or e-mailing it.

Taking it to the Next Level

We have finished our lessons on Microsoft Access, although tripling the size of this chapter (and, consequently, the weight and price of this book!) would not be difficult.

One you master the basics of Access, and get comfortable with designing queries, forms, and reports, here are some avenues for you to explore on your road to Access mastery. A simple Google search or a search of Microsoft's knowledge base at **http://support.microsoft.com** will get you started.

- XOR, EQV, and IN operators in queries
- The versatile IIF function. There are dozens of ways it can make your life easier.

- PivotTable and PivotChart Views for tables and queries. PivotTables and PivotCharts provide another way to quickly aggregate large datasets. We explore them in the Excel chapter, but Access uses them as well.

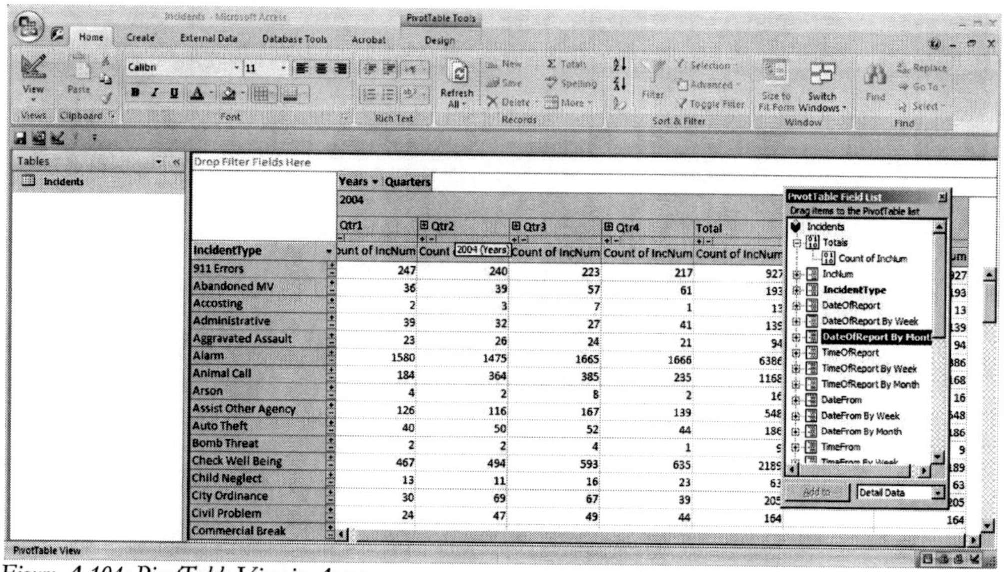

Figure A-104: PivotTable View in Access

- Queries based on queries

- Find Duplicate and Find Unmatched queries

- Parameter queries and queries that draw their criteria from forms

- Adding charts to reports

- Basic Visual Basic for Applications (VBA) coding

- Splitting Access databases

CHAPTER 2

Microsoft Excel

EXCEL MAY BE THE TOOL MOST COMMONLY USED BY THOSE analyzing crime. This versatile program can serve as a data repository, filter and sort data, "clean" data, aggregate data, perform every kind of statistical calculation imaginable, and create attractive charts, graphs, and reports. First released in 1987, Excel quickly came to dominate the spreadsheet market.

Like Access, Excel can import and link to data in a number of different formats. Power-analysts often use Access to filter and query large datasets, and then export the results to Excel for advanced statistical procedures.

In this chapter, we provide an introduction and an overview to Excel. The reader learns how to enter data, manipulate it with formulas, create charts, link to multiple data elements on a single sheet, import data, analyze data, and automate tasks with macros.

What's New in Excel 2007?

These are the most significant new features of Excel 2007:

- As with all of the Office 2007 applications, Microsoft has replaced menus and toolbars with the "ribbon" interface at the top of the screen.

- Excel's new XML file format, .xlsx, offers better integration with other systems that read XML data.

- Row and column limits have been raised significantly. Excel 2003 had a column limit of 256; Excel 2007 allows 16,384. Whereas Excel 2003 limited you to 65,536 rows, in Excel 2007, you can use up to 1,048,576. Excel 2003's row limit was a significant obstacle to crime analysis for even medium-sized agencies. With Excel

2007, all except the largest agencies should be able to use Excel for most of their non-relational needs.

- Conditional formatting has been expanded to allow a limitless number of rules from Excel 2003's three and a far greater selection of formats, including symbologies.

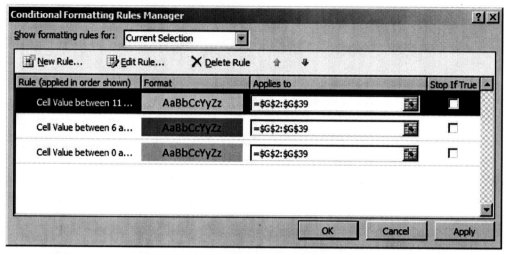

Figure E-1: conditional formatting options have been expanded in Excel 2007

- There are more sorting and filtering options, including the ability to sort and filter by color, the ability to filter by more than one value at a time without going to a custom filter, and automatic recognition of date parts when filtering. You can now sort by up to 64 levels instead of Excel 2003's three levels.

- A new "Data Tools" option group has automated tools for removing duplicates values within your data, for checking data for errors, and for testing out the different results obtained by multiple formulas ("What-If Analysis")

- Excel helps more with formulas:

  o Formula autocomplete makes it easier to find the formula you want. Just start typing a few letters, and all matches automatically appear.

  o You can include structured references (named ranges) within a formula.

  o Formulas can be more complex, with 64 nested functions instead of Excel 2003's seven.

- Once you get used to charting, you will generally find it improved. The default styles are much more attractive, and if you just want a quick and simple chart, you no longer need to navigate through several steps. You can now change the chart type for individual data series on the fly.

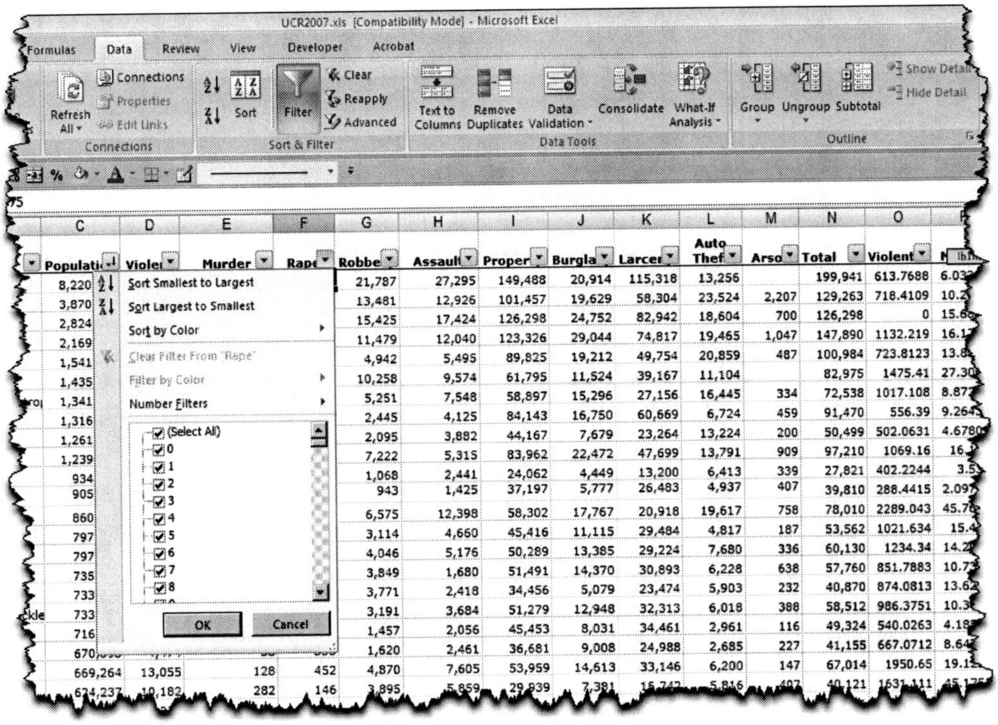

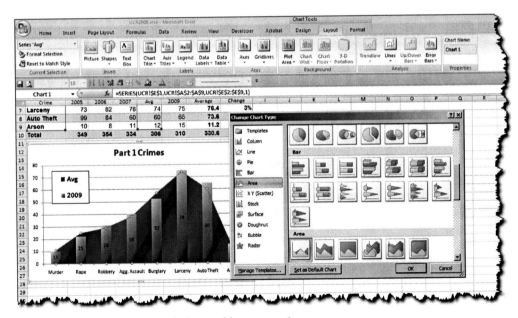

Figure E-2: there are more filtering and data analysis options in Excel 2007

Figure E-3: charts are faster, better-looking, and have more options

- PivotTables and PivotCharts have been completely redesigned. Notably, instead of dragging fields into the PivotTable, you drag them around the various areas in the PivotTable pane. Most users adept with the old 2003 PivotTable style will find the new style maddening, but there are some new capabilities to compensate, including easier sorting and filtering. Users who never used PivotTables in Excel 2003 may, in fact, find the newer interface more intuitive.

- Word and PowerPoint now use Excel as their default charting programs, replacing the old Microsoft Graph. Charts created in Excel can thus be animated in PowerPoint.

- Excel will no longer save data in DBF format. This may cause trouble for some users of ArcGIS and CrimeStat who are comfortable with manipulating their data in Excel.

- There is a new Page Layout View, comparable to Word's, that allows you to work within the spreadsheet as normal but shows you exactly how the result will look on the printed page.

- Excel 2003's Analysis ToolPak has been fully integrated into the Excel function library. There are also five new functions: IFERROR, AVERAGEIF, AVERAGEIFS, SUMIFS, and COUNTIFS.

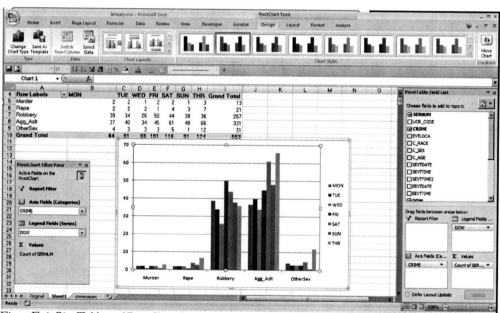

Figure E-4: PivotTables and PivotCharts have a completely different interface

A Tour of Excel

To begin our lessons:

»**Step 1:** Launch Excel.

The default Excel file—that is, what you get when you first launch Excel, is the *workbook*. Each workbook can store multiple *worksheets*, or spreadsheets. When you first start a new Excel workbook, it has three worksheets, called "Sheet1," "Sheet2," and "Sheet3," available with tabs at the bottom of the screen. You begin on "Sheet1." You can both re-name the three default sheets and add additional sheets (the maximum number is determined by your available memory).

Each worksheet has a maximum of 16,384 *columns* (referenced with letters) and 1,048,576 *rows* (referenced with numbers). Where each row and column intersect is a *cell*, referenced by its column and row (e.g., A15). A cell can store text, numbers, dates, times, and other types of data, or it can store calculations and expressions that depend on data in other cells. Each cell can display up to 1,024 characters but can store up to 32,767. All told, an Excel workbook can store a vast amount of information.

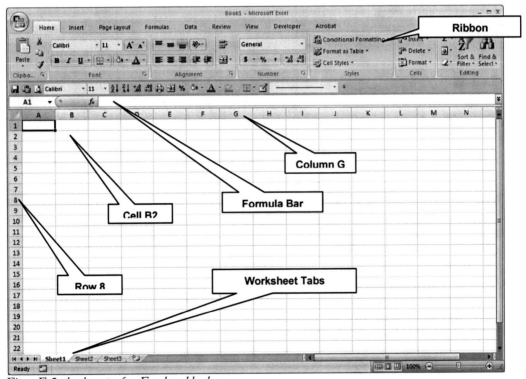

Figure E-5: the elements of an Excel workbook

Like all Office applications, Excel has a number of options available under **Office Button | Excel Options**. These settings control the way that the program behaves.

When something seems amiss in a spreadsheet, or does not work in a way you would expect, the cause is often an errant option. For now, we will leave the options alone until we understand Excel a bit better.

Spreadsheet Templates

By default, starting Excel puts you in a blank workbook. **Office Button | New** gives you additional options, including the option to create a new workbook based on a template.

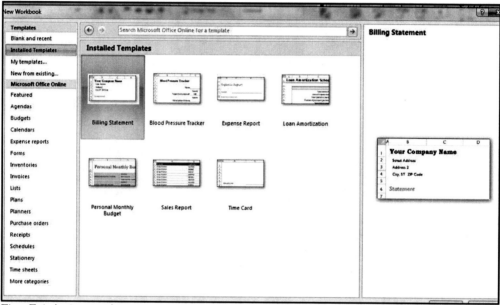

Figure E-6: choosing a template

The "Installed Templates" option access templates installed with Microsoft Office, and there are several. You may have additional templates on your network, and you can access thousands more on Microsoft Office Online, including categories as varied as menus, quizzes, and student ID cards.

Templates are designed for specific, common tasks. They open with many formatting and formula options already established, and most of the sheet may be *protected* so that you can only enter and change data in specified cells. Though templates can be very useful for specific purposes—some of the options are calendars, invoices, receipts, and time sheets— we will be performing the lessons in this chapter from scratch.

We also caution that you should verify formulas before relying on any template, particularly those created by other users.

Entering and Formatting Data

We begin by creating a simple spreadsheet showing UCR Part 1 crimes in 2008 and 2009.

»**Step 1:** In a blank workbook, click in cell **A2** and type "Murder"; note that the word appears in both the cell and the formula bar. You can edit it in either location.

»**Step 2:** Replicate Figure E-7 by typing the rest of the crimes and the numbers in the indicated cells.

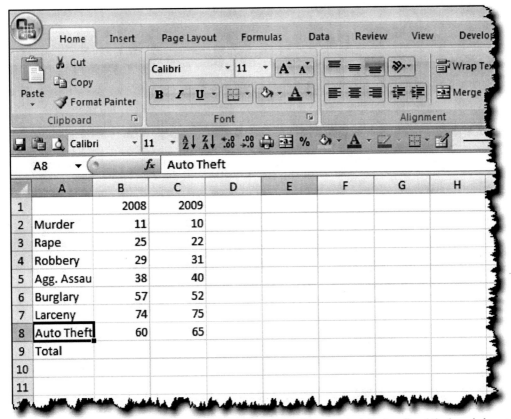

Figure E-7: your first spreadsheet. Note how the words "Auto Theft" appear both in the cell and the formula bar at the top.

»**Step 3:** Save the file via **Office Button | Save** or **CTRL-S**. Navigate to **C:\BPOffice\Excel** and call the file **UCR2009.xls**.

Now that we have some data in the spreadsheet, we can set some formatting options. These include column width, row height, font, text size, background, and borders. To begin with, the width of your Column A may be too short to accommodate the length of text you entered into it. You can select Column A and choose **Home | Cells | Format | Column Width** to manually change it, but there is a simpler way:

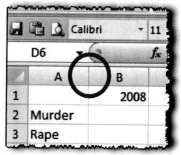

»**Step 4:** Double-click on the border between Columns A and Column B (Figure E-8). This will re-size Column A to fit the contents.

To set font options for the text, we have to select all the cells we want to affect. Selecting a single cell is easy: click on it. There are several ways to select multiple cells:

Figure E-8: double-click on the border between two columns to automatically re-size them.

- To select all the cells in a column, click on the letter at the top of the column.

- To select all the cells in a row, click on the number to the left of the row.

- To select multiple columns, click on the first column, hold down the mouse button, and drag to the last column.

- To select multiple rows, click on the first row, hold down the mouse button, and drag to the last row.

- To select a block of cells, click the cell in one of the block's corners (e.g., the upper left-most corner), hold down the mouse button, and drag to the opposite corner. *Or,* click the cell in one corner, hold down the **SHIFT** key, and click in the opposite corner.

- To select non-contiguous cells (e.g., cells not next to each other), hold down the **CTRL** key and click on them one at a time.

- To select non-contiguous columns, rows, or blocks of cells, use one of the methods above to select the first range, hold down the **CTRL** key, and use one of the methods to select the next range.

»**Step 5:** Click in Cell A1 and drag to cell C9 to select the entire range.

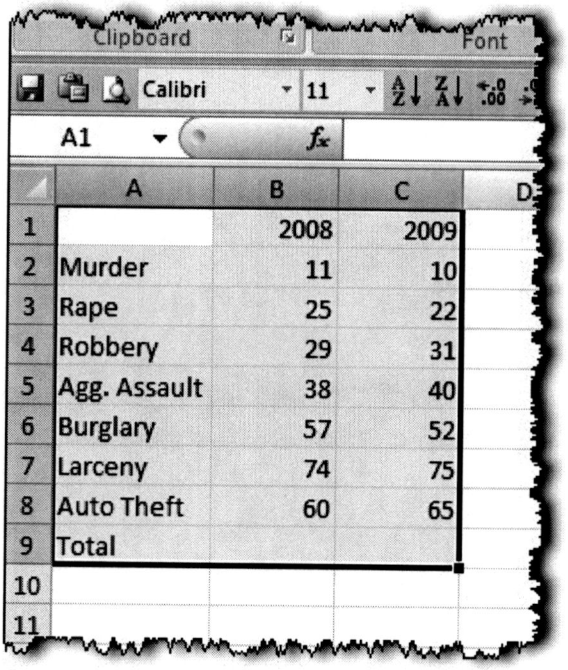

Figure E-9: selecting a range of cells

In your Excel career, you will probably visit the **Font**, **Alignment**, and **Number** groups on the **Home** ribbon frequently. It is here that you can set both formatting and data options for the cells in your spreadsheet.

The **Font** and **Alignment** groups all deal with cosmetic options, but the **Number** group is crucial: it specifies how you want Excel to treat data entered into the cells. As you type into the cells, Excel does its best to figure out whether you're typing text, numbers, dates, or some other kind of data. Here, however, you can tell Excel explicitly what you're entering.

Changing the "Number" type can have significant effects on how your data is displayed. For instance, look at Figure E-10 to see how a series of numbers entered in Column A as "General" (the default) changes as different number types are selected for Columns B through J.

General	Number	Currency	Accounting	Short Date	Time	Percentage	Fraction	Scientific	Text
525	525.00	$525.00	$ 525.00	06/08/1901	00:00:00	52500.00%	525	5.25E+02	525
100	100.00	$100.00	$ 100.00	04/09/1900	00:00:00	10000.00%	100	1.00E+02	100
13180	13180.00	$13,180.00	$ 13,180.00	01/31/1936	00:00:00	1318000.00%	13180	1.32E+04	13180
0.75	0.75	$0.75	$ 0.75	01/00/1900	18:00:00	75.00%	3/4	7.50E-01	0.75
1.5	1.50	$1.50	$ 1.50	01/01/1900	12:00:00	150.00%	1 1/2	1.50E+00	1.5
0.43	0.43	$0.43	$ 0.43	01/00/1900	10:19:12	43.00%	3/7	4.30E-01	0.43

Figure E-10: the differences the "Number" options can make

Changing "Number" types will become important in later lessons. For now:

»**Step 6:** Set the font to Arial, 12 point.

»**Step 7:** Select Column A (the crime type), Row 1 (the "Year" row), and Row 9 (the "Total" row) by clicking at the top of Column A, holding down the **CTRL** key, and clicking to the left of on Row 1 and then to the left of Row 9.

»**Step 8:** Bold your selection **B** .

»**Step 9:** Re-size the columns as in Step 4 as necessary.

Note that we have a "Total" row but no totals. We can tell Excel to add up all of the numbers in each column with a *formula*. In later lessons, we'll type in our formulas manually, but for now we can use an easy Excel tool.

»**Step 10:** Select Cells B2 through C9.

»**Step 11:** Click the "AutoSum" tool at **Home | Editing**: Σ AutoSum ▾ .

The total for the two columns will be calculated and entered in Row 9 (Figure E-11).

	A	B	C	D
1		2008	2009	
2	Murder	11	10	
3	Rape	25	22	
4	Robbery	29	31	
5	Agg. Assault	38	40	
6	Burglary	57	52	
7	Larceny	74	75	
8	Auto Theft	60	65	
9	Total	294	295	
10				
11				
12				

B2 = 11

Figure E-11: selecting a range and using the AutoSum tool. In doing so, we have to take care not to accidentally include the years in the range, or Excel will try to include them as part of the sum.

What Excel did for us was to insert formulas into Cells B9 and C9. What we see in the spreadsheet is the result of those formulas. If you click in either Cell B9 or C9 however, you will see the formula itself displayed in the formula bar. The formula in Cell B9, for instance, is **=SUM(B2:B8)**. The formulas are dynamic: if you change any of the crime numbers, the "Total" row will update accordingly. We will learn much more about formulas in future lessons.

As a final formatting option, we can add borders* and shading or patterns to our cells. These were available to us in the **Font** group, but it's often easier to use the pre-existing "Styles," which is quick and easy, and helps establish consistency from one spreadsheet to the next.

»**Step 12:** Select Cells A1 through C9.

»**Step 13:** Choose **Home | Styles | Format As Table**.

»**Step 14:** Select the format that most appeals to you (we chose the fifth option under "Medium"). The data range should already be correct.

The formatting will change the font, text size, text color, borders, shading, and alignment to match the style.

»**Step 15:** Replace the "Column1" heading with "Crime."

»**Step 16:** Admire your handiwork, then save your Excel workbook.

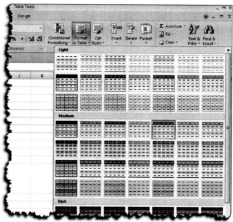

Figure E-12: table formatting styles

---

* The borders or lines that we already see around each cell are called *gridlines*. They assist you, when looking at the spreadsheet, to pick out each cell, but unless you tell Excel otherwise, they do not print with the spreadsheet.

Using Formulas that Calculate Statistics

In these lessons, we will use formulas to calculate more complex statistics in our UCR spreadsheet.

»**Step 1:** Insert three additional columns to the left of Column B by right-clicking on the Column B header and choosing "Insert" three times. Title these columns "2005," "2006," and "2007." Re-size the columns as appropriate. Fill them in with the numbers in Figure E-13, and repeat Steps 10 and 11 in the previous lesson (selecting cells B2 through D9 this time) to get the sums.

»**Step 2:** Add two columns to the right of the 2009 figures, in Columns G and H, titled "Average" and "Change."

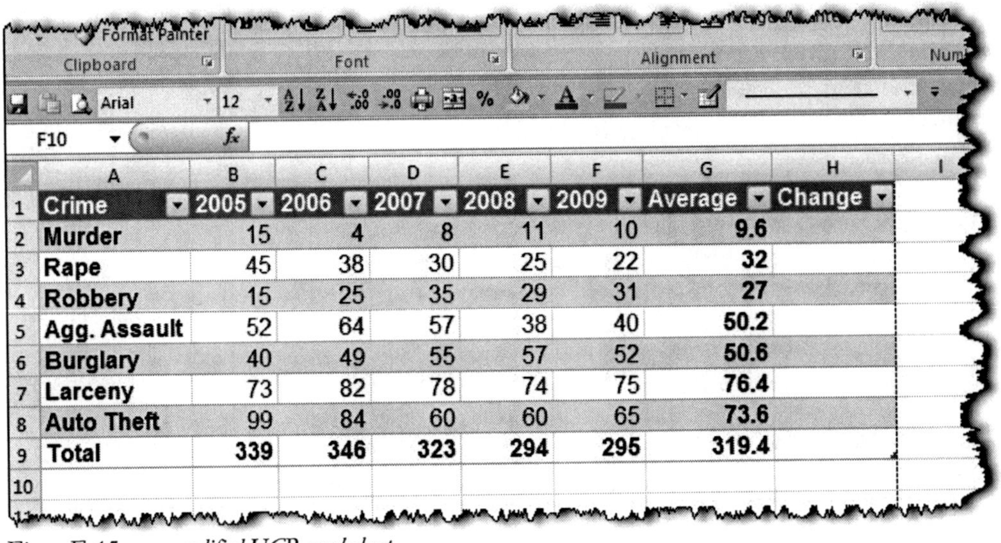

	A	B	C	D	E	F	G	H	I
1	Crime	2005	2006	2007	2008	2009	Average	Change	
2	Murder	15	4	8	11	10	9.6		
3	Rape	45	38	30	25	22	32		
4	Robbery	15	25	35	29	31	27		
5	Agg. Assault	52	64	57	38	40	50.2		
6	Burglary	40	49	55	57	52	50.6		
7	Larceny	73	82	78	74	75	76.4		
8	Auto Theft	99	84	60	60	65	73.6		
9	Total	339	346	323	294	295	319.4		
10									

Figure E-15: your modified UCR worksheet.

The "Average" and "Change" columns will of course require formulas. There are two ways to add these formulas:

1) Type them in ourselves
2) Use Excel's "Insert Function" wizard.

We'll begin with the second option.

»**Step 3:** Click in Cell G2 (the average for the "Murder" category). Click the "Insert Function" button next to the formula bar fx .

Excel gives us two ways to find the function we want: we can type in a description of what we're looking for, or we can select by category.

»Step 4: If the "AVERAGE" function does not appear in the "Most Recently Used" list, select "Statistical" from the "Category" drop-down (Figure E-16).

»Step 5: Select the "AVERAGE" function and click "OK."

Excel returns you to your worksheet where a "Function Arguments" dialog opens up (Figure E-17). In this box, you type the range of cells that contains the numbers you

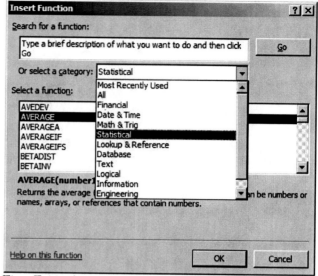

Figure E-16; selecting statistical functions

want to average. Excel has already selected all of the numeric cells to the left of the "Average" column: B2:F2. Excel is correct in its assumption of the range. If we wanted to change the range, we could click on the 🔢 box and do so.

»Step 6: Accept B2:F2 as the cell range by clicking "OK."

Figure E-17: arguments for your "Average" function

The average number of murders per year (9.6) is calculated and appears in Cell G2, and Excel automatically fills the same formula down for all of our crimes.

Once you learn how functions work, you may find it easier to simply type them rather than using the "Insert Function" wizard. While Cell G2 shows us the *result* of the formula, clicking on the cell displays the formula itself in the formula bar. The formula is **=AVERAGE(B2:F2)**.

Figure E-18: the formula displayed in the formula bar.

This formula illustrates how most functions work in Excel. All formulas are preceded by an equals sign (=) which lets Excel know that a function or calculation follows. The next element is often (but not always) the name of a function, such as "AVERAGE" or "SUM." If we're using a function, we immediately follow it with a set of parentheses (), inside which is the range of cells the function applies to. A range of cells is indicated with the first cell reference, a colon, and the last cell reference (i.e., B2:F2 includes cells B2, C2, D2, E2, and F2). Noncontiguous cells or ranges are indicated by separating them with a comma. Any of the following are valid formulas (though not necessarily for this worksheet):

=SUM(A1:A16)
=AVERAGE(B3,B4,B6,B8)
=MEDIAN(A7:A9,A11)
=MODE(C2:C10,D3:D11)

Some functions require an additional argument after the cell range (the cell range and the argument are separated by a comma). For instance, the ROUND function, which rounds a number to a specified number of decimal places, needs an argument that tells Excel how many decimal places to round it to:

=ROUND(A3,2) rounds the value in Cell A3 to two decimal places.

Functions can also be nested inside each other. For instance:

=ROUND(AVERAGE(B2:F2),0) would calculate the average of Cells B2–F2, and then round this figure to the nearest whole number (no decimal places).

Not all formulas use functions. The simple formula **=B2+C2** adds those cells together, while **=C2-B2** makes a simple subtraction. Just as in regular mathematics, parentheses indicate order of operations: **=(F2-B2)/B2** subtracts B2 from from F2 first, *then* divides by B2, while **=F2-B2/B2** would divide B2 by itself before subtracting it from F2. (Unless you use parentheses to indicate otherwise, Excel multiples and divides before adding and subtracting.)

For Column H ("Change"), we need to type in a formula. There is no function to calculate change from one time period to another.

»**Step 7:** Click in Cell H2 and type **=(F2-B2)/B2**. When finished, hit **ENTER**.

The result of this formula shows the change in murder between 2005 and 2009, the standard formula for which is **(New-Old)/Old**. As before, Excel automatically fills the formula down for the range of our formatted table (if it did not, we would have to auto-fill the formula, as on Page 132).

We want Excel to treat the values in the "Change" column (Column H) as percentages rather than decimal numbers.

> **»Step 8:** Select Cells H2–H9. At **Home | <u>Number</u>**, change the type from "General" to "Percentage," or just use the "Percent Style" button: %.

If you later decide that you want to increase or decrease the number of decimal places, the "Increase Decimal" and "Decrease Decimal" tools at **Home | <u>Number</u>** are a quick way to do it. They increase or decrease the number of displayed decimal places by one, each time you click them.

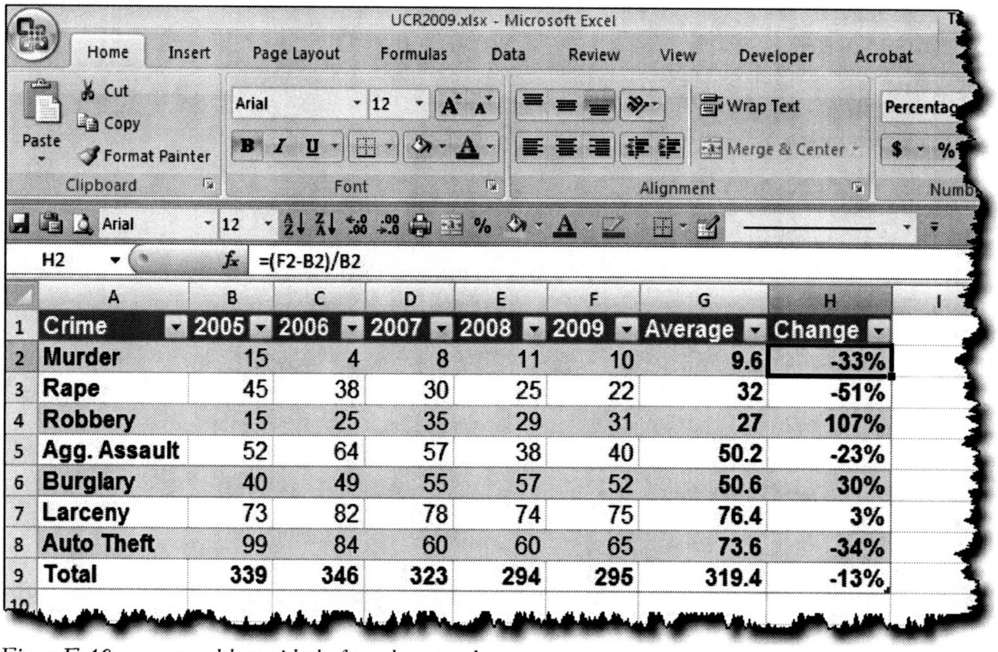

	A	B	C	D	E	F	G	H
1	Crime	2005	2006	2007	2008	2009	Average	Change
2	Murder	15	4	8	11	10	9.6	-33%
3	Rape	45	38	30	25	22	32	-51%
4	Robbery	15	25	35	29	31	27	107%
5	Agg. Assault	52	64	57	38	40	50.2	-23%
6	Burglary	40	49	55	57	52	50.6	30%
7	Larceny	73	82	78	74	75	76.4	3%
8	Auto Theft	99	84	60	60	65	73.6	-34%
9	Total	339	346	323	294	295	319.4	-13%

Figure E-19: your spreadsheet with the formulas entered

Now that we have the percentage change from 2005 to 2009, we can use *conditional formatting* to indicate increases or decreases. Conditional formatting applies a certain format (font size, style, or color; background; border) to a cell based on its value. We can use it to tell Excel to show increases in red text and decreases in blue text.

> **»Step 9:** Select Cells H2–H9. Choose **Home | <u>Styles</u> | Conditional Formatting | Highlight Cells Rules | Greater Than.**

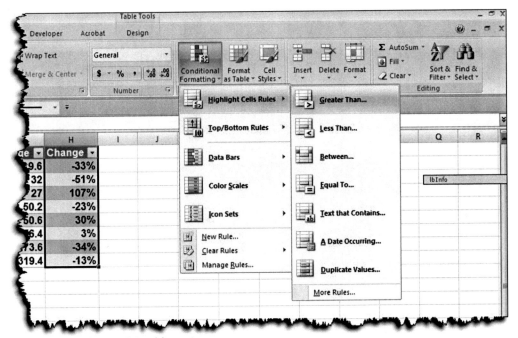

Figure E-20: applying conditional formatting

»**Step 10:** Tell Excel to "format cells that are GREATER THAN" 0% with "Red Text," as in Figure E-21. Then click "OK."

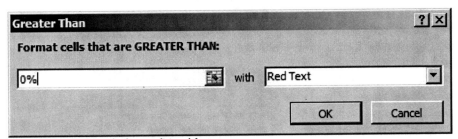

Figure E-21: applying the first conditional format

»**Step 11:** With Cells H2–H9 still selected, choose **Home | Styles | Conditional Formatting | Highlight Cells Rules | Less Than**.

»**Step 12:** Tell Excel to "format cells that are LESS than" 0%. In the "with" box, we don't see our desired option (blue text), so choose "Custom Format" in the drop-down.

»**Step 13:** In the "Format Cells" box on the "Font" tab, use the "Color" field to apply a blue color. Then click "OK" twice.

You should now see the conditions you entered applied to the percentages in Column H.

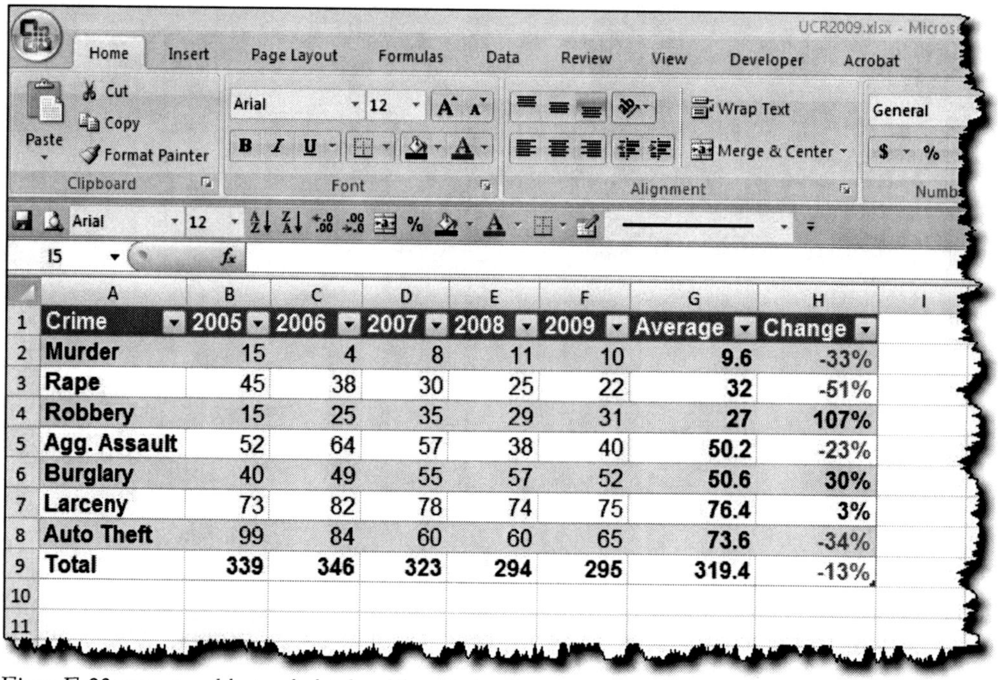

Figure E-22: your spreadsheet, calculated and formatted

There are a lot of other conditional formatting options. Excel greatly expanded the abilities of conditional formatting in the 2007 version, allowing you to use very complex criteria. Moreover, where you were limited to three conditional formats in Excel 2003, in Excel 2007 you are only limited by your computer's memory. Finally, while Excel 2003's only formatting options were text style and color and background color, in 2007 you can modify the data type and add symbols to the fields based on conditional formatting.

To see all of the conditional formatting options available, choose **Home | Styles | Conditional Formatting | New Rule**. You will see multiple categories of options, including the ability to write your own formula. After applying rules, you can always use **Home | Styles | Conditional Formatting | New Rule** to modify or delete them.

»**Step 14:** Save and close your spreadsheet.

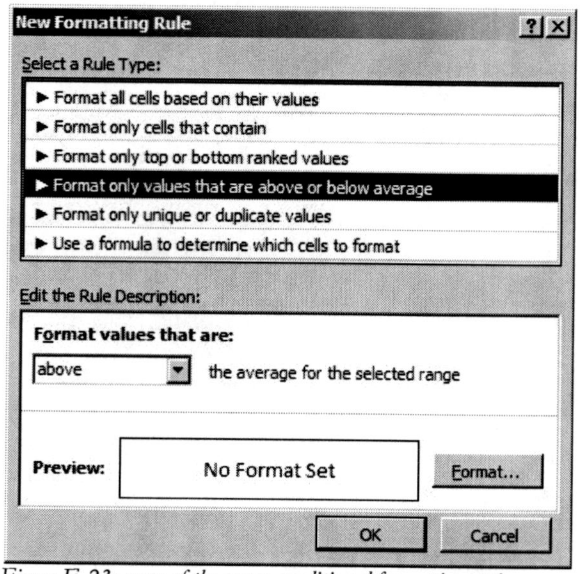

Figure E-23: some of the many conditional formatting options

Common Crime Analysis Formulas

Table E-1 illustrates some of the more common formulas and functions used by crime analysts.

After you have reviewed them, open the file at **C:\BPOffice\Excel\TexasUCR.xls**, which shows 2007 Uniform Crime Report statistics for the state of Texas. The first sheet, "Lesson," shows only the UCR statistics with blank columns for different calculations. Fill in blank columns with the proper formulas. The second sheet, "Solution," gives you the solution to the formulas. *Try doing it yourself before looking at the solutions!*

Some of the examples in the table refer to this sample spreadsheet:

	A	B	C	D	E	F
1	Crime	2005	2006	2007	2008	2009
2	Murder	15	4	8	11	10
3	Rape	45	38	30	25	22
4	Robbery	15	25	35	29	31
5	Agg. Assau	52	64	57	38	40
6	Burglary	40	49	55	57	52
7	Larceny	73	82	78	74	75
8	Auto Theft	99	84	60	60	65
9	Total	339	346	323	294	295
10						
11	Population	115,806				

Name	Formula/Function	Example
Average (Mean)	AVERAGE(*range*)	=AVERAGE(B2:F2)
Clearance Rate	Crimes/Crimes Cleared	(not shown on sheet)
Correlation (Pearson's *r*)	CORREL(*range1,range2*)	=CORREL(B7:F7,B9:F9)
Crime Per 1000 Population	Crime/Population*1000	=F9/$B$11*1000
Difference	New-Old	=F3-B3
Median	MEDIAN(*range*)	=MEDIAN(B5:F5)
Mode	MODE(*range*)	=MODE(B8:F8)
Percent Change	(New-Old)/Old	=(F4-E4)/E4
Percent of Total	Category/Total	=F7/F9
		=F7/SUM(F2:F8)
Standard Deviation	STDEV(*range*)	=STDEV(B3:F3)
Sum	SUM(*range*)	=SUM(B2:B8)
		=SUM(B2:B5) – Violent Only
		=SUM(B2:F8)
Z-Score	(Category-AVG(*range*))/STDEV(*range*)	=(F6-AVG(B6:F6)/STDEV(B6:F6)

Table E-1: common crime analysis formulas

Absolute and Relative References

The formula for crimes per 1000 population uses an *absolute reference*. Most references (including all the other ones in the examples above) are *relative references*, meaning that if you copy and paste them, or fill them to other cells, Excel will adjust the row and column references according to the number of columns or rows the copied formula cell is from the original formula cell. This is often helpful, as we saw when we filled the "average" and "change" formulas on our UCR spreadsheet.

Occasionally, however, we don't want the formula to adjust. Consider Figure E-24. Here we have several cells showing crime totals, but only one cell for the population. In Cell B11, we have entered the formula =**B9/B10*1000**.

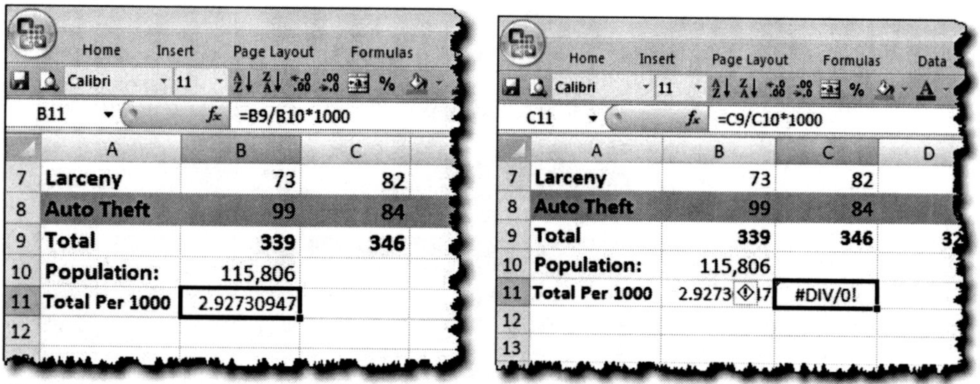

Figure E-24: copying a formula with a relative reference can sometimes result in an error

If we now try to fill this formula to Cell C11, however, we get an Excel error message, because Excel has adjusted our reference from Cell B10 to Cell C10. Since there's nothing in C10, the formula does not work properly.

The solution is to use an absolute reference for fixed cells, like the "Population" cell. Although we *do* want the first half of the formula to adjust as we move across the columns (i.e., B9 should become C9 for 2006, D9 for 2007, and so on), the second half should remain fixed on B10.

We indicate absolute references in Excel with dollar signs ($) before the column (e.g., $B10), if we want the column to be absolute, before the row (e.g., B$10), if we want the row to be absolute, or both (e.g., $B$10), if we want both column and row to be absolute. In our case, we want both column and row to have an absolute reference.

In Figure E-25, we have adjusted the formula to use an absolute reference, and the results are much different.

Typing the dollar signs can become cumbersome. Excel gives you a shortcut to absolute references: after you type (or click) the cell reference, tap the **F4** key.

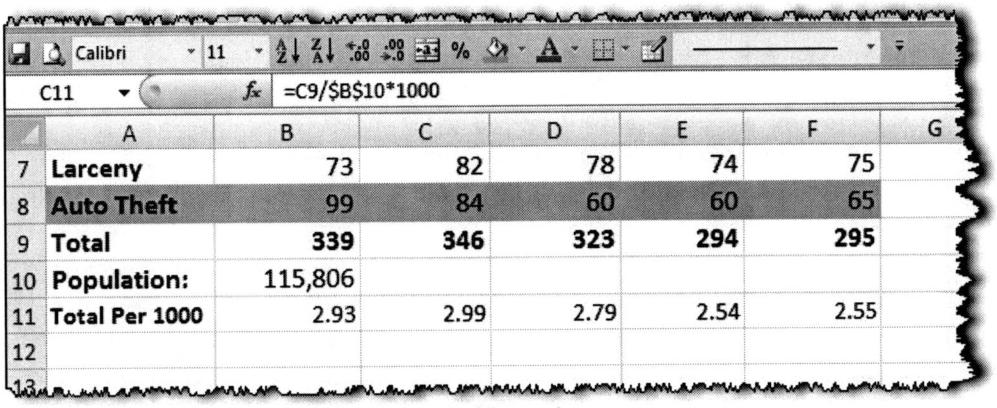

Figure E-25: an absolute reference makes the formula fill correctly

Using Functions that Manipulate Text

There are a number of Excel functions that re-arrange text. This section covers some of the most useful.

»**Step 1:** Open **C:\BPOffice\Excel\addresses.xlsx**.

You have here a spreadsheet with addresses separated into three fields: number, direction, and street name. Most records management systems will export data this way. But this is not useful for geocoding—most GIS systems require an address in a single field. The solution is to *concatenate* the address parts—to combine them into a single field.

»**Step 2:** Title Column D (Row 2), "Address 1"

»**Step 3:** Type this formula into Cell D3: **=CONCATENATE(A3," ",B3," ",C3)**
There are spaces in between the quotes—make sure you type those in.

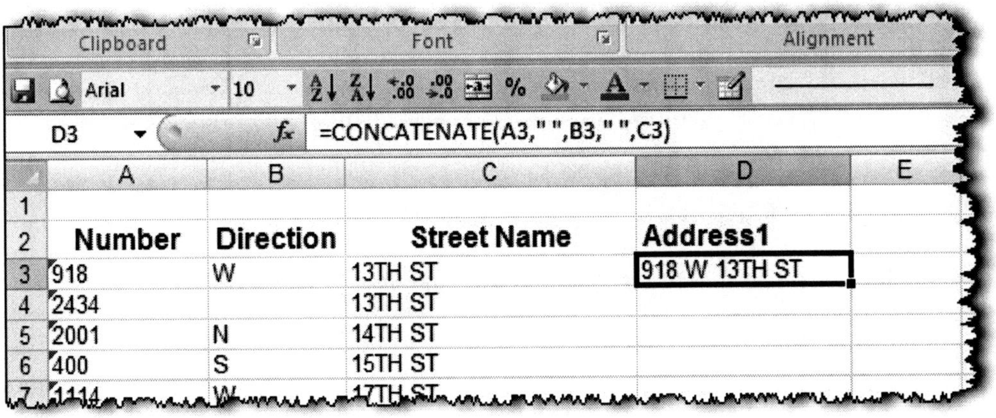

Figure E-26: a concatenated address field

When we had our data formatted as a table, in the UCR example, Excel automatically filled our formula down for the range of cells. It doesn't do so here, so we have to do it manually.

> »**Step 4:** Using one of the selection methods on Page 114, select Cells D3 to D103 and **CTRL-D** or **Home | Editing | Fill | Down** to fill the formula down the entire range of rows.

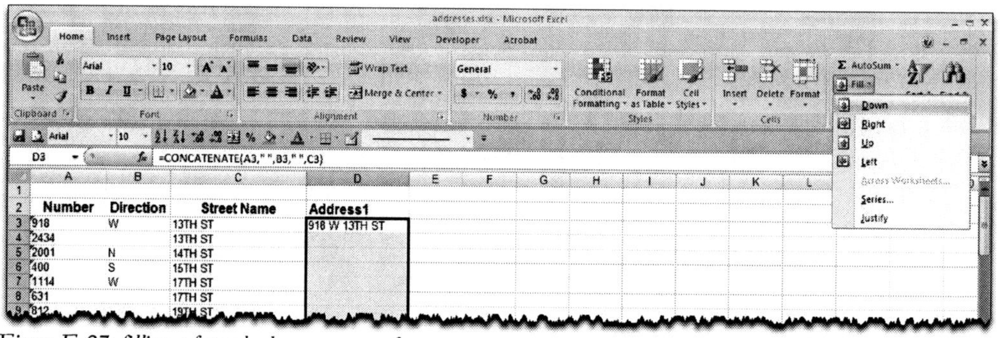

Figure E-27: filling a formula down a range of rows

When you **fill** a formula, Excel automatically adjusts the column references for every column you fill it across, and it automatically adjusts the row references for every row you fill down. It usually gets it right, but it's worth taking a moment to select some of the cells and spot-check them before moving on. Also, as we saw in the last lesson, sometimes you want to use an absolute reference to *prevent* Excel from adjusting the cell references.

Columns A–C have been combined in a single field, and for most, this will be enough. But there's a small problem: some of our addresses (for instance, Row 4) have no "direction." What happens is, Excel concatenates the address number, a space, nothing, another space, and the street name. Note how the second address (Row 4) has two spaces between the address number and the street—this may confuse some GIS systems.

There are two ways we can solve this problem: with an *if* function, or with a *trim* function.

IF allows us to specify conditions in our formula. We can tell Excel: if there is no direction, just join the number and the street name; otherwise, join the number, the direction, and the street name.

The syntax for an IF function is:

=IF(*condition,what to do if condition is true,what to do if condition is false*)

We want to tell Excel to do one thing if cell B3 is empty, and another thing if B3 is not. The way we signify "empty" in an Excel formula is: **=""** (that is, an open and closed quote, with nothing in between). So the full formula for Row 3 is:

=IF(B3="",CONCATENATE(A3," ",C3),CONCATENATE(A3," ",B3," ",C3))

The other option is the TRIM function. TRIM removes double-spaces from within a string of text. It also removes any excess spaces from the beginning and the end of a string of text. The TRIM option, for Row 3, is:

=TRIM(CONCATENATE(A3," ",B3," ",C3))

»**Step 5:** Title Column E (Row 2), "Address 2." Enter one of the formulas above into Cell E3.

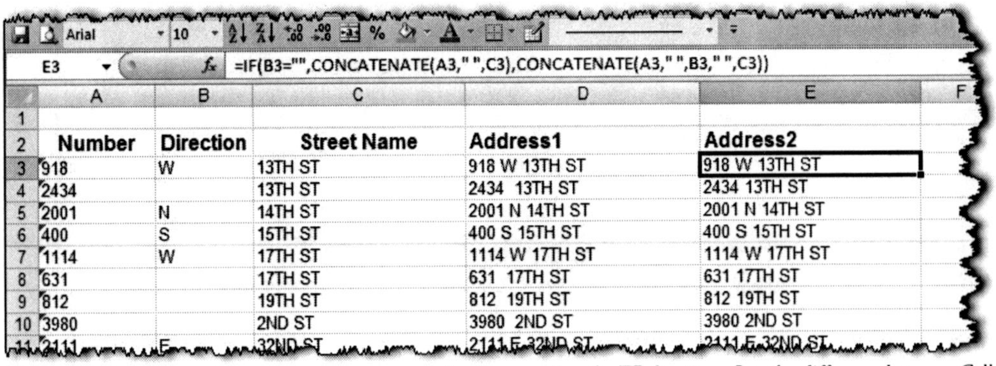

	A	B	C	D	E	F
1						
2	**Number**	**Direction**	**Street Name**	**Address1**	**Address2**	
3	918	W	13TH ST	918 W 13TH ST	918 W 13TH ST	
4	2434		13TH ST	2434 13TH ST	2434 13TH ST	
5	2001	N	14TH ST	2001 N 14TH ST	2001 N 14TH ST	
6	400	S	15TH ST	400 S 15TH ST	400 S 15TH ST	
7	1114	W	17TH ST	1114 W 17TH ST	1114 W 17TH ST	
8	631		17TH ST	631 17TH ST	631 17TH ST	
9	812		19TH ST	812 19TH ST	812 19TH ST	
10	3980		2ND ST	3980 2ND ST	3980 2ND ST	
11	2111	E	32ND ST	2111 E 32ND ST	2111 E 32ND ST	

Formula bar: E3 f_x =IF(B3="",CONCATENATE(A3," ",C3),CONCATENATE(A3," ",B3," ",C3))

Figure E-28: our second attempt at a concatenated address, using the IF function. See the difference between Cells D4 and E4?

»**Step 6:** Fill this formula down to Row 103.

We're happy with our "Address2" column. In fact, we no longer really need the first three columns. But we can't delete them, since the formula in Column E depends on them. Yet we may want to fix this concatenated address in place, rather than having it rely on other cells. There is a way to do this.

»**Step 7:** Select Column E by clicking on the "E" at the top of the column.

»**Step 8: CTRL-C** to copy the column to the clipboard.

»**Step 9:** Choose **Home | Clipboard | Paste** (click on the arrow underneath the "paste" icon) and **Paste Values** (figure E-29).

This sequence of commands will replace a column of formulas with a column of fixed values that the formulas calculated. There are even further options under **Home | Clipboard | Paste | Paste Special**: formats only, everything except borders, and so on. If the cells contain numbers, you can even perform mathematical operations on them. There are times when finding these options can save a great deal of time and frustration.

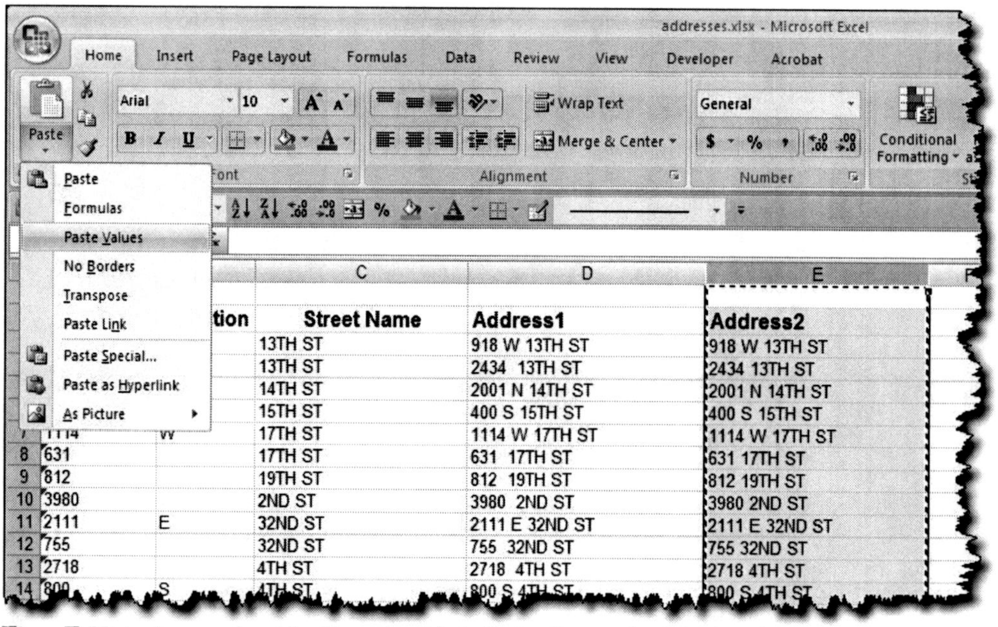

Figure E-29: pasting over the original formulas with the "values," or results of the formula

One of the more interesting "Paste Special" options is the "Transpose" feature. If you select a block of cells, this will allow you to transpose their rows and columns (rows become columns and columns become rows), as in Figure E-30.

»**Step 10:** Note now that if you click in any of the cells in Column E, you will see that they contain the actual addresses, not the formulas.

»**Step 11:** Save the addresses spreadsheet and close it.

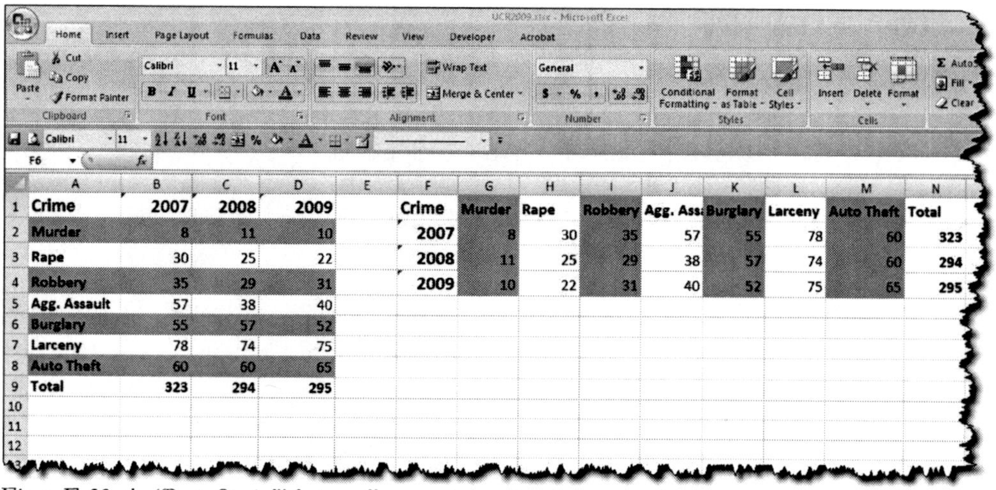

Figure E-30: the "Paste Special" feature allows you to transpose columns and rows

There are many other functions that work with text. They include the following:

CLEAN(*cell*)	Removes non-printing characters from text
EXACT(*cell1,cell2*)	Checks whether two cells match each other and returns "True" or "False"
LEFT(*cell,characters*)	Returns a specified number of characters from the beginning of a text string
RIGHT(*cell,characters*)	Returns a number of characters from the end of a text string
LEN(*cell*)	Returns the number of characters in a text string
LOWER(*cell*)	Converts all the characters in a cell to lower case
UPPER(*cell*)	Converts all the characters in a cell to upper case
PROPER(*cell*)	Makes the first letter in each word upper case, others lower case

These functions, as well as more complex ones such as REPLACE and SUBSTITUTE, can be invaluable for data cleaning. We have provided a sample spreadsheet at **C:\BPOffice\Excel\datacleaning.xlsx** that illustrates some of these examples.

Using Functions that Manipulate Dates and Times

Excel stores dates and times as decimal numbers, in which the integer portion of the number represents the number of days since January 1, 1900, and the decimal part of the number represents the percentage of the 24-hour clock from midnight.

For instance, 12:00 noon on May 31, 2005 is stored as 38503.5. May 31, 2005 is 38,503 days from January 1, 1900, and 12:00 is .5 or 50% of the way through the day.

If you enter only a date in a field, Excel stores only the integer part of the number. If you enter only a time, Excel stores only the decimal part of the number.

Storing dates and times as numbers makes it easy to perform calculations. For instance, if you subtract 05/01/2005 from 05/31/2005, behind the scenes Excel simply subtracts 38,473 from 38,503. The answer, of course, is 30. Similarly, if you subtract 12:00 from 18:00, behind the scenes Excel subtracts .50 from .75. The answer—.25—converts to 06:00 in the Excel time system. The only trick is to make sure the field that contains the formula is formatted correctly—as a number when subtracting dates or date/times, and as a time when subtracting times alone. It can get confusing.

This lesson covers some of the more common calculations and functions that can be performed with dates and times.

»**Step 1:** Close all open spreadsheets and open the spreadsheet at **C:\BPOffice\Excel\calls.xlsx**.

This spreadsheet represents a sample of calls for service received in a small jurisdiction on New Year's Eve and Day, 2009. The dates and times of the call receipt, dispatch, and arrival are stored in combined fields (if they were separated into dates and times, we could add them). We want to know how long it took to dispatch and to respond to each call.

> **»Step 2:** In Cell F2, add a new column title "Dispatch Time." In Cell G2, type "Transit Time," and in Cell H2, type "Total Time." Expand the width of the columns to accommodate your text.

At this point (depending on your screen resolution), you will probably find that the used part of your worksheet has extended far enough to the right of the page that you have to scroll. At the very least, you will have to scroll down to reach the end of the records. But when you scroll right or down, you lose the identifying information to help you figure out where you are in your spreadsheet. That is, if you scroll down, you lose your column titles, and if you scroll right, you lose the incident numbers.

The following step will "freeze" the row and column headers as you scroll.

> **»Step 3:** Click in Cell B2. Choose **View | Window | Freeze Panes | Freeze Panes**.

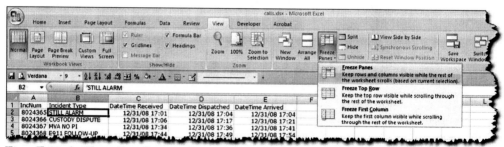

Figure E-31: the "Freeze Panes" command keeps the row and column headers fixed

The "Freeze Panes" command freezes all rows *above* the cell you have selected, and all columns to the *left* of the cell you selected. This is why we selected Cell B2 in Step 3—so that we would freeze Row 1 and Column A.

Having accomplished this task, the actual formulas for the time differences are simple:

> **»Step 4:** In Cell F2, type: **=D2-C2**

> **»Step 5:** In Cell G2, type: **=E2-D2**

> **»Step 6:** In Cell H2, type: **=E2-C2**

> **»Step 7:** Select Cells F2–H56 and choose **Home | Editing | Fill | Down**. The formulas in all three columns should copy down to Row 56.

At first glance, it doesn't look like you got the results you wanted. Depending on your settings, you may see decimal numbers (0.002106481), scientific notation (6.94444E-05), or nonsensical dates (01/0/00 0:03). The answer is simply a matter of formatting.

»**Step 8:** Select Columns F, G, and H. On the **Home | Number** group, set the number type to "Time."

	F	G	H
	Dispatch Time	Transit Time	Total Time
:04	0.002106481	6.94444E-05	0.00217593
:21	0.007708333	0.002395833	0.01010417
:41	0.001203704	0.00337963	0.00458333
:54	0.003506944	0.003402778	0.00690972
:53	0.001273148	0.003483796	0.00475694
:04	-0.01819444	0.000104167	-0.0180903
:59	0.002384259	6.94444E-05	0.0024537
:08	0.001111111	0.003125	0.00423611

	F	G	H
	Dispatch Time	Transit Time	Total Time
04	00:03:02	00:00:06	00:03:08
21	00:11:06	00:03:27	00:14:33
41	00:01:44	00:04:52	00:06:36
54	00:05:03	00:04:54	00:09:57
53	00:01:50	00:05:01	00:06:51
04	00:00:48	00:00:09	00:00:57
59	00:03:26	00:00:06	00:03:32
08	00:01:36	00:04:30	00:06:06
15	00:01:49	00:05:58	00:07:47

Figure E-32: the results don't seem to be what you want…but it's all a matter of formatting

Now you have the dispatch, transit, and total times calculated for this 24 hour period. We can do a few final calculations to make it more relevant.

»**Step 9:** Scroll down to Cell E57. In it, type "Average." In Cell E58, type "Minimum," and in Cell E59, type "Maximum."

»**Step 10:** Select Cells E57–E59, bold them **B** and right-justify them ≡.

»**Step 11:** In Cell F57, type the following formula: **=AVERAGE(F2:F56)**

»**Step 12:** In Cell F58, type the following formula: **=MIN(F2:F56)**

»**Step 13:** In Cell F59, type the following formula: **=MAX(F2:F56)**

»**Step 14:** Select Cells F57–H59. Fill the formulas right by typing **CTRL-R**.

You now have the average, minimum, and maximum times for all three of your calculated categories.

	Font			Alignment			Number			Styles	

=AVERAGE(F2:F56)

	B	C	D	E	F	G	H	I
	Type	DateTime Received	DateTime Dispatched	DateTime Arrived	Dispatch Time	Transit Time	Total Time	
	PI	1/1/09 13:31	1/1/09 13:34	1/1/09 13:38	00:02:34	00:03:50	00:06:24	
	M/V	1/1/09 14:11	1/1/09 14:12	1/1/09 14:22	00:01:11	00:09:59	00:11:10	
		1/1/09 15:17	1/1/09 15:19	1/1/09 15:20	00:02:08	00:00:07	00:02:15	
	ARDS	1/1/09 16:24	1/1/09 16:25	1/1/09 16:28	00:01:41	00:02:43	00:04:24	
				Average	00:02:59	00:06:17	00:09:16	
				Minimum	00:00:18	00:00:03	00:00:56	
				Maximum	00:21:18	01:15:06	01:17:03	

Figure E-33: calculating average, minimum, and maximum call times

There are a few functions that manipulate dates and times. One of the most useful is the TEXT function, the syntax of which is:

=TEXT(*cell***,"** *format***")**

The "format," which you enclose in quotes can draw out the month, year, day, weekday, and any combination thereof from a date. For instance, the following examples would have the indicated results on Cell C2, which has a date of 12/31/2008:

Formula	Result
=TEXT(C2,"yyyy")	2008
=TEXT(C2,"yy")	08
=TEXT(C2,"mm")	12
=TEXT(C2,"mmm")	Dec
=TEXT(C2,"mmmm")	December
=TEXT(C2,"dd")	31
=TEXT(C2,"ddd")	Wed
=TEXT(C2,"dddd")	Wednesday
=TEXT(C2,"yyyymmdd")	20081231
=TEXT(C2,"yyyy-mmm")	2008-Dec

There are also a couple of helpful time functions:

=HOUR(C2)	17
=MINUTE(C2)	1
=SECOND(C2)	26

Extracting parts of dates or times can become valuable when we later create filters, groupings, and pivot tables. You can practice any or all of these formulas in Columns I onward.

»**Step 15:** When you are finished, save and close your spreadsheet.

You may sometimes receive date and time data in a format that Excel doesn't understand, such as text (e.g., "700PM") or a number (e.g., 20050718). You will not be able to perform calculations on these dates and times until you make Excel understand them as such.

Fortunately, Excel has a couple of formulas that will help you convert text or numeric dates and times to actual dates and times. These are DATEVALUE and TIMEVALUE. These will convert something that *looks* like a date or time ("07/18/05") into an Excel date or time (38551, which represents the date 07/18/2005).

The trouble is getting the "bad" date or time into a format that looks like a date or time as far as Excel is concerned. This means turning 20050718 into "07/18/2005" and turning "700PM" into "7:00 PM" or "19:00"—with colons, slashes and everything.

There are related functions called DATE and TIME. DATE will supply an Excel date if you supply the parts (month, day, year), and TIME will supply an Excel time if you supply the hours, minutes and seconds.

So how do you get your text or number date or time into a format that Excel can recognize with DATEVALUE, TIMEVALUE, DATE, or TIME? It usually involves the use of the LEFT, RIGHT, MID, and other functions, and perhaps some calculations. Figure E-34 shows the **timeconversion.xlsx** spreadsheet, included in your sample files, which uses all four functions.

	A	B	C	D	E	F	G	H
1	Text Date	Excel Date	Text Time	Excel Time	Number Date	Excel Date	Number Time	Excel Time
2	07/15/05	07/15/2005	300PM	15:00	20050705	07/05/2005	1500	15:00
3	07/17/05	07/17/2005	900AM	9:00	20050717	07/17/2005	900	9:00
4	08/13/05	08/13/2005	830PM	20:30	20050813	08/13/2005	2030	20:30
5	10/10/2004	10/10/2004	400AM	4:00	20041010	10/10/2004	400	4:00
6	09/12/99	09/12/1999	950PM	21:50	19990912	09/12/1999	2150	21:50
7	8/15/65	08/15/1965	637AM	6:37	19650815	08/15/1965	637	6:37
8	1/1/50	01/01/1950	114PM	13:14	19500101	01/01/1950	1314	13:14
9	01/01/50	01/01/1950	230AM	2:30	19500101	01/01/1950	230	2:30

Figure E-34: converting text or numeric dates and times to Excel dates and times

Column B uses the DATEVALUE function to convert the entries in Column A, which already look like dates, into Excel dates. The formula is simple:

=DATEVALUE(*text string*)
=DATEVALUE(A2)

Converting the text times in Column C is more difficult. To recognize them as times, Excel needs a colon between the hours and minutes and a space between the minutes and the AM/PM identifier. So "300PM" needs to become "3:00 PM." The formula that makes this possible CONCATENATEs (joins together) a combination of LEFT, RIGHT, and MID functions to put everything in the proper place:

=TIMEVALUE(*text string*)
=TIMEVALUE(CONCATENATE(LEFT(C2,1),":",MID(C2,2,2)," ",RIGHT(C2,2)))

Column F similarly uses the LEFT, RIGHT, and MID functions, but in this case we're using a DATE function to specify what parts of the numeric string represent months, days, and years:

=DATE(*month,day,year*)
=DATE(LEFT(E2,4),MID(E2,5,2),RIGHT(E2,2))

Finally, Column H converts the numeric time into an Excel time. This particular conversion presents a challenge, because some of the numbers are three digits (when the hour is a single digit), and some are four (when the hour is two digits). Therefore, we cannot use a LEFT function to extract the hour unless we throw in a complicated IF function as well. Instead, we can calculate the hour by dividing the number by 100 (Excel doesn't round the result; it just takes the integer), and the minutes using a RIGHT function:

=TIME(*hour, minutes, seconds*)
=TIME(G2/100,RIGHT(G2,2),0)

After you enter these formulas, you may need to go to **Format | Cells** and change the formatting to date or time to see the actual date or time rather than the underlying Excel number.

Charts

If a picture is worth a thousand words, a well-designed chart is worth a thousand numbers. Charts can convey clearly and cleanly what numbers only provide through careful interpretation.

Excel provides many different types of charts. In this section, we look at a few of them.

>**Step 1:** Open your **C:\BPOffice\Excel\UCR2009.xlsx** file.

Our first chart will compare 2008 and 2009 UCR figures for each type of crime. The first step in creating any chart is to select the cells (including their labels) that have the data you're charting.

>**Step 2:** Select Cells A1:A8 and E1:F8. Remember, hold down the CTRL key to select multiple ranges.

>**Step 3:** Choose **Insert | <u>Charts</u> | Column** (Figure E-35).

The many chart types available to you include column, bar, line, pie, XY scatter, doughnut, and radar charts. The simple column chart is one of the easiest and most effective. While line charts and pie charts only makes sense with specific types of data, you can represent almost anything with a column chart.

It may be tempting to create three-dimensional column, bar, and pie charts. Certainly, they seem to look more attractive. But they can actually be misleading and difficult to read, and the subtleties of shading that produce the three-dimensional appearance do not reproduce well on photocopiers. We strongly recommend sticking to two-dimensional charts. If you really want to use 3-D for aesthetic reasons, make them with a shallow depth.

»Step 4: Select the "clustered column" option (the first one).

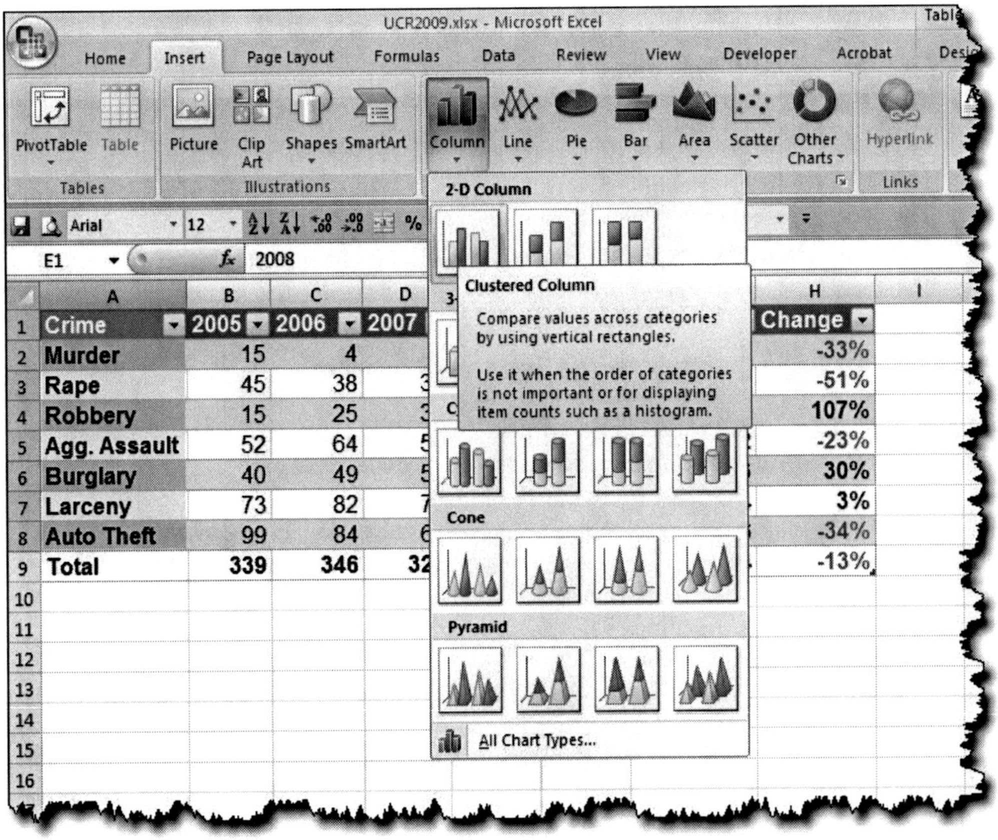

Figure E-35: creating a new column chart

A difference between Excel 2003 and Excel 2007 becomes immediately apparent. While Excel 2003 walked you through a series of dialog options before showing you the final result, Excel 2007 immediately drops the chart of your choosing into your spreadsheet. You set the options *after* the chart has appeared.

»Step 5: Use the handles in the corners to re-size it, and drag it so that it fits snugly under the data table (Figure E-36).

»Step 6: With the chart selected, choose **Chart Tools | Layout | Labels | Chart Title | Above Chart**. Click within the title and rename it "Part 1 Crimes."

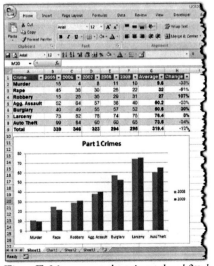

Figure E-36: your new chart, inserted and fitted

Several elements comprise your chart. You can adjust the color, size, and appearance of each of them. These elements include:

- The *Chart Area*, or background
- The *Chart Title*
- The *Plot Area*, or the background behind the series representations
- The *Gridlines*, major and minor
- The *Series Representations*, which are in our case columns
- The *Value Axis*, running vertically along the left, and its title
- The *Category Axis*, running horizontally along the bottom, and its title
- The *Legend*
- Any *Data Labels* you attach to your series representations

Figure E-38 shows these various elements on a modified version of our chart. Clicking on these various elements selects them, allowing you to make changes.

»**Step 7:** Select the columns representing 2008 crimes by clicking on one of them. As shown in Figure E-37, selectors appear on the columns indicating that they are selected.

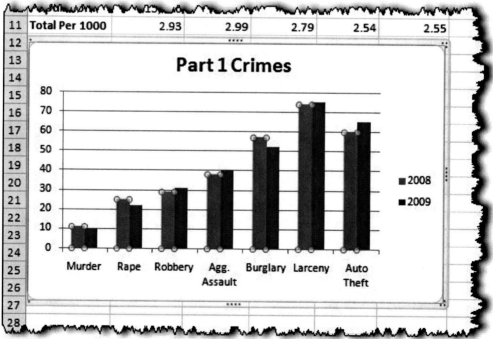

Figure E-37: as you select elements of your chart, different selectors appear to show what is selected

»**Step 8:** Go to Chart Tools | Format. On the Shape Styles group, use the "Shape Fill," "Shape Outline," and "Shape Effects" to experiment with different styles.

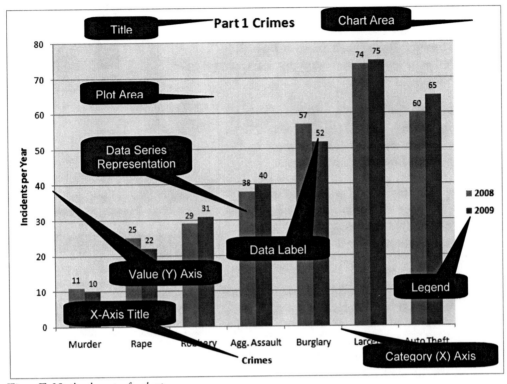

Figure E-38: the elements of a chart

Although almost all of the options you need to format parts of your chart can be found in the **Chart Tools** ribbon, there's another way to get at the options for a specific object.

»**Step 9:** Right-click on one of the bars representing 2009 and choose "Format Data Series."

There are many options in the "Format Data Series" box. We are going to use only a few of them, but we encourage you to explore the chart options liberally. Remember: you can always re-load or choose **CTRL-Z** to undo mistakes.

»**Step 10:** On the "Fill" group, click through the selections to see the various options and stop on "Gradiant Fill."

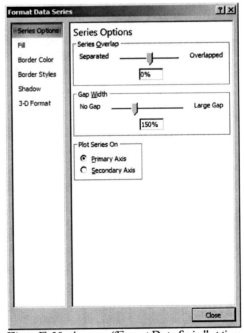

Figure E-39: the many "Format Data Series" options

»Step 11: Under "Preset Colors," choose the "Fire" option (fourth column, second row) or whatever else appeals to you. Play with the other settings if you want to see what they do.

»Step 12: Click on the "Series Options" group, change the "Overlap" from 0% to 30% (either use the slider or type in the box). When finished, click "Close."

»Step 13: Right-click on one of the 2008 bars, Choose "Format Data Series," and select which fill options you like. Use a color that contrasts with 2009. Then "Close" the options box.

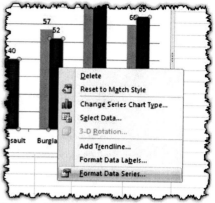

Figure E-40: formatting a data series

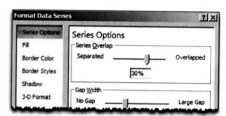

Figure E-41: changing the overlap

»Step 14: Click on the Legend and drag it to the upper left-hand corner of the plot area, to occupy the blank space there. Use the font options at **Home | Font** to increase the font of the legend to 14 and to bold it. Use the handles on the legend to increase the size to accommodate the new text.

»Step 15: Right-click on the legend and choose "Format Legend." You will see the dialog box looks similar to the one for the data series. Click on the "Fill" and give it a "Solid Fill" that is white. Then click on "Border Color" and give it a "Solid Line," black. "Close" when done.

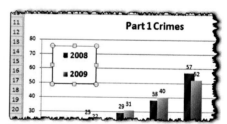

Figure E-42: moving and re-sizing the legend

»Step 16: Select the plot area by clicking within it (but not on a gridline). Use the handle on the right sides to click and drag the plot area to expand into the blank space where the legend was.

»Step 17: Right-click on one of the 2008 bars and choose "Add Data Labels" repeat for one of the 2009 bars. (When you right-click on one bar, it should select all the bars in the series.)

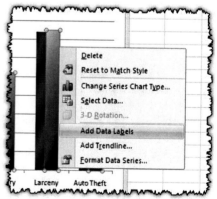

Figure E-43: adding data labels

When you are finished, your chart should look like Figure E-44.

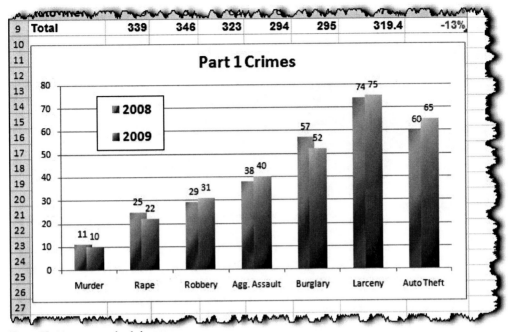

Figure E-44: your completed chart

In our second charting example, we'll create a pie chart that shows the share of the Part 1 Crime total that each individual crime had in 2004.

»**Step 18:** Select Cells A1–A8 *and* F1–F8. Since these cells are non-contiguous (i.e., you have to skip Columns B, C, D, and E), you must first select A1–A8, then hold down the **CTRL** key and choose C1–C8.

»**Step 19:** Choose **Insert | Charts | Pie** and chose the first option. A basic pie chart appears.

A pie chart has some, but not all, of the elements of the column chart. For instance, there are no axes, and the series representation is in wedges instead of columns.

Figure E-45: inserting a pie chart

Before we do anything, let's move this chart to a separate sheet so it's easier to work with.

»**Step 20:** Right-click on a blank part of the chart and choose "Move Chart." Select "New Sheet" and click "OK"

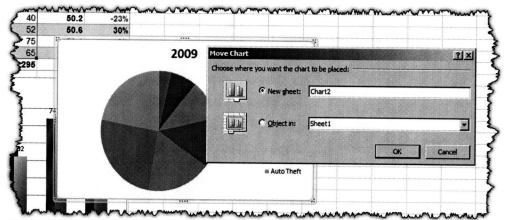

Figure E-46: moving your chart to a new sheet

The legend has a few too many categories to make it useful. Let's add the categories directly to the pie wedges instead.

»Step 21: Right-click on one of the wedges and choose "Add Data Labels." The counts appear—not helpful. Right-click again and choose "Format Data Labels." Un-check the box that says "Value" and instead click the boxes labeled "Category Name" and "Percentage." Then "Close."

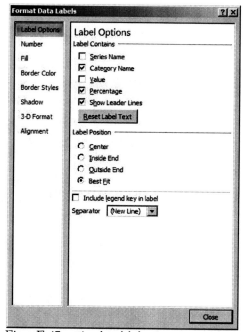

The labels don't look so bad at this point, but they could stand to be a little larger.

»Step 22: If you un-selected the data labels after the previous step, click on one again to select them all. If they are already selected, move on to the next step.

»Step 23: Use the font options at **Home | Font** to increase the font size to 14.

Figure E-47: setting data label options

»Step 24: Select the legend and tap the **DELETE** key. The legend is superfluous with the data labels.

So far, we have been selecting data series and labels by clicking on one of them, which by default selects them all. But if we want to select only a single series representation (in this case, a single wedge) or a single data label at a time, we can do that.

»**Step 25:** Click on one of the pie wedges. All of them will select. Wait a second, then click on the same wedge a second time, and only it will be selected. Use **Chart Tools | Format | Shape Styles | Shape Fill** to give it the color you want. Repeat with the other wedges of the pie.

When you're finished, you might find that the black text does not show up very well on some of your darker pie pieces.

»**Step 26:** Click on one of the labels on a dark wedge. All of the labels will select. Wait a second, then click on the same label a second time, and only it will be selected. Use **Home | Font |** to change the font color to white. Repeat for any other labels on a dark pie wedge.

You can use this same click-wait-click technique to select a single column in a column graph, a single section of line on a line chart, and so on. You can then change the appearance and formatting of your selections independent of the other series representation elements. This is useful if you want one particular column to have its own color or formatting to make it stand out.

»**Step 27:** Finally, change the title from "2009" to "Part 1 Crimes in 2009" by clicking in it and typing new text. Use the Formatting toolbar to increase the side of the font and bold it.

Your pie chart should now resemble Figure E-48.

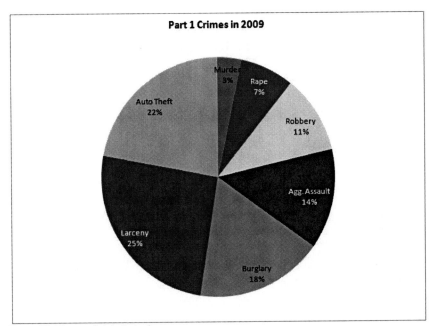

Figure E-48: your finished pie chart

Adding New Data to an Existing Chart

Once created, a chart maintains a live link to the data used in its creation. If the data changes, the chart will change accordingly. But how do you add new data?

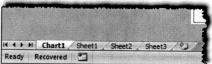

Figure E-49: your workbook tabs after adding the pie chart and moving it to a new sheet

We are missing one Part 1 crime on our spreadsheet: arson. We will add this crime and adjust both of our charts to incorporate this additional offense, but first let's work on managing the multiple sheets we now have in our workbook.

When you moved the pie chart to a new sheet, it created a new tab at the bottom of your workbook called "Chart1." "Sheet1" contains the UCR crimes data. Neither is very descriptive.

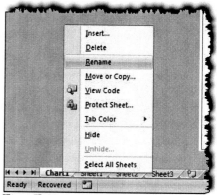

Figure E-50: re-naming a sheet

> **»Step 1:** Right click on the "Chart1" tab in the bottom left-hand corner and choose "Rename." The word "Chart1" will highlight. Type "2009Pie" over it.

> **»Step 2:** Right click on the "Sheet1" tab in the bottom left-hand corner and choose "Rename." Type "UCR."

Sheets 2 and 3 don't have anything on them. We don't need them. If we later need more worksheets, we can always add them with the ⬚ button.

Figure E-51: your worksheet tabs after performing "maintenance"

> **»Step 3:** Right-click on the "Sheet2" tab and choose "Delete." Repeat for "Sheet3."

Now we're ready to add data.

> **»Step 4:** If not already there, switch back to your spreadsheet by clicking the "UCR" tab. Select Row 9 (the "Total") row. Choose **Home | Cells |Insert**. Excel should insert a row above the row you had selected.

> **»Step 5:** You should now have a blank row in between "Auto Theft" and "Total." Fill it in with the data in Figure E-52. The two formulas should fill in automatically.

What will not adjust automatically is the "Total" row formula. Notice how in Figure E-52 there's a little mark in the upper-left-hand corner of each "Total" cell. Microsoft calls this a "tag." Whenever you see a tag, it indicates that Excel thinks there's some kind of error with the formula. In many cases, Excel is wrong, but it is correct in this case.

7	Larceny	73	82	78	74	75	76.4	3%
8	Auto Theft	99	84	60	60	65	73.6	-34%
9	Arson	10	8	11	12	15	11.2	50%
10	Total	339	346	323	294	295	319.4	-13%
11							
12		Part 1 Crimes					
13							

Figure E-52: populating the data in your new "Arson" row. Note the "tags" in the total row now.

»Step 6: Click in the "Total" cell for 2005. Note that a little exclamation point appears to the left of the cell. Hover your pointer over it and you will get a drop-down menu. Select it. Excel tells you what it thinks the error is, and it is correct. Choose "Update Formula" to include adjacent cells.

»Step 7: Fill the formula across the cells to the right by selecting Cells B10 to F10 and typing **CTRL-R.**

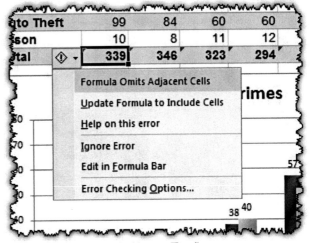

Figure E-53: verifying and addressing Excel's error tag

Note that after you fill the formula, which includes the "Arson" figures, the little marks go away.

We now want to add some of this new data to the existing charts. There are two ways to accomplish this:

1) Right-click on the chart and choose "Select Data" and adjust the series references
2) Copy and paste the new data

The second option is easier and a bit more fun.

»Step 8: Select Cells A9, E9, and F9 (hold down the CTRL key and click on them one at a time).

»Step 9: Choose **Home | Clipboard | Copy**.

»Step 10: Click on your "Part 1 Crimes" column chart and choose **Home | Clipboard | Paste**.

A new category label for "Arson" should appear, with the appropriate columns above it.

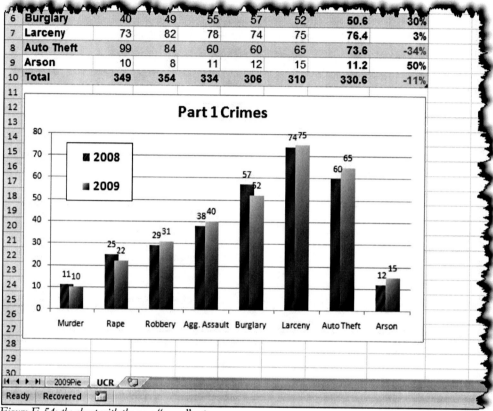

Figure E-54: the chart with the new "arson" category

»Step 11: Select Cells A9 and C9 (you will have to click Cell A9, hold down the **CTRL** key, and click Cell C9) and choose **Home | Clipboard | Copy**.

»Step 12: Click on your pie chart tab at the bottom of the screen. Select the chart and choose **Home | Clipboard | Paste**.

A new wedge will be added to your pie with the arson data. Other percentages will adjust accordingly.

Pasting a Chart in Word or PowerPoint

Often you will want to present the results of your charts in a Word report or a PowerPoint presentation. Doing so is quite simple: select the chart in Excel, choose

Home | Clipboard | Copy (or **CTRL-C**), switch to your Word document or PowerPoint presentation, and **Home | Clipboard | Paste** (or **CTRL-V**) it in the desired location.

By default, both Word and PowerPoint paste the chart *as* a chart (not a picture), meaning it retains the original data. Once it's pasted, you can still modify the formatting or the underlying data, with all of the same options as you have in Excel, simply by double-clicking on it and getting access to the **Chart Tools** ribbon group. Unlike with Word and PowerPoint 2003, which used the somewhat-clunky Microsoft Graph as their chart editors, Word and PowerPoint 2007 use Excel itself as their chart editor, making a much more seamless transition.

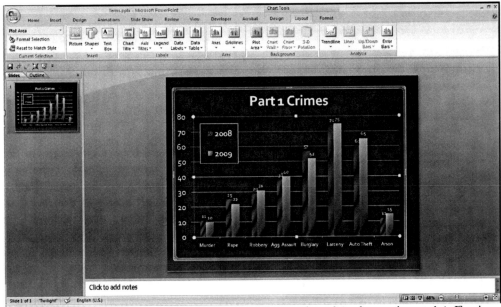

Figure E-55: in Word and PowerPoint 2007, you have all the same chart editing features that you do in Excel

But with **Home | Clipboard | Paste | Paste Special**, you have an even *more* advanced option: to paste it as a link. When you click the "Paste Link" option, you tie the image in Word or PowerPoint to the original Excel chart. If the chart later changes in Excel, those changes will update in the Word or PowerPoint file. If, however, the Excel file is deleted or renamed, you will get an error the next time you open the Word or PowerPoint file that contains the link, and you will be left with only a picture.

In case for some reason you don't want to paste the chart as a chart, "Paste Special" also gives you the opportunity to paste it as an image.

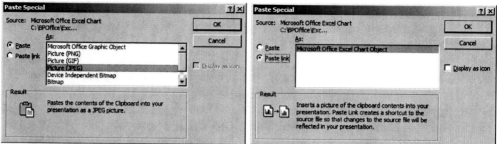

Figure E-56: the "Paste Special" option in Word and PowerPoint gives you the ability to paste your chart as a chart, an image, or as a link to the original chart

Other Chart Types

We have explored only a few of the chart types available in Excel. We encourage you to use the sample data provided or your own data to experiment with other chart types. There are many.

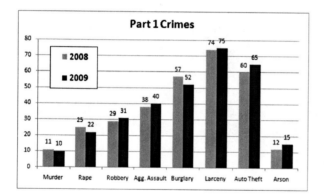

Bar charts or *column charts* are best for showing simple volume by category, as in our "Part 1 Crimes" example. You can have more than one column per category (e.g., 2008 and 2009), but more than three is not recommended.

Stacked bar charts or *stacked column charts* expand on column charts by showing the contribution of one or more categories to a whole.

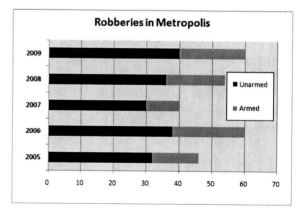

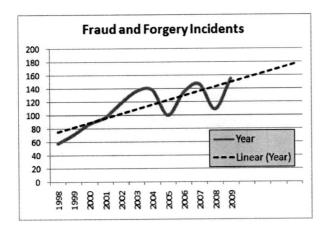

Line charts and area charts show a linear progression, for instance by month or by year. You can add different types of trendlines to them that project future occurrences based on past ones.

Pie charts and donut charts show the relationship of parts to a whole. They are best limited to no more than six categories.

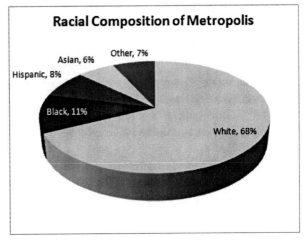

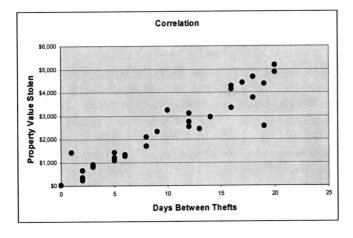

Scatter charts compare two numeric values to show relationship or correlation.

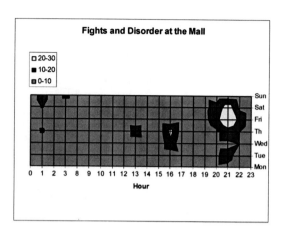

Surface charts show relationships between two categories, such as time of day and day of week.

Data Analysis

So far in this chapter, we have experimented primarily with calculations and charting based on numeric data already aggregated. Excel also has a number of features that make it ideal for the analysis for raw crime data. You can aggregate, filter, and cross-tabulate data in Excel just as you can do in Access.

Like Access, Excel may often save a crime analyst from an outdated or poorly-designed records management system (RMS). Even analysts with good RMSes, however, may frequently use Excel to analyze data obtained from external sources, such as a web site, another agency, or a spatial query in a geographic information system (GIS).

One major limitation of analysis in previous versions of Excel was its row and column limits: 65,536 rows and 256 columns in Excel 2003. But in Excel 2007, Microsoft increased the row limit to one million and the column limit to 16,000, so Excel is now able to analyze all but the largest data tables.

One significant limitation remains, however: Excel, unlike Access, can only work with one table at a time. You cannot join multiple tables the way you can in an Access query. In Excel, you can analyze information about crimes, or information about people, but (unlike Access) not crimes and people simultaneously. You will still need Access for your relational database needs. And because Excel does not have the same features with validation rules, input masks, and lookup tables as Access, we still recommend that you use Excel to analyze data but not to store or enter it.

Sorting

This lesson demonstrates how Excel can be used to organize and make better sense out of large amounts of data.

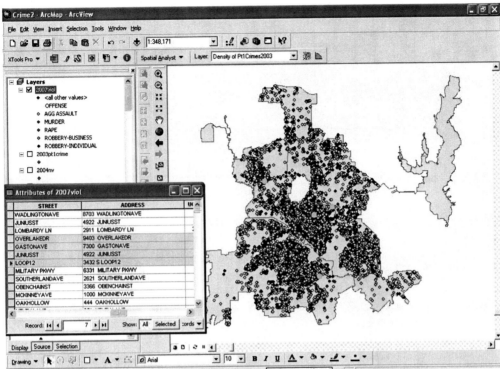

Figure E-63: the analyst has used ArcGIS to select all crimes that occurred within 1000 feet of a school. Excel is an ideal program to quickly import and analyze this data.

»**Step 1:** Open **C:\BPOffice\Excel\January.xlsx**.

This spreadsheet mimics a data export from a records management system, showing all the violent offenses that occurred in January 2009 in a large Texas city. There are two sheets: "Original" and "crimenames."

The spreadsheets in this workbook mimic what a crime analyst might encounter, with perplexing field names, baffling numeric codes, and blank and missing data.

We will puzzle through it, beginning with the "Original" sheet. We will sort, subtotal, and cross-tabulate this data. We begin by *sorting*.

»**Step 2:** Click anywhere in the spreadsheet and choose **Data | Sort & Filter | Sort**.

»**Step 3:** Sort by the UCR_CODE field, on "Values," in "A to Z" order.

»**Step 4:** Click "Add Level" twice. For the second two rows, enter "SEVTDATE" ("Start Event Date") and "SEVTIME" (Figure E-64).

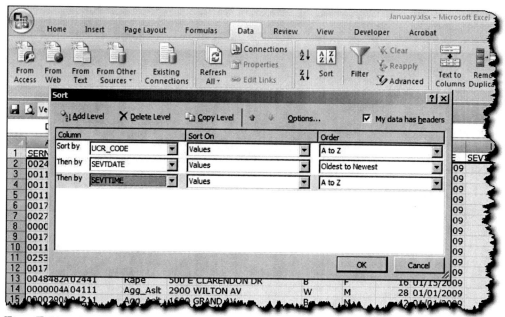

Figure E-64: setting sort options

The sort runs. The result is that the most serious UCR offenses (those with lower codes) are grouped at the top of the sheet, and then put in order of date and time.

> **»Step 5:** Practice with more sorts using the fields in the spreadsheet. Try combinations of ascending and descending sorts. When finished, click within the "SERNUM" column (don't select the column, just click on one of the cells within it), and click the "Sort Ascending" button at **Data | <u>Sort & Filter</u>**. Both the "Sort Ascending" and "Sort Descending" buttons are quick and easy ways to sort by a single column at a time.

When sorting data, beware of the warning message in Figure E-65. This occurs when you select a *range* of cells (as opposed to a single cell) and then click the "Sort Ascending" or "Sort Descending" button. If you continue with the sort, you will sort the cells you have selected but not the related cells adjacent to them. If we performed this operation on the SEVTDATE field, for instance, the dates would sort, but they would no longer appear on the correct rows with the rest of the data associated with those incidents. More than one analyst has rendered useless hours of work with a careless

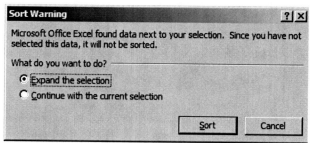

Figure E-65: you usually want to click "Cancel" when you see this warning

sort! There are times that you may want to sort data in one column but not in adjacent columns, but usually when you see this message you want to click "Cancel," undo your selection, and start over. In some previous versions of Excel, you did not get an error message and might not realize your mistake until hours later, or never.

Excel generally sorts data in the way you would expect and desire: text in alphabetical order, numbers in numerical order, dates and times in chronological order. But there are times in which you may want to use a different order. A good example is the DOW field in the current spreadsheet. DOW stands for "Day of Week." If you click in this field and "Sort Ascending," Friday will move to the top of the list, followed by Monday, and then Saturday. Why? Because this is the order that the days occur in an alphabetical sort. But it probably isn't what you want.

Excel allows *custom lists* to deal with such custom sort jobs. The day of week list comes with Excel by default. Here's how to use it:

»**Step 6:** Click within your spreadsheet and choose **Data | Sort & Filter | Sort**. In the "Sort By" box, choose "DOW," but in the "Order" box, choose "Custom List." Select the second custom list, which begins "Sun, Mon, Tue..." and then "OK" twice.

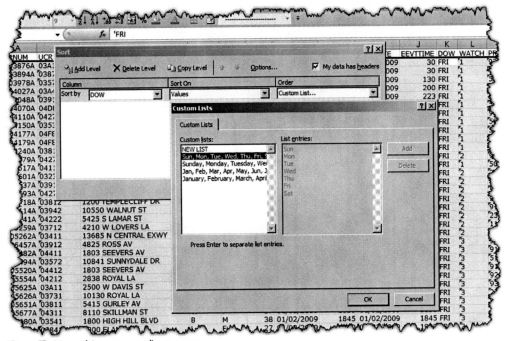

Figure E-66: applying a custom list to a sort

What if you wanted Monday first? You can add your own custom lists to those that come with Excel. We'll add two: one for a Monday-first DOW sort, and one for a textual crime sort. There are two ways to create custom lists: type them into cells, or type them directly into the "Custom Lists" box. We'll do both.

»Step 7: At the bottom of the workbook, to the right of the worksheet tabs, click on the "Insert Worksheet" button to add a new worksheet to the workbook.

»Step 8: Starting in Cell A1, type the following offenses, one per row (Figure E-52): Murder, Rape, Robbery, Agg_Aslt, Burglary, Theft, Auto_Theft.

»Step 9: Select Cells A1–A7 (the range containing the values you just typed) and choose **Office Button | Excel Options.** On the "Popular" tab, choose "Edit Custom Lists."

»Step 10: Verify that the cell range to "Import" is **$A$1:$A$7**. Click the "Import" button. The list should appear before you, and you will now be able to use it when sorting by a textual "crime type" field.

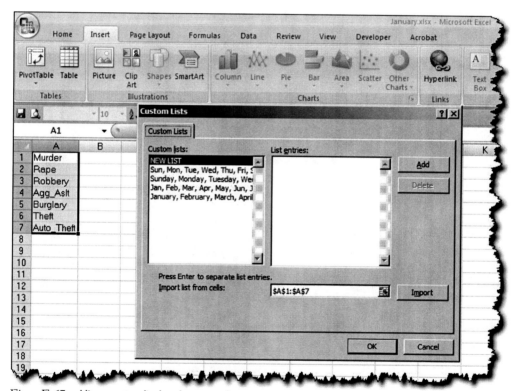

Figure E-67: adding a custom list based on a typed range

While we're in this dialog box, we'll explore the other means of creating a custom list: type it in yourself.

»**Step 11:** In the "Custom lists" box, click "NEW LIST."

»**Step 12:** In the "List entries" box, type the list in Figure E-68, hitting **ENTER** between each day.

»**Step 13:** When finished, click the "Add" button. You now have two custom list options for sorting days of the week.

Now that you know how to create custom lists, more examples from your own agency probably leap to mind. Precinct names, races, sexes, city and town names, shift names, ranks, and premise types are all good candidates for custom lists.

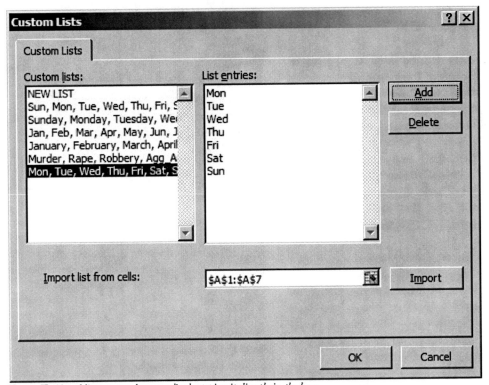

Figure E-68: adding a second custom list by typing it directly in the box

»**Step 14:** Adapt Step 6 to use your new custom lists on the DOW field and the CRIME field on the "crimenames" sheet.

Subtotals

Subtotals help you aggregate data by category. They expand on sorting by applying a count or other function on records in each sorted category. Before you subtotal by a field, you must sort by that field.

»Step 1: On the "Original" sheet, click within the WATCH (shift) field. Click the "Sort Ascending" ⌷ button at **Data | Sort & Filter** to sort this field in order by watch.

»Step 2: Choose **Data | Outline | Subtotal**.

»Step 3: Fill out the "Subtotal" dialog as follows: "At each change in WATCH, use function Count, Add subtotal to Premise." Accept the defaults for the checkboxes and click "OK."

»Step 4: A Subtotal bar appears to the left of the screen. Ignore it for now. Scroll down to Row 202, and you will see the result of your Subtotal: a count of offenses in Watch 1 (200) appears under the PREMISE column (as in your "Subtotal" dialog at the point that the Watch 1 offenses end. You will find the same subtotal at Rows 318, 656, and 668.

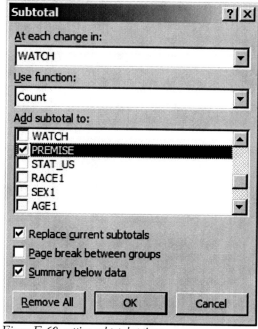

Figure E-69: setting subtotal options

The Subtotal bar on the left allows you to show *only* the subtotals, to quickly determine how many offenses occurred on each watch. As you click on the appropriate buttons, it "rolls up" the individual records so that only the subtotals remain.

THR	1	913	S
WED	1	503	S
MON	1	503	C
	1 Count	200	
THR	2	213	S
THR	2	501	E
THR	2	501	E
THR	2		

Figure E-70: a count of offenses on Watch 1 appears at the point that the watch changes from 1 to 2

»Step 5: Click on the "1" button on the subtotal bar. *All* offenses are rolled up into one "Grand Total" row. Click on the "2" button, and you see each subtotal. Clicking on "3" returns you to a line-by line recording of each offense. While you are at Level 2 (Figure E-57), you can use the ⊞ symbols to show only the records on a particular watch. Finish your exploration on Level 2.

Figure E-71: the subtotal bar

With the subtotals summarized before you (as in Figure E-72), you can now create a quick pie chart showing the percentage of offenses on each watch. However, you can *not* simply select the range of cells that shows the counts. Even though Rows 2–201, 203–317, and so on are not visible, they will still be selected if you click on Cell L202 and drag to Cell M668. The way around this is to select each cell individually.

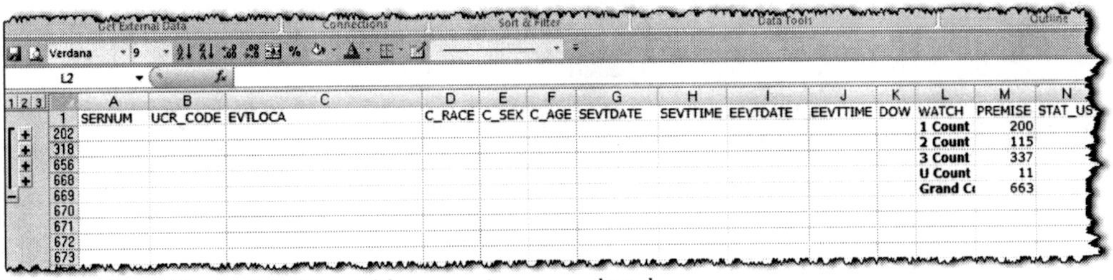

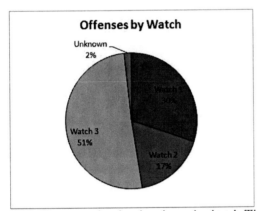

Figure E-72: clicking on Level 2 quickly summarizes your subtotals

»**Step 6:** Click on Cell L202, hold down the **CTRL** key and, keeping the **CTRL** key depressed, click Cells M202, L318, M318, L656, M656, L668, and M668.

»**Step 7:** Choose **Insert | Charts | Pie**. Follow the steps you learned before to create a pie chart (Figure E-73).

Offenses by Watch

Unknown 2%

Watch 1 30%

Watch 3 51%

Watch 2 17%

Figure E-73: a pie chart based on the watch subtotals. The data labels were originally "1 Count," "2 Count," etc., but we clicked in and typed over them.

In the example above, we used the subtotals to count offenses, but there are other subtotal options, including sum, average, minimum, maximum, and standard deviation. Only numeric fields can be used for anything but "Count," however.

»**Step 8:** Click within the spreadsheet and choose **Data | Outline | Subtotal**. This time, at each change in WATCH, use function "Average" and add it to C_AGE (complainant's age). Click "OK."

»**Step 9:** Click on the Level 2 grouping **2**, and you will see that the average complainant age is 29.14. It varies only slightly among the three watches.

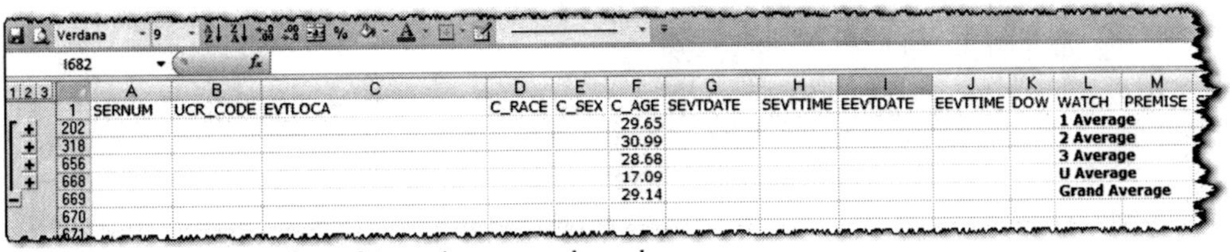

Figure E-74: an average of complainants' ages on each watch

»Step 10: When finished, choose **Data | Outline | Subtotal** and click "Remove All" to return the spreadsheet to its original state.

Non-count subtotals are particularly valuable for property value information. Within a few minutes, you can calculate the average, maximum, minimum, and total value of stolen property for each offense, each watch, each district, and so on.

As further exercises, we encourage you to perform other sorts and subtotals on this data. Options include:

- Sort by the premise type
- Sort and subtotal by DOW (day of week)
- Using the "crimenames" sheet, sort by the CRIME and use subtotals to calculate the average age of complainants for each crime

Filtering

Excel's filtering options are a quick way to drill-down into your data. It can be useful for finding crime patterns or analyzing problems. Though Excel filters are not as advanced as Access filters, they still allow a lot of flexibility.

»Step 1: If it is not already open, open **C:\BPOffice\Excel\January.xlsx**. Select the "crimenames" sheet.

»Step 2: Choose **Data | Sort & Filter | Filter**.

Your column headers become a series of drop-down menus. Clicking on any of them will give you a list of all values in that column, as well as a few other options (Figure E-75).

Checking any of the actual values (e.g., "A," "B") will hide any rows that do not match those values. "Blanks" shows you only records with no values in that field. There are also special text, number, and date filters that let you write more complex expressions, for instance searching for all dates within a particular range.

Assume that we have a rape series in which young black females are being victimized. We want to find all of the incidents in the series.

»Step 3: Click on the drop-down menu for C_RACE (complainant's race) and un-check all except "B" (the easiest way is to un-check "Select All" and then select "B"). The records filter so that only the 276 rows with a "B" for race are shown. Now click on the drop-down for C_SEX and choose "F" (un-check "M"), and you get only the 114 records with black females as victims. Note that the drop-down arrows on the filtered columns change to a tiny funnel, indicating a filter is in place.

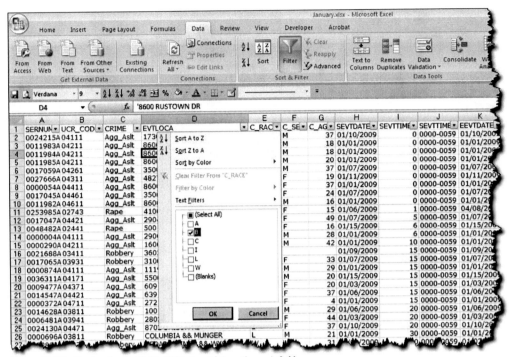

Figure E-75: filtering by the C_RACE (complainant's race) field

»**Step 4:** Click on the drop-down menu for C_AGE and choose "Number Filter" and "Between." Set your custom filter to find C_AGE greater than or equal to 15 AND less than 26 (Figure E-61). You should now filter down to 49 records.

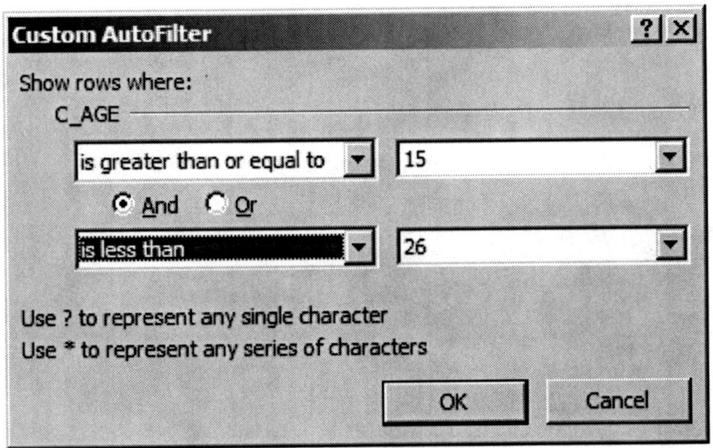

Custom AutoFilter   **? ✕**

Show rows where:
    C_AGE

| is greater than or equal to ▼ | 15 ▼ |

       ● And   ○ Or

| is less than ▼ | 26 ▼ |

Use ? to represent any single character
Use * to represent any series of characters

            OK   Cancel

Figure E-76: applying a "Custom AutoFilter" to age

»**Step 5:** Click on the drop-down menu for CRIME check only "Rape." You will be left with eight incidents of rape to black female victims between the ages of 15 and 26 (Figure E-77).

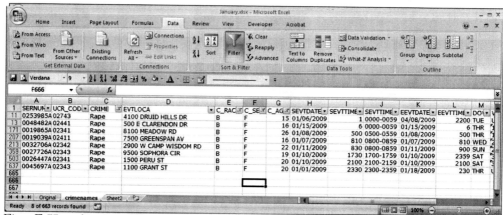

Figure E-77: combinations of filters can help you find patterns of offenses

Unlike when subtotaling, when you filter data, you *can* click and drag to select a range of cells, and copy and paste (or create a chart based on) *only* those cells, not the hidden ones.

»**Step 6:** When finished, choose **Data | <u>Sort & Filter</u> | Clear** ⚔ Clear to remove the filters.

It's worth experimenting a little more with different filters to see what you can discern from this data. Try using different filters to find:

1) The top 10 oldest complainants in the list.

2) All incidents on "Bonnie View Road." This requires a text filter (Figure E-78).

3) All incidents between January 1 and January 10. This requires a date filter (Figure E-79).

4) All robberies on Watch 3 with female victims.

5) Robberies in which the victim's race and sex are unknown ("Blanks").

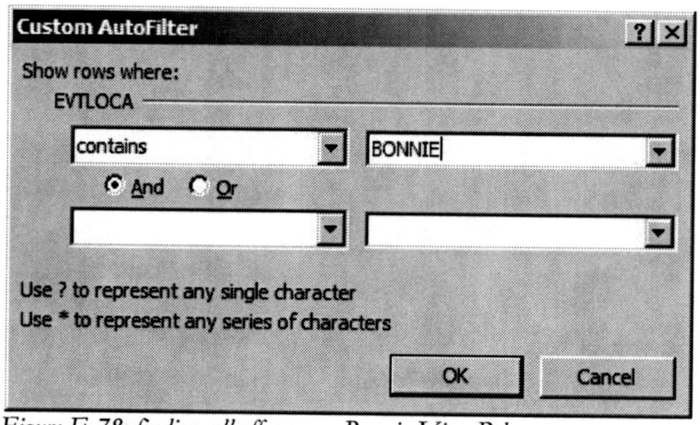

Figure E-78: finding all offenses on Bonnie View Rd

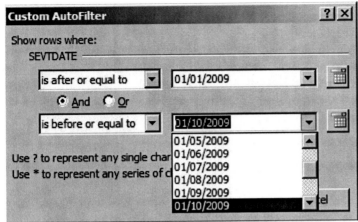

Figure E-79: using a Custom AutoFilter to find all incidents between January 1 and January 10

Remember to choose **Data | Sort & Filter | Clear** when you are finished.

PivotTables

PivotTables aggregate and cross-tabulate data and, as such, they can quickly make sense of a large amount of it. You can use them to find correlations or relationships between different types of data.

To illustrate pivot tables, we will be using another sample file, again mimicking an export from a records management system (RMS). In this case, we're opening a dBASE (.dbf) file, a common interchange format.

>>**Step 1:** Choose **Office Button | Open**. Navigate to **C:\BPOffice\Excel**, and in the "Files of type" box, choose "dBase Files (*.dbf)."

As you're making this selection, note all of the different file types that Excel can read: web pages, XML, text, Access, Microsoft Query, Lotus 1-2-3, Quattro Pro, dBASE, and so on. Essentially, Excel can recognize anything that stores data in columns and rows.

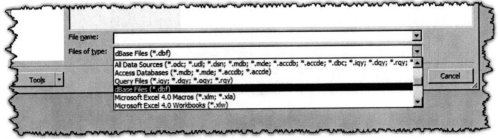

Figure E-80: Excel can open a host of different file types

A Note on Excel 2007 and DBF Files

Excel 2003 allowed you to both open and save files in .dbf format. Excel 2007 will open dbf files but will not allow saves. This is very unfortunate because dBASE remains a fairly common interchange type, and it is very familiar to crime analysts using ArcGIS shape files. We hope Excel re-introduces this capability in future versions. You can still export to dBASE format from Access.

»**Step 2:** Choose **C:\BPOffice\Excel\October.dbf** and open it.

Similar to our "January" file, this file contains all Part 1 crimes in a large Texas city in October of 2008. There are 7,878 records in the file. We're going to make sense of this vast amount of data with pivot tables.

»**Step 3:** Choose **Insert | Tables | Pivot Tables**.

As the options on the following dialog box (Figure E-81) indicate, in creating your PivotTable or PivotChart, you are not limited to the data within your existing Excel workbook. Instead, you can draw data from database connections and other sources. In our case, we want to base our PivotTable on the data in the worksheet, and by default Excel selects the data in the active worksheet.

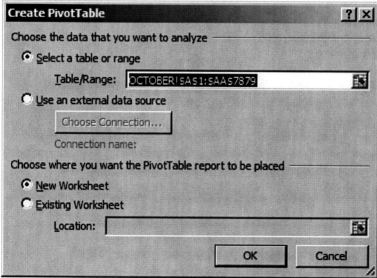

Figure E-81: the first stage of creating a PivotTable or PivotChart allows you to draw data from external sources

»**Step 4:** Accept the defaults and click "OK."

The result is a blank PivotTable grid, a field list, and a PivotTable toolbar (Figure E-82).

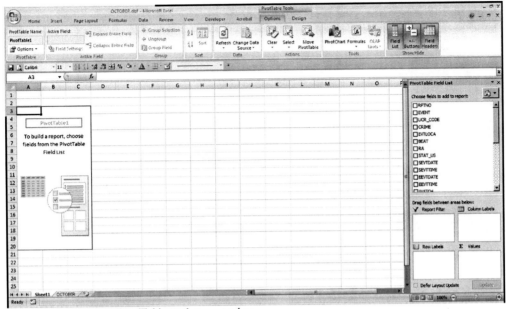

Figure E-82: your virgin PivotTable, ready to accept data

At this point, we construct the PivotTable checking the fields we want to aggregate by or summarize, and by moving them around the "Row Labels," "Column Labels," and "Values" boxes. We can also filter by fields by adding them to the "Report Filter" box.

»**Step 5:** Put a checkmark next to the CRIME field, then the WATCH field, then the RPTNO field. Excel gets it all wrong by putting the WATCH field as a row heading and summing (rather than counting) the report numbers.

»**Step 6:** In the "Row Labels" box, click on WATCH and drag and drop it into the "Column Labels" box.

»**Step 7:** In the "Values" box, click on the drop-down menu next to "Sum of RPTNO." Choose "Value Field Settings" and change the setting to COUNT rather than SUM (Figure E-83).

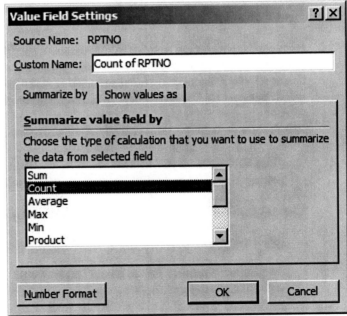

Figure E-83: changing the aggregation for RPTNO to COUNT

With that change made, our PivotTable ends up showing us the number of crimes that have occurred within each watch in October 2008 (Figure E-84). The "U" indicates the watch was unknown.

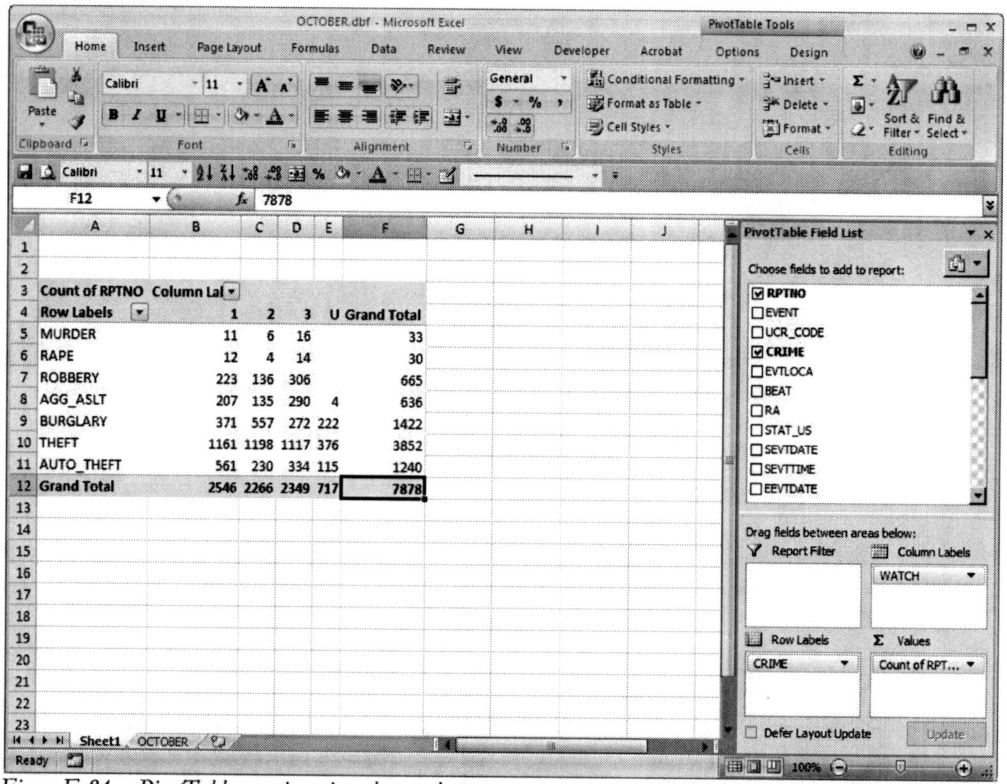

Figure E-84: a PivotTable counting crimes by watch

In choosing which field to drop in the center of the PivotTable to COUNT, always pick a field that *always* has something in it. Excel will not count blank fields. For this reason, we chose RPTNO, because every crime has a report number. If we had chosen C_SEX, we would have gotten lower numbers because not all records have a complainant sex.

PivotTables are very flexible—we can easily change the fields in our cross-tabulation.

»**Step 8:** Un-check the CRIME field in the field list, and check the BEAT field instead. You are now looking at a cross-tabulation of beats and watches.

You can sort data in a PivotTable just like in a regular Excel spreadsheet.

»**Step 9:** Click within Column F (the "Grand Total" column) and click the "Sort Descending" button $^{Z}_{A}\downarrow$ at **PivotTable Tools | Options | Sort**. The beats with the highest crime totals now appear first. Looks like Beat 322 is highest.

You can also write formulas outside the PivotTable that reference cells within it. For instance, we have the total number of offenses in each beat, but perhaps we might want to know the average number of offenses among all the beats.

>**Step 10:** Scroll down to Cell F238. In it, type the following formula: **=AVERAGE(F5:F236).** (Note that when you click outside the PivotTable, your PivotTable field list and options disappear from the right-hand side of the screen. To get them back, just click within the PivotTable again.) You should find that the average number of offenses on each beat is 33.96 (Figure E-73). We could use a similar formula in Cell G237 to find the average number of offenses on each watch.

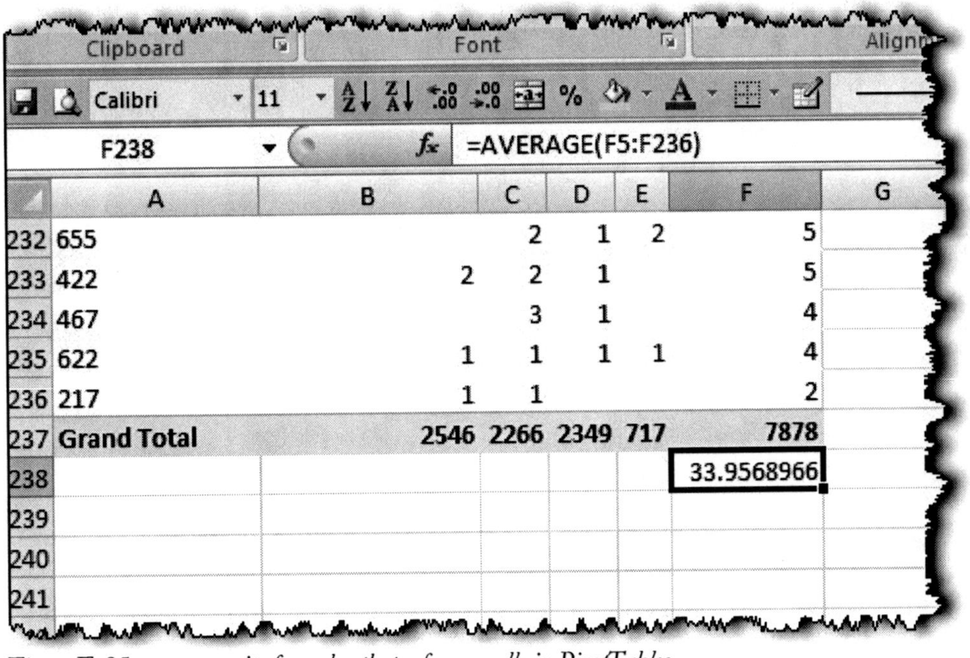

						F	G
Clipboard			Font				Align
Calibri	11			%			
F238		f_x	=AVERAGE(F5:F236)				
	A	B	C	D	E	F	G
232	655		2	1	2	5	
233	422	2	2	1		5	
234	467		3	1		4	
235	622	1	1	1	1	4	
236	217	1	1			2	
237	**Grand Total**	2546	2266	2349	717	7878	
238						33.9568966	
239							
240							
241							

Figure E-85: you can write formulas that reference cells in PivotTables

You do not have to see all the values in the categories you have added to your cross-tabulation. Perhaps we do not care about offenses that occurred on unknown watches.

>**Step 11:** Scroll back up to the top. Click on the "Column Labels" drop-down menu in Cell B3 and uncheck the "U" watch. The "U" ("Unknown") column disappears, and we are left with only incidents on known watches. Use the same procedure to bring back the "U" column.

PivotTables allow multiple grouping levels.

>**Step 12:** Check the box next to the RA field in the Field List. Excel adds it to the "Row Labels" box, which is what we want.

The PivotTable now has hierarchical row headings, showing first the BEAT and its totals, and then the totals for the RAs that make up each beat. Note that you can collapse the RAs by clicking on the little ⊟ symbol before each beat.

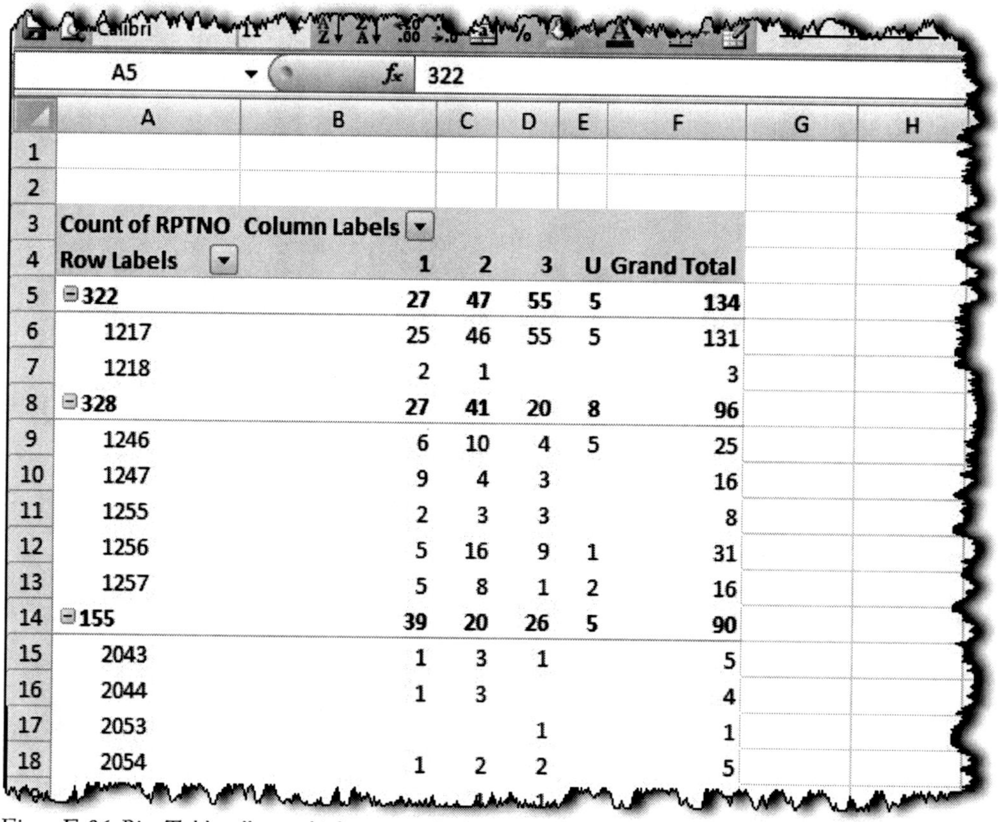

	A	B	C	D	E	F	G	H
		A5	▼		f_x	322		
1								
2								
3	Count of RPTNO	Column Labels ▼						
4	Row Labels ▼		1	2	3	U Grand Total		
5	⊟322		27	47	55	5	134	
6	1217		25	46	55	5	131	
7	1218		2	1			3	
8	⊟328		27	41	20	8	96	
9	1246		6	10	4	5	25	
10	1247		9	4	3		16	
11	1255		2	3	3		8	
12	1256		5	16	9	1	31	
13	1257		5	8	1	2	16	
14	⊟155		39	20	26	5	90	
15	2043		1	3	1		5	
16	2044		1	3			4	
17	2053				1		1	
18	2054		1	2	2		5	

Figure E-86: PivotTables allow multiple grouping levels

Finally, the "Report Filter" field allows even more filtering options.

»**Step 13:** Check the box next to "Crime." Excel adds it to the "Row Labels," which isn't what we want. Drag it from there and drop it in "Report Filter." Note that the CRIME field appears up in Cell A1.

»**Step 14:** Click on the drop-down menu in Cell B1 and select "Robbery" to study only robberies by beat and watch (Figure E-87). Then click the menu again and select "(All)."

»**Step 15:** Use what you've learned about filtering and sorting to look only at auto theft. Which beat has the highest number of auto thefts? Swtich back to "(All)" when you're finished.

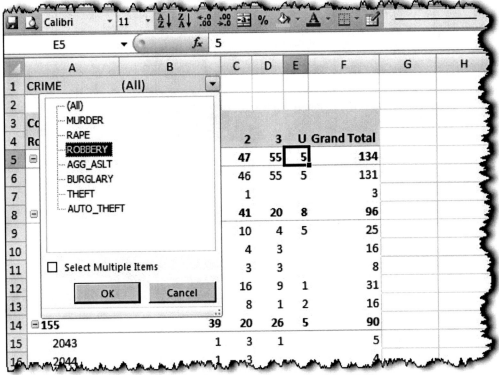

Figure E-87: Report filters allow additional filtering options for more detailed analysis

The key to the effective use of PivotTables is maximizing your speed. By dragging different fields in and out of the Row Labels, Column Lables, Report Filters, and Values, you can very quickly summarize large datasets.

»**Step 16:** Un-check the boxes next to "BEAT" and "RA" in the field list. Drag the CRIME field from the "Report Filter" and in to the "Row Labels" box. You should once more be cross-tabulating crimes by watch.

Styles can give a PivotTable a more attractive appearance.

»**Step 17:** Select your PivotTable by clicking on Cell A3. Choose one of the styles from **PivotTable Tools | Design | PivotTable Styles** to give it an attractive appearance, as in Figure E-89. We chose the third option under "Medium."

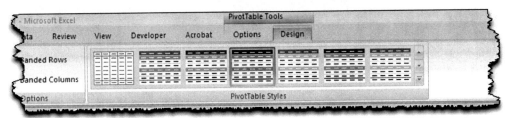

Figure E-88: PivotTable styles

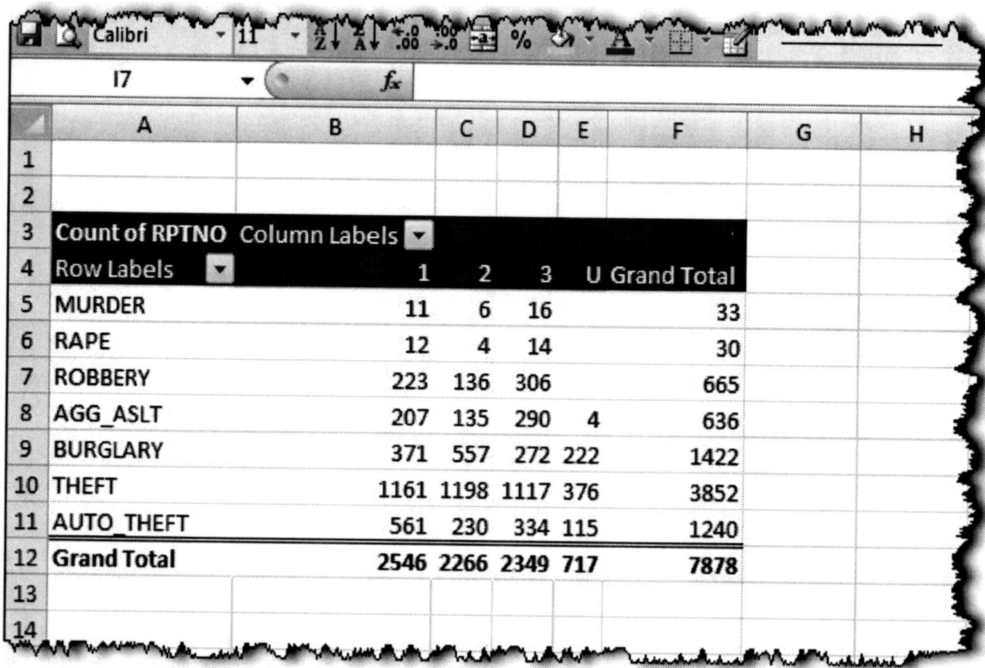

	A	B	C	D	E	F	G	H
1								
2								
3	**Count of RPTNO**	Column Labels ▾						
4	Row Labels ▾		1	2	3	U Grand Total		
5	MURDER		11	6	16	33		
6	RAPE		12	4	14	30		
7	ROBBERY		223	136	306	665		
8	AGG_ASLT		207	135	290	4	636	
9	BURGLARY		371	557	272	222	1422	
10	THEFT		1161	1198	1117	376	3852	
11	AUTO_THEFT		561	230	334	115	1240	
12	**Grand Total**		2546	2266	2349	717	7878	
13								
14								

Figure E-89: your PivotTable with AutoFormatting applied.

To really make an attractive PivotTable, you may want to change your column headings from ALL CAPS, abbreviations, or police lingo to terms that make more sense to the average reader. You can adjust these headings within the PivotTable without affecting the original data (see Figure E-90).

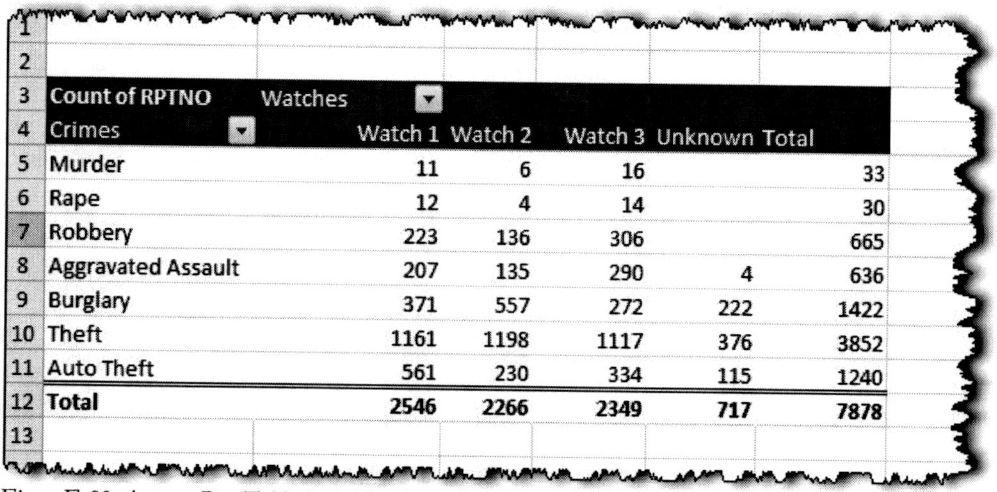

1							
2							
3	**Count of RPTNO**	Watches ▾					
4	Crimes ▾		Watch 1	Watch 2	Watch 3	Unknown	Total
5	Murder		11	6	16		33
6	Rape		12	4	14		30
7	Robbery		223	136	306		665
8	Aggravated Assault		207	135	290	4	636
9	Burglary		371	557	272	222	1422
10	Theft		1161	1198	1117	376	3852
11	Auto Theft		561	230	334	115	1240
12	**Total**		2546	2266	2349	717	7878
13							

Figure E-90: the same PivotTable, but with more understandable headings

Finally, let's assume that you're curious about those six murders on Watch 2.

»Step 18: Double click on Cell C5, which has a figure of "6" in it.

Excel creates a new worksheet (Figure E-91) with all of the records that make up the aggregate you double-clicked on. To get rid of the worksheet, just right click on its tab and choose "Delete."

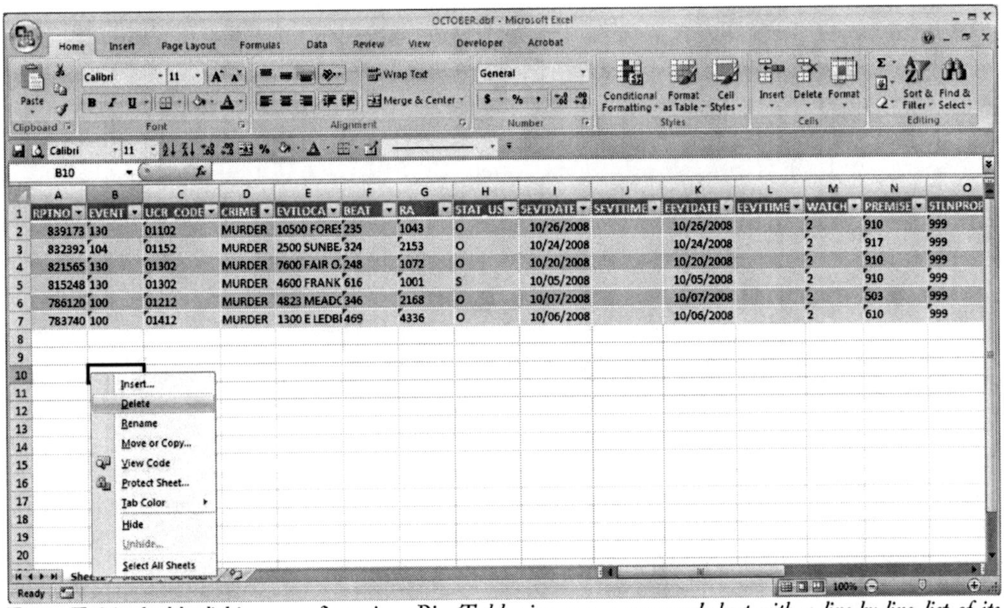

Figure E-91: double-clicking on a figure in a PivotTable gives you a new worksheet with a line-by-line list of its contents. Delete it when you're through.

You can copy and paste your PivotTable into other applications, such as Microsoft Word, to include in a bulletin or report. Just as in pasting charts, you can use **Home | Clipboard | Paste | Paste Special** to "Paste Link" to the Excel spreadsheet so that as the PivotTable changes, the Word document that uses it changes to reflect the updates.

Once you understand how to create PivotTables, detailed comparative analysis of large datasets becomes fairly simple. Try comparing day of week to hour of day, hour of day to beat, beat to race of offender, race of offender to race of victim, race of victim to property value stolen, and so on. Use page fields to filter all of these comparisons by specific types of crime. There are innumerable examples of valuable PivotTable ideas.

We encourage you to continue to use the "October" file to look for relationships between different categories.

»Step 19: When you are finished, **File | Save As** and save your file as an Excel spreadsheet—even in Excel 2003, which could save as dBASE files, PivotTables would not save with the file—at **C:\BPOffice\Excel\October.xlsx**.

PivotCharts

PivotCharts are similar to PivotTables in that they summarize data, and you can drag around categories freely. The various options for creating PivotCharts are similar to regular charts, though you have a few more restrictions (such as chart type).

PivotCharts require a PivotTable, so although you can create one directly from **Insert | Tables | PivotTable** (click the drop-down menu beneath the button) **| PivotChart**, it's easier just to use an existing PivotTable if you have one, which we do.

>**Step 1:** If it is not already open, open **C:\BPOffice\Excel\October.xlsx**, which you saved in the previous lesson. Go to the sheet with the PivotTable (probably "Sheet1").

>**Step 2:** Click outside the PivotTable, in Cell G3.

>**Step 3:** Click **Insert | Charts| Column.** Click the drop-down menu beneath the "Column" button and choose the second option, a stacked column chart.

Excel inserts a chart next to your PivotTable and provides you with a "PivotChart Filter Pane" (you may have to drag this off the chart itself), as in Figure E-93. The PivotChart's data is based on the data in the PivotTable, so the "Filter Pane" is tied directly to the data in the table.

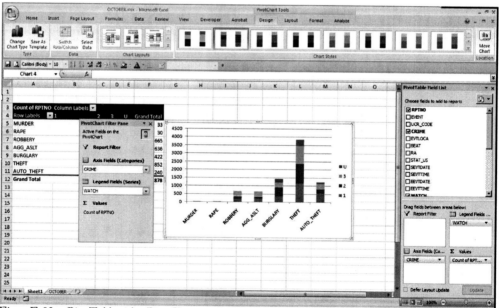

Figure E-92: a PivotTable with a PivotChart.

>**Step 4:** On the PivotChart Filter Pane, click on the "Legend Fields (Series)" drop-down. Un-check the "U" option, so only known watches are visible.

You can modify the data shown on the chart by making changes to the data in the PivotTable.

»**Step 4:** Click within the PivotTable (off the chart). In the options to the right, drag "CRIME" out of the "Row Labels" and into the "Report Filter." Drag the "WATCH" field from the "Column Labels" and into the "Row Labels." Your chart should change to one showing the number of crimes per watch (Figure E-93).

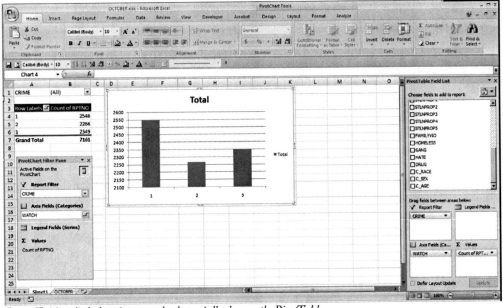

Figure E-93: a little dragging around substantially changes the PivotTable

»**Step 5:** Either in Cell B1 or on the "Report Filter" on the "PivotChart Filter Pane," click the drop-down and choose "Burglary." Now you're seeing how burglary breaks down by watch.

Perhaps we want to see the chart as a separate object.

»**Step 6:** Right-click on the chart and choose "Move Chart" and "New Sheet."

The chart now occupies its own worksheet, but it is still linked to the PivotTable on Sheet1. You can make changes to the data on either sheet, and it will be reflected in both the chart and the table. Try it.

Again, we encourage you to use the "October" workbook or any of the other workbooks we've used so far to explore additional PivotTable and PivotChart options.

Importing Data from Other Sources

We have seen how Excel can open data in several different formats. Excel's flexibility and ease-of-use make it an ideal tool for importing data, cleaning it, and passing it on to another application.

Example 1: Crime Statistics from the FBI's Internet Site

Analysts are frequently asked to compare their jurisdictions to other, similar ones. For decades, a primary source of crime statistics from other agencies has been the FBI's *Crime in the United States*, an annual publication of Uniform Crime Reporting (UCR) figures.

Analysts once had to hand-enter this data in spreadsheets, but in recent years the FBI has provided its UCR tables to the public in Microsoft Excel format.

»**Step 1:** Use your Internet browser to go to **http://www.fbi.gov**. On the left-side navigation bar, click on "Reports and Publications." At the bottom of the "Reports" page, you should see a heading that reads "On Statistics." Under this heading, click on "Uniform Crime Reports: Crime in the United States."

You should see statistics in several categories and several years. Most of the links open in Adobe Portable Document Format (PDF) and cannot be converted to Excel without a complicated process of selecting the text, pasting it into Excel, and splitting columns. However, all of the tables under the "Crime in the United States" category are in Excel format already.

»**Step 2:** Click on "2007." After a warning, the site takes you to a table of contents for the 2007 *Crime in the United States*. Click on "Go to Offense Tables."

On the right, under "Data Tables," you see a list of tables from the UCR report. All of these are available in Excel.

»**Step 3:** Click on "Table 8." When the "Table 8: Offenses Known to Law Enforcement" screen appears, click on "Download Excel." Choose "Save File" and save it to **C:\BPOffice\Excel** and name it **UCR2007.xls** (this is an Excel 2003 version of the file).

»**Step 4:** Close your Internet browser, launch Excel, and open the file you just saved.

The data isn't quite ready for manipulation. The FBI designed these spreadsheets to be looked at rather than analyzed. (For crime analysis purposes, it would have been better if they hadn't bothered with the headings and had put the state in its own field next to the city.) You could copy and paste a single state from this spreadsheet into a new one, but to analyze all the data, we need to remove some of the "features" of the sheet, including the headings and the merged cells.

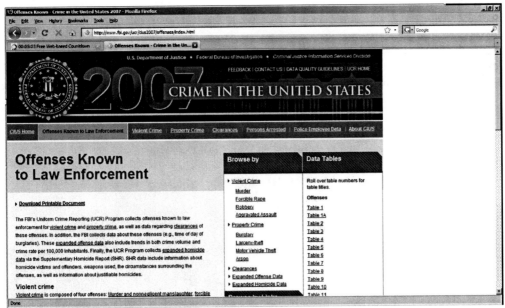

Figure E-94: the FBI's Uniform Crime Report tables for 2007

Table 8

Offenses Known to Law Enforcement

by State by City, 2007

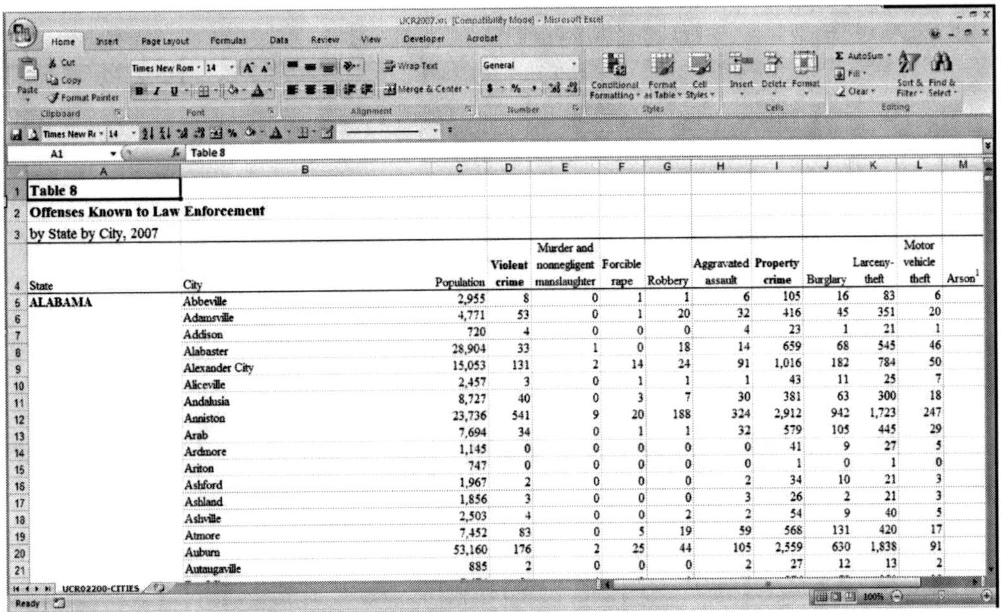

State	City	Population	Violent crime	Murder and nonnegligent manslaughter	Forcible rape	Robbery	Aggravated assault	Property crime	Burglary	Larceny-theft	Motor vehicle theft	Arson[1]
ALABAMA	Abbeville	2,955	8	0	1	1	6	105	16	83	6	
	Adamsville	4,771	53	0	1	20	32	416	45	351	20	
	Addison	720	4	0	0	0	4	23	1	21	1	
	Alabaster	28,904	33	1	0	18	14	659	68	545	46	
	Alexander City	15,053	131	2	14	24	91	1,016	182	784	50	
	Aliceville	2,457	3	0	1	1	1	43	11	25	7	
	Andalusia	8,727	40	0	3	7	30	381	63	300	18	
	Anniston	23,736	541	9	20	188	324	2,912	942	1,723	247	
	Arab	7,694	34	0	1	1	32	579	105	445	29	
	Ardmore	1,145	0	0	0	0	0	41	9	27	5	
	Ariton	747	0	0	0	0	0	1	0	1	0	
	Ashford	1,967	2	0	0	0	2	34	10	21	3	
	Ashland	1,856	3	0	0	0	3	26	2	21	3	
	Ashville	2,503	4	0	0	2	2	54	9	40	5	
	Atmore	7,452	83	0	5	19	59	568	131	420	17	
	Auburn	53,160	176	2	25	44	105	2,559	630	1,838	91	
	Autaugaville	885	2	0	0	0	2	27	12	13	2	

Figure E-95: the "Offenses Known to Law Enforcement" table in Excel

»**Step 5:** Select the entire spreadsheet by clicking on the box above Row 1 and to the left of Column A . Click on **Home | <u>Alignment</u> | Merge & Center** to un-merge the cells.

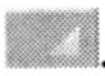

»**Step 6:** Select the top three rows in the spreadsheet and choose **Home | <u>Cells</u> | Delete**.

Unfortunately, the FBI has designed the spreadsheet to only include the state's name at the beginning of the list of cities for that state. This is fine when you're just viewing the sheet, but if we want to sort the data, we will no longer be able to tell what city each state belongs to. Fortunately, we can overcome this with a simple formula.

»**Step 7:** Select Column B and choose **Home | <u>Cells</u> | Insert**. This will insert a new column between the existing "State" field and the "City" field.

»**Step 8:** Type "State" in Cell B1 and the following formula in Cell B2: **=IF(A2="",B1,A2)**

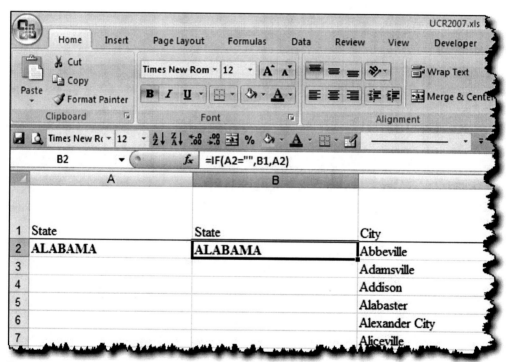

Figure E-96: a formula to fill the proper state down the range of cities

»**Step 9:** Select Cells B2 through B8660 and choose **Home | <u>Editing</u> | Fill | Down.**

»**Step 10:** While you're at the bottom of the spreadsheet, either delete the eight footnotes (Rows 8661 through 8668) or cut and paste them on a different worksheet.

»**Step 11:** Return to the top of the worksheet (CTRL-HOME is a quick way), right-click on Column B and choose "Copy." Then immediately right-click on Column B again and choose "Paste Special" and "Values." Finish off by right-clicking on Column A and choosing "Delete."

Now that we have the states in place, we can do some basic sorting and data manipulation.

»**Step 12:** Click on any cell in Column C and click the "Sort Descending" $\begin{smallmatrix}Z\\A\end{smallmatrix}\downarrow$ tool at **Data | Sort & Filter** (this tool and its "Sort Ascending" counterpart are good candidates for adding to your Quick Access Toolbar).

The result is a "cleaned" spreadsheet with the highest-population cities at the top. New York City should be first, followed by Los Angeles and Chicago. One hundred and two American cities with populations greater than 200,000 have reported to the UCR. Let's confine our analysis to those cities.

»**Step 13:** Choose **Data | Sort & Filter | Filter**.

As we saw before, the AutoFilter drop-down menus become available at the tops of our columns.

»**Step 14:** Click the drop-down menu in Cell C2 and choose "Number Filters" and "Greater Than."

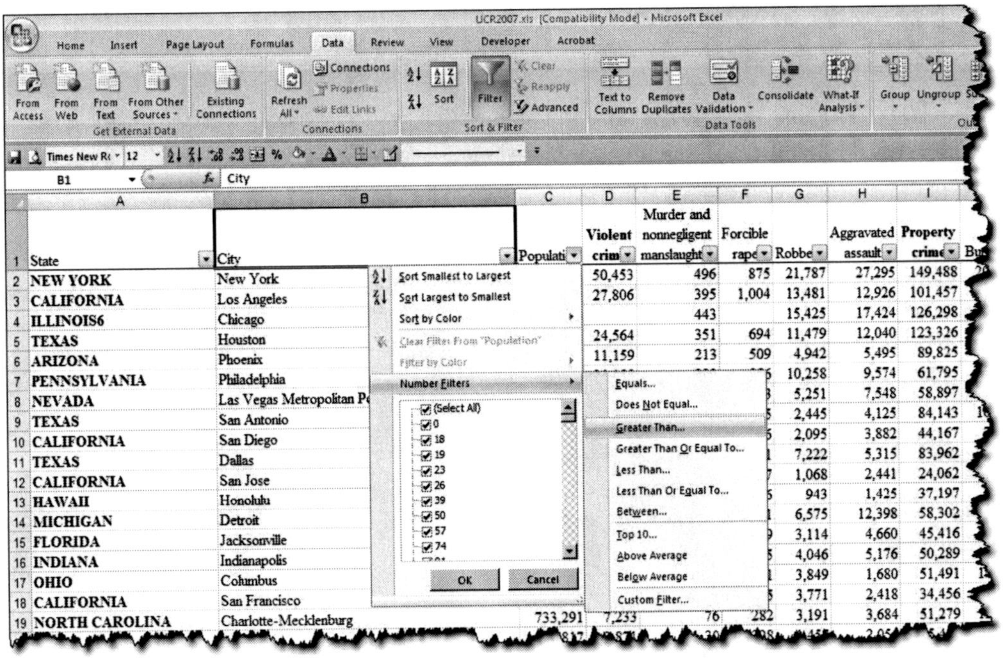

Figure E-97: filtering by the population field

»**Step 15:** In the "Custom AutoFilter" box (Figure E-98), look for all rows where Population "is greater than" 200000. Then click "OK."

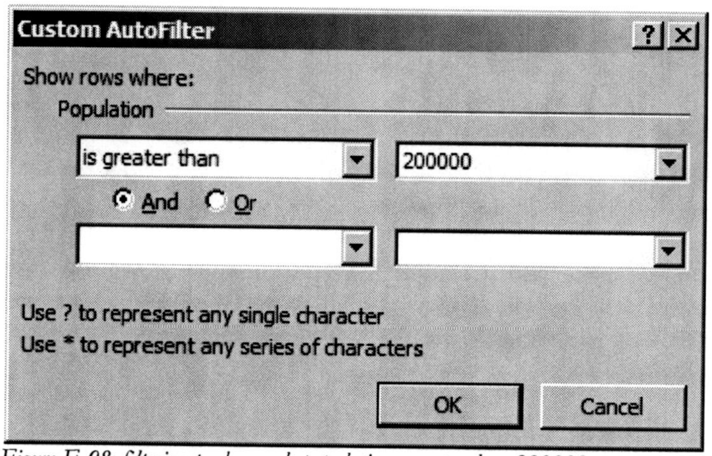

Figure E-98: filtering to show only populations greater than 200000

With our top 102 cities, we will calculate the total crime per 1000 persons. To do so, we need to create two columns—total crime and crimes per 1000—and enter the appropriate calculations.

»**Step 16:** Chicago did not report its rape total in 2003. As such, its violent crime total cannot be calculated, and therefore the total crime cannot be calculated. Right-click on Chicago's row (4) and choose "Delete."

»**Step 17:** Click in Cell C2 and **View | Window | Freeze Panes | Freeze Panes** so that the column and row headings remain fixed.

»**Step 18:** Title Column N "Total Crime" and Column O "Crimes Per 1000."

To calculate the total crime, we will simply add the Violent Crime (Column C) and Property Crime (Column H) totals.

»**Step 19:** In Cell N2, enter **=D2+I2**

»**Step 20:** In Cell O2, enter **=N2/C2*1000**

The crime rate per 1,000 residents is the total crime divided by the population multipled by 1,000.

»**Step 21:** Select Cells N2 through O103 and use **CTRL-D** to fill the formula down through the range of cells.

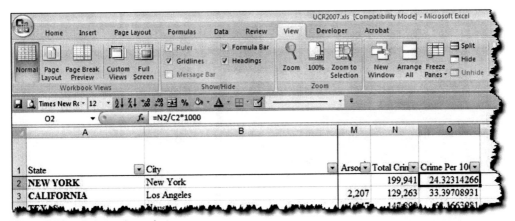

Figure E-99: calculating the total crime

»**Step 22:** Finally, use the "Sort Descending" ⍖ tool at **Data | Sort & Filter** to sort by the "Crimes per 1000" column.

The results show that St. Louis, MO; Orlando, FL; and Birmingham, AL have the highest crime rates of the big cities, and that Irvine, CA; Glendale, CA; and New York City have the lowest rates (Tucson doesn't count because it didn't report a property crime total).

It took 27 minutes for your authors to get from the last paragraph to this one, because we started playing with the data and couldn't stop. We encourage you to do the same. Change the filter to apply to all cities and towns with more than 25,000 people. Sort by the total crime rate (watch your wallet while in Myrtle Beach). Calculate the violent crime rate and sort by that (had you ever *heard* of Saginaw, Michigan before now?). There are many, many issues involved in comparing cities this way, and we caution analysts against using superficial statistics like this to draw any conclusions, but it is a starting point, and it only took us a few minutes to get there.

Example 2: Data from Census.Gov

The United States Census bureau has a wealth of information to provide to a crime analyst. Their web site contains population data as well as commerce-related data, including both past trends and future estimates. The resources on the Census Bureau's web site (www.census.gov) is compatible with Excel and, in some cases, a geographic information system (GIS).

The "American Fact Finder" site has a variety of information related to housing,

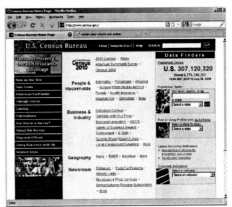

Figure E-100: www.census.gov

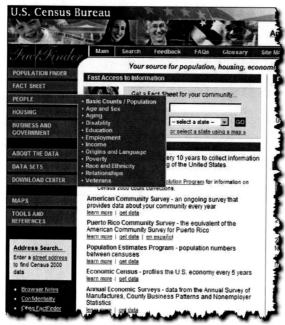

Figure E-101: finding census data with the American FactFinder.

business and people. In particular there are a number of data sets available with information related to census boundaries as well as survey information. In our example, we have selected "People" and "Basic Counts/Population." Once we select that link we will choose "Rankings of Total Population: for all states."

Choosing this link brings up an HTML-formatted table of state populations with population estimates (Figure E-102). This table can easily be brought into Excel for analysis, either by copying and pasting the table from the browser window to Excel, or by clicking the "Print/Download" link at the top of the page and choosing Excel in the resulting pop-up window (Figure E-103) or one of several other compatible formats. Note that unlike the FBI, the Census Bureau allows you the option to download just the data, with formatting and footnotes stripped.

Geographic Comparison Table

You are here: Main ▸ Data Sets ▸ Data Sets with Geographic Comparison Tables ▸ Geography ▸ Tables ▸ Results

Print / Download | Related Items

View this table...
for other geographies

Other tables...
select another table

United States -- States
GCT-T1-R. Population Estimates (geographies ranked by estimate)
Data Set: 2008 Population Estimates

NOTE: For information on errors stemming from model error, sampling error, and nonsampling error, see: http://www.census.gov/popest/topics/methodology.

| Rank | Geographic area | Population Estimates | | | | | | | | | Estimates Base | Census 2000 |
		July 1, 2008	July 1, 2007	July 1, 2006	July 1, 2005	July 1, 2004	July 1, 2003	July 1, 2002	July 1, 2001	July 1, 2000	April 1, 2000	April 1, 2000
	United States	304,059,724	301,290,332	298,362,973	295,560,549	292,892,127	290,210,914	287,726,647	285,039,803	282,171,936	281,424,602	281,421,906
1	California	36,756,666	36,377,534	36,121,296	35,885,415	35,629,666	35,307,398	34,916,496	34,507,030	33,998,767	33,871,650	33,871,64
2	Texas	24,326,974	23,843,432	23,367,534	22,811,128	22,424,884	22,062,119	21,713,397	21,333,928	20,946,049	20,851,811	20,851,82
3	New York	19,490,297	19,429,316	19,367,028	19,336,376	19,301,113	19,230,877	19,161,573	19,088,220	18,998,429	18,976,816	18,976,45
4	Florida	18,328,340	18,199,526	18,019,093	17,702,476	17,313,811	16,937,337	16,652,679	16,340,734	16,047,246	15,982,813	15,982,37
5	Illinois	12,901,563	12,825,809	12,759,673	12,704,063	12,665,718	12,611,047	12,565,228	12,510,596	12,437,888	12,419,660	12,419,293
6	Pennsylvania	12,448,279	12,419,930	12,388,055	12,351,881	12,335,052	12,317,647	12,298,775	12,284,522	12,285,041	12,281,052	12,281,05
7	Ohio	11,485,910	11,477,641	11,458,390	11,450,954	11,445,095	11,430,306	11,410,582	11,391,298	11,363,719	11,353,160	11,353,14
8	Michigan	10,003,422	10,049,790	10,083,878	10,093,266	10,090,280	10,065,881	10,037,303	10,004,341	9,955,148	9,938,492	9,938,44
9	Georgia	9,685,744	9,523,297	9,318,715	9,093,968	8,910,741	8,732,924	8,583,674	8,418,592	8,230,053	8,186,812	8,186,45
10	North Carolina	9,222,414	9,041,594	8,845,343	8,661,061	8,523,199	8,409,660	8,311,263	8,199,913	8,078,824	8,046,500	8,049,313
11	New Jersey	8,682,661	8,653,126	8,640,218	8,634,657	8,620,770	8,589,562	8,547,410	8,490,942	8,430,913	8,414,360	8,414,350
12	Virginia	7,769,089	7,698,775	7,628,347	7,546,725	7,454,688	7,363,300	7,276,785	7,188,251	7,104,354	7,079,025	7,078,515
13	Washington	6,549,224	6,449,511	6,380,529	6,254,579	6,179,845	6,110,202	6,055,613	5,987,181	5,911,104	5,894,143	5,894,12
14	Arizona	6,500,180	6,353,421	6,178,251	5,961,239	5,750,475	5,585,512	5,449,195	5,303,632	5,166,810	5,130,607	5,130,632
15	Massachusetts	6,497,967	6,467,915	6,443,424	6,434,343	6,437,414	6,441,440	6,433,043	6,407,269	6,362,583	6,349,113	6,349,097
16	Indiana	6,376,792	6,335,862	6,294,124	6,248,569	6,210,801	6,178,826	6,146,974	6,123,942	6,091,392	6,080,522	6,080,485
17	Tennessee	6,214,888	6,149,116	6,068,306	5,983,211	5,906,936	5,849,583	5,799,093	5,753,497	5,703,094	5,689,270	5,689,28

Figure E-102: census population estimates

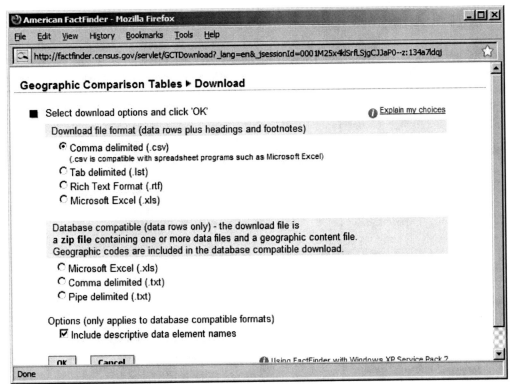

Figure E-103: downloading census tables to Excel

```
CBSA,MDIV,STCOU,NAME,LSAD,CENSUS2000POP,ESTIMATESBASE2000,POPESTIMA
,,,,,,,,,,,,,,,,,,,,,,,,,,,,,,,,,,,,,,,,,,,,,,,,,,,,,,,,,,,,,,,,,,,
,,,Metropolitan Statistical Area,,,,,,,,,,,,,,,,,,,,,,,,,,,,,,,,,,,,
,,,,,,,,,,,,,,,,,,,,,,,,,,,,,,,,,,,,,,,,,,,,,,,,,,,,,,,,,,,,,,,,,,,
10180,,,"Abilene, TX",Metropolitan Statistical Area,160245,160241,16
10180,,48059,"Callahan County, TX",County or equivalent,12905,12905,
10180,,48253,"Jones County, TX",County or equivalent,20785,20785,20
10180,,48441,"Taylor County, TX",County or equivalent,126555,126551
10420,,,"Akron, OH",Metropolitan Statistical Area,694960,694962,695
10420,,39133,"Portage County, OH",County or equivalent,152061,15206
10420,,39153,"Summit County, OH",County or equivalent,542899,542901
10500,,,"Albany, GA",Metropolitan Statistical Area,157833,157868,15
10500,,13007,"Baker County, GA",County or equivalent,4074,4074,4054
10500,,13095,"Dougherty County, GA",County or equivalent,96065,9606
10500,,13177,"Lee County, GA",County or equivalent,24757,24757,2488
10500,,13273,"Terrell County, GA",County or equivalent,10970,10970,
10500,,13321,"Worth County, GA",County or equivalent,21967,22000,21
10580,,,"Albany-Schenectady-Troy, NY",Metropolitan Statistical Area,
10580,,36001,"Albany County, NY",County or equivalent,294565,294565
10580,,36083,"Rensselaer County, NY",County or equivalent,152538,155
10580,,36091,"Saratoga County, NY",County or equivalent,200635,20063
10580,,36093,"Schenectady County, NY",County or equivalent,146555,14
10580,,36095,"Schoharie County, NY",County or equivalent,31582,31582
10740,,,"Albuquerque, NM",Metropolitan Statistical Area,729649,72964
10740,,35001,"Bernalillo County, NM",County or equivalent,556678,556
10740,,35043,"Sandoval County, NM",County or equivalent,89908,90584
10740,,35057,"Torrance County, NM",County or equivalent,16911,16910
10740,,35061,"Valencia County, NM",County or equivalent,66152,66152
10780,,,"Alexandria, LA",Metropolitan Statistical Area,145035,14503
10780,,22043,"Grant Parish, LA",County or equivalent,18698,18696,18
10780,,22079,"Rapides Parish, LA",County or equivalent,126337,12653
10900,,,"Allentown-Bethlehem-Easton, PA-NJ",Metropolitan Statistica
10900,,34041,"Warren County, NJ",County or equivalent,102437,102438
10900,,42025,"Carbon County, PA",County or equivalent,58802,58803,5
```

Figure E-104: a comma-separated value (CSV) file with population estimates for statistical areas.

Below the table is a link titled "Population Estimates Program." This link will take you to a site that contains a variety of Excel compatible data. We will choose "Estimates Data." This link will provide us with a variety of estimates based on different geography such as state or metropolitan area. We will choose the "Totals" link below "Metropolitan and Micropolitan Statistical Areas." This link will provide us with a number of estimate links, including annual estimates of population, population change, maps and other useful information. The site provides file layout and CSV files, which open directly to Excel.

Tactical Analysis

A primary goal of tactical crime analysis is to capture a serial offender before he commits another crime in a series. This can be accomplished, in part, through the art and science of *forecasting*—specifically, forecasting the most likely date, time, and location of the next incident in a series. Location forecasting is done with GIS software, but time and date forecasting can be accomplished in Excel.

Forecasting is a detailed discipline of crime analysis. Even when done correctly, it is often unsuccessful. Many articles have been written about its various aspects, and nothing in the following pages should be taken by the reader to encompass all of it. These exercises will cover some of the more basic, elementary methods of forecasting, with the understanding that a crime analyst should expand his or her knowledge in this area.

»**Step 1:** Open **C:\BPOffice\Excel\robberyseries.xlsx**.

Here, you'll find a fairly basic convenience store robbery series. Our goals are to suggest a likely date and time of the next offense.

»**Step 2:** Extract the day of week for each date. This is accomplished with the TEXT function. Enter into Cell C4 **=TEXT(B4,"ddd")** and fill it down for the range of cells in Column C.

We now calculate the number of days that have elapsed from one offense to the next. The formula is simple.

»**Step 3:** In Cell D5, enter **=B5-B4**. Fill this formula down through Cell D25, and Excel will adjust the cell references by one row for each row it fills down.

	A	B	C	D	E	F	G	H
1	Convenience Store Robbery Series							
2								
3	IncNum	Date	DOW	Interval	Time	Location	Money Stolen	
4	2009-34098	03/10/2009	Tue	--	18:30	1502 E Broadway	$1,120	
5	2009-34117	03/17/2009	Tue	7	17:25	1454 S Main St	$1,130	
6	2009-34118	03/21/2009	Sat	4	19:00	1903 S First St	$1,370	
7	2009-34269	03/26/2009	Thu	5	20:00	1989 N Fourth St	$1,420	
8	2009-34325	04/02/2009	Thu	7	20:25	1048 N Third St	$1,700	
9	2009-34381	04/11/2009	Sat	9	21:45	1336 E Kimberly Ave	$980	
10	2009-34435	04/16/2009	Thu	5	19:35	1419 W Elm St	$1,390	
11	2009-34484	04/24/2009	Fri	8	20:15	1004 S Minnesota Blvd	$1,060	
12	2009-34533	04/30/2009	Thu	6	20:45	1580 S Antioch Rd	$1,150	
13	2009-34587	05/04/2009	Mon	4	20:25	1289 E Santa Fe Dr	$1,650	
14	2009-34644	05/12/2009	Tue	8	21:25	1744 E College Blvd	$1,580	
15	2009-34699	05/21/2009	Thu	9	17:18	1612 W Broadway	$1,140	
16	2009-34748	05/28/2009	Thu	7	22:38	1799 N Main St	$1,430	

Figure E-105: the convenience store robbery series with our new calculations

Before we move on to any statistical calculations, take a look at the results (Figure E-105) and apply your common sense. Does the robber seem to prefer any particular days of the week? Well, nine Thursdays and six Tuesdays seem to indicate some preferences. How often does he strike? It looks like he hits about once a week on average. He's struck twice in one week before, but it's pretty rare. So you might suggest to officers to watch convenience stores next Tuesday and Thursday.

But there are mathematical ways that we can come up with the same answer, as well as look at the most likely time of the next offense.

In Figure E-106, we add a number of cells to the spreadsheet and calculate the values for those cells.

»**Step 4:** Add the cells to your spreadsheet necessary to match Figure E-106. The formulas and their explanations are given on the next two pages.

22	2009-35086	07/02/2009	Thu			23:47	1745 S Ocean Ave
23	2009-35140	07/10/2009	Fri	8		20:00	1706 N Newbury St
24	2009-35197	07/15/2009	Wed	5		20:20	1740 N Ridgecrest Dr
25	2009-35256	07/21/2009	Tue	6		19:10	1248 W Old Post Rd
26							
27			Average	6	20:09		
28			Minimum	2	17:18		
29			Maximum	9	23:47		
30			St Dev	1.86	01:33:49		
31							
32			Next Hit				
33			Min Earliest	07/23/2009	17:18		
34			1 StDev Earliest	07/25/2009	18:36		
35			1 StDev Latest	07/29/2009	21:43		
36			Max Latest	07/30/2009	23:47		
37							
38							
39							

Figure E-106: calculations to forecast the next offense

Cell	Formula	Explanation
D27	=AVERAGE(D5:D25)	Calculates the average number of days between offenses
D28	=MIN(D5:D25)	Shows the smallest number of days elapsed between offenses
D29	=MAX(D5:D25)	Shows the longest period of days that has elapsed between offenses
D30	=STDEVP(D5:D25)	Calculates the standard deviation, from the average, of the days between offenses. The standard deviation essentially helps measure the "usual" range of days between offenses. With an average of 6 and a standard deviation of 2, the usual range of days between offenses is 4 to 8. In a normal distribution, 68% of all numbers will fall within one standard deviation of the mean. That is, 68% of all the days between offenses are between 4 and 8. (Note: STDEVP, rather than STDEV, is used when you have an entire population, not a sample, of data.)

E27	=AVERAGE(E4:E25)	This calculates the average time of offense. Because Excel stores times as decimal numbers, it's easy for the program to calculate the average of those numbers and to render the result as a time.
E28	=MIN(E4:E25)	The earliest time at which an offense was committed
E29	=MAX(E4:E25)	The latest time at which an offense was committed
E30	=STDEV(E4:E25)	The normal deviation from the average time.

Based on these initial statistics, we can now calculate the range of dates and times in which the next offense will most likely occur. The most inclusive method is to use the minimum and maximum values. Since the robber has always struck within nine days of the last offense, but never before at least two days have elapsed, it's a safe bet that his next strike will be between two and nine days from now—that is, we simply add the MIN and MAX to the date of the most recent offense. However, he is *most likely* to strike within the range represented by one standard deviation from the mean, which is between four and eight days. The same consideration applies to the time.

We therefore enter a series of formulas that calculate both the min/max range for the next offense and a range represented by one standard deviation.

Cell	Formula	Explanation
D33	=B25+D27	Adds the minimum number of days to the date of the last offense
D34	=B25+D26-D29	Adds the average number of days to the last offense, then subtracts one standard deviation
D35	=B25+D26+D29	Adds the average number of days to the last offense, then adds one standard deviation
D36	=B25+D28	Adds the maximum number of days to the last offense
E33	=E27	Pretty simple—takes the earliest time of occurrence
E34	=E26-E29	Subtracts the standard deviation from the average time
E35	=E26+E29	Adds the standard deviation to the average time
E36	=E28	Repeats the maximum time

The result of all this work with averages, standard deviations, minimums, and maximums? Unless the robber does something he's never done before, he will strike again between July 23 and July 30. He is *most likely* to strike between July 25 and July 29. Again, unless the robber completely alters his pattern, he will hit between 17:18 and 23:47, because he has never struck earlier or later. Again, however, the most likely time of the next offense will be between 18:36 and 21:43.

Predicting future offenses by applying averages and standard deviations to both times and days between offenses has been a crime analysis technique for decades.[*] But it is not the only, or even necessarily the best, method of making a prediction. Some series exhibit an

---

[*] See for instance Steven Gottlieb, Sheldon Arenberg, and Raj Singh, *Crime Analysis: From First Report to Final Arrest* (Montclair, CA: Alpha Publishing, 1994), 395–438.

increasing or decreasing "tempo" in the days between hits, or a cyclical pattern. We encourage analysts to educate themselves further about the science of temporal analysis.[°]

We will present one further option here. Occasionally, the number of days between hits is related to some other variable, such as the dollar value of the property stolen in each crime. We can calculate the *correlation* between these two variables.

»**Step 5:** In Cell F27, type "Correlation." In Cell G27, enter this formula: **=CORREL(D5:D25,G4:G24)**

The function calculates the correlation of the range to the left of the comma (D5:D25) with the range to the right of the comma (G4:G24). The row references are slightly different because the dollar value stolen in the previous crime predicts the days between hits for the next crime. Since no crime has occurred after July 21, we exclude from consideration the dollar value in this incident.

The result, as we see in figure E-107, is that there is a correlation of 0.79 between the two sets of variables. A result of 1 would indicate a perfect direct correlation (as one goes up, the other goes up); a result of -1 is a perfect inverse correlation (as one goes up, the other goes down), and 0 would be absolutely no correlation whatsoever. Our result, a positive 0.79, indicates a fairly strong correlation.

	B	C	D	E	F	G	H
					fx =B25+G30		
22	07/02/2009	Thu	9	23:47	1745 S Ocean Ave	$1,600	
23	07/10/2009	Fri	8	20:00	1706 N Newbury St	$1,190	
24	07/15/2009	Wed	5	20:20	1740 N Ridgecrest Dr	$1,560	
25	07/21/2009	Tue	6	19:10	1248 W Old Post Rd	$750	
26							
27		Average	6	20:09	Correlation	0.793816023	
28		Minimum	2	17:18	Slope	0.005888185	
29		Maximum	9	23:47	Y-Intercept	-1.23158297	
30		St Dev	1.86	01:33:49	Days Till Next	3.18	
31					Predicted Date	07/24/2009	
32		Next Hit					
33		Min Earliest	07/23/2009	17:18			
34		1 StDev Earliest	07/25/2009	18:36			
35		1 StDev Latest	07/29/2009	21:43			
36		Max Latest	07/30/2009	23:47			
37							

Figure E-107: calculating the date of the next offense based on the correlation between dollar value and days

The final step in this *regression analysis* is to then predict the date of the next offense based on the dollar value stole ($750) in the most recent. This is done by fist calculating the *slope* and the *y-intercept* of the sets of data, then multiplying the dollar value of the last incident

---

[°] For a good place to start, see Dan Helms, "Temporal Analysis," in *Exploring Crime Analysis: Readings on Essential Skills* (Overland Park, KS: International Association of Crime Analysts, 2004), 220–262.

by the slope and adding the y-intercept. We will refer you to a statistics text for the theory behind these calculations,[*] but the formulas for this spreadsheet are:

Cell	Formula	Explanation
G28	=SLOPE(D5:D25,G4:G24)	Calculates the slope of the two arrays
G29	=INTERCEPT(D5:D25,G4:G24)	Calculates the (theoretical) point on the y-axis that the x-axis would intercept if the value of x was 0. In other words, if the robber got no money, he would strike next in -1.23 days. As we said, it's theoretical.
G30	=G25*G28+G29	The predicted number of days until the next hit
G31	=B25+G30	The last hit plus the predicted days

The result—July 24, 2009—is within the full range of dates we predicted earlier, but it lies outside the "most likely" range that starts on July 25. Why the contradiction? Because although he usually doesn't strike again so soon, he's never done so badly, financially, as he did in the last incident. Since we've discovered that the dollar value of the robbery has some predictive value in the number of days before the next incident, it seems likely that he might strike again sooner rather than later.

In the end, all of this analysis must be translated to the operational level. What do we tell the shift commanders and their troops? We might merge our initial observations, our range calculations, and our correlation calculations, in a simple paragraph: "All other things being equal, I would recommend July 25–29 as the most likely date frame for the next incident, but since he escaped with so little cash in the last incident, it seems more likely that he will strike sooner. His last hit was on a Tuesday, and he is known to favor Thursdays, so I would recommend extra attention to convenience stores on Thursday, July 23 between 18:30 and 21:45. If he does not strike, I recommend continued attention through Wednesday, July 29, with special attention on Tuesday, July 28."

Analyzing Crimes with a Span of Time

The time calculations in the previous exercise assume that we know the exact time the incident occurred. This is usually the case with violent or confrontational crimes such as robbery. But for many property crimes, we don't know the exact time, only a span of time from the "earliest" possible time (e.g., when the victim left his house) to the "latest" time (e.g., when the victim came home and found the front door pried open).

Some analysts solve this problem by calculating the "midpoint time" or "split time"—that is, the time at the center of the range. If the victim parked his car at 16:00 and returned at 18:30 to find it stolen, the midpoint is 17:15. While this technique may work adequately for small time ranges, when the range is large, the "midpoint" values are meaningless.

---

[*] See Jamie Price and Donald W. Chamberlayne, "Descriptive and Multivariate Statistics" in *Exploring Crime Analysis: Readings on Essential Skills* (Overland Park, KS: International Association of Crime Analysts, 2004), 277–299.

An alternate, better, but more complicated solution for time spans has been coined *aoristic analysis* by Dr. Jerry Ratcliffe.* With this method, we determine the number of hours within a crime's time range, and then assign a weight to each hour equal to its portion of the total crime. For instance, if a crime occurred between 12:00 and 16:00 (four hours), then the hours 12, 13, 14, and 15 each get a weight of 0.25, or one-quarter of the crime. If the crime occurred over a 16-hour period, then each hour gets only a weight of 0.0625, or one-sixteenth of the total crime.

With this method we assign a higher weight to hours when the time of the crime is known and less weight to hours in which the exact time is unknown, thus resulting in a more accurate calculation of the "most likely" time of an offense. This result has implications for both a short-term crime series and a long-term crime problem.

Consider the example in Figure E-108. Here we have a series of 10 daytime burglaries. For only one incident do we know the exact time. The rest are unknown. Some of the remainder have a short range, but others have a long range.

In columns E and F, we extract the hour from each time using the **HOUR** function—the formula in Cell E3 is **=HOUR(C3)**. In Column F, we calculate the total number of hours in the range by subtracting the earliest hour from the latest hour and adding 1—the formula in Cell G3 is **=(F3-E3)+1**. Finally, we see what weight each hour in the range is going to get in Column H—the formula in Cell H3 is **=1/G3**.

	A	B	C	D	E	F	G	H
1			**Daytime Burglary Series**					
2	**IncidentNum**	**Date**	**EarliestTime**	**LatestTime**	**Ehour**	**Lhour**	**Hours**	**Weight**
3	2009-31700	08/01/2009	09:00	16:59	9	16	8	0.125
4	2009-31750	08/07/2009	12:30	16:30	12	16	5	0.200
5	2009-31800	08/12/2009	08:00	17:30	8	17	10	0.100
6	2009-31850	08/19/2009	07:00	18:59	7	18	12	0.083
7	2009-31900	08/23/2009	14:15	14:15	14	14	1	1.000
8	2009-31950	08/31/2009	06:45	15:30	6	15	10	0.100
9	2009-32000	09/03/2009	02:00	22:59	2	22	21	0.048
10	2009-32050	09/07/2009	10:00	15:59	10	15	6	0.167
11	2009-32100	09/12/2009	09:00	16:30	9	16	8	0.125
12	2009-32150	09/14/2009	07:00	17:45	7	17	11	0.091

Figure E-108: the beginning of an aoristic distribution

---

* The basic concept is found in Steven Gottlieb, Sheldon Arenberg, and Raj Singh, *Crime Analysis: From First Report to Final Arrest* (Montclair, CA: Alpha Publishing, 1994), 429–434. It is expanded and given its present term in Jerry H. Ratcliffe and Michael J. McCullagh, "Aoristic Crime Analysis" in *International Journal of Geographical Information Science* 12:7 (1998), 751–764 and other articles by Jerry Ratcliffe available at http://www.jratcliffe.net.

The next step is to create a column for each hour of the day, then assign the weight to it *if* the hour falls between the earliest hour and the latest hour. In Figure E-109, we see how that is done.

In Column I, Row 3—the midnight hour for the first incident—we ask: does the hour at the top of this column (0) fall in between the earliest hour (Cell E3) or the latest hour (Cell F3)? If so, assign this hour the weight in Cell H3; otherwise, give it a weight of 0. The specific formula for this expression is:

=IF(AND(I$2>=$E3,I$2<=$F3),$H3,0)

In plain text, it reads: "If the hour at the top if the column is greater or equal to the earliest hour *and* less than or equal to the latest hour, put the figure 0.125 in this cell; otherwise, put a 0 in this cell."

	Verdana	· 10													
J4					*fx*	=IF(AND(J$2>=$E4,J$2<=$F4),$H4,0)									
	A	B	C	D	E	F	G	H	I	J	K	L	M	
1			**Daytime Burglary Series**												
2	**IncidentNum**	**Date**	**EarliestTime**	**LatestTime**	**Ehour**	**Lhour**	**Hours**	**Weight**	**0**	**1**	**2**	**3**	**4**	
3	2009-31700	08/01/2009	09:00	16:59	9	16	8	0.125	0	0	0	0	0	
4	2009-31750	08/07/2009	12:30	16:30	12	16	5	0.200	0	0	0	0	0	
5	2009-31800	08/12/2009	08:00	17:30	8	17	10	0.100	0	0	0	0	0	
6	2009-31850	08/19/2009	07:00	18:59	7	18	12	0.083	0	0	0	0	0	
7	2009-31900	08/23/2009	14:15	14:15	14	14	1	1.000	0	0	0	0	0	
8	2009-31950	08/31/2009	06:45	15:30	6	15	10	0.100	0	0	0	0	0	
9	2009-32000	09/03/2009	02:00	22:59	2	22	21	0.048	0	0	0.05	0.05	0.05	0
10	2009-32050	09/07/2009	10:00	15:59	10	15	6	0.167	0	0	0	0	0	
11	2009-32100	09/12/2009	09:00	16:30	9	16	8	0.125	0	0	0	0	0	
12	2009-32150	09/14/2009	07:00	17:45	7	17	11	0.091	0	0	0	0	0	
13								**Total**	**0**	**0**	**0**	**0**	**0**	
14														
15														

Figure E-109: assigning a weight to each hour of the day

Since hour 0 does not fall between 9 and 16 (the range in the first row), the cell gets a 0.

Note that the formula uses *absolute references*, represented by the dollar signs ($). This way, when we copy the formula to other cells, it adjusts only in the way that we want it to adjust. For instance, if we used simply "I2" instead of "I$2," when we copied the formula to the second row, it would adjust it to "I3" and give us an invalid result. So the dollar sign in front of the 2 makes sure the formula stays on Row 2, where the hours are. We *do* want it to adjust the column reference as we copy the row to Columns J:AF, so we don't put the dollar sign in front of the column.

However, we *do* put the dollar sign in front of the column reference when we refer to $E3, $F3, and $H3, because in this case, as we copy the formula down to other rows, we want it to adjust the row reference but *not* the column reference.

Finally, note in Figure E-109 that we have totaled each hour column to give a total "weight" for that hour of the day. When we graph this total, as we do in Figure E-110, we see that the series is most active between 10:00 and 17:00, with a definite peak around 13:00–15:00. This is vital information for deployment.

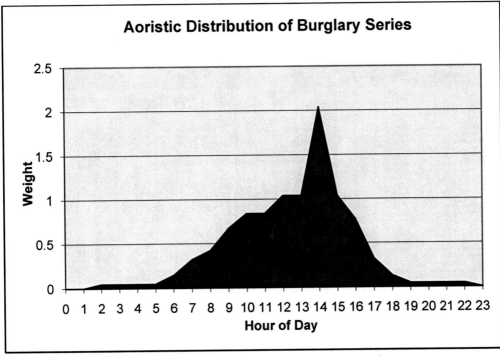

Figure E-110: a charted distribution of the burglary series

The aoristic distribution shown in Figures E-105 to E-107 can be found at **C:\BPOffice\ Excel\aoristic1.xls**. You can open this file and see how it works for yourself.

This spreadsheet works well for crimes that occur during the day, but what about crimes that cross midnight? That is, that occur, for instance, between 22:00 and 02:00? In this case, the spreadsheet would fail. Column G would fail to calculate the number of hours properly, and no weights would appear under the hours of the day. For more complicated time series, we need a formula that first evaluates whether the second hour occurs on the next day, and makes adjustments accordingly.

The spreadsheet at **C:\BPOffice\Excel\aoristic2.xls** has daytime and nighttime crimes combined in the same distribution. The relevant formulas use an IF statement to first evaluate whether the crime crosses midnight, and then apply the appropriate formulas. Because, as we saw a couple pages ago, the formula to assign weights to the hours *already* uses an IF statement, we end up with several IF statements "nested" inside each other:

=IF($G4>=$F4,IF(AND(I$3>=$F4,I$3<=$G4),1/$H4,0),IF(OR(I$3<=$G4, I$3>=$F4),1/$H4,0))

Again, take your time with the spreadsheet and break down the statement until you understand what it is doing. Even if you don't understand right away, you can still copy its syntax for use in your own aoristic analysis efforts.

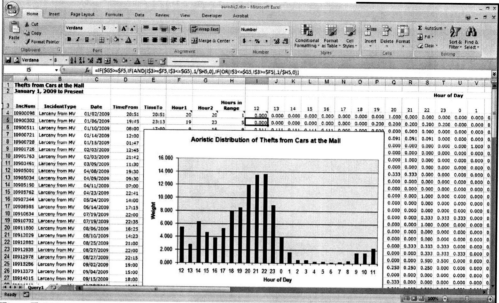

Figure E-111: a second aoristic distribution, with some crimes that "cross midnight."

Crime Series Exercise

It is Tuesday, November 25, 2008. A Robbery lieutenant has brought you the following 12 offenses that she recognizes as a pattern. She wants you to know that it is the primary goal of the police department to catch these criminals. These offenses are occurring in one of the most influential neighborhoods in the city. The mayor has told the chief to make this priority one. Your job is to tell the lieutenant where, when, and how to catch these criminals. You should calculate the average time that the offenses are occurring and the standard deviation. This will give you much better insight on the time and day(s) to deploy the officers. Any other information you need is contained in the reports.

GOOD LUCK!!

October 2008

Sun	Mon	Tue	Wed	Thu	Fri	Sat
			1	2	3	4
5	6	7	8	9	10	11
12	13	14	15	16	17	18
19	20	21	22	23	24	25
26	27	28	29	30		

November 2008

Sun	Mon	Tue	Wed	Thu	Fri	Sat
						1
2	3	4	5	6	7	8
9	10	11	12	13	14	15
16	17	18	19	20	21	22
23	24	25	26	27	28	29
30						

Offense #1

Service Number:	1414A
Offense Beat:	634
Watch:	3rd
Date:	October 3, 2008
Time:	19:00
Day of Week:	Friday
Offense Type:	Aggravated Robbery
Offense Location:	7504 Jupiter
Type Premise:	House
Property taken:	Rolex watch, Diamond necklace, 2 diamond rings, and cash
Method of Operation:	Drove behind complainants and robbed them at gunpoint
Suspect Vehicle:	1984 White Chevrolet 2 dr. with Texas plates
Weapons used:	2 automatic pistols
Suspect description:	2 White males, 30-35, 6' tall, thin, medium complexion, with brown hair wearing jeans and dark shirts

On October 4, 2008 the complainant pulled into his driveway in the rear of the house and was cornered by the listed suspects. He was driving a 2007 Lexus Coupe. Both suspects pointed weapons (pistols) at the complainant and his wife. They demanded valuables. They received the listed property and had the complainants place the valuables into a bag. The suspects drove off in the listed vehicle. The complainant had been shopping at the Forestwood Shopping Center before driving home.

Offense #2

Service Number:	1496A
Offense Beat:	634
Watch:	3rd
Date:	October 4, 2008
Time:	20:00
Day of Week:	Saturday
Offense Type:	Aggravated Robbery
Offense Location:	7452 Horizon
Type Premise:	House
Property taken:	Rolex watch, mens diamond ring, and cash
Method of Operation:	Drove behind complainants and robbed them at gunpoint
Suspect Vehicle:	1991 White Chevrolet 2 dr.
Weapons used:	2 pistols
Suspect description:	2 White males, 30s, 6' tall, thin

On October, 4, 2008 the complainant pulled into his driveway in the rear of the house and was cornered by the listed suspects. He was driving a 2008 Mercedes Benz. Both suspects pointed weapons (pistols) at the complainant and his wife. They demanded valuables. They received the listed property. The suspects drove off in the listed vehicle. The complainant had been shopping at the Garland Shopping Center before driving home.

Offense #3

Service Number:	1562A
Offense Beat:	632
Watch:	3rd
Date:	October 9, 2008
Time:	18:30
Day of Week:	Thursday
Offense Type:	Aggravated Robbery
Offense Location:	7610 Marian Circle
Type Premise:	House
Property taken:	Diamond necklace, mens diamond ring and diamond necklace
Method of Operation:	Drove behind complainants and robbed them at gunpoint
Suspect Vehicle:	1998 White 2 dr.
Weapons used:	2 guns
Suspect description:	2 White males, 38-40, 6'-6' 3", 200-240 pounds, with brown hair wearing jeans

On the listed date and time the complainant pulled into his driveway in the rear of the house and was cornered by the listed suspects. He was driving a 2007 Mercedes Benz. The suspects pointed weapons at the complainant. They received the listed property and had the complainants place the valuables into a bag. The suspects drove off in the listed vehicle. The complainant had been shopping at the Forestwood Shopping Center before driving home.

Offense #4

Service Number:	1625A
Offense Beat:	632
Watch:	3rd
Date:	October 11, 2008
Time:	19:25
Day of Week:	Saturday
Offense Type:	Aggravated Robbery
Offense Location:	7002 Bridal Wreath.
Type Premise:	House
Property taken:	Ladies watch, fur coat, diamond ring, and cash
Method of Operation:	Drove behind the victim and robbed them in their driveway
Suspect Vehicle:	1997 White Chevrolet Malibu 2 dr. with Texas plates
Weapons used:	2 pistols
Suspect description:	2 White males, 30-35, 6' tall, thin

At the listed time and date the complainant pulled into his driveway in the rear of the house and was cornered by the listed suspects. She was driving a 2008 BMW. Both suspects pointed weapons at the complainant and her husband. They received the listed property and had the complainants place the valuables into a bag. The suspects drove off in the listed vehicle. The complainant had been shopping at the Willow Way Shopping Center before driving home.

Offense #5

Service Number:	2571A
Offense Beat:	632
Watch:	3rd
Date:	October 17, 2008
Time:	20:15
Day of Week:	Friday
Offense Type:	Aggravated Robbery
Offense Location:	7620 Marian
Type Premise:	House
Property taken:	Rolex watch, Diamond ring, and cash
Method of Operation:	Drove behind complainant's vehicle and robbed them at gunpoint
Suspect Vehicle:	1998 White Chevrolet 2 dr.
Weapons used:	2 guns
Suspect description:	2 White males, 40s, 6' tall

On the listed date and time the complainant pulled into his driveway in the rear of the house and was cornered by the listed suspects. He was driving a 2008 Rolls Royce. Both suspects pointed weapons at the complainant. They demanded valuables. They received the listed property and had the complainants place the valuables into a bag. The suspects drove off in the listed vehicle. The complainant had been shopping at the Garland Shopping Center before driving home.

Offense #6

Service Number:	2495A
Offense Beat:	632
Watch:	3rd
Date:	October 21, 2008
Time:	18:50
Day of Week:	Tuesday
Offense Type:	Aggravated Robbery
Offense Location:	7005 Bridal Wreath
Type Premise:	House
Property taken:	Ladies Rolex watch, Diamond ring, fur coat and cash
Method of Operation:	Drove behind complainant's vehicle and robbed at gunpoint
Suspect Vehicle:	1998 White Chevrolet 2 dr.
Weapons used:	2 guns
Suspect description:	2 White males, 40s, 6' tall

On the listed date and time the complainant pulled into his driveway in the rear of the house and was cornered by the listed suspects. He was driving a 2008 Lexus. Both suspects pointed weapons at the complainant. They demanded valuables. They received the listed property and had the complainants place the valuables into a bag. The suspects drove off in the listed vehicle. The complainant had been shopping at the Garland Shopping Center before driving home.

Offense #7

Service Number:	2775A
Offense Beat:	632
Watch:	3rd
Date:	October 25, 2008
Time:	19:50
Day of Week:	Saturday
Offense Type:	Aggravated Robbery
Offense Location:	6870 Winding Creek
Type Premise:	House
Property taken:	Ladies Rolex watch, Diamond ring and cash
Method of Operation:	Drove behind complainant's vehicle and robbed him at gunpoint
Suspect Vehicle:	1997 White Chevrolet Malibu 2 dr. with Texas plates
Weapons used:	2 guns
Suspect description:	2 White males, late 30s, 6' tall

On the listed date and time the complainant pulled into his driveway in the rear of the house and was cornered by the listed suspects. He was driving a 2006 Mercedes. Both suspects pointed weapons at the complainant. They demanded valuables. They received the listed property and had the complainants place the valuables into a bag. The suspects drove off in the listed vehicle. The complainant had been shopping at the Forestwood Shopping Center before driving home.

Offense #8

Service Number:	2802A
Offense Beat:	632
Watch:	3rd
Date:	November 1, 2008
Time:	20:15
Day of Week:	Saturday
Offense Type:	Aggravated Robbery
Offense Location:	7612 Marian.
Type Premise:	House
Property taken:	Rolex watch, diamond ring, and cash
Method of Operation:	Drove behind complainant and robbed him at gunpoint
Suspect Vehicle:	1997 White Chevrolet Malibu 2 dr.
Weapons used:	2 automatic pistols
Suspect description:	2 White males, 40s

On November 1, 2008 the complainant pulled into his driveway in the rear of the house and was cornered by the listed suspects. He was driving a 2008 Rolls Royce. Both suspects pointed weapons (pistols) at the complainant. They demanded valuables. They received the listed property and had the complainants place the valuables into a bag. The suspects drove off in the listed vehicle. The complainant had been shopping at the Garland Shopping Center before driving home.

Offense #9

Service Number:	3025A
Offense Beat:	632
Watch:	3rd
Date:	November 7, 2008
Time:	19:15
Day of Week:	Friday
Offense Type:	Aggravated Robbery
Offense Location:	7619 Marian
Type Premise:	House
Property taken:	Rolex watch, diamond ring, and cash
Method of Operation:	Drove behind complainant and robbed him at gunpoint
Suspect Vehicle:	1996 White Chevrolet Malibu 2 dr.
Weapons used:	2 pistols
Suspect description:	2 White males, 40s

On November 7, 2008 the complainant pulled into his driveway in the rear of the house and was cornered by the listed suspects. He was driving a 2007 BMW. Both suspects pointed weapons at the complainant. They demanded valuables. They received the listed property and had the complainants place the valuables into a bag. The suspects drove off in the listed vehicle. The complainant had been shopping at the Forestwood Shopping Center before driving home.

Offense #10

Service Number:	3625A
Offense Beat:	632
Watch:	3rd
Date:	November 15, 2008
Time:	19:15
Day of Week:	Saturday
Offense Type:	Aggravated Robbery
Offense Location:	7004 Bridal Wreath
Type Premise:	House
Property taken:	Rolex watch, diamond ring, and cash
Method of Operation:	Drove behind complainants and robbed them at gunpoint
Suspect Vehicle:	1997 White Chevrolet 2 dr. with Texas plates
Weapons used:	2 pistols
Suspect description:	2 White males, 40, 6' tall, thin, medium complexion, with brown hair wearing jeans and dirty dark shirts

At the above listed date and time the complainant pulled into his driveway in the rear of the house and was approached by the listed suspects. He was driving a Mercedes Benz. Both suspects pointed weapons (pistols) at the complainant and his wife. They demanded valuables. They received the listed property and had the complainants place the valuables into a bag. The suspects drove off in the listed vehicle. The complainant had been shopping at the Garland Shopping Center before driving home.

Offense #11

Service Number:	3715A
Offense Beat:	634
Watch:	3rd
Date:	November 19, 2008
Time:	20:30
Day of Week:	Wednesday
Offense Type:	Aggravated Robbery
Offense Location:	7508 Jupiter
Type Premise:	House
Property taken:	Rolex watch, Diamond necklace, 2 diamond rings, and cash
Method of Operation:	Drove behind complainants and robbed them at gunpoint
Suspect Vehicle:	1997 White Chevrolet 2 dr. with Texas plates
Weapons used:	2 automatic pistols
Suspect description:	2 White males, 30-35, 6' tall, thin, medium complexion, with brown hair

On the listed date and time the complainant pulled into his driveway in the rear of his house and was confronted by the listed suspects. He was driving a 2008 Lexus Coupe. Both suspects pointed weapons (pistols) at the complainant and his wife. They demanded valuables. They received the listed. The suspects drove off in the listed vehicle. The complainant had been shopping at the Forestwood Shopping Center before driving home.

Offense #12

Service Number:	3910A
Offense Beat:	634
Watch:	3rd
Date:	November 22, 2008
Time:	19:15
Day of Week:	Saturday
Offense Type:	Aggravated Robbery
Offense Location:	7450 Horizon
Type Premise:	House
Property taken:	Rolex watch, Diamond necklace, diamond ring, and cash
Method of Operation:	Drove behind complainants and robbed him at gunpoint
Suspect Vehicle:	1997 White Chevrolet 2 dr. with Texas plates
Weapons used:	2 pistols
Suspect description:	2 White males, 38-39, 6' tall, thin, medium complexion, with brown hair

On the listed date and time the complainant pulled into his driveway in the rear of his house and was confronted by the listed suspects. He was driving a 2007 Mercedes. Both suspects pointed weapons at the complainant and his wife. They demanded valuables. They received the listed. The suspects drove off in the listed vehicle. The complainant had been shopping at the Garland Shopping Center before driving home.

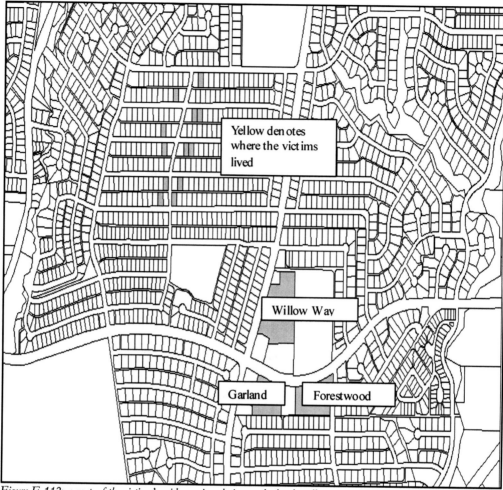

Figure E-112: a map of the victims' residences in relation to the local malls

Here are some questions to consider as you analyze this series:

1. What characteristics are common among the offenses? What are the common elements among suspect and victim descriptions, *modus operandi*, vehicle descriptions, property taken, and so on?

2. Can you predict what days have the highest probability of future offenses? In what time range are they likely to occur?

3. Do you see any common geographic factors in the victims' residences and travel routes?

4. Based on your answers to questions 1–3, what would you tell the investigative lieutenant and the officers working for her? How would you recommend deploying officers?

Sheet Linking

Throughout this chapter, we have used various *cell references* to calculate data based on ranges of cells, and to display or use those calculations in other locations on the same sheet. But what about combining data from multiple worksheets?

Excel users must often link data from various worksheets onto a single sheet to summarize the data. You can link to data on the same sheet, in another sheet in the same workbook, or in another Excel workbook.

»Step 1: Open **C:\BPOffice\Excel\2007CrimeOfficerPopulation.xlsx.**

This spreadsheet summarizes data published by the FBI's Uniform Crime Reporting Program in 2008, concerning the year 2007. For agencies that reported both crime figures and personnel figures, and that have a population greater than 10,000 residents, it shows crime, officer, and personnel totals. There are 2,806 agencies listed.

The sheet then uses Excel formulas to calculate, for each agency, the number of crimes per 1000 residents, the number of officers per 1000 residents, the number of officers per 1000 crimes, the number of total personnel per 1000 residents, and the number of personnel per 1000 crimes.

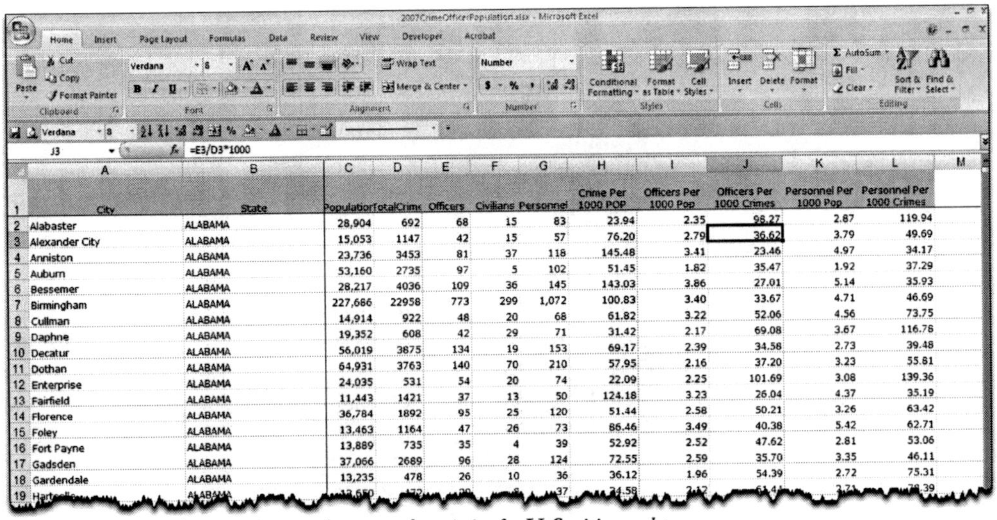

	City	State	Population	TotalCrime	Officers	Civilians	Personnel	Crime Per 1000 POP	Officers Per 1000 Pop	Officers Per 1000 Crimes	Personnel Per 1000 Pop	Personnel Per 1000 Crimes
2	Alabaster	ALABAMA	28,904	692	68	15	83	23.94	2.35	98.27	2.87	119.94
3	Alexander City	ALABAMA	15,053	1147	42	15	57	76.20	2.79	36.62	3.79	49.69
4	Anniston	ALABAMA	23,736	3453	81	37	118	145.48	3.41	23.46	4.97	34.17
5	Auburn	ALABAMA	53,160	2735	97	5	102	51.45	1.82	35.47	1.92	37.29
6	Bessemer	ALABAMA	28,217	4036	109	36	145	143.03	3.86	27.01	5.14	35.93
7	Birmingham	ALABAMA	227,686	22958	773	299	1,072	100.83	3.40	33.67	4.71	46.69
8	Cullman	ALABAMA	14,914	922	48	20	68	61.82	3.22	52.06	4.56	73.75
9	Daphne	ALABAMA	19,352	608	42	29	71	31.42	2.17	69.08	3.67	116.78
10	Decatur	ALABAMA	56,019	3875	134	19	153	69.17	2.39	34.58	2.73	39.48
11	Dothan	ALABAMA	64,931	3763	140	70	210	57.95	2.16	37.20	3.23	55.81
12	Enterprise	ALABAMA	24,035	531	54	20	74	22.09	2.25	101.69	3.08	139.36
13	Fairfield	ALABAMA	11,443	1421	37	13	50	124.18	3.23	26.04	4.37	35.19
14	Florence	ALABAMA	36,784	1892	95	25	120	51.44	2.58	50.21	3.26	63.42
15	Foley	ALABAMA	13,463	1164	47	26	73	86.46	3.49	40.38	5.42	62.71
16	Fort Payne	ALABAMA	13,889	735	35	4	39	52.92	2.52	47.62	2.81	53.06
17	Gadsden	ALABAMA	37,066	2689	96	28	124	72.55	2.59	35.70	3.35	46.11
18	Gardendale	ALABAMA	13,235	478	26	10	36	36.12	1.96	54.39	2.72	75.31

Figure E-113: population, crime, and personnel statistics for U.S. cities and towns

Assume that we work for the Dallas Police Department, and we want to summarize some of this data on the worksheet titled "Summary."

»Step 2: At the bottom of the screen, click on the tab for the "Summary" worksheet.

The summary sheet asks us for the figures for Dallas alone, all Texas agencies, and all U.S. agencies. We will fill these figures with references to the other worksheet.

»**Step 3:** At the bottom of the screen, click on the tab for the "USA" worksheet.

By returning to the "USA" worksheet, we see that Dallas is at Row 2390. Texas occupies Rows 2345–2551, and the entire spreadsheet takes up Rows 2–2807. The relevant columns occupy Columns H–L.

To reference another worksheet, we simply put the worksheet name and an exclamation point in front of the cell reference. So where we would normally type, if we were referencing cells on the same worksheet:

=C2
=D2/C2*1000
=AVERAGE(I2:I2807)

We now type, from a different worksheet:

=USA!C2
=USA!D2/USA!C2*1000
=AVERAGE(USA!I2:I2807)

»**Step 3:** With this in mind, fill out the cells on the "Summary" sheet with the formulas below.

Cell	Formula
B4	=USA!H2390
B5	=USA!I2390
B6	=USA!J2390
B7	=USA!K2390
B8	=USA!L2390
B11	=AVERAGE(USA!H2345:H2551)
B12	=AVERAGE(USA!I2345:I2551)
B13	=AVERAGE(USA!J2345:J2551)
B14	=AVERAGE(USA!K2345:K2551)
B15	=AVERAGE(USA!L2345:L2551)
B18	=AVERAGE(USA!H2:H2807)
B19	=AVERAGE(USA!I2:I2807)
B20	=AVERAGE(USA!J2:J2807)
B21	=AVERAGE(USA!K2:K2807)
B22	=AVERAGE(USA!L2:L2807)

The result, shown in Figure E-114, is that Dallas has a significantly higher crime rate than the U.S. and Texas averages (as we might expect for a large city), and that while its staffing is higher than the U.S. and Texas averages by *population*, it is lower than both by *crime*.

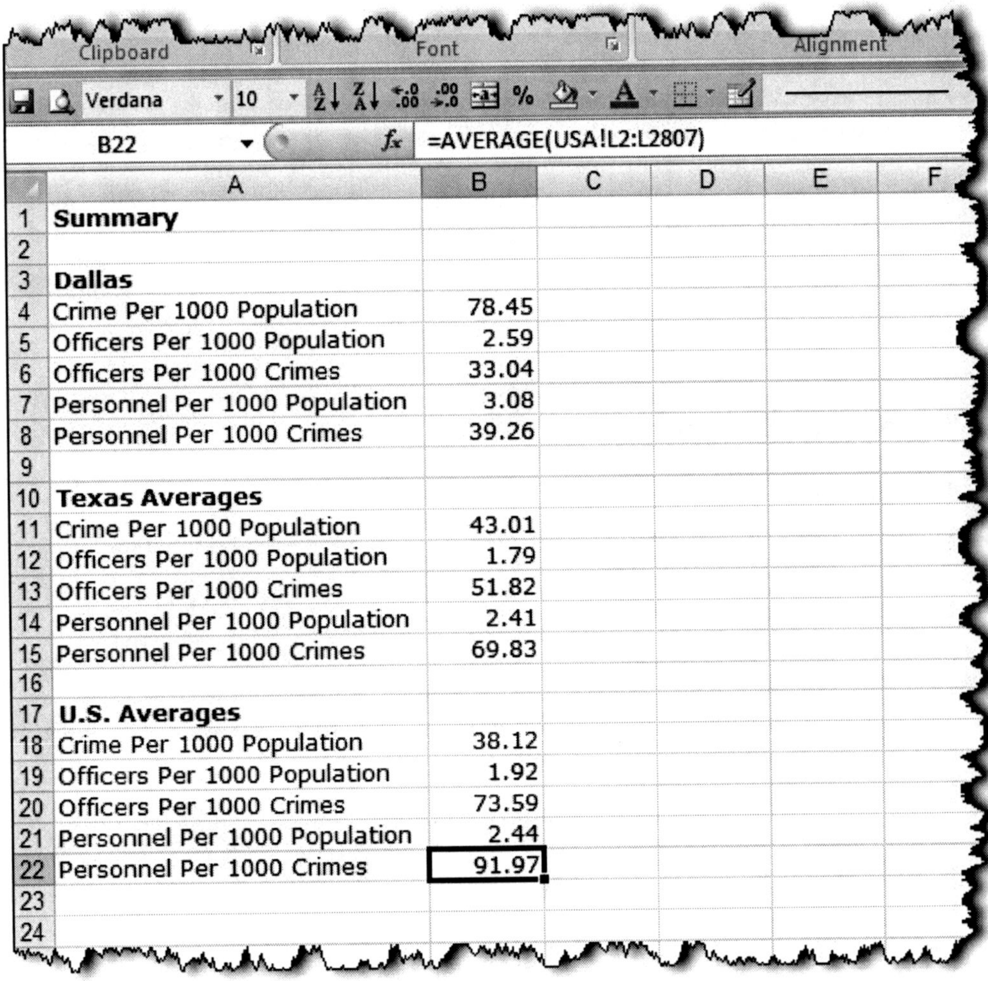

Figure E-114: using sheet linking to summarize data

Finally, you can also reference cells contained in other workbooks, as long as the workbook location and name do not change. The syntax for linking to another workbook is:

='FilePath\[filename.xlsx]worksheetname'!CellRef

For instance:

='C:\BPOffice\Excel\[2007CrimeOfficerPopulation.xlsx]USA'!B2

Macros

Excel macros allow you to record a series of steps and replay them. Macros are best when you must perform the same series of functions regularly. In this example, we're going to record a macro that finds errors and replaces them with correct values—valuable if we will frequently have to clean a data extract from a records system, for example.

To use macros, we must turn on a ribbon tab that does not activate itself with the default installation of Excel.

»**Step 1:** Launch Excel if it is closed. If it is open, close any open workbooks.

»**Step 2:** If you do not have a "Developer" tab on your ribbon, choose **Office Button | Excel Options**. Click on the "Popular" option on the right and check the box (third one down) that reads "Show Developer tab in the Ribbon."

Figure E-115: the Developer ribbon options, once enabled.

»**Step 3:** Choose **Developer | Code | Record Macro**.

»**Step 4:** Name your macro "CleanAddresses." Save it in your Personal Macro Workbook and enter the description shown in Figure E-112. Click "OK."

The macro now starts *recording*. Any steps that you take at this point will become part of your permanent macro. Therefore, we want to avoid any extraneous steps.

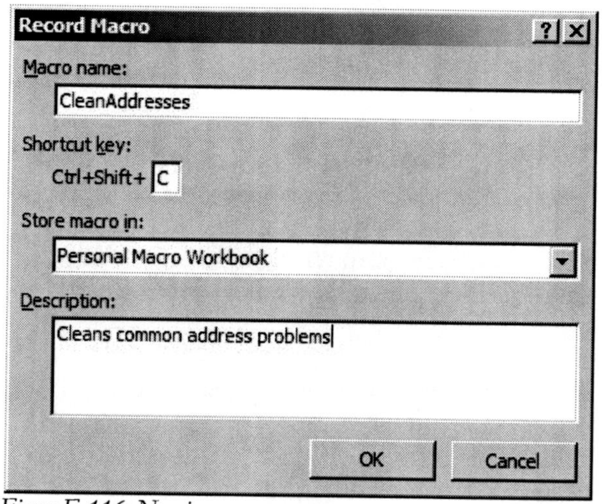

Figure E-116: Naming your new macro

»**Step 5:** Choose **File | Open**. Navigate to **C:\BPOffice\Excel** and open **crimeextract.xlsx**.

The assumption in this exercise is that "crimeextract" is an export from your records management system. You will frequently receive an RMS extract with this name, and you will have to perform the same data cleaning procedures on it each time.

»**Step 6:** Click within Column C and choose **Home | Editing | Find & Select | Replace**. Replace "S Westmoreland" with "N Westmoreland" and "Replace All." Repeat twice, replacing "Dallasnorthpkw" with "Dallas N Pkwy" and "N Central Exwy" with "Central Exwy."

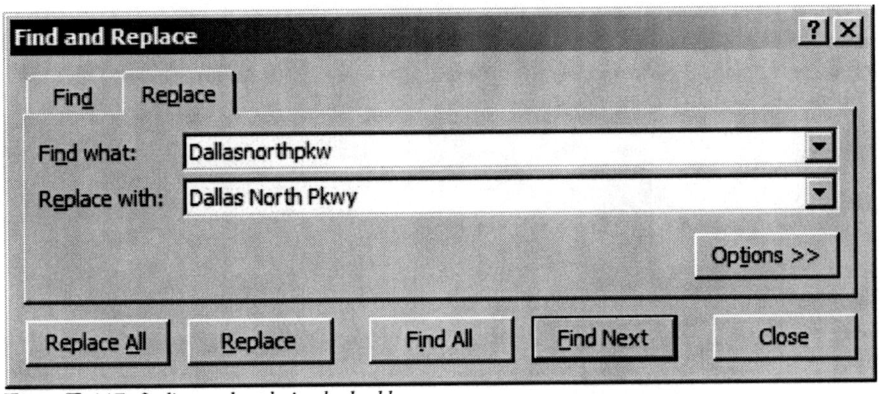

Figure E-117: finding and replacing bad addresses

»**Step 7:** Sort the spreadsheet in order of UCR code by clicking in the Column B and then the "Sort Ascending" button ![sort icon] at **Data | Sort & Filter**.

»**Step 8:** Stop the macro by choosing **Developer | Code | Stop Recording**.

»**Step 9:** Now: close the spreadsheet *without saving your changes* (the macro will be saved; just not the changes you performed to the data while recording it).

»**Step 10:** Choose **Developer | Code | Macros**, select "CleanAddresses" and click "Run." Instantly, Excel will open the file and make the find-replace changes.

There are innumerable uses for macros. Set one up to go through the procedures involved in importing a text file you will frequently access. Set up another to fill your worksheet with the calculations necessary in the "Aoristic Analysis" example above. Use another to create a common type of chart, setting the formatting and coloring. Any time you must accomplish the same task, using the same procedures, on a regular basis, a macro is a superb time-saver.

The downside of macros is that malicious programmers can use them to sneak viruses onto your computer. For this reason, Excel offers different levels of macro security, accessible at **Developer | Code | Macro Security**. Here, you can tell Excel only to allow macros in certain locations, or with certain authentication protocols, to run.

Spreadsheet Layout and Printing

We have covered many of the ways to analyze, chart, and calculate data in Excel. But Excel is also meant for finished, printed reports, and it offers a number of features that make your printed product attractive and professional.

The first is the *print area*, which you can set by selecting the range of cells you want to print and choosing **Page Layout | Page Setup | Print Area | Set Print Area**. This limits the printed page to only the cells that you choose, excluding those that might be useful for on-screen analysis, but not for a printed report. To include a chart in the print area, you must include the cell beneath the upper-left corner of the chart (Figure E-118).

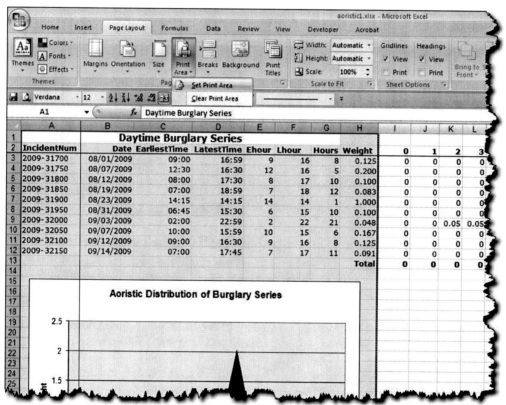

Figure E-118: this selected print area includes the chart, because the cell containing the upper-left-hand corner of the chart is among those selected

The **Page Layout** tab in the ribbon contains most of the rest of the options you'll need for printing your spreadsheet. These include (on various groupings):

- **Orientation:** some spreadsheets look better in portrait view, others in landscape
- Paper **size:** regular "letter" (8.5 x 11), legal, or any other options you desire
- **Margins**

- **Scaling:** to make your spreadsheet better fit on the page, you can tell Excel to expand or shrink it by a certain percent, or to fit it to a specific number of pages

- Background colors and pictures

- Whether to show gridlines or not

- Text to display in the **header** and **footer**, and its color and formatting

- Rows or columns to repeat on every page

Figure E-119: the Page Layout tab in Excel

The **Page Setup**, **Scale to Fit**, and **Sheet Options** groups all have buttons in the lower right-hand corners ◱ that take you to the "Page Setup" sheet, which has even more options.

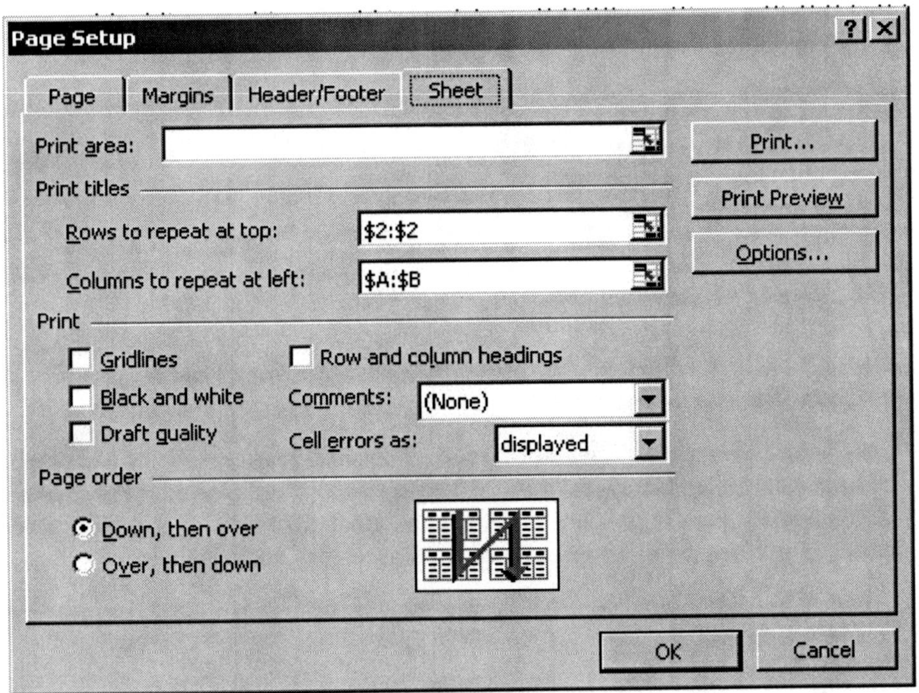

Page Setup

Page | Margins | Header/Footer | Sheet

Print area: [   ]

Print titles

Rows to repeat at top: [$2:$2]

Columns to repeat at left: [$A:$B]

Print

☐ Gridlines   ☐ Row and column headings

☐ Black and white   Comments: [(None) ▼]

☐ Draft quality   Cell errors as: [displayed ▼]

Page order

◉ Down, then over

○ Over, then down

[Print...] [Print Preview] [Options...]

[OK] [Cancel]

Figure E-120: the "Page Setup" screen in Excel.

On the "Sheet" tab, we have the ability to specify certain rows to appear at the top of each page, such as the header rows in a long list of records. We can also specify certain columns to appear at the right of each page. A check box allows us to specify whether the gridlines between cells should print (if not, the only borders that appear between cells will be the ones that we set through the "Borders" button at **Home | Font |** ▦ ▾.

The "Cell errors as" option lets us tell Excel that, for printing purposes, any calculation errors should be blank or annotated with "N/A" rather than printing "#DIV/0! or whatever the applicable error is.

Taking it to the Next Level

Excel is a large application with many functions, and it makes sense that the Excel chapter is the longest in the book. Having completed these exercises, you should be at an intermediate, if not advanced, level with Excel. We hope that the exercises have not only shown you specific examples of how Excel can make law enforcement employees more efficient at their tasks, but have also given you dozens of ideas for further applications.

Here are some advanced Excel topics for you to explore after you have mastered the basics of this chapter:

- More advanced functions and formulas. Excel comes with almost 350 built-in functions; we only explored about a dozen. Moreover, you can next functions within functions within functions to create very complex statistical models.

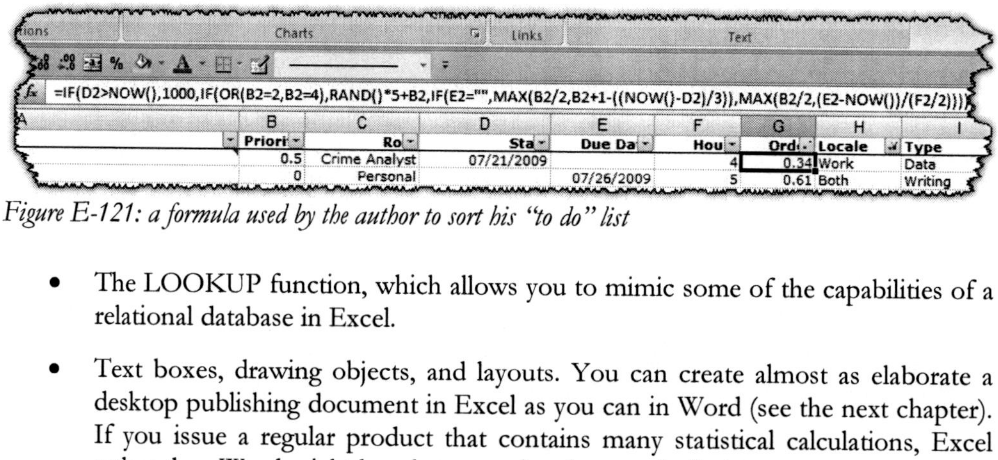

Figure E-121: a formula used by the author to sort his "to do" list

- The LOOKUP function, which allows you to mimic some of the capabilities of a relational database in Excel.

- Text boxes, drawing objects, and layouts. You can create almost as elaborate a desktop publishing document in Excel as you can in Word (see the next chapter). If you issue a regular product that contains many statistical calculations, Excel rather than Word might be a better option for your bulletin or report.

- Connecting to data in Access, XML, and text formats, from ODBC connections, and on web sites.

- Inserting OLE objects into an Excel workbook.

- Using named ranges.

- "What-If" analysis

- Formula auditing

CHAPTER 3

Microsoft Word

Word is a desktop publishing application that can be used to create and disseminate almost any type of bulletin, report, and other publication imaginable.

Greatly advanced from the "word processing" applications of yesteryear, which limited users to text, Word can incorporate photographs, charts, graphs, tables, and drawing objects. Word documents can be made interactive, with sounds, movies, and hyperlinks. Newer versions can provide automatic translations of text, and can convert documents directly to web pages. It is one of the most versatile, easy-to-use applications ever developed for the personal computer. This book was entirely written, formatted, and laid out in Microsoft Word.

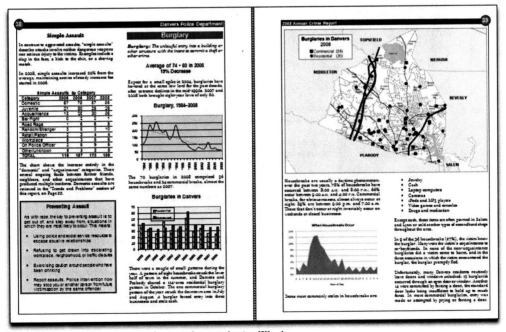

Figure W-1: pages from an annual report, formatted using Word

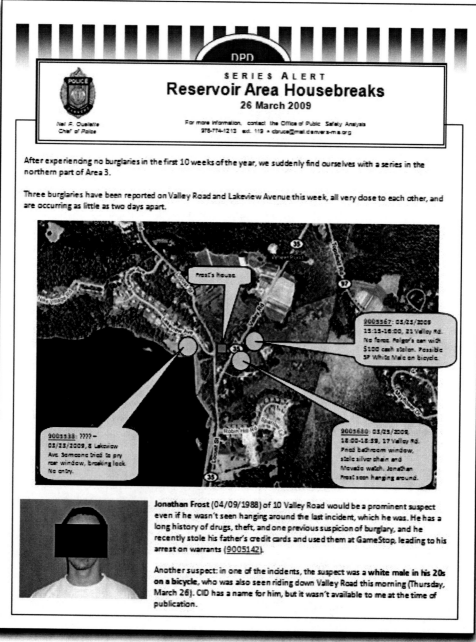

Figure W-2: a crime bulletin from the Danvers (MA) Police Department, created in Word. This single page includes drawing objects, tables, borders, text formatting, callout boxes, and images to create a professional-looking publication.

Figure W-3: a brochure for the International Association of Crime Analysts, created with a word template.

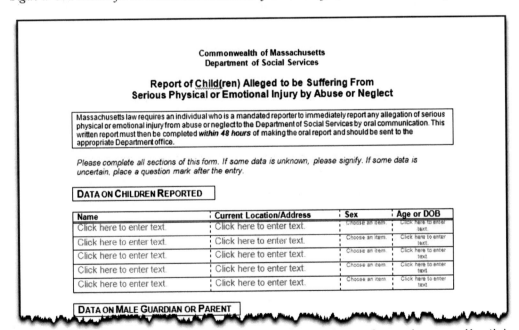

Figure W-4: templates save a great deal of time. Most of a police agency's paper forms and reports could easily be rendered as Word templates.

What's New in Word 2007?

These are the most significant new features of Word 2007:

- As with all of the Office 2007 applications, Microsoft has replaced menus and toolbars with the "ribbon" interface at the top of the screen.

- The new file format (.docx) is an XML format that reduces file size and has certain other advantages over the old .doc format. Word supports backwards compatibility, however, and you can still save your files in Word 2003 format.

- There are many new templates, including "pre-formatted content," or individual page and section templates, for things like cover pages, headers, footers, tables, and equations.

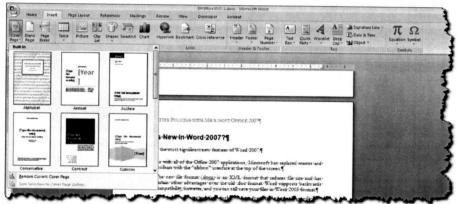

Figure W-5: some of the new "template"-style features of Word 2007 include cover pages.

- New "SmartArt" shapes allow you to create varies diagrams and graphics—including flow charts, organizational charts, and Venn diagrams—very quickly.

- Word 2007 uses Excel (rather than Microsoft Graph) to create and manage charts. Therefore, full Excel charting functionality is present in Word.

- Review, tracking, and commenting options have been expanded to make it easier to review, compare, accept, or reject changes.

- Word now supports automatic saving of documents in PDF format.

Figure W-6: Word 2007 will save documents in Adobe PDF format

Creating a Crime Bulletin

Basic use of Word is simple: launch it and start typing. Without any special training or fanfare, you can create simple documents, reports, and letters.

»**Step 1:** Launch Microsoft Word 2007 [w].

Opening Word usually presents you with a blank document. Getting started is easy: click in the document and start typing. Creating a simple list, paragraph, or business letter is a snap—but if that was all there was to Word, this chapter wouldn't be necessary.

»**Step 2:** Choose **Office Button | Open** or **CTRL-O** and navigate to **C:\BPOffice\Word\bulletin.docx**. Open it.

You should be presented with a brief paragraph describing a burglary series in the city of Metropolis (Figure W-7). Before we continue, to make sure that everyone is seeing the same thing, we need to review a few options.

»**Step 3:** Choose **Office Button | Word Options**.

You are presented with a set of options as thorough as any Microsoft Office application. As you become proficient in Word, we encourage you to visit these options from time-to-time and see if you can improve your efficiency with them.

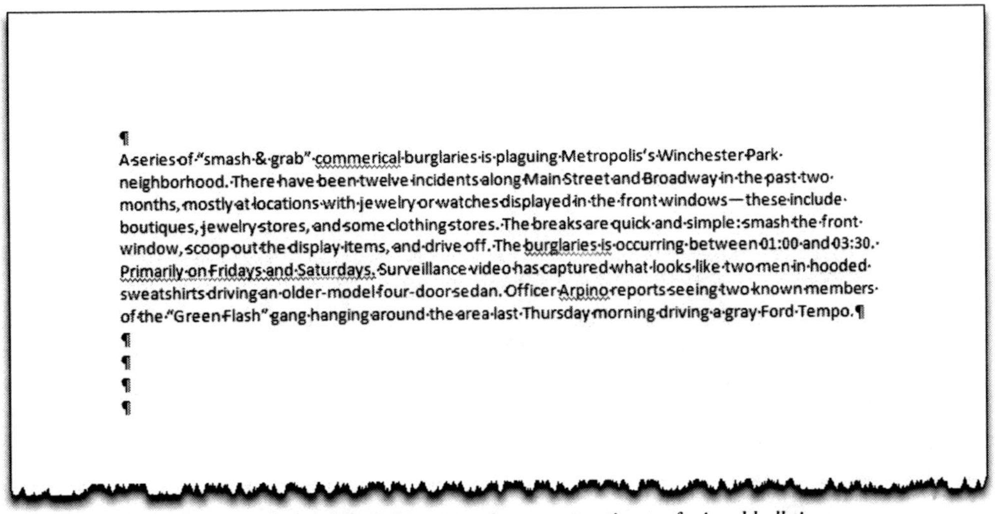

¶
A·series·of·"smash·&·grab"·commerical·burglaries·is·plaguing·Metropolis's·Winchester·Park·
neighborhood.·There·have·been·twelve·incidents·along·Main·Street·and·Broadway·in·the·past·two·
months,·mostly·at·locations·with·jewelry·or·watches·displayed·in·the·front·windows—these·include·
boutiques,·jewelry·stores,·and·some·clothing·stores.·The·breaks·are·quick·and·simple:·smash·the·front·
window,·scoop·out·the·display·items,·and·drive·off.·The·burglaries·is·occurring·between·01:00·and·03:30.·
Primarily·on·Fridays·and·Saturdays.·Surveillance·video·has·captured·what·looks·like·two·men·in·hooded·
sweatshirts·driving·an·older·model·four·door·sedan.·Officer·Arpino·reports·seeing·two·known·members·
of·the·"Green·Flash"·gang·hanging·around·the·area·last·Thursday·morning·driving·a·gray·Ford·Tempo.·¶
¶
¶
¶
¶

Figure W-7: the brief paragraph that we're going to turn into an attractive, professional bulletin

»**Step 4:** Click on the "Proofing" option group. Make sure these options are checked: "Check spelling as you type" and "Check grammar as you type" (Fig. W-8).

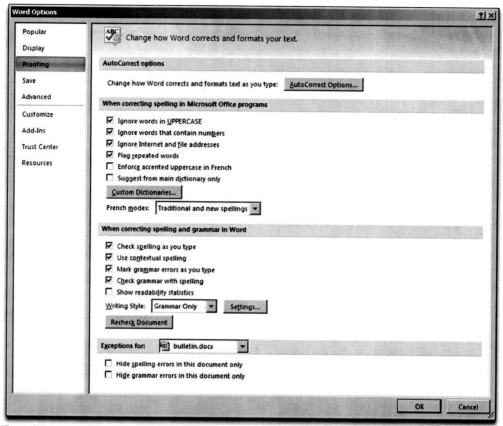

Figure W-8: setting Word's proofreading options.

It is these options that produce the little red squiggles under questionable spelling and grammatical errors. With these options turned on, you should see a few in the "bulletin" document. We'll cover these in a little bit.

View and Layout Options

There are a few view and layout options that we should explore before we begin working. The first is the *zoom level*, available from **View | Zoom | Zoom** or the "Zoom" bar in the lower right-hand corner of the screen. Normally, users prefer to work at 100%, so that the size of text and images on the screen is identical to the size of text and images that will be printed. However, users with small monitor resolutions (e.g., 800 x 600) or large page layouts may prefer to work at less than 100% so that more of the document appears on the screen. Conversely, users with poor eyesight may prefer to adjust their zoom to more than 100%. Our zoom will be set to 100% through most of these lessons. If you wish to change your zoom, simply adjust the zoom slider.

Figure W-9: the zoom slider appears in the lower right-hand corner

Word users seem to be divided evenly between those who prefer to see their *formatting marks*, and those who prefer to hide them. Formatting marks show a ¶ whenever there is a pargraph, a · whenever there is a space, a → when there is a tab, and so on. These marks are visible only in the on-screen document, and not on the printed version or in the print preview. Figure W-10 shows the difference between a screen with formatting marks and one without them.

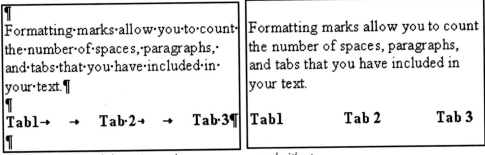

Figure W-10: text with formatting marks.................and without

The advantage to showing your formatting marks is that you know exactly how many carriage returns you have entered between paragraphs, exactly how many spaces between words, and so on. Formatting marks often help troubleshoot text that seems to be behaving badly—an errant tab or carriage return may be throwing it off.

But some users find that formatting marks "clutter" the screen and make it difficult to differentiate "real" text and symbols from the formatting marks. Whichever style you prefer, you can toggle the formatting marks on and off with the "Show/Hide ¶" button ¶ at **Home | Paragraph**.

Word offers you five "views," not including Print Preview. All of them are accessible at **Views | Document Views** or by using the view options to the left of the zoom slider.

- **Print Layout** view is the preferred view for most desktop publishing work. It shows, more or less, exactly the way the document will look when printed, including headers, footers, columns, and image positioning.

- **Full Screen Reading** maximizes screen space for reading and commenting on documents. It does so at the expense of precise layouts—shoving images and drawing objects hither and yon—so it's best for text-only documents.

- **Web Layout** shows you the way your document will look if converted to HTML.

- **Outline** view can be useful for long documents with chapter and section headings. The view allows you to expand, collapse, and easily drag sections of your document.

- ▤ **Draft** view is the same as "normal" view in previous versions of Word. It shows only the text of your document without images, headers and footers, drawing objects, or any layout formatting.

Print Preview, accessible from the **Office Button | Print | Print Preview,** shows you exactly what the document will look like when printed.

The nature of most Microsoft Word use in crime analysis, which often involves images, headers, drawing objects, and other desktop publishing elements, usually requires users to work in the Print Layout view. These lessons require it.

»**Step 5:** Toggle among the different views, and finish with **View | Document Views | Print Layout.**

Paper Size, Orientation, and Margins

Word has very flexible options for paper size, paper orientation, and document margins.

»**Step 6:** Click on the **Page Layout** tab on the ribbon.

The "Margins" button under **Page Setup** allows you to adjust the document's internal margins. The default settings—one inch all around—is good for a letter or report, but probably too much for a crime bulletin.

»**Step 7:** Click on **Page Layout | Page Setup | Margins | Narrow** (Figure W-11) to change the margins to 0.5 inches all around.

"Orientation" allows you to specify whether your document is oriented in a vertical "Portrait" format (like a regular book or letter) or a horizontal "Landscape" format (like some maps or certificates). You can have both landscape and portrait pages in the same document by inserting a *section break* between them. We will explore this later.

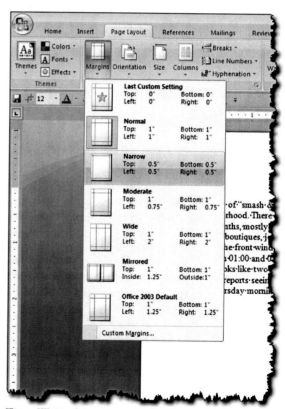

Figure W-11: choosing a smaller margin

Using the "Size" button, we can adjust our paper size, in case we want to layout and print our document on a legal or 11 x 17 piece of paper. Our document is currently set to 8.5 x 11—regular "letter" size.

>**Step 8:** Save your document at **Office Button | Save.**

As you work in Word, we encourage you to *save* your document frequently. **CTRL-S** is a handy keyboard shortcut for saving—get in the habit of pressing this combination as you finish each paragraph or major change. It only takes a second to save; it can take hours to recover a lost document.

"Save As" allows you to save a copy of your document under a different file name. This is handy if you want to use last week's crime bulletin as your basis for this week's bulletin. Just open last week's document, choose **Office Button | Save As**, save it with this week's name, and start making your changes.

Undo: Your Best Friend

One of your authors, working on this section about mid-evening on a Friday, just took a brief Haagen-Dazs break. He returned to find his cat sleeping on the warm laptop keyboard. As cats do, she had apparently "kneaded" the surface a bit before settling down for her nap, and in doing so, managed to select and delete several pages of text, replacing it with random keystrokes (she did not, alas, manage to write "Hamlet" on her first try).

Your author could have thrown up his hands, given up, and gone to play "Half-Life" for the rest of the night. Frankly, he was thinking about doing that anyway. But he didn't. Instead—after hurling the cat out of the room—he used his "nuclear option": "Undo." As the name suggests, it un-does the last thing that you did, returning your document to the way it was before you started. Don't like where you pasted that text? "Undo" and try again. Accidentally crop that picture too much? "Undo." Did you just execute an ill-advised "Replace?" "Undo" to get back the original text.

"Undo" cannot be found on the ribbon in Word 2007. Instead, Microsoft added it to the default "Quick Access Toolbar." Its icon looks like this: , and if you click on the arrow, it removes the previous action. If you click on the drop-down menu to the right of the arrow, you can see a list of recent actions that you can un-do. If you deleted the icon from your Quick Access Toolbar, like we did, memorize the keyboard shortcut: **CTRL-Z**.

Almost all programs have an "Undo" command, but none of them are as thorough as Word. In some, you can undo only your most recent action. In others, like Excel and Access, you can undo multiple actions, but certain actions (e.g., saving the document, creating a chart) interrupt the chain. In Word, however, there seems to be no limit to the number of actions that you can undo, and nothing except closing the document breaks the "undo" chain. You can work on a document for hours, then hold down **CTRL-Z** and watch all your changes disappear, one by one, until you end up with the same blank document you started with. You can even do this after you've saved it.

This is particularly helpful when you, for instance, start with last week's crime bulletin in order to create this week's. After working for a couple of hours, you realize that you forgot to save the document under a new name, and you've been saving over the old bulletin. No problem! Just **Office Button | Save As** and save the document under it's new name, then undo all your actions, then **Office Button | Save As** again under the old name.

If you're half as ham-handed and absent-minded as us, there are dozens of opportunities to use "Undo" in an average day. We suggest making **CTRL-Z** second nature to you.

Fonts

The *font* is one of the first options you'll want to set as you create a Word document. In Windows, the term "font" refers to the typeface, or the graphic design applied to the text, as well as the spacing and pitch. Many fonts are fairly standard, suitable for most documents; others are stylized and meant for specific purposes; still others are actually symbol sets. Here are some examples of fonts:

Calibri

Times New Roman

Arial

Georgia

Impact

Rockwell Extra Bold

Monotype Corsiva

Σψμβολ (Symbol)

✳✠■℀♎✠■℀♦ (Wingdings)

Batang

Comic Sans MS

Broadway

Windows comes with several hundred fonts, which are stored in the **C:\Windows\Fonts** folder. These fonts are available to all Windows applications. You can add more fonts to the folder by purchasing them on CD or downloading them. There are many thousand fonts in existence. Some people like to load up on fonts, but as you do so, remember two things:

1. If you plan to share your document electronically, and the user who receives it does not have the font on his computer that you used, it will look very different to him. He may not be able to read it at all.

2. The more fonts you have installed, the longer it will take applications to load.

Regular text (non-symbol) fonts come in two varieties: *serif* and *sans serif* ("without serif"). Serifs are the little stylized markings that appear at the ends of letters in some typefaces— the "foot" at the bottom of a capital "T", a bit of a curve at the end of a "y." Look at the list above. Times New Roman and Georgia are both serif fonts, while Arial and Calibri have no serifs. See the difference?

Experts recommend that you use no more than two or three fonts per document, usually one for headings and one for text. The heading is usually a sans serif font and the text is a serif font. Look at the two examples below, and you should see a remarkable stylistic difference between them. We suspect you'll agree that the first example is the better one.

Example 1	**Example 2**
This sample uses a header in Arial and a text in Times New Roman. We think you'll agree that it looks more natural and pleasing to the eye than Example 2, which reverses these fonts.	This sample uses a header in Times New Roman and a text in Arial. We think you'll agree that it looks less natural and pleasing to the eye than Example 1, which reverses these fonts.

Figure W-12: two different font styles in a document

Flip through any professional published book, and though you sometimes find serif fonts used as headings, you very rarely find a sans serif font used in the text body.

The default font in Office 2007 applications is Calibri, a new font designed specifically for Office 2007. It is a sans serif font, but it has rounded corners and stems and other stylizations that make it suitable for purposes that would normally suggest a serif font. Because it is relatively new, it has a fresh look about it, but to us nothing says "boooooooring!" more than simply using the default font.

»**Step 9:** Select the text, and the blank paragraphs after the text, by clicking at the beginning and dragging to the end.

»**Step 10:** At **Home | Font**, use the "Font" tool `Georgia ▾` to change the font to Georgia. Use the "Font Size" tool `11 ▾` to change the size to 11 point.

The "Font Size" tool gives you a drop-down menu with the most common font sizes, but you are not limited to these options: you can type in your own size, and you can even type half-sizes, like 9.5 or 11.5. Sometimes a reduction of half a point is all that's needed to keep a few lines of text from spilling onto an additional page.

Formatting Text

Before we start formatting, we'll add some additional text to the bulletin.

»**Step 11:** Enter a couple of carriage returns (**ENTER**) at the top of the bulletin.

»Step 12: Two paragraphs from the top, and two paragraphs above the text (see Figure W-13 for exact placement), add a title: "Smash & Grab Commercial Burglary Series"

We now want to format the new text, as well as the text we already have. Word has innumerable options for formatting text, including:

Bold

Italics

Underlining

Text Color

Background Color (or "Highlight")

~~Strikethrough~~

Subscript and Superscript

Shadow

Emboss

Engrave

SMALL CAPS

ALL CAPS

Any Combination of the Above

ANY COMBINATION OF THE ABOVE

The most common options, including bold **B**, italics *I*, underlining **U**, font color **A**, and highlight, are available right on **Home | Font**. Others are available by selecting the little button at the lower right of the **Home | Font** group, or by typing **CTRL-D**.

»Step 13: Select the title and make it Arial, 14 point, bold with this succession of tools Arial | 14 | **B**.

»Step 14: Bold key words in the text that should jump to an officer's attention: **Smash & Grab, Winchester Park, Main Street, Broadway, jewelry, watches, between 01:00 and 03:30, Fridays and Saturdays, two men in hooded sweatshirts, Green Flash, gray Ford Tempo.**

An officer simply scanning the bolded words would understand the gist of the story.

Finally, we want to set *Text Alignment at* **Home | Paragraph**, where we can specify whether text is aligned to the left margin or right margin, *justified* on both margins, or centered on the page. Usually, text looks best when justified.

»Step 15: Select the text (not the title) and click **Home | Paragraph | Justify**.

Your bulletin should now resemble Figure W-13.

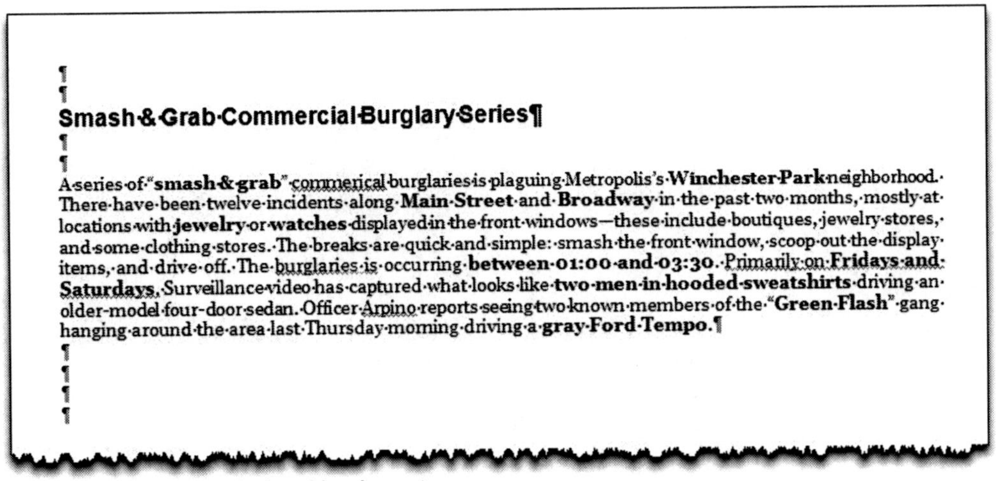

¶
¶
Smash·&·Grab·Commercial·Burglary·Series¶
¶
¶
A·series·of·"smash·&·grab"·commerical·burglaries·is·plaguing·Metropolis's·Winchester·Park·neighborhood.· There·have·been·twelve·incidents·along·Main·Street·and·Broadway·in·the·past·two·months,·mostly·at· locations·with·jewelry·or·watches·displayed·in·the·front·windows—these·include·boutiques,·jewelry·stores,· and·some·clothing·stores.·The·breaks·are·quick·and·simple:·smash·the·front·window,·scoop·out·the·display· items,·and·drive·off.·The·burglaries·is·occurring·between·01:00·and·03:30.·Primarily·on·Fridays·and· Saturdays.·Surveillance·video·has·captured·what·looks·like·two·men·in·hooded·sweatshirts·driving·an· older-model·four-door·sedan.·Officer·Arpino·reports·seeing·two·known·members·of·the·"Green·Flash"·gang· hanging·around·the·area·last·Thursday·morning·driving·a·gray·Ford·Tempo.¶
¶
¶
¶
¶

Figure W-13: the formatted, aligned burglary series story

Spelling and Grammar

You've probably noticed by this point that there are some mistakes in the text. "Commercial" is spelled incorrectly in the first sentence; mid-way through, it reads "burglaries is" instead of "burglaries are," and the sentence that begins with "Primarily" is a fragment. Moreover, Word has annotated these mistakes for us with some red squiggly lines under the text. These squiggles are the result of the "Check spelling as you type" and "Check grammar as you type" options under **Office Button | Word Options**. If you don't have these options turned on, you can choose **Review | Proofing | Spelling and Grammar** to run a spell check and grammar check any time you want.

You can right-click on "flagged" words to see Word's list of potential corrections, or you can simply type the corrections yourself.

> **»Step 16:** Right-click on "commerical" in the first sentence. Left-click on the first option ("commercial") to replace the incorrect text with correct text (Figure W-14).
>
> **»Step 17:** Right-click on the flagged text "burglaries is" and replace it with the suggested correction "burglaries are."

commercial
Ignore
Ignore All
Add to Dictionary
AutoCorrect
Language
Spelling...
Look Up...
Cut
Copy
Paste

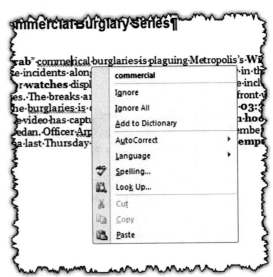

Figure W-14: Word's automatic spelling and grammar checks will flag error and suggest corrections

Word doesn't know exactly how to fix the fragment sentence "Primarily on Fridays and Saturdays," so we'll have to do it manually.

»Step 18: Delete the period before "Primarily" and replace it with a comma, then change the upper-case "P" in "Primarily" to a lower-case "p"—the sentence should now read "…between 01:00 and 03:30, primarily on Fridays…," and the squiggles should go away.

The only squiggle left is under "Arpino," a proper name that Word doesn't recognize. Word almost never recognizes proper personal names, which means these squiggles will appear often in crime bulletins and lists of suspects. Here, we have two options: we can right-click on it and choose "Ignore All," and Word will stop flagging this word within the current document; or we can right-click on it and choose "Add to Dictionary," and Word will now recognize this name in this document and all future documents. It makes sense to do this with officers at your agency, since their names will probably appear frequently in your products.

»Step 19: Right-click on the flagged word "Arpino" and choose "Add to Dictionary."

AutoCorrect

Type the following text as a new paragraph under the existing paragraph. Type it *exactly* as written here, even though there are a lot of mistakes.

> THe tabel below shows supsects known to have comited this type of burglary in the past. the last two--Bruce and Stallo--are members of the "Green Flash" gang.

You now have a paragraph full of spelling errors, right? Wrong! Your paragraph should be pristine. It will read:

> The table below shows suspects known to have committed this type of burglary in the past. The last two—Bruce and Stallo—are members of the "Green Flash" gang.

What happened? Word applied its "AutoCorrect" feature to the text as you were typing it. Among other things, AutoCorrect, by default:

- Replaces two initial capitals (a common typo) with correct case: "The" instead of "THe"

- Replaces common misspellings with corrections: "tabel" with "table" and "supsects" with "suspects."

- Replaces lower-case letters after a period with upper-case: "…past. The…" instead of "…past. the…"

- Replaces double-dashes with "M-dashes": "—" instead of "--"

- Replaces straight quotes with "curly quotes": " instead of "

All of these options are customizable under **Office Button | Word Options | Proofing | AutoCorrect Options**. Some of them you may wish to turn off. We personally find "Automatic bulleted lists" and "Automatic numbered lists" to be annoying. But we encourage you to add liberally to "Replace text as you type" list. Put in your own common spelling mistakes or, more importantly, anything you have to type frequently that you'd like to be able to abbreviate; for instance, your name—how about AutoCorrecting with "Mark A. Stallo" every time you type "MAS?" (Our Trinidad friends will want to avoid this one, of course, lest they find themselves "playing Mark A Stallo" around

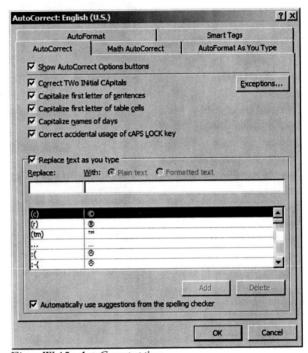

Figure W-15: AutoCorrect options

Carnival time.) Are you sick of typing "Thank you for your time and consideration" at the end of every letter? With AutoCorrect, you can just type "tyfyt" and the words will magically appear.

AutoCorrect replaces only *whole words*, not parts of words. So with the example above, you don't have to worry about AutoCorrect giving you "Merry ChristMark A. Stallo."

Most people don't know about AutoCorrect, so it's perfect for pranks. Trust us, you haven't lived until you've seen your co-worker Rachel tear her hair out trying to figure why every time she types her own name, Word replaces it with "Repulsive Rachel."

WordArt

Text formatting can only accomplish so much. For truly stylish text, we need to turn to WordArt—a mini-application accessible from the "Drawing" toolbar of Word, Excel, and

PowerPoint. WordArt can create decorative text that is shadowed, skewed, rotated, stretched, and arranged into pre-defined shapes.

»**Step 1:** Click in the first paragraph of your document, above the title of the crime series.

»**Step 2: Choose Insert | Text | WordArt.**

WordArt presents you with a selection of initial styles (Figure W-16). Some of them are a bit wacky, and since this is supposed to be a professional document, we're going to go with a fairly subdued style— the second-to-last on the bottom row, which is labeld "WordArt Style 29."

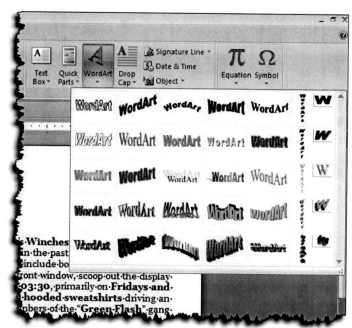

Figure W-16: selecting WordArt

»**Step 3:** Select your preferred style and click "OK."

On the next fairly Spartan screen, you simply type your text and set a couple of basic formatting options.

»**Step 4:** Type "Crime Bulletin" and click "OK."

Your new WordArt will appear. Along with it—when selected—you have a new WordArt ribbon (Figure W-17). The WordArt ribbon includes additional options for formatting your WordArt, including a "WordArt Shape" ⬛ Change Shape ▾ tool that allows you to shoe-horn your WordArt into pre-defined geometric shapes (Figure W-18). Some of these might be fun on a garage sale or golf tournament flyer, but we won't use them in our crime bulletin.

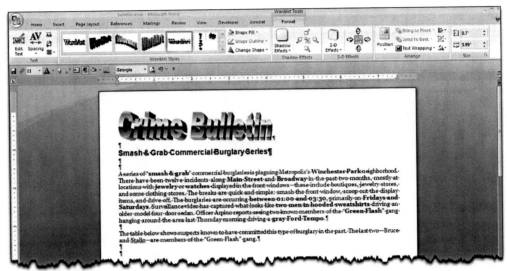

Figure W-17: WordArt and the WordArt ribbon

Figure W-18: some of the interesting but wholly unnecessary shapes possible with the "WordArt Shapes" button

Inserting Images

Word's desktop extensive desktop publishing capabilities allow it to incorporate almost every conceivable image format, and to make several advanced edits to images. Images can be copied and pasted into Word from almost any other application, including those posted in the Internet. In our case, we're going to insert one from a file.

»**Step 1:** Click in a blank paragraph beneath your new WordArt. Choose **Insert | Illustrations | Picture.**

»**Step 2:** Navigate to **C:\BPOffice\Word\policebadge.jpg** and "Insert."

A very small badge will appear in your document. When you double-click on it, the Picture Tools ribbon should automatically appear (Figure W-19).

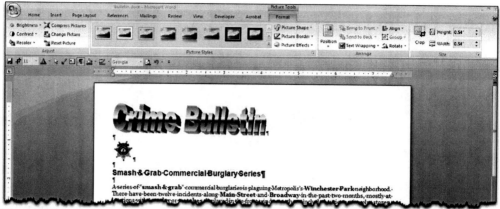

Figure W-19: a picture with the Picture Tools ribbon

The Picture Tools ribbon has some amazing options. You can adjust color, contrast, and brightness, crop and rotate the image, and give it a border and background color.

Figure W-20: to resize a picture, click and drag one of the "handles" in the corners

One of the most important options in editing pictures does not require the Picture Tools ribbon: resizing. To increase or decrease the size of the image, click on one of the "handles" in the corner (Figure W-20) and drag it in or out. (Don't use the handles on the top or sides—this will expand the picture vertically or horizontally and distort it. The corner handles make sure the picture "scales" properly.)

>**Step 3:** Drag one of the handles to expand the size of the badge until it is about the same height as the "C" in "Crime Bulletin."

There are some important options for how the picture appears in the document under **Picture Tools | Format | <u>Arrange</u> | Text Wrapping.** The options are "In line with text," "Square," "Tight," "Behind Text," "In Front of Text," "Top and bottom," and "Through." The most common options are "In line with text" and "Square."

In your bulletin, the text is currently "In line with text," which means that Word treats the image like a character in a very large font. "Square" allows the text to *wrap* around the image. You can see examples in this book. Figures W-17 and W-19 are in line with text: they occupy their own paragraphs. The "Bold" symbol **B** in this line is also in line with the text, which is why the line containing is a bit longer than the other lines in the paragraph—the image is the same size as a character in a 14-point font.

In contrast, Figures W-16 and W-29 are in "Square" mode, with the text wrapped around them. If we moved those pictures to other locations the document, the text would obediently straighten itself out in the old location, and wrap around it in the new location.

»Step 4: Select the badge image and choose **Picture Tools | Format | Arrange | Text Wrapping**. Choose "Square" (Figure W-21).

You should see an immediate change as the text (including any empty paragraphs) around the image change to wrapping around the badge.

»Step 5: Click on the badge and drag it to the top of the page, to appear at the left end of the "Crime Bulletin" title.

At the conclusion of this exercise, your bulletin should resemble Figure W-22. We will learn more about working with images in subsequent sections. It is important to note that the same properties that apply to images also apply to other types of

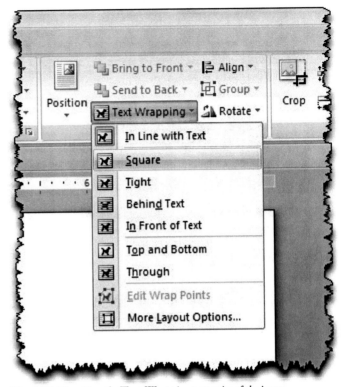

Figure W-21: setting the Text Wrapping properties of the image

objects in Word: charts, WordArt, drawing objects, and so on. All can be resized, cropped, wrapped, placed in line with text, given borders and background colors, and so on.

Figure W-22: your bulletin with a title and badge

Drawing Objects

Another entry in Word's arsenal of desktop publishing capabilities is the ability to add Drawing objects—lines, rectangles, circles, stars, arrows, callout boxes, and free-form drawings—to a document. All of them are accessible from **Insert | Illustrations**, and we'll use a few in these lessons.

»**Step 1:** Click on **Insert | Illustrations | Shapes**. Find the "Rectangle" shape ▭ , which is the second option under "Basic Shapes." Your cursor should change to a cross-hair. Click and drag a box around the badge and title at the top of your bulletin, all the way to the right margin.

The new box covers and blocks the title and badge. This is not a problem; we'll fix it in a moment.

»**Step 2:** Double-click your rectangle to get the "Drawing Tools" ribbon.

Note here the options in the **Shape Styles** group. "Shape Fill" ◊ Shape Fill ▾ refers to the color or pattern in the middle of the object—by default, it's white. "Shape Outline" ◙ Shape Outline ▾ refers to the border of the object—right now, it's a thin black.

»**Step 3:** Use Drawing **Tools | Format | Shape Styles |** ◊ Shape Fill ▾ to give the object a light blue background.

»**Step 4:** Use ◙ Shape Outline ▾ to give the image a dark (we chose dark red) border with a weight of 1½.

»**Step 5:** With the rectangle still selected, choose **Drawing Tools | Format | Arrange |** ☒ Text Wrapping ▾ **| Behind Text**

Your image now appears *under* the badge and title, giving your bulletin a nice heading. Only one problem remains—the ugly white background to the badge image. We can fix this by making the white color *transparent* in the image.

»**Step 6:** Click on the badge picture.

»**Step 7:** Choose **Picture Tools | Format | Adjust |** ✎ Recolor ▾ **| Set Transparent Color.**

»**Step 8:** Click anywhere on the white background of the badge image.

The white background becomes transparent, and we end up with a pretty good looking header if we do say so ourselves (Figure W-23).

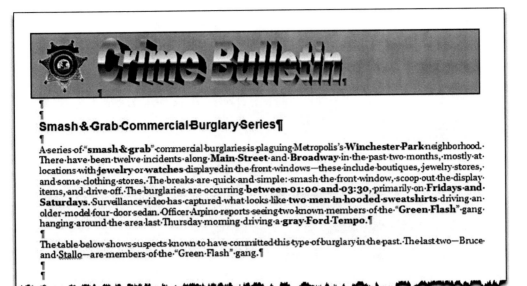

Figure W-23: your bulletin now has an attractive header

Text Boxes

We end up with some blank space to the right of the header in which we can put some additional information about our bulletin. We want to add some text which "floats" to the right of the "Crime Bulletin" title. To accomplish this, we need a *text box*.

Text boxes are essentially text that Word treats (for some purposes) like a picture: you can drag it around and position it, give it a border and background, and choose to wrap other text around it.

»Step 1: **Choose Insert | Text | Text Box | Draw Text Box.** Your cursor changes to a crosshair.

»Step 2: Click and drag to draw a small box in the right end of the header.

The default text box has a white fill and a black border. We can deal with that in a second. First:

Figure W-24: inserting and typing in a text box

»Step 3: Click in the text box and type "Created by the Crime Analysis Unit," **ENTER**, and "999-555-1212," ENTER, and "For law enforcement use only!" Your words may extend beyond the boundaries of the box. That's okay.

»Step 4: Select the text box by clicking on its border. Use the **Home | Font** to change the text to 9-point Georgia Georgia ▾ 9 ▾ . Use **Home | Paragraph | Justify** ☰ to give it a centered alignment.

»Step 5: With the text box still selected, choose **Text Box Tools | Format | Text Box Styles |** Shape Fill ▾ to give the box a transparent fill ("No Fill"). Use Shape Outline ▾ to give it no border ("No Outline").

Figure W-25: our completed header

We note once again that there are multiple ways to accomplish the same thing in any Office application. To create the exact same look as the header above, we could have inserted a three-column one-row table, given it a light blue fill and a thick border around it, inserted the badge in the first column ("In line with text"), the WordArt in the second, and the text in the third, and sized the columns. If you prefer working with tables, this might have been a better option. Again, there's no "right" way to accomplish a task.

Tables

Tables have always been an easy-to-understand way to present records. As Word has improved from version to version, tables have only gotten better. With the current version's ability to split and merge cells, you can create a highly compartmentalized layout for your information

The basic use of tables is to arrange data or information elements side-by-side, as we do below with photos and information about possible suspects in our series.

»Step 1: Click a couple of paragraphs below the commercial burglary story.

»Step 2: Choose **Insert | Tables | Table**.

»Step 3: Drag across four columns and two rows and click (Figure W-26).

A new table will appear on the screen, with thin black lines around the cells. We're going to insert information into this table. The top row will contain photographs, and the bottom will contain information to go with the photographs.

>**Step 4:** Click in the first cell in the first row and choose **Insert | Illustrations | Picture**.

>**Step 5:** Navigate to **C:\BPOffice\Word\MacDougal.jpg** and choose "Insert."

>**Step 6:** Repeat the process in the second cell with **C:\BPOffice\Word\Caldwell.jpg** and in the third cell with **C:\BPOffice\Word\Bruce.jpg**.

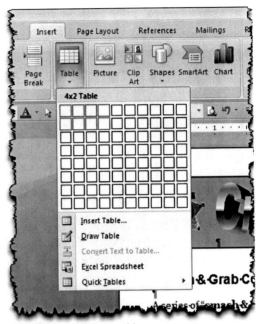

Figure W-26: inserting a table.

Whoops! The Bruce picture is pretty big, isn't it? And it shows much more of our subject than we need to see.

>**Step 7:** Click on the Bruce photograph and choose **Picture Tools | Format | Size | Crop**. Thick black lines appear on the sides and corners of the picture. Click and move them to reduce the picture to just the head and chest of the subject. When finished, click off the photo to remove the "Crop" action, then click on it again and re-size it to fit the size of the other images.

>**Step 8:** Repeat Steps 6 and 7 with the **C:\BPOffice\Word\Stallo.jpg** image

Figure W-27: with "crop" selected, the regular handles in the corners and sides of the photograph change to cropping handles.

>**Step 9:** In the second row, under the photos, type the attributes shown in Figure W-32. Then select the table by clicking on the table selector in its upper left-hand corner (⊞) and change the font to 10-point Georgia, centered. Select each of the names and **bold** them.

| Robert·MacDougal¶
DOB·07/12/1930¶
1505·Teg·Down·Meads¶
Edinburgh,·Scotland¤ | Linus·Caldwell¶
DOB·03/10/1970¶
2157·Lake·Shore·Dr¶
Chicago,·IL¤ | Christopher·W.·Bruce¶
DOB·02/12/1973¶
120·Ash·Street¶
Danvers,·MA¤ | Mark·A.·Stallo¶
DOB·09/18/1962¶
1005·South·Hollow¶
Southlake,·TX¤ |

Figure W-28: our four nefarious burglars, cropped and positioned in the table, with their names and data

»Step 10: With the table selected, choose **Table Tools | Design |** ⊞ Borders ▾ and click on the "Borders" tab. By default, the "All" setting is selected, meaning there are borders around each cell.

»Step 11: Use the diagram on the right of this screen to click off the horizontal borders, leaving only the vertical borders between columns (Figure W-29). Then click "OK."

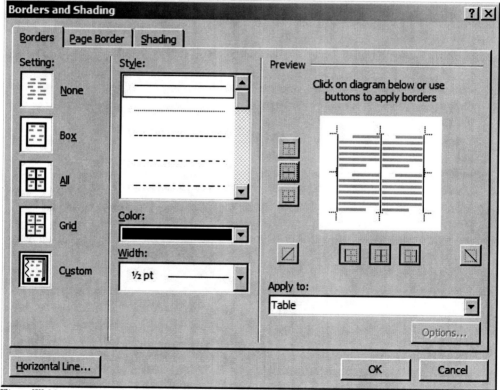

Figure W-29: you can use the "Borders" diagram to click and specify exactly where you want your borders. We're applying this to the entire table, but you can do it for a single column, row, or cell as well.

The end result will look like Figure W-30. Note that there is a light blue dashed gridline running horizontally at the top and bottom of the table and between the rows. This is only Word's way of telling us where the table's borders are—these dotted lines do not print (check out Print Preview).

Figure W-30: our table, formatted and centered, with the horizontal borders removed

Inserting a Database

Word will allow us to insert records from a database into our document. We can create a query within the database and insert the results of the query, or we can design the query within Word to pull out the records that we want. However, the tool that we need to do so is one of the few tools not contained in the ribbon. We need to add it to the Quick Access Toolbar.

Depending on your own preferences, you may have left the Quick Access Toolbar above the ribbon, or you may have moved it below the ribbon (Figure W-31). You may have retained the default tools, or you may have added tools of your own. Although it "fits" better above the ribbon, we usually put it beneath the ribbon to make it easier to access.

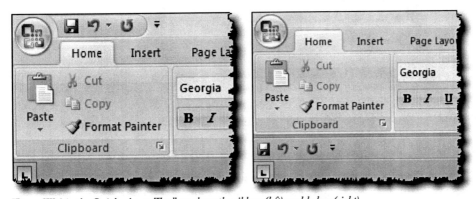

Figure W-31: the Quick Access Toolbar above the ribbon (left) and below (right).

»**Step 1:** Click the drop-down arrow to the right of the Quick Access Toolbar, whatever its position. (At this point, you might want to choose either "Show Above Ribbon" or "Show Below Ribbon" to move it.) Choose "More Commands."

In the dialog box that follows (Figure W-32), you can specify which commands that you want to see on the Quick Access Toolbar. We'll leave you to adjust this as you desire, but for the purposes of this lesson:

»**Step 2:** In the drop-down menu under "Choose Commands From," select "Commands Not in the Ribbon." Scroll down until you find "Insert Database." Select it and click the "Add" button. Then click "OK."

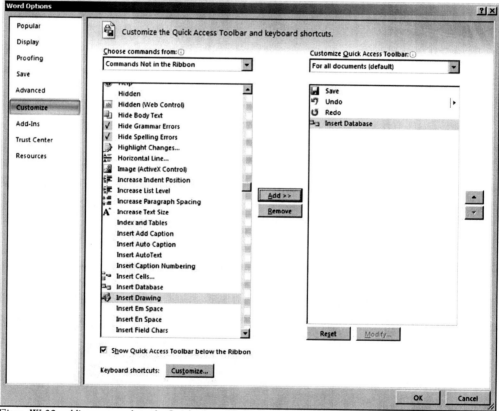

Figure W-32: adding commands to the Quick Access Toolbar.

The "Insert Database" tool ⬛ should now be in your Quick Access Toolbar.

»**Step 3:** Click a couple of paragraphs below our table of photographs

»**Step 4:** Click the "Insert Database" tool ⬛ on the Quick Access Toolbar.

»Step 5: Click the "Get Data" button.

»Step 6: At the bottom of the screen, change "Files of type" to "Microsoft Access 2007 Database." Navigate to **C:\BPOffice\Access\RMS.accdb** and click "Open."

»Step 7: Click "Query Options."

On the tabs in the "Query Options" dialog, we tell Word what records and what fields to bring over from the database, and how to format the result. We only want commercial burglaries that occurred at jewelry stores after July 1, 2005, which we signify with the querying properties in Figure W-33. Figure W-34 shows how to sort the data, and in Figure W-35, we see how to specify what fields we want.

»Step 8: Use Figures W-33, W-34, and W-35 to set the options, then click "OK."

»Step 9: Click "Insert Data."

The final option is crucial. Make sure you check the box that reads "Insert Data as Field" (Figure W-36). This will establish a link to the original data source—a link that we can refresh simply by typing **F9**. That means as new records are added to the series in the database, we can easily add them to our Word bulletin.

The resulting table isn't formatted very well. No problem:

»Step 10: Select the table and use the Formatting toolbar to set the font to 8-point  Georgia 8 . Bold the top row (with the field names).

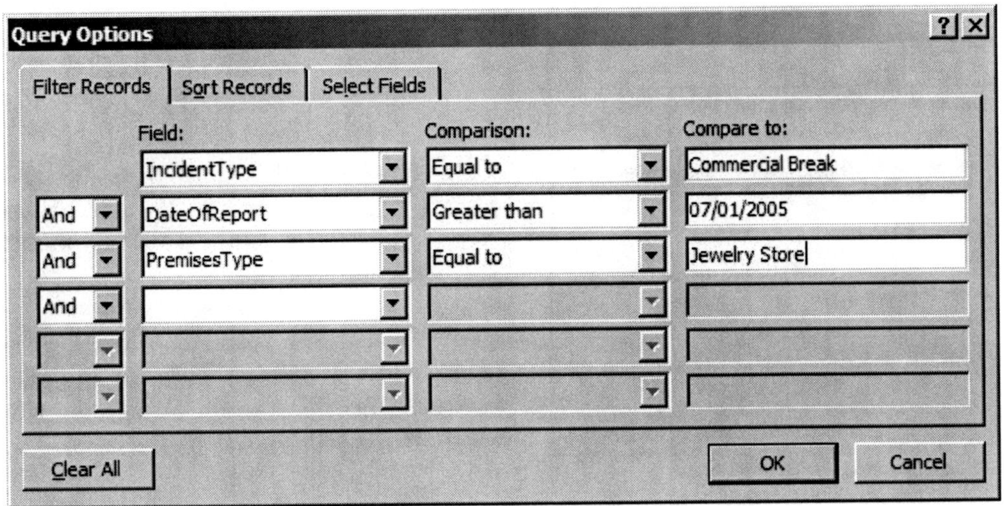

Figure W-33: specifying what records to insert from our database

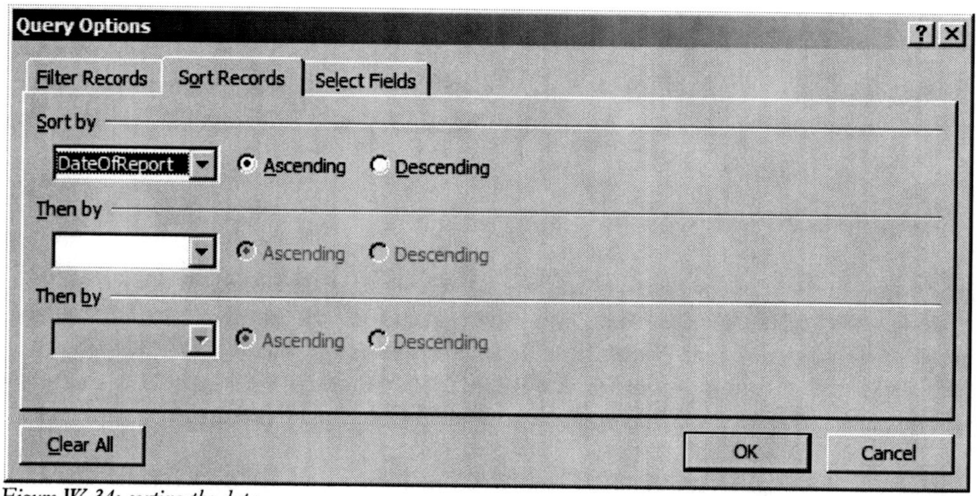

Figure W-34: sorting the data

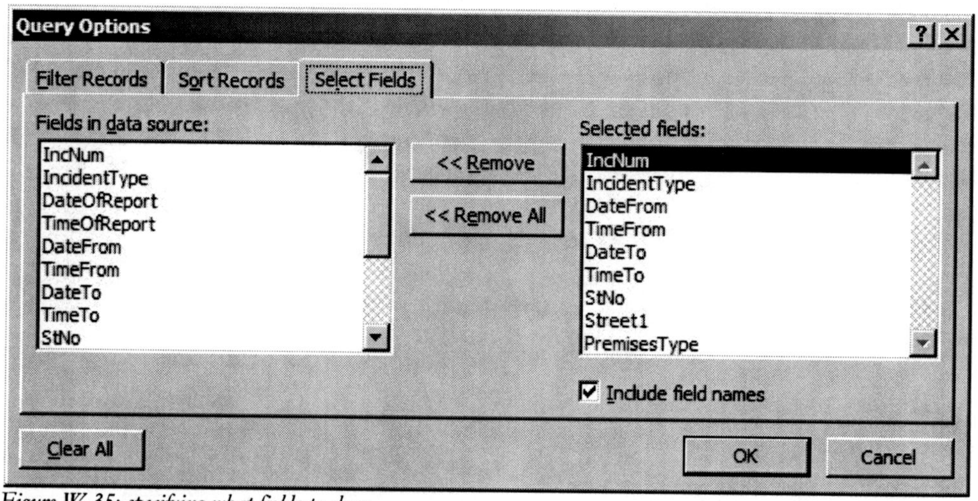

Figure W-35: specifying what fields to show

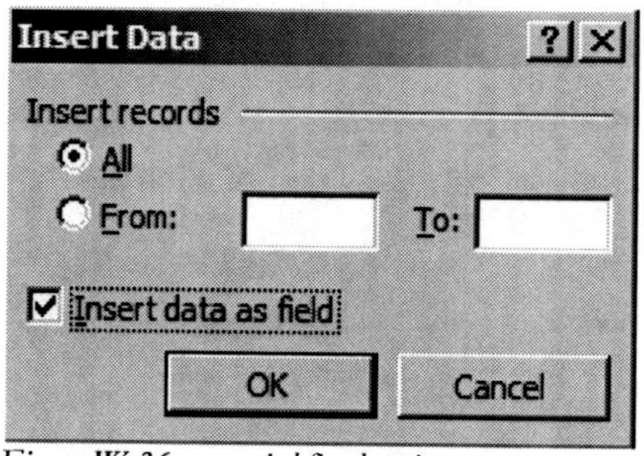

Figure W-36: a crucial final option

»Step 11: Select the table with the table selector (⊕). Right-click on the selector and choose **AutoFit | AutoFit to Contents**. Now it should fit on one page.

»Step 12: With the table still selected, go to **Table Tools | Design | Table Styles | Borders.** Use the diagram to give the table horizontal borders but not vertical ones.

»Step 13: A couple of paragraphs above the table, add a title: "Incidents in the Series." Make it Arial, 12-point, bold.

Figure W-37 shows the results of the table work, and Figure W-38 shows the bulletin at this point in Print Preview. It's shaping up quite handsomely.

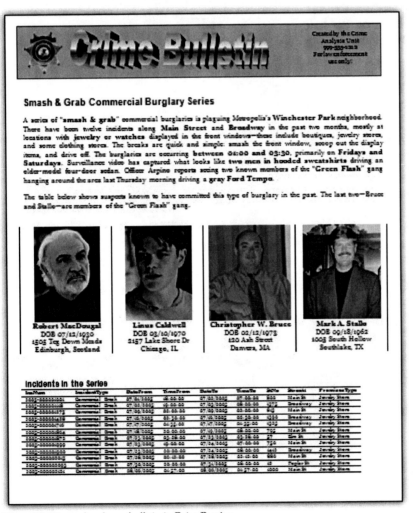

Incidents·in·the·Series¶

IncNum¤	IncidentType¤	DateFrom¤	TimeFrom¤	DateTo¤	TimeTo¤	StNo¤	Street¤	PremisesType¤	¤
2005-000001001¤	Commercial·Break¤	7/1/2005¤	18:00:00¤	7/2/2005¤	07:00:00¤	800¤	Main·St¤	Jewelry·Store¤	¤
2005-000001118¤	Commercial·Break¤	7/2/2005¤	19:00:00¤	7/3/2005¤	08:00:00¤	1375¤	Broadway¤	Jewelry·Store¤	¤
2005-000001275¤	Commercial·Break¤	7/9/2005¤	02:00:00¤	7/9/2005¤	02:00:00¤	815¤	Main·St¤	Jewelry·Store¤	¤
2005-000001426¤	Commercial·Break¤	7/16/2005¤	02:30:00¤	7/16/2005¤	02:30:00¤	1390¤	Broadway¤	Jewelry·Store¤	¤
2005-000001710¤	Commercial·Break¤	7/17/2005¤	01:35:00¤	7/17/2005¤	01:35:00¤	1325¤	Broadway¤	Jewelry·Store¤	¤
2005-000001864¤	Commercial·Break¤	7/18/2005¤	20:00:00¤	7/19/2005¤	08:00:00¤	795¤	Main·St¤	Jewelry·Store¤	¤
2005-000001872¤	Commercial·Break¤	7/23/2005¤	03:28:00¤	7/23/2005¤	03:28:00¤	57¤	Elm·St¤	Jewelry·Store¤	¤
2005-000001900¤	Commercial·Break¤	7/23/2005¤	20:00:00¤	7/24/2005¤	08:00:00¤	1412¤	Broadway¤	Jewelry·Store¤	¤
2005-000001999¤	Commercial·Break¤	7/23/2005¤	19:00:00¤	7/24/2005¤	07:00:00¤	750¤	Main·St¤	Jewelry·Store¤	¤
2005-000002015¤	Commercial·Break¤	7/28/2005¤	02:12:00¤	7/28/2005¤	02:12:00¤	880¤	Main·St¤	Jewelry·Store¤	¤
2005-000002098¤	Commercial·Break¤	7/30/2005¤	20:00:00¤	7/31/2005¤	08:00:00¤	12¤	Poplar·St¤	Jewelry·Store¤	¤
2005-000002121¤	Commercial·Break¤	8/6/2005¤	01:57:00¤	8/6/2005¤	01:57:00¤	1000¤	Main·St¤	Jewelry·Store¤	¤

Figure W-37: the result of all our work on the inserted database table

Figure W-38: our handsome bulletin in Print Preview

Section Breaks and Landscape Formatting

What our bulletin lacks most at this point is a map of the series. Assume for the purposes of this exercise that we have recently created such a map in ArcGIS or MapInfo. The map is quite large, and in a landscape orientation. We want it to take up the full second page, which we therefore also want to put in landscape orientation.

To combine two orientations in a single document, we have to insert a *section break* in between the portrait pages and the landscape pages. All of the options under the **Page Layout** tab and in a few other locations can apply to individual sections as well as to the document as a whole. Section breaks are how we delineate these various sections.

»**Step 1:** Add a few carriage returns (**ENTER**) after the table of incidents on the first page. It's okay if they go on to a second page.

»**Step 2:** Click in a paragraph after the table—but still on the first page—and choose **Page Layout | Page Setup | Breaks ▾**, and choose "Next Page" under "Section Breaks" (Figure W-39).

A line will appear indicating a section break, and if a second page did not already exist, it will now be forced.

»**Step 3:** Click within the second section (on the second page) and choose **Page Layout | Page Setup | Orientation | Landscape.**

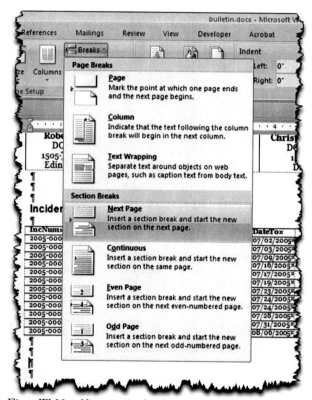

Figure W-39: adding a section break

Now that we have a second page in landscape orientation (Figure W-40), conditions are right for inserting our map.

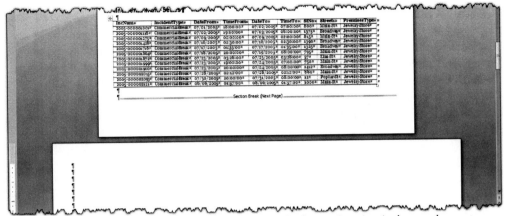

Figure W-40: with a section break, we can combine portrait and landscape orientations in the same document

»**Step 4:** Click within the second page and choose **Insert | Illustrations | Picture**. Navigate to **C:\BPOffice\Word\burglarymap.bmp** and "Insert" it.

»**Step 5:** Select the image and center it on the page with **Home | Paragraph | Center** ≣.

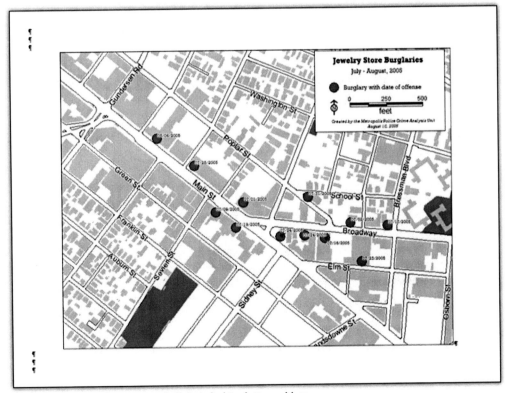

Figure W-41: now with a map, our bulletin is looking better and better

Callout Boxes

Callout boxes are a special type of drawing object that allow us to "point" to parts of an image and annotate them. These are extremely useful when you insert a map into a bulletin and want to call attention to various features on the map.

»**Step 1:** Click on **Insert | Illustrations | Shapes** and choose the second option under "Callouts" 💬 .

»**Step 2:** Point to anywhere on the map, click, and drag to draw the callout. It doesn't really matter where you position the callout at this point; you can adjust it later.

A callout box is like a text box with a pointer attached to it. In terms of formatting and setting text formats, it works exactly like a text box. But the pointer and the "text box" part of the callout can move independently of each other. To move the pointer, click the little yellow diamond and its end and drag it. To move the text box, click on the border of the box and drag it. To move both at the same time, click on the "trunk" leading from the text box to the pointer and drag it.

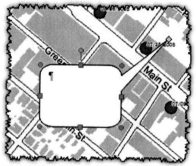

Figure W-42: a callout box on a map

»**Step 3:** Click within the callout box and type: "Two males in hooded sweatshirts fled this incident in a four-door sedan."

»**Step 4:** Click the border of the text box to select it, and use the tools at **Home | Font** to set the font to 9-point Georgia.

»**Step 5:** Resize the box as needed using the handles on the sides. Now drag the pointer to the incident on Main Street on 07/28/2005, and position the text box in a location where it does not obscure any of the incidents.

»**Step 6:** Repeat Steps 1-5 to add a second callout box pointing to the intersection of Elm Street and Main Street. Note in this box, "Officer Arpino saw two 'Green Flash' members hanging around this area."

Check Figure W-43 for an example of how your second page should now look. You will also find callout boxes in PowerPoint and Excel, and they are a great way to annotate maps, charts, graphs, photographs, and other representations of data.

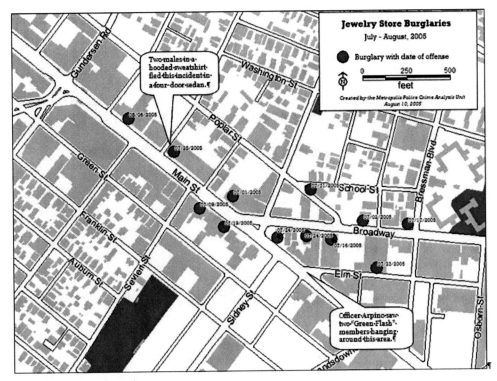

Figure W-43: your annotated map

Inserting an Excel Chart

The final element that we will add to our crime bulletin is a chart showing the distribution of offenses over the hour of the day. We will float it above the lower left-hand corner of the map, in which there are no incidents nor features of use to us.

The chart we will insert has been pre-created in Microsoft Excel, and it is called "Aoristic Distribution of Incidents by Hour." *Aoristic analysis* is a term coined by Jerry Ratcliffe that describes a method of "weighing" the likelihood that each incident occurred during a particular hour. Incidents that occurred in a "tighter" time frame receive more weight for each hour than incidents that are spread out over a long time frame. We have covered the theory of aoristic analysis in the Excel chapter, on Pages 188-192.

If you did not already have an Excel chart, you could create one directly in Microsoft Word by choosing **Insert | Illustrations | Chart.** This opens Excel *within* Word, creates a basic chart from sample data, which you can then edit to your design.

In our case, we have already created the chart in Excel, so we simply need to insert it.

»Step 1: Click at the bottom of the second page of the bulletin, in a blank paragraph.

»Step 2: Choose **Insert | Text | Object**.

»Step 3: Click on the "From File" tab and then click the "Browse" button. Navigate to **C:\BPOffice\Excel\aoristic.xls** and "Insert" it.

»Step 4: Check the box that reads "Link to file" and click "OK."

"Link to file" establishes a *live* link to the Excel workbook so that if data changes in the chart, the changes will be updated in the Word document that includes it.

The Excel chart appears, but on a new page and somewhat larger than we intended.

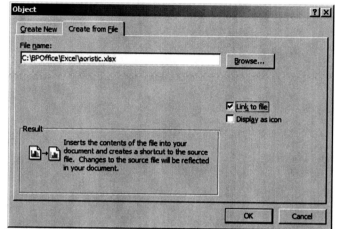

Figure W-44: inserting an Excel workbook into Word

»Step 5: Select the chart and use the handles in the corners to shrink it to a size small enough to fit into the lower left-hand corner of the map.

»Step 6: Right-click on the chart and choose "Format Object." On the "Colors and Lines" tab, give the object a white fill. On the "Layout" tab, position it "In front of text."

»Step 7: Click and drag the chart onto the lower left-hand corner of the map. Re-size it as necessary.

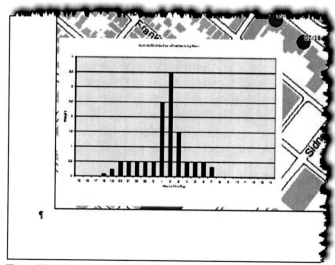

Figure W-45: your map with the Excel chart on top of it

The act of shrinking the chart made the chart title and the axis titles almost unreadable, but we can fix that by opening Excel within Word and making our edits.

»**Step 8:** Double-click on the chart to open Excel within Word.

»**Step 9:** Select the chart title and axis titles and increase the font to 14.

»**Step 10:** Save and close the chart. Then right-click on the chart in the Word document and choose "Update Link."

The chart titles in your Word document should now be more readable. Figure W-46 shows the entire page.

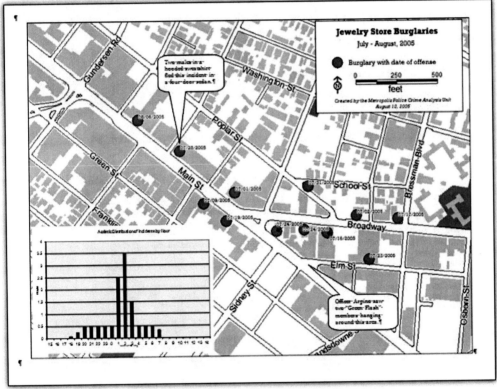

Figure W-46: the final second page, with the map, callout boxes, and a chart

Columns

Some writers prefer text in two columns. There is nothing inherently better about a two-column format except that it sometimes makes for more interesting page layout. We will change our single-column paragraphs on the first page to a double-column format.

»Step 1: Return to the first page of the bulletin. Select all the text in the two paragraphs, starting with "A series of…" and ending with "…members of the 'Green Flash' gang."

»Step 2: Choose **Page Layout | Page Setup | Columns | More Columns**. Enter 2 in the "Number of columns" box, and check the box that says "Line between" (Figure W-47). Then click "OK."

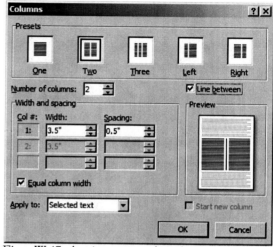

Columns are set section-by-section, so to accommodate your request, Word inserts section breaks at the beginning and end of the paragraphs of text. The sections above and below remain in single-column format, while the text switches to two-column (Figure W-48).

Figure W-47: changing to a two-column format

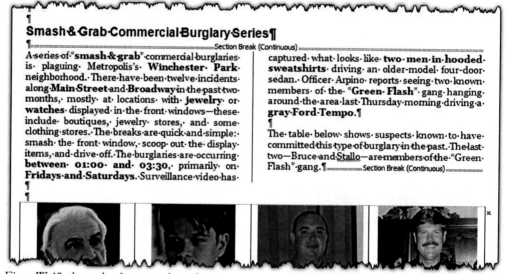

Figure W-48: the results of our two-column change

You can manually insert section breaks, then change the number of columns by choosing **Page Layout | Page Setup | Columns** *without* selecting anything first. But it's usually easier to type the text first, then set the number of columns and allow Word to insert the section breaks.

The end result of all of this work is a pretty decent-looking bulletin, shown in Print Preview view in Figure W-49. Make sure you save your bulletin before closing it.

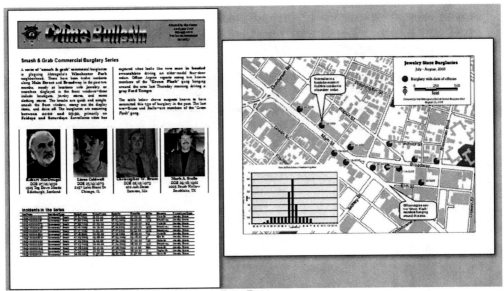

Figure W-49: our final two-page crime bulletin in Print Preview

Templates and Forms

In this section, we look at how a police agency can increase its efficiency through the use of form templates. As we noted in the introduction, most of the paper forms used by police departments could easily be converted to Word templates, allowing for quicker completion and dissemination than hand-written pieces of paper. And unlike paper, Word forms can be saved on the computer and changed at a later date.

A *template* is a special type of Word document saved as a "document template" or .dotx file. When you double-click on a template, or choose it from **Office Button | New**, you create a new Word document based on the template. The template itself remains unchanged in its original location.

Templates can be *protected* so that the only elements users can add or change are responses in form fields—the titles and the boilerplate text remain locked. This prevents a novice user from accidentally messing up the template with careless typing.

The template we'll create in this lesson is a "shift report," akin to those that many agencies require their shift commanders to submit at the end of a shift.

»**Step 1:** Close all open documents and start a new document in Word with **Office Button | New** (if you are re-launching Word after closing it, you don't have to do anything—you should have a new blank document before you).

»Step 2: Choose **Office Button | Save As**. At the bottom of the "Save As" screen, name the document "shiftreport" and make sure that you set the "Save as type" option to "Document Template (*.dotx)." Save the document in **C:\BPOffice\Word.** (Figure W-50).

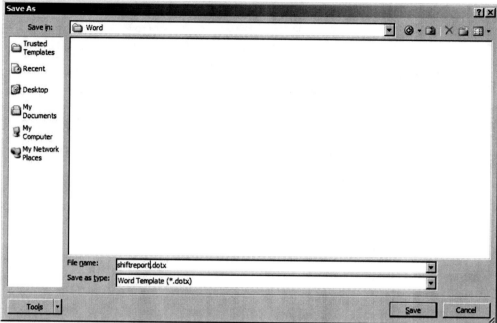

Figure W-50: saving the new document as a template

»Step 3: Enter a few blank paragraphs to give yourself some space to work. Then, at the top of the page, enter a title: "Shift Report." Make it Arial, 22-point, bold , and center it on the page . Use the keyboard shortcut **CTRL-SHIFT-K** to make the title SMALL CAPS.

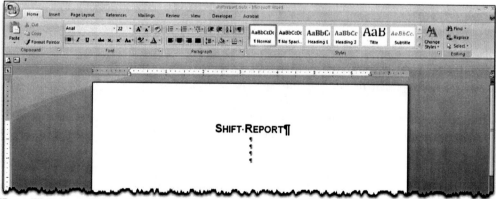

Figure W-51: the beginning of a new template

At this point, creating the template is a matter of typing the text we *always* want to appear interspersed with *fields* for text that will change each time the template is filled out. We can use tables (with our without borders) to align text and keep it in our desired layout.

Inserting fields is done from **Developer | Controls**, but we have to turn on the Developer tab before we can do anything else.

>**Step 4:** Choose **Office Button | Word Options**. Click "Popular" on the left and check the box that says "Show Developer Tab in Ribbon."

Creating a form for uses to fill out is a matter of choosing the correct control and inserting it in the form at the appropriate location. Your control options are:

Aa Rich-text field

Aa Regular text field

Picture

Combo box

Drop-down list*

Date picker

Building block gallery

Legacy tools: field types that existed in Word 2003

Figure W-52: the "Controls" section of the Developer tab

>**Step 5:** Leave a blank paragraph after the title. On the next line, type "Report of the "—here, insert a drop-down field 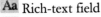—"shift on "—here, insert a date picker field .

>**Step 6:** On the next line, type "Submitted by **Aa** to **Aa**."

>**Step 7:** If not already, center both lines on the page (at **Home | Paragraph**). Make the text (and all the paragraphs that follow) your font choice—we're using 12-point Calibri.

As the user of the template enters information into these form fields, it will appear in the font and style that we select for the field at this point. We may want to **bold** all the entries in the fields to distinguish them from the text around them.

---

* The difference between a combo box and a drop-down list is that the combo box allows users to enter something not on the list while a drop-down list does not. Functionally, they are the same control.

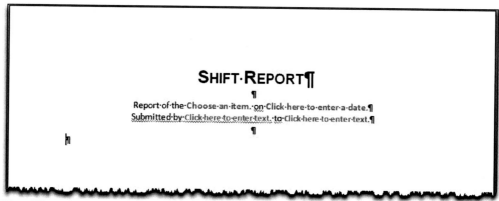

Figure W-53: the beginnings of a template, with several form fields

»Step 8: Select each of the form fields by clicking on them, then bold them with **B** or **CTRL-B**.

Each of the fields we enter in a template has a series of options, accessible from the "Properties" button [Properties] at **Developer | Controls**. These options include the default value (if any) and, for drop-down fields, the options that will appear in the drop-down list.

> **»Step 9:** Click in the first field (after "Report of the"), and click the "Properties" button.

> **»Step 10:** Add the options "Day," "First Half," and "Last Half" to the list by clicking "Add" and typing them in the box (Figure W-54).

The next step is to format the date field.

> **»Step 11:** Click on the control that reads "Click here to enter a date." Click **Developer | Controls | Properties.** Where it reads "Display the date like this," change it to the second option ("Weekday, month, day, year").

The last two text boxes we'll leave alone. We could have made them combo boxes and put in a list of all supervisors who

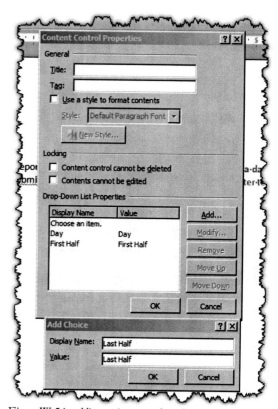

Figure W-54: adding options to a drop-down menu

might be reporting, as well as a list of all commanders they might be reporting to. But we would have to edit the template every time a promotion changed the command structure.

The rest of the page, the supervisor will use to comment on everything that happened during the shift. We need to make a break between the initial part of the template, and its form fields, and the latter part of the template, where free text is allowed.

»Step 12: Leave two blank paragraphs after the "Submitted by" line. Click in the third paragraph, making sure you have at least two or three more paragraph marks after this point (hit **ENTER** a few times if you don't). Choose **Page Layout | Page Setup | Breaks | Section Break | Continuous**.

»Step 13: Finally, we *protect* the first section of the document to allow changes only in the form fields themselves. Choose **Developer | Protect | Protect Document | Restrict Formatting and Editing**. A dialog box opens to the right.

»Step 14: Check the box under "Editing Restrictions" and allow only "Filling in Forms" for the document. Click on the little hyperlink beneath it that says "Select Sections" and select only Section 1. "OK" this box and then click "Yes, start enforcing protection." Enter no password and click "OK."

At this point, you will not be able to change any of the text under the "Shift Report" heading (try!). But you will be able to add text in Section 2.

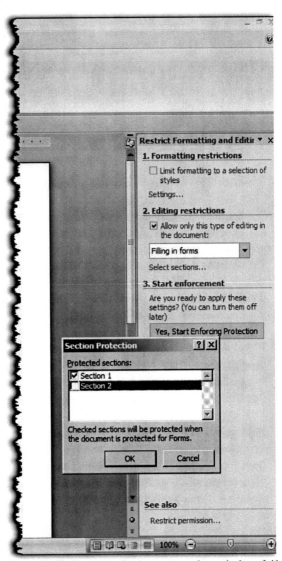

Figure W-55: protecting the document so that only form field entries can be made in Section 1.

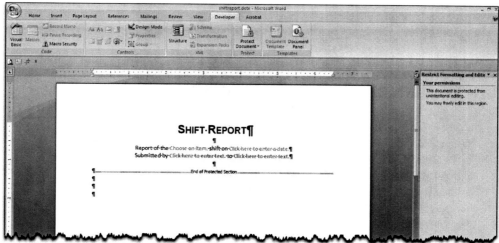

Figure W-56: the finished template

»**Step 15:** Save and close the template.

We can now do any number of things with this template, including creating a shortcut to it on our supervisors' desktops. But whether we double-click on the shortcut to open it, or use Windows Explorer or "My Computer" to find the original file in **C:\BPOffice\Word**, when we double-click on it, Word does not *open* the file, as it does with a regular Word document. Instead, it creates a copy of the template with a regular Word document extension (.docx). Thus, no matter what changes we make to the file, the original template remains unchanged.

If you do want to open the original template, to make changes to it, we must open Word, then choose **Office Button | Open**, change the "Files of type" to "document template," and go find it. We must also click "Stop Protection" at **Developer | Protect | Protect Document** if we want to make changes to the first section.

This lesson was a rather easy introduction to making templates. As Figure W-4 shows, templates can be much more complex and advanced, mimicking any paper form you may have. As Figure W-4 also shows, tables offer an excellent way to lay out templates. Sometimes, in fact, they are the only way. Most agencies' arrest reports and incident reports—if not already computerized—can be rendered into Word templates with skilled use of tables.

Advanced Pictures and Drawing Objects

In creating the crime bulletin, we explored the use of drawing objects, such as rectangles and circles, text boxes, and images. Together, these features can be used to create advanced images, diagrams, and layouts.

We present here a series of documents created by Sergeant Robert Newton of the Dallas Police Department for use in tactical planning and operations. They illustrate how a Word document and its drawing objects can accomplish the same things that special programs, costing tens of thousands of dollars, purport to do.

The first of them, Figure W-57, assists police called to the scene of a barricaded person. The operator can quickly draw the shape of the building, and then drag the unit numbers (represented by floating text boxes) around the building to represent their locations. The operator saves the document periodically (with a time stamp) so that later the incident, and the officers' actions, can be reconstructed.

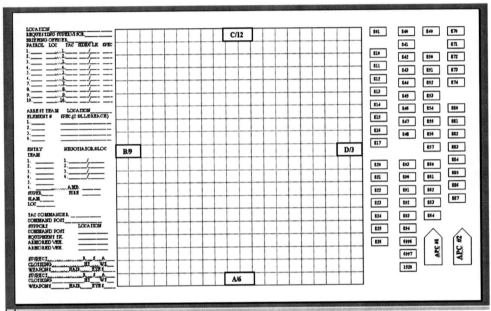

Figure W-57: the barricaded person tactical map. * *The operator can drag units from the right to show their locations. Fields on the left track crucial information about the incident, such as the officers' names, the negotiator, and equipment needed and at the scene.*

This tactical document can be combined with satellite imagery from online sources, including **www.maps.google.com**. The operator can find the location, switch to a "satellite" image, and use Windows's "print screen" option (**ALT-PRNT SCRN**) to capture the image. He can then paste it into the tactical map and use Word's cropping tools to reduce it to the appropriate size.

---

* All documents in this section are copyright Sergeant Robert Newton, Dallas Police.

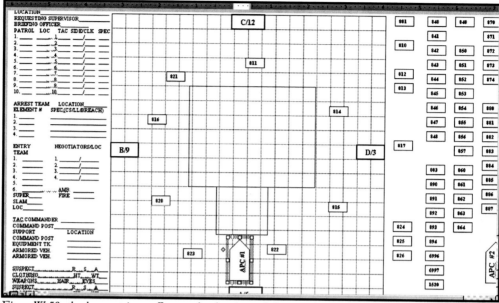

Figure W-58: the document in use. Rectangular drawing tools have produced a simple building, around which eight officers have been strategically placed. The tactical vehicle is preparing for a frontal assault on the complex.

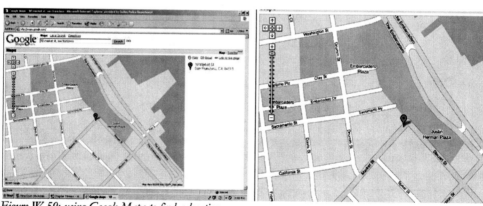

Figure W-59: using Google Maps to find a location

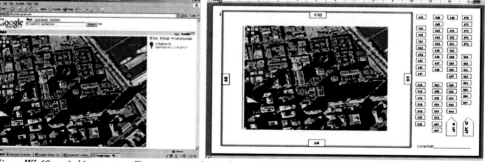

Figure W-60: switching to a satellite map, pasted into the tactical map document

The second example is similar to the "barricaded person" document, but it begins with a pre-drawn diagram of an airplane. This document is used to monitor a tactical situation involving a 737 aircraft. Like the barricaded person map, the operator can drag units around the aircraft and show their positions, and he can record pertinent information about the incident and its participants to the left.

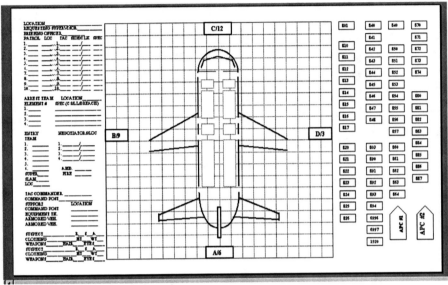

Figure W-61: the aircraft tactical template

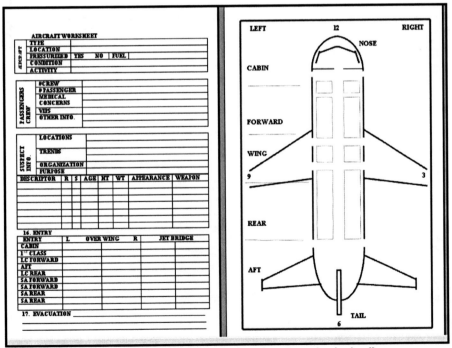

Figure W-62: a related form records all information about the actions taken by the officers

The final example from Sergeant Newton concerns some diagrams used to calculate distance, angle, wind speed, and other important factors for a sniper.

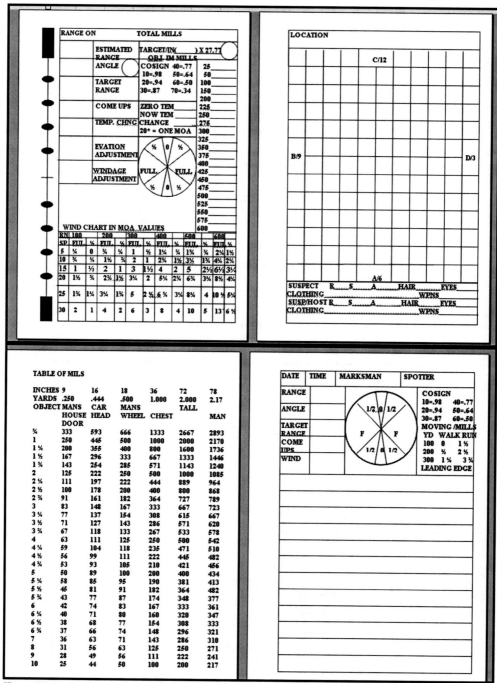

Figure W-63: documents to assist snipers in calculating key factors before making a shot

In the last example in this section, we see how drawing objects can supplement images and data from a geographic information system (GIS). With combinations of line and polygon objects, the analyst can create high-definition diagrams of buildings, a shopping mall, and apartment complex, a city service center, and so on. Such diagrams could serve useful in the depiction of a crime series, trend, or problem. For simply illustrating an area, a combination of Google maps and Word drawing tools can serve as well as a multi-thousand dollar GIS.

The example below diagrams a construction site. The darker buildings (orange, if you're viewing an electronic version of this book) are open, with material unsecured, and the lighter buildings (gray) are secured.

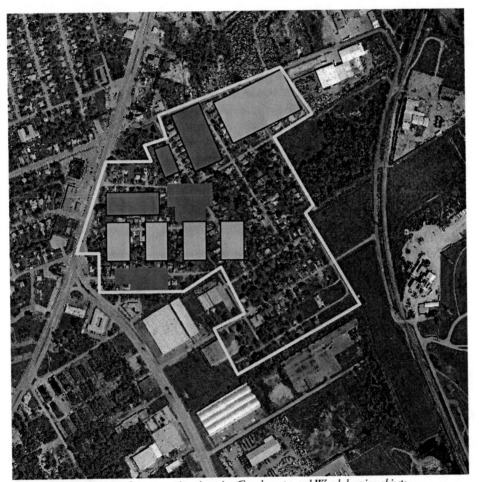

Figure W-64: a diagram of a construction site using Google maps and Word drawing objects

Labels and Mail Merge

Assume you have a letter to send to a thousand of your residents. Before modern Word processing applications, you had two options: manually type a thousand different names and addresses on a thousand different letters and envelopes, or send out a generic "Dear Resident" letter.

Word allows us two crucial time-saving operations: the ability to publish both mailing labels and multiple copies of letters based on a spreadsheet or database of names and addresses. In our example, we are preparing a letter to be sent to multiple offenders with active warrants,

We will begin by assuming that we have already written the letter; we just need to insert the appropriate variable fields and print it.

»**Step 1:** Open **C:\BPOffice\Word\warrantletter.docx**. Here we have a basic letter informing an offender about the existence of an arrest warrant. All that's missing is an address for the offender, the warrant and service numbers, and the information about the detective in the final paragraph.

»**Step 2:** Choose **Mailings | <u>Start Mail Merge</u> | Select Recipients | Use Existing List**.

»**Step 3:** In the dialog box that follows, navigate to **C:\BPOffice\Word\warrantnames.xlsx** and open it.

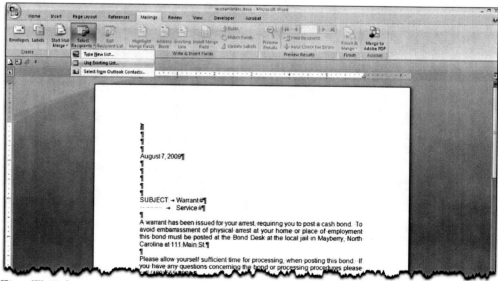

Figure W-65: Starting a mail merge

»Step 4: You should only have one table to select; just make sure that the option "First row of data contains column headers" is checked.

Nothing happens at first, but new options become available to us at **Mailings | Write & Insert Fields**, and the next step becomes possible.

»Step 5: Click on **Mailings | Start Mail Merge | Edit Recipient List**.

In the screen that comes up (Figure W-66), we are asked to select the recipients of our letter from the list. By default, all of them receive it (which is what we want). But we can un-check names that should not get it. To assist in this process, Word allows us to sort and filter our various columns. It also has a routine that automatically searches for possible duplicate names.

Mail Merge Recipients

This is the list of recipients that will be used in your merge. Use the options below to add to or change your list. Use the checkboxes to add or remove recipients from the merge. When your list is ready, click OK.

Data Source		Name	Address	City	State
warrantnames.xlsx	✔	Mary, Gilberto	801 Burnside Dr.	Smithville	North Carolina
warrantnames.xlsx	✔	Jones, Fred	10846 Mandalay	Jonesville	North Carolina
warrantnames.xlsx	✔	Hernandez, Susan	4884 Turtle Creek Blvd.	Jonesville	North Carolina
warrantnames.xlsx	✔	McKinney, Mark	1614 Tommy Court	Smithville	North Carolina
warrantnames.xlsx	✔	Ramirez, John	6100 Town and Ctry	Smithville	North Carolina
warrantnames.xlsx	✔	Ramos-Cordova	11610 N. Central Expy	Mayberry	North Carolina
warrantnames.xlsx	✔	Romo, Kim	4806 Ridgeline Drive	Mayberry	North Carolina
warrantnames.xlsx	✔	Aims, Stan	4140 Stag	Mayberry	North Carolina
warrantnames.xlsx	✔	Smith, Beth	9946 Appletree	Mayberry	North Carolina
warrantnames.xlsx	✔	Jerro, Ravinder	4449 Willow Ln.	Mayberry	North Carolina
warrantnames.xlsx	✔	Suey,Frederick	9868 Denton Dr	Mayberry	North Carolina
warrantnames.xlsx	✔	Mary, Walter	6860 Phoenix	Mayberry	North Carolina

Data Source

warrantnames.xlsx

Refine recipient list

- Sort...
- Filter...
- Find duplicates...
- Find recipient...
- Validate addresses...

Edit...   Refresh

OK

Figure W-66: selecting the recipients of the warrant letter

»Step 6: Click "OK" to send the letter to all the names.

At this point, if we did not already have a letter, we would write it in the blank document. Since we already have the letter written, we just need to insert the mail merge fields in the appropriate location.

»Step 7: Click a couple of paragraphs below the date on the letter, and click **Mailings | <u>Write & Insert Fields</u> | Insert Merge Field**. In the pop-up box that comes up (Figure W-67), choose "Name."

»Step 8: Click in the paragraph below the new «Name» entry in the letter, and repeat Step 7 to add "Address," then again to add "City," "State," and "Zip" on one line. Manually type a comma-space between "City" and "State" and a space between "State" and "Zip." When finished, the header of your letter should look like Figure W-68.

»Step 9: Repeat Step 67 to add the "Warrant Num," and "Service" after the indicated locations in the letter's header, and the "Detective" name and "Phone" after the indicated locations in the letter's final paragraph.

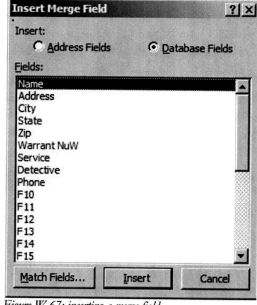

Figure W-67: inserting a merge field

»Step 10: Click on **Mailings | <u>Preview Results</u> | Preview Results** to see what your warrant letters will look like. Word will insert the merge fields from the first record. Make any changes you need and save and close the document.

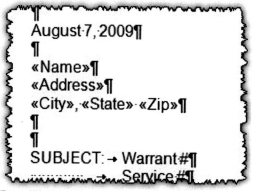

Figure W-68: the letter header, with our fields inserted

To actually print the letters, we would use **Mailings | <u>Finish</u> | Finish & Merge**, but you probably don't want to do that. If you did, you have options to:

- Create individual documents for each letter
- Print letters for each record
- Send letters for each record by e-mail.

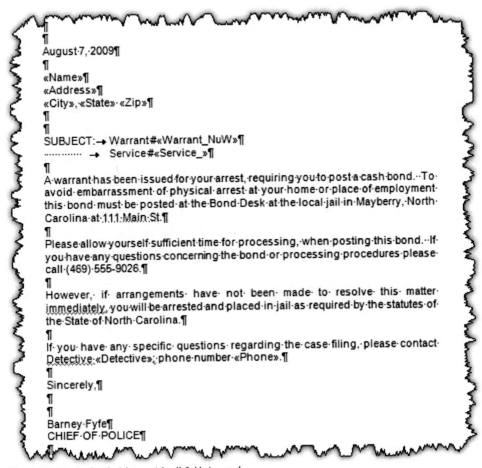

¶
August·7,·2009¶
¶
«Name»¶
«Address»¶
«City»,·«State»·«Zip»¶
¶
¶
SUBJECT:→ Warrant#«Warrant_NuW»¶
············ → Service#«Service_»¶
¶
A·warrant·has·been·issued·for·your·arrest,·requiring·you·to·post·a·cash·bond.··To·
avoid·embarrassment·of·physical·arrest·at·your·home·or·place·of·employment·
this·bond·must·be·posted·at·the·Bond·Desk·at·the·local·jail·in·Mayberry,·North·
Carolina·at·111·Main·St.¶
¶
Please·allow·yourself·sufficient·time·for·processing,·when·posting·this·bond.··If·
you·have·any·questions·concerning·the·bond·or·processing·procedures·please·
call·(469)·555-9026.¶
¶
However,· if· arrangements· have· not· been· made· to· resolve· this· matter·
immediately,·you·will·be·arrested·and·placed·in·jail·as·required·by·the·statutes·of·
the·State·of·North·Carolina.¶
¶
If·you·have·any·specific·questions·regarding·the·case·filing,·please·contact·
Detective·«Detective»;·phone·number·«Phone».¶
¶
Sincerely,¶
¶
¶
Barney·Fyfe¶
CHIEF·OF·POLICE¶

Figure W-69: the finished letter with all fields inserted

Labels

The same basic process allows us to also produce envelopes and mailing labels from a list of names. There are different options when we produce labels, and the most crucial, shown in Figure W-70, is what type of label we have. No matter where you buy your perforated, pre-glued mailing labels, somewhere on the packaging should be a manufacturer's name and code that corresponds with the prepared list in Word.

»**Step 11:** Open a new document in Word (**Office Button | New | Blank Document**).

»**Step 12:** Click **Mailings | Start Mail Merge | Labels**.

»**Step 13:** In the "Label Options" dialog (Figure W-70), chose Avery 8162.

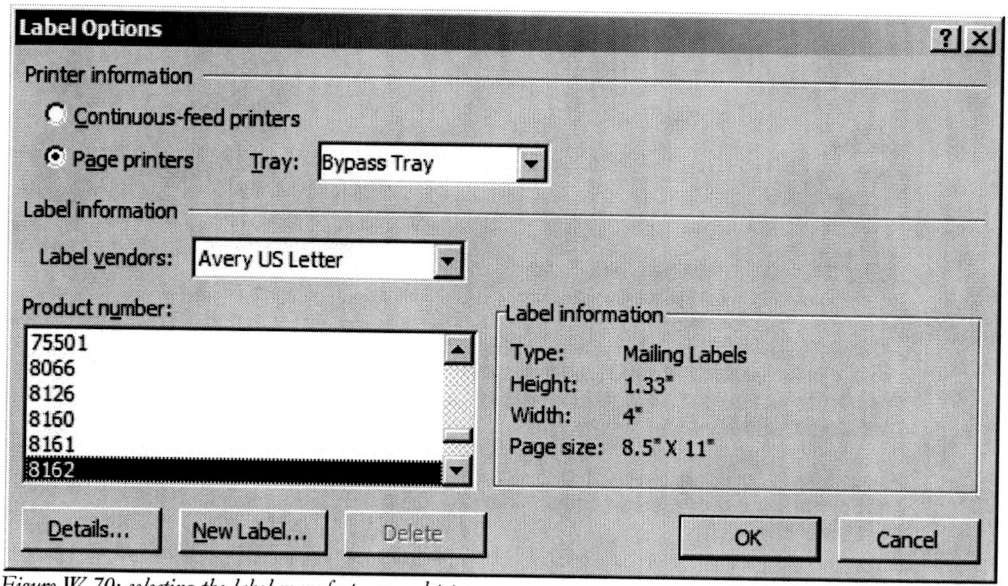

Figure W-70: selecting the label manufacturer and type

A page of blank labels appears. Just as with the letter, we need to select our data source.

> **»Step 14:** Click **Mailings | <u>Start Mail Merge</u> | Select Recipients | Use Existing List**. Navigate to **C:\BPOffice\Word\warrantletters.xlsx**. Choose the sheet and click "OK."

We only need to set up the mailing in the first label. Word will automatically apply what we set up here to all the other labels with the «Next Record» annotation.

> **»Step 15:** Use **Mailings | <u>Write & Insert Fields</u> | Insert Merge Field** to set up the first label as in Figure W-71. Select the label fields and go to **Home | Font** to make them Arial, 14-point fonts, bolded.

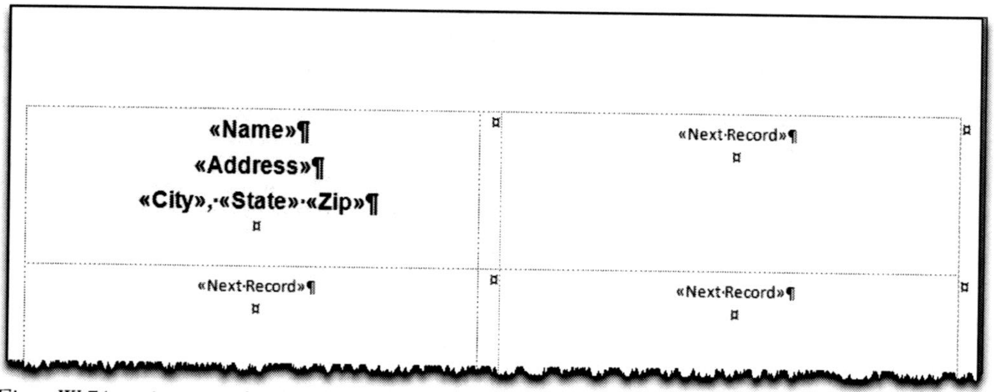

Figure W-71: setting up mailing labels

»**Step 16:** Use **Mailings | <u>Preview Results</u> | Preview Results** to see what the labels will look like. It's a little misleading because it shows all but the first label as blank, which will not be the case.

Again, if we were going to print them for real, we would then choose **Mailings | <u>Finish</u> | Finish & Merge.** You probably don't want to waste your paper, though.

To create envelopes and labels *without* a mail merge, we simply choose **Mailings | <u>Create</u> | Envelopes** or **Labels**. Here, we can print a single envelope or a single sheet of labels, but we must manually type in the information.

In Office 2007, Word includes the option to automatically print postage on envelopes, provided that you have electronic postage software and an account with a provider like Stamps.com.

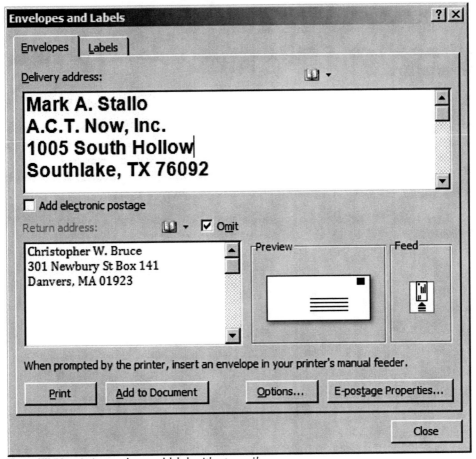

Figure W-72: printing envelopes and labels without a mail merge

Taking it to the Next Level

Microsoft Word has come a long way, from its origins as a simple "word processor" to its modern-day incarnation as a full desktop publishing and document production program, able to accommodate just about any design and layout that the user demands. Its uses in policing are legion: crime bulletins, posters, alerts, annual reports, flyers, community notifications, tactical mapping, and many, many more. We hope that these lessons have opened your eyes to the enormous potential of this program.

Here are some topics to explore to move beyond the lessons in this book:

- Use **styles** to quickly apply formatting changes to large parts of your document at a single pass.

- There are so many options available in **"Find and Replace"** that many crime analysts use Microsoft Word to help clean data.

- Investigate the different diagramming options under **Insert | <u>Illustrations</u> | SmartArt**.

- Try out the different **shapes** available under **Insert | <u>Illustrations</u>**.

- Especially if you are a current or future student, explore the **References** tab to see how Word helps with footnotes, endnotes, citations, and captions. Word can automatically convert your sources, citations, and references between APA, MLA, Chicago, and other styles. If you are writing a book, the options at **References | <u>Index</u>** will allow you to create and manage a detailed index.

- Like Excel, Word supports **macros** and Visual Basic for Applications (VBA) code.

CHAPTER 4

Microsoft PowerPoint

PowerPoint is the world's premier presentation software. Within this software are a variety of tools that assist presenters in enhancing an idea or delivering it in such a manner that leaves its intended impression on the audience.

PowerPoint is a natural outgrowth of "slide shows" (using slide projectors) and projected overhead transparencies—expensive and time-consuming options in the pre-PowerPoint era. Today, it is uncommon to attend a seminar, lecture, or conference and *not* see a PowerPoint presentation.

But while PowerPoint presentations may be common, *good* PowerPoint presentations are still rare. When used properly, PowerPoint can greatly enhance a presentation; when used improperly, PowerPoint can cripple it. Some common PowerPoint "sins" include:

- Too much text crammed on the slide
- Presenter reading the slide instead of facing the audience
- Animation and sound overload
- Too many slides
- Poor choice of colors, fonts, and backgrounds

We hope that the lessons in this chapter will help you create *good* PowerPoint presentations. We include some references to further reading on presentations in general.

Before we begin the lessons, let's take a look at a few presentation examples. Figure P-1 shows a title slide from a presentation given by one of the authors at the Massachusetts Association of Crime Analysts conference in 2009. Figure P-2 is an example of combining text and images on a slide to illustrate a point.

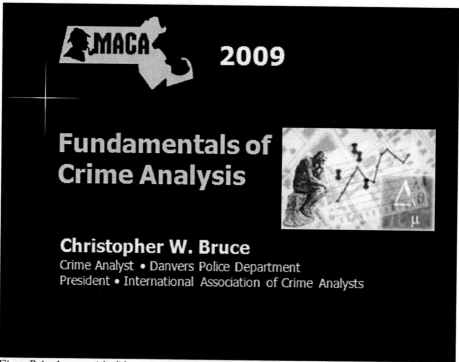

Figure P-1: A strong title slide can get your presentation to a great start

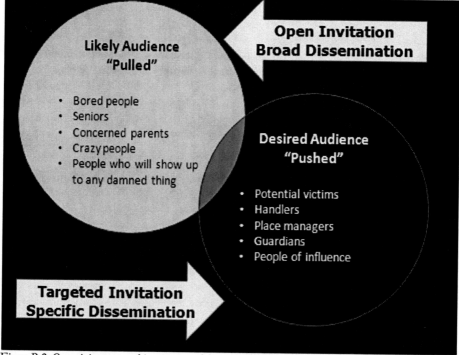

Figure P-2: Organizing text and images on a slide can be a fine art

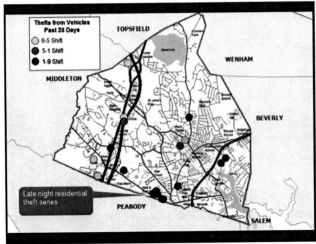

Figure P-3: a slide from COMPSTAT meeting

In Figure P-3, we see how crime mapping can be incorporated in a PowerPoint presentation to powerful effect—suitable for discussion in a COMPSTAT meeting or similar forum.

Finally, Figure P-4 illustrates how animation can bring in elements one at a time, as the presenter chooses to explain them.

1. Speaker: "Routine Activities Theory posits that when a motivated offender…"

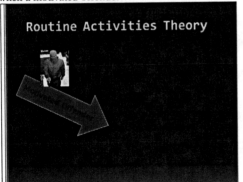

2. "…encounters a suitable target…"

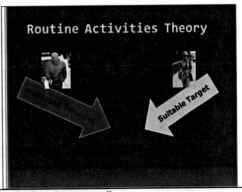

3. "…at a time and place with an absence of capable guardianship…"

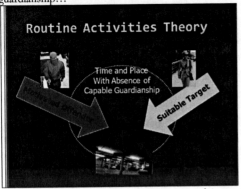

4. "…the crime occurs."

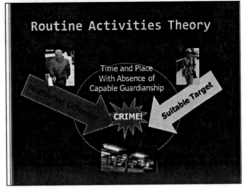

Figure P-4: examples of slide animation to explain a point

What's New in PowerPoint 2007?

These are the significant new features of PowerPoint 2007:

- As with all of the Office 2007 applications, Microsoft has replaced menus and toolbars with the "ribbon" interface at the top of the screen.

- The new file format (.pptx) is an XML format that reduces file size and has certain other advantages over the old .ppt format. PowerPoint supports backwards compatibility, however, and you can still save your files in PowerPoint 2003 format or earlier

- As with Word 2007, PowerPoint 2007 uses Excel (rather than Microsoft Graph) to create and manage charts. Therefore, full Excel charting functionality is present in PowerPoint.

- PowerPoint 2007 offers new and improved effects, themes, layouts, and formatting options, including galleries of pre-defined "Quick Styles," layouts, and table formats.

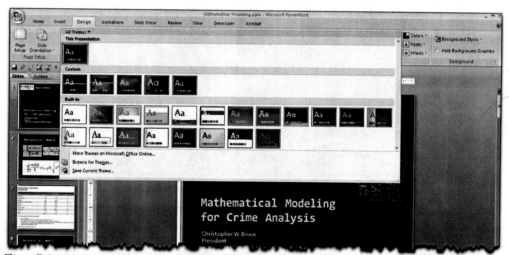

Figure P-5: rather than limiting you to a series of cheesy "presentation templates," PowerPoint 2007 allows you to fine-tune the overall themes and styles of the presentation.

- When you switch from one theme to another in your presentations, PowerPoint does a better job of adjusting the background, text, graphics, charts, and tables on each slide to reflect the new theme. New graphics, tables, charts, WordArt, and other features do a better job of matching the theme when you insert them.

- The "Master" view has been greatly expanded so you can create custom layouts with placeholders for different slide topics.

- Effect options for graphics, WordArt, and charts have been expanded to allow three-dimensions, shading, reflections, and glows. A new "SmartArt" option works the same way it does in Word, allowing you to insert pre-formatted flowcharts, diagrams, and other designs.

- You can "publish" slides that you want to use again and again to a "Slide Library" allowing quick creation of a new presentation from existing slides. The presentation *links* to the Slide Library, meaning that when you update slides in the library, all presentations that use those slides will be updated.

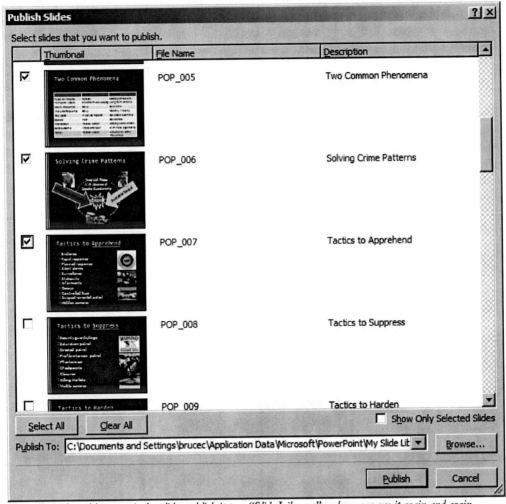

Figure P-6: if you like a particular slide, publish it to a "Slide Library," and you can use it again and again.

Creating a Presentation

Creating a PowerPoint presentation is similar to creating a Word document: you can just open the application and start typing, or you can start by choosing a template.

>**Step 1:** Launch Microsoft PowerPoint 🔲. A blank presentation automatically appears, with no design formatting.

We know one presenter who always uses blank white slides, but most prefer to add some panache to their presentations. PowerPoint comes with a number of themes installed, and more can be found at **www.microsoft.com**, by searching **www.google.com**, or by creating your own. We'll apply one of PowerPoint's existing themes. We can do it from **Design | Themes**, but you actually get more options this way:

>**Step 2:** Choose **Office Button | New**.

The "New Presentation" dialog (Figure W-7) has a number of options for determining the overall look and feel of your presentation. "Installed Templates" and "Installed Themes" will let you choose from a handful of pre-existing templates and themes (the two are similar, except that templates contain multiple slides and the themes just set the background and font styles. "My Templates" pulls templates from the "Templates" directory on your computer. "New From Existing" will create a brand new presentation using the same styles as another presentation on your computer. Finally, you can download templates and themes in different categories from "Microsoft Office Online."

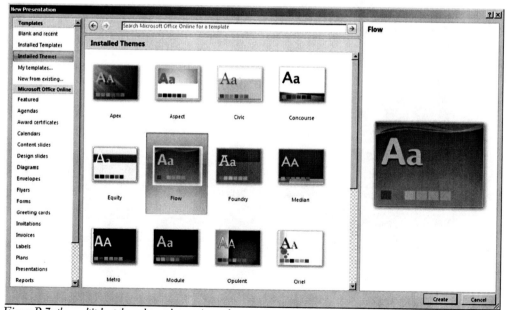

Figure P-7: the multiple style and template options when creating a new presentation

»**Step 3:** Choose any of the templates or themes that you prefer. If you want your presentation to look like the book lessons, click on "Installed Themes" and then the "Flow" template. Then click "Create." Your blank presentation will change to one with the theme applied.

Step 4: Click where it says "Click to add title" and type "2009 Crime Trends."

Step 5: Click where it says "Click to add subtitle" and type "Presented by the Crime Analysis Unit."

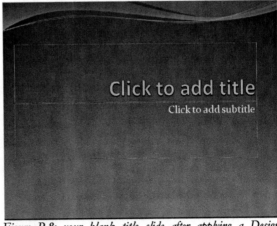

Figure P-8: your blank title slide after applying a Design Template

The default text, font style, and color are set by the theme. If you want to change them, you need to select the text and use the options at **Home | Font** and **Home | Paragraph**.

Step 6: Select your "2009 Crime Trends" text and change the color to a dark red at **Home | Font | Font Color** (A). Left-justify the "2009 Crime Trends" title at **Home | Paragraph | Align Text Left** ( )

Figure P-9: your finished title slide

Both the title and the subtitle are contained in text boxes that can be adjusted in size and moved within the slide. To move a box, place your cursor on its edge until you get a crosshair. Then click and drag the box to any location. To resize a text box, click on one of the "handles" on the sides or corners.

Proceeding through the rest of your presentation is a simple matter of adding new slides, typing in text, and inserting images, charts, graphs, and other visual aids.

Step 7: Click **Home | Slides | New Slide**.

The default "Title and Content" slide appears, but it is not the only option that we have for a slide layout.

Step 8: Click **Home | <u>Slides</u> | Layout.**

The drop-down menu (Figure P-10) offers nine different slide layouts:

- **Title Slide**, for the beginning of your presentation

- **Section Header**, like a title slide, but for sub-sections of your presentation

- **Title and Content**, the default style and the one you will use most often for any slide with a heading and text, graphics, charts, tables, or media below

- **Two Content**, like Title and Content, but with the content arranged in two columns

- **Comparison**, identical to Two Content, but with a separate title above each content

- **Title Only**, which allows you to use most of the slide to draw or add your own content

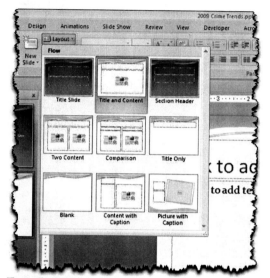

Figure P-10: different slide layout options

- **Content with Caption**, ideal for content with some explanatory text next to it.

- **Picture with Caption**, a stylized slide for a photo with a small title and text next to it

- **Blank**, a blank slide (except for images and colors defined by the theme)

These text and content layouts define the way a slide looks when you first start to put things into it. You are not, however, constricted by these layouts—after choosing one, you're free to add, delete, and move elements. If you don't like any of the pre-defined layouts, you can always use Title Only or Blank layouts and add your own material. Most users, however, will use Title and Content for most of the slides.

»Step 9: Click through the other text and content layouts to see what they look like, but finish by returning to the "Title and Content."

»Step 10: Click where it says "Click to add title" and type "Summary and Highlights."

The box on the lower half of the screen allows you to simply click and start adding text *or* to click one of the little object images in the center and add a table, a chart, a graphic, a picture, clip art, or a media (sound or video) clip. We will use all of them at some point.

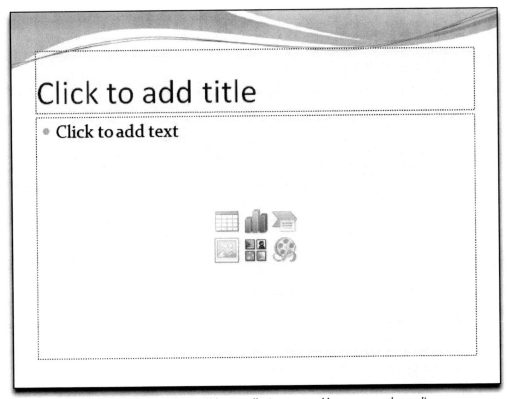

Figure P-11: the standard "Title and Content" layout, allowing you to add text or any other media

Step 11: Where the slide reads "Click to add text," type the following bullet points, hitting **ENTER** after each:

- Most crimes are average
- Rape is at its lowest level in five years
- Robbery is slightly high
- Arson is at its highest level in five years
- Other crimes are normal

When finished, your slide should look like Figure P-12.

On the next slide, we'll add some crime data from an Excel chart showing crime statistics

Step 12: Choose **Home | <u>Slides</u> | New Slide** again.

Step 13: On the new slide, go to **Home | <u>Slides</u> | Layout** and set the layout to "Title Only"

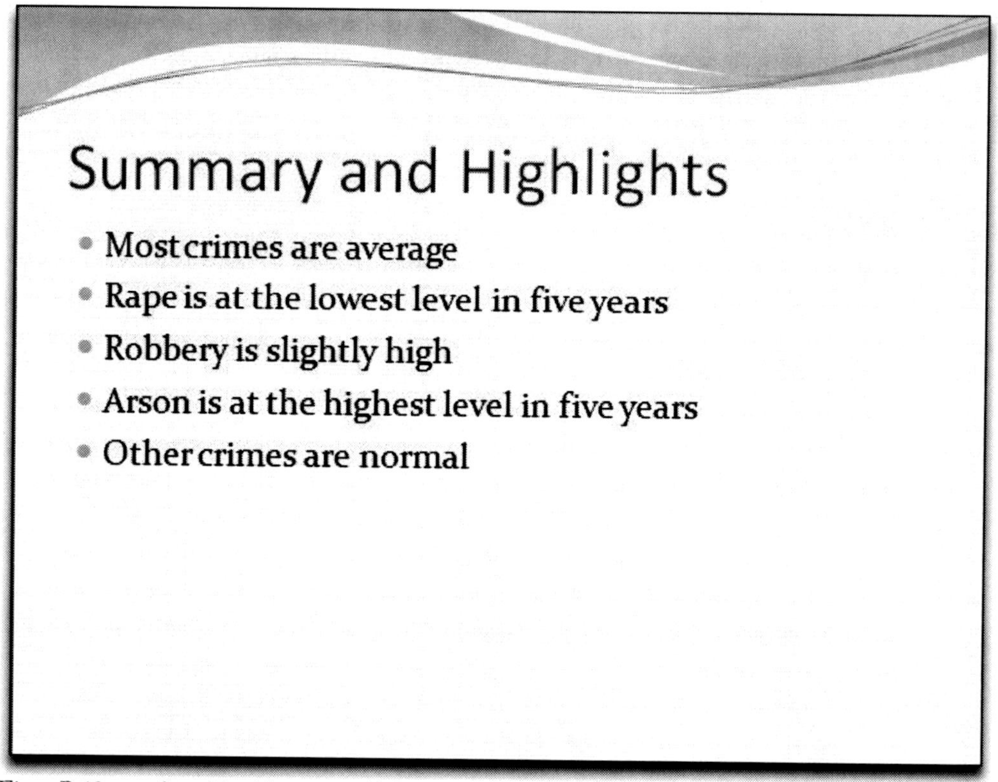
Summary and Highlights
Most crimes are average
Rape is at the lowest level in five years
Robbery is slightly high
Arson is at the highest level in five years
Other crimes are normal

Figure P-12: your first slide with content added

Step 14: Type the title as "2005-2009 Crime Statistics"

Step 15: Launch Excel and **Office Button | Open** the file at **C:\BPOffice\PowerPoint\crimestats.xls**.

2005-2009 Crime Statistics

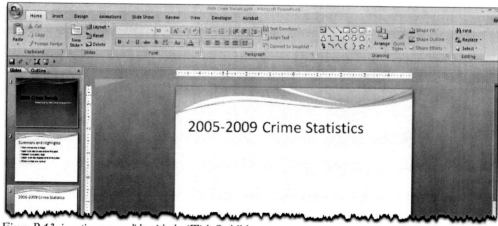

Figure P-13: inserting a new slide with the "Title Only" layout

Step 16: Select the statistics (Cells A2:F11). Choose **Home | Styles | Format as Table** and apply the "Medium 3" style to the cells (Figure P-12). Turn off the filters by going to **Data | Sort & Filter | Filter**.

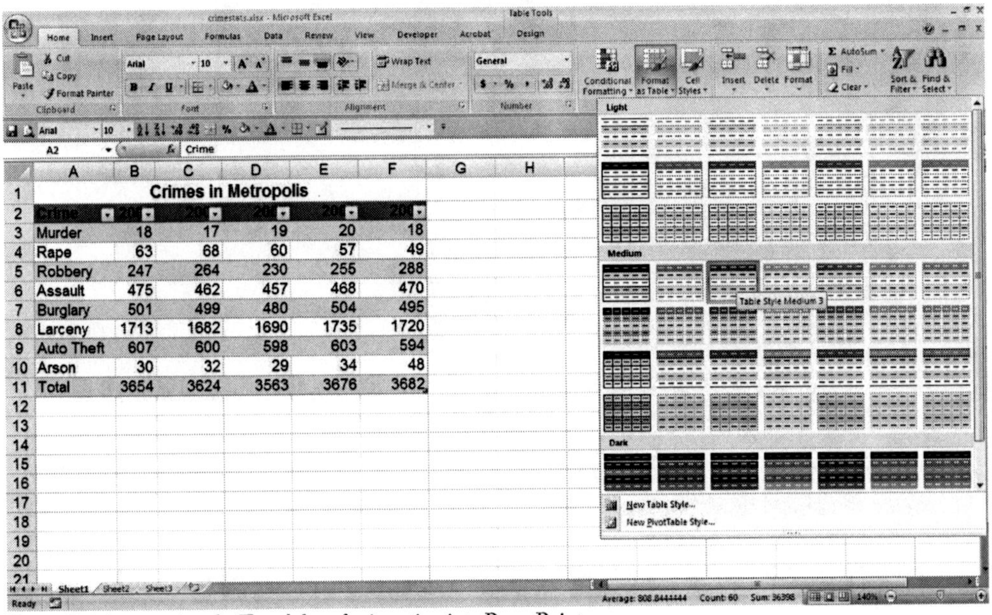

Figure P-14: preparing the Excel data for insertion into PowerPoint

Step 17: With the Excel cells selected, choose **Home | Clipboard | Copy**. Return to the third slide in your PowerPoint presentation and choose **Home | Clipboard | Paste** (click the arrow at the bottom) **| Paste Special**.

As we saw in the Word lessons, there are several options available with "Paste Special." The default is "Microsoft Office Excel Worksheet Object"—this is what PowerPoint would have chosen if you had simply used "Paste" instead of "Paste Special." In this case, PowerPoint would store the pasted number as an Excel workbook, embedded in the presentation. Even if you were to delete the original Excel file and close the presentation, you could later double-click on the table, PowerPoint would launch Excel *within* PowerPoint, and you could change the numbers.

Other options include the ability to paste the data as a picture (useful if you want to later resize it as a whole) and as various types of text.

We're going to use an altogether different option: "Paste Link." By clicking on this radial button (see Figure P-15), Excel pastes the data as a link to the original spreadsheet. If the data in the spreadsheet changes, so will the data on our PowerPoint slide.

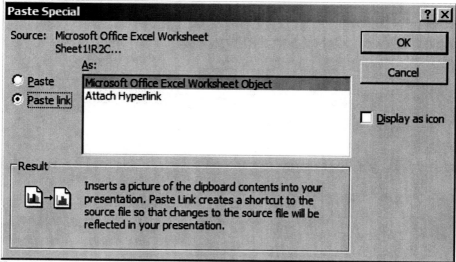

Figure P-15: pasting the Excel data as a link to the original spreadsheet

Step 18: Select the "Paste Link" option and click "OK." Afterwards, you can close the Excel workbook. Save the changes that you made.

Step 19: The resulting image in PowerPoint is quite small. Click on it and use the handles in the corners to expand its size.

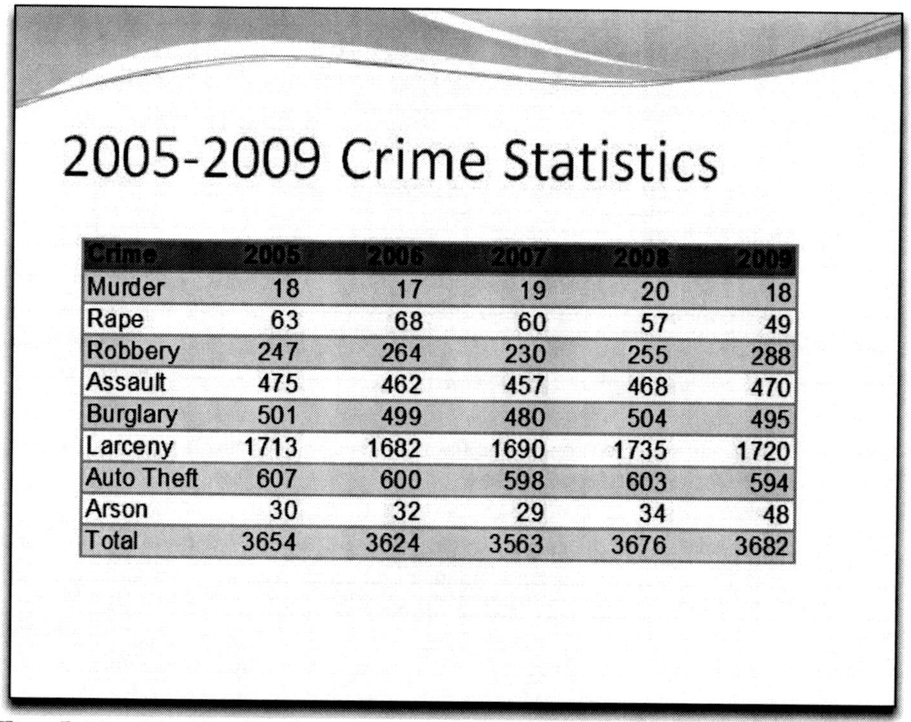

2005-2009 Crime Statistics

Crime	2005	2006	2007	2008	2009
Murder	18	17	19	20	18
Rape	63	68	60	57	49
Robbery	247	264	230	255	288
Assault	475	462	457	468	470
Burglary	501	499	480	504	495
Larceny	1713	1682	1690	1735	1720
Auto Theft	607	600	598	603	594
Arson	30	32	29	34	48
Total	3654	3624	3563	3676	3682

Figure P-16: a slide with an Excel spreadsheet embedded in it

With this data pasted as a link, we can change it or its formatting at any time by double-clicking on the table in the PowerPoint slide. This will cause the original file to open in Excel. At this point, we're going to return to Excel create a chart.

Step 20: Double-click on the crime data table in your PowerPoint slide. The **crimestats.xls** spreadsheet should open.

Step 21: Select Cells A2:A10, hold down the **CTRL** key, and select Cells E2:F10 (the crime names and all the numbers for 2008 and 2009.

Step 22: Choose **Insert | Charts | Column** and pick the first option. Move the chart so that it does not cover any of the data. Choose **Chart Tools | Layout | Labels | Chart Title | Above Chart**, give it the title "Crimes in 2008 and 2009" and click "Finish." Re-size the chart and use your knowledge from the Excel exercises to change the font and colors to your preferences.

Step 23: Select the chart. Choose **Home | Clipboard | Copy**. Return to PowerPoint and choose **Home | Slides | New Slide**. At **Home | Slides | Layout**, select the "Blank" content layout and use **Home | Clipboard | Paste | Paste Special** to paste the chart as a link. Re-size it to fill the slide.

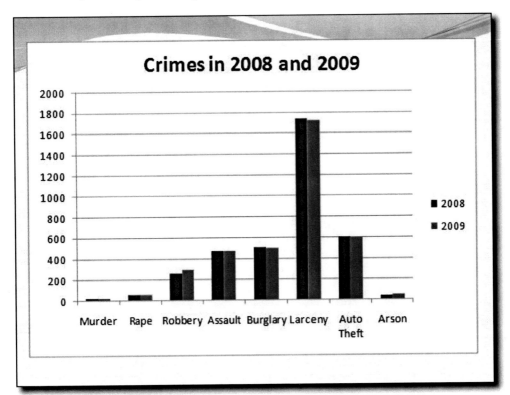

Figure P-17: a new chart slide for your presentation

Step 24: Save and close the Excel spreadsheet. Then save your PowerPoint presentation as **C:\BPOffice\PowerPoint\2009CrimeTrends.pptx**.

Creating a Chart in PowerPoint

In previous versions of PowerPoint, it made a difference whether you created the chart in Excel or in PowerPoint—specifically, you could animate charts created in PowerPoint but not in Excel. With PowerPoint 2007, there is no difference, and PowerPoint in fact uses Excel as its chart maker. Nonetheless, it's a good idea to see how to create a chart directly from PowerPoint, in case you don't want to store a separate Excel file.

Step 1: Choose **Home | Slides | New Slide** to add fifth slide to your presentation. At **Home | Slides | Layout**, apply the "Title and Content" layout. Click where it says "Click to add title" and type "Increase in Robberies."

Step 2: In the content area, click on the chart icon, in the middle of the top row.

Step 3: PowerPoint asks you what type of chart you want to create. Choose a column chart, first option.

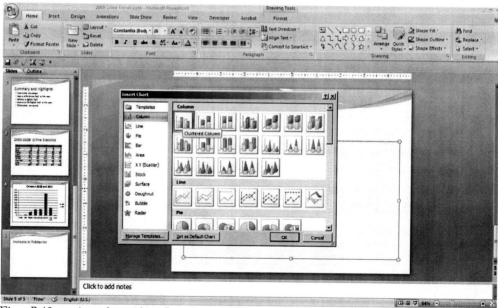

Figure P-18: creating a chart within a PowerPoint slide

At this point, PowerPoint opens up Excel so you can type the data for the chart. Note that the title of the Excel workbook is "Chart in Microsoft Office PowerPoint"; the data you type here will be embedded within your presentation, not stored as a separate file.

Step 4: Fill in the chart data as in Figure P-19. As you do so, delete or type over the instruction that says "To resize chart data range, drag lower right corner of range"; more on that below. Do not delete Column D ("Series 3"), even though we will not be using it.

You tell PowerPoint what part of the data to chart by dragging the corner of the thin blue box that surrounds some of the data.

Step 5: Click the handle in the bottom-right corner of the thin blue box and drag the box so that it covers cells A1 through C13.

	A	B	C	D	E	F	G
1		Average	2009	Series 3			
2	Jan	26	24	2			
3	Feb	28	22	2			
4	Mar	21	20	3			
5	Apr	18	18	5			
6	May	15	16				
7	Jun	20	18				
8	Jul	13	15				
9	Aug	12	18				
10	Sep	17	29				
11	Oct	21	32				
12	Nov	26	35				
13	Dec	32	41				
14							
15							
16							
17							

Figure P-19: typing in the robbery data for your PowerPoint chart

You do not delete any of the sample data in the spreadsheet. Type over it if you want to use that space, but do not delete it. Otherwise, Excel will constantly give you an error message. Microsoft has confirmed that this is a problem but has not fixed it yet.

At this point, if you wanted to save this spreadsheet for permanent use, you could so at **Office Button | Save As**. But to use it in PowerPoint, you don't even need to save it; you just close it. However, one confusing aspect of PowerPoint using Excel for its charting is that if you have another Excel spreadsheet open on your computer, when you close your PowerPoint-based spreadsheet, instead of returning to PowerPoint, Windows will take you to your other Excel spreadsheet. You will have to return to PowerPoint manually at this point.

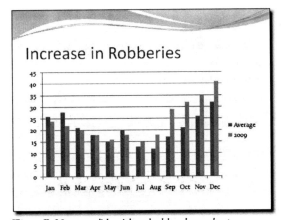

Figure P-20: your slide with a double column chart

Step 6: Close the spreadsheet and return to your PowerPoint presentation. You should have a double column chart (Figure P-20).

Step 7: Right-click on one of the bars, in any month, representing the average (i.e., the first set). Choose "Change Series Chart Type" and choose an area chart. Modify the colors and fonts of the chart using the options at **Home | Font** and **Chart Tools | Format | Shape Styles**. When finished, your chart should look similar to Figure P-21.

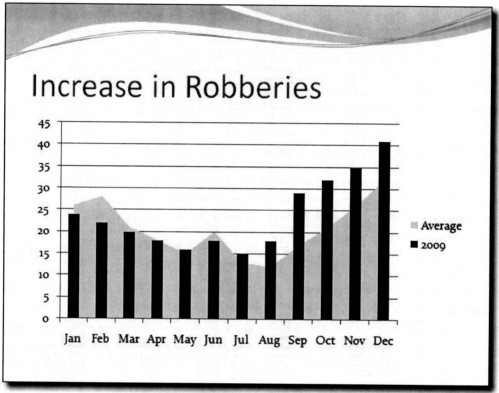

Figure P-21: the chart we just created in PowerPoint. It clearly shows that the robbery increase started in later summer and got worse in the fall

Slides with Tables

Data arranged in tabular format looks just as good on a slide as it does in a printed report. Previous versions of PowerPoint used Word's table tools to embed a Word table, but modern versions have their own table-creation abilities.

Step 1: Choose **Home | Slides New Slide** to add Slide 6. Use the layout called "Title and Content." You have to scroll down a ways to find it. Make the title "Recent Arson Series."

Step 2: Click on the "Insert Table" button (the first one) in the center of the slide. Make it four columns and five rows (Figure P-22).

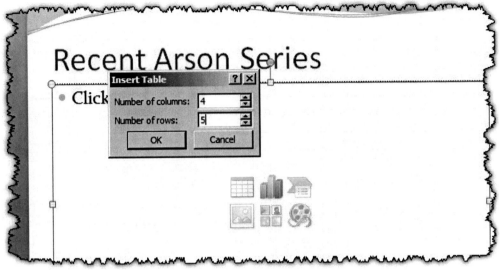

Figure P-22: inserting a table

Step 3: Fill in your table with the information in Figure P-23. Select the table by clicking on its border and change the font to 20-point Calibri.

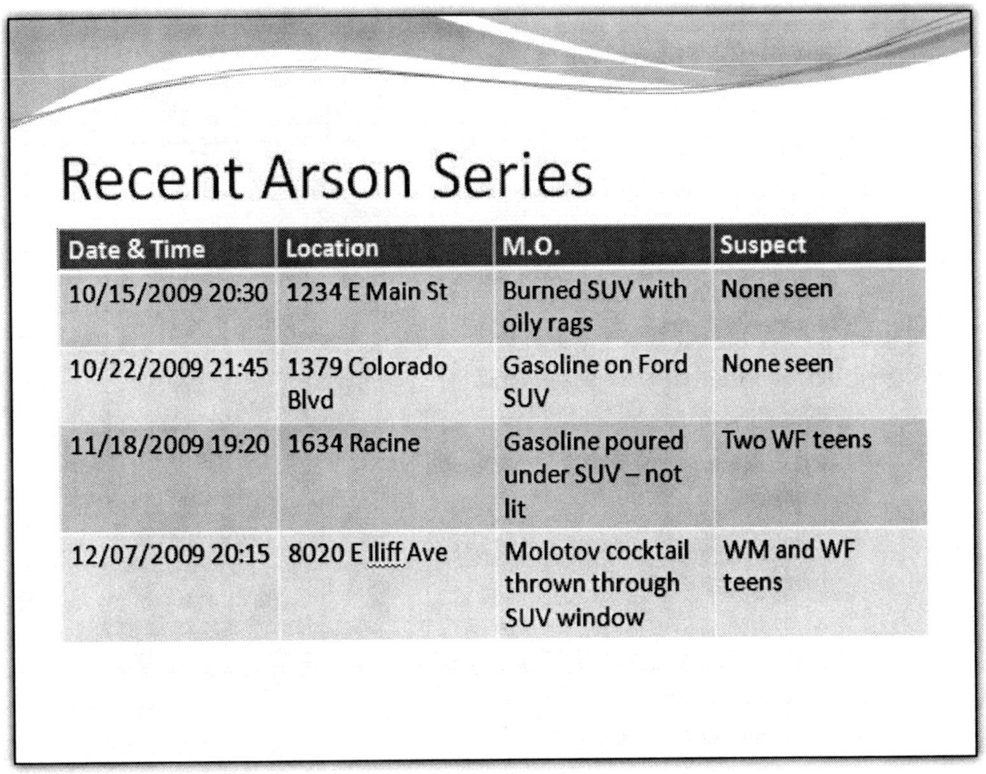

Recent Arson Series

Date & Time	Location	M.O.	Suspect
10/15/2009 20:30	1234 E Main St	Burned SUV with oily rags	None seen
10/22/2009 21:45	1379 Colorado Blvd	Gasoline on Ford SUV	None seen
11/18/2009 19:20	1634 Racine	Gasoline poured under SUV – not lit	Two WF teens
12/07/2009 20:15	8020 E Iliff Ave	Molotov cocktail thrown through SUV window	WM and WF teens

Figure P-23: a slide containing a table with arson series information

Slides with Images

Like Word, PowerPoint can accommodate a large variety of image formats, including .jpg, .gif, .tif, and .bmp images. Images can be copied and pasted into PowerPoint from almost any source, including Web pages, and PowerPoint shares Microsoft's Clip Art gallery. PowerPoint also has the same Picture tools as Word, meaning images can be adjusted for brightness and contrast, rotated, resized, and cropped.

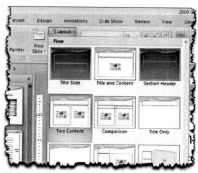

Figure P-24: a two-content layout

Step 1: Choose **Home | Slides | New Slide**. At Home | Slides | Layout, choose "Two Content." Title the slide "Crime at Christmas."

Step 2: In the content section on the right, click on the "Clip Art" button (bottom middle). In the search box, search for "Christmas" and choose any image that appeals to you (we chose the Santa Claus head). Enlarge the picture to take up more space on the right of the slide.

Step 3: In the left content area, where it says "Click to add text," add the following bullet points:

- Pocketpicking increased in Metropolis Square

- Thefts from cars were epidemic at the Metropolis Mall

- Extra security at Shrek's reduced shoplifting

- Violent purse snatching pattern identified downtown

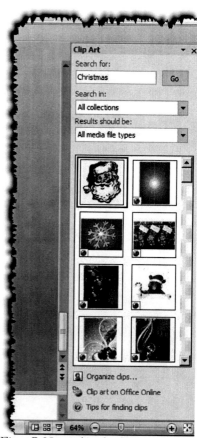

Figure P-25: searching for clip art

Increase the borders of the text box and adjust the font as you desire. When finished, your slide should look like Figure P-26.

Figure P-26: a finished slide with two content: text and clip art

Organizational Charts

PowerPoint comes with a pre-defined templates called "SmartArt" for things like organization charts, lists, pyramids, Venn diagrams, and other special layouts of text and graphics.

> **Step 1:** Choose **Home | Slides | New Slide** and at **Home | Slides | Layout**, choose "Title and Content." Title the slide "Downtown Pocketpicking Gang."

> **Step 2:** In the content section, click on the "Insert SmartArt Graphic" button (third on the top row).

> **Step 3:** Click around in the dialog box (Figure P-27) to see some of the different SmartArt graphics available to you. When you're done exploring, click on the "Hierarchy" category on the left and choose the first option: "Organization Chart."

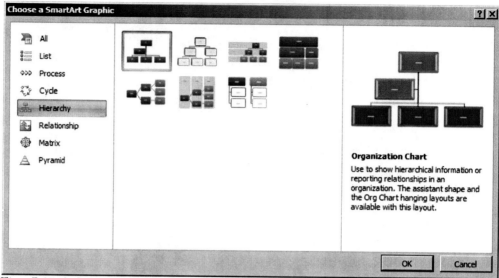

Figure P-27: the SmartArt gallery

A basic organization chart appears in your slide along with an Organization Chart panel to help you automatically organize the people on your chart. Indent people beneath other people with the **TAB** key to create different levels of individuals within the organization.

Step 4: Organize your pocketpicking gang as in Figure P-28.

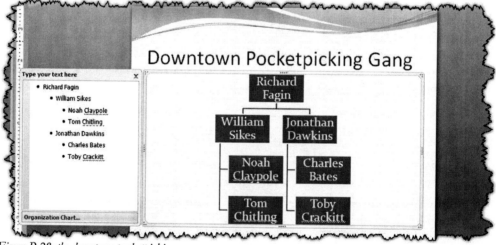

Figure P-28: the downtown pocketpicking gang

Step 5: Change the colors and styles to match your preferences. You can do it manually at **Home | <u>Font</u>** and **SmartArt Tools | Format | <u>Shape Styles</u>**, or you can have PowerPoint do it for you at **SmartArt Tools | Design | <u>Layouts</u>** and **SmartArt Tools | Design | <u>SmartArtStyles</u>**.

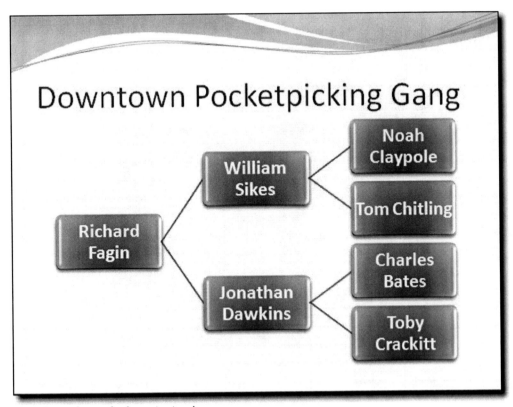

Figure P-29: the completed organization chart

Media Slides

The final type of slide allows us to add various media—images, videos, and sounds.

> **Step 1:** Choose **Home | <u>Slides</u> | New Slide**. Choose the "Title and Content" layout. Title it, "Smash & Grab Suspects."

> **Step 2:** In the content area, click on the "Insert Media Clip" button. Browse to **C:\BPOffice\PowerPoint\brick.wmv** and "OK" to insert it. When PowerPoint asks how you want the movie to start in the slide show, choose "When Clicked."

> **Step 3:** Enlarge the size of the video by clicking and dragging one of the handles in the corners.

Figure P-30 shows the completed slide. You will see the video when you run the presentation.

Figure P-30: a completed media slide

Other Slide Layouts and Drawings

We have explored several of the slide layout types available in PowerPoint. Though the slide layouts are helpful, it is important to remember that you are not limited to them. You can choose a "Blank" layout every time, and add your own text and objects using the "Text Box" tool at **Insert | Text | Text Box**, the objects at **Insert | Illustrations**, and the other selections from the **Insert** tab. You can choose layouts but later delete the helpful "Click here to…" elements.

Figure P-31: the Insert tab has all of the tools you need to design your own slide layouts

We will explore how to create a slide on our own with these features. In the example in Figure P-33, we use combinations of rectangles, ovals, shapes, and block arrows to create a "flow chart" indicating the progression of a crime problem.

Step 1: Choose **Home | <u>Slides</u> | New Slide**. Select a "Title Only" layout and title the slide "Health Club Theft Problem."

Step 2: Use the tools at **Insert | <u>Illustrations</u> | Shapes** tools to replicate the diagram in Figure P-33. You will find the shapes you need under the "Basic Shapes," "Stars and Banners," and "Block Arrows" headings. Just click on the shapes and start typing to add text.

Step 3: Use the tools at **Drawing Tools | Format | <u>Shape Styles</u>** to give the shapes the color that you desire, and the tools at **Home | <u>Font</u>** to adjust the text. You can also right-click on the shapes and choose "Format Shape" for more options.

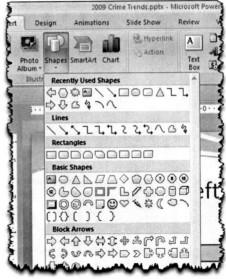

Figure P-32: some of the drawing options available

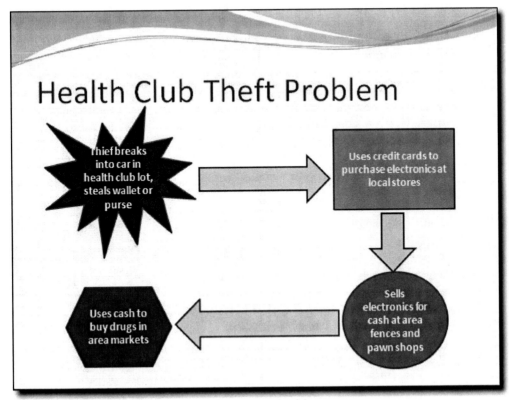

Figure P-33: liberal use of illustrations can produce an attractive slide

You can "Group" different drawing objects on a slide so that they move and re-size as a single object. To do so, hold down the **SHIFT** key while clicking on each object, then click on **Drawing Tools | Format | <u>Arrange</u> | Group**.

Notes

Below each slide in Normal view, PowerPoint displays a "Notes" pane, in which you can annotate each slide. This capability is useful for several reasons.

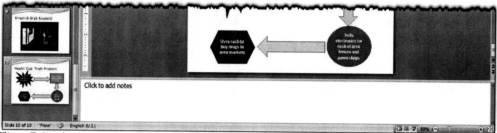

Figure P-34: the notes box

- Some speakers prefer to use a printed copy of their presentation as a guide when speaking. PowerPoint allows you to print the slides with the notes, so you will have them in front of you when you speak.

- When you run the presentation (see "Giving the Presentation" below), you can set it up to show you a normal view on your laptop, including your notes, but a presentation view on the projector.

- You may want to offer your slides, along with the notes, as a handout to your audience. Annotating each slide allows audience members to recall the meaning and context of the visual aids depicted on your slides.

- Many conference presenters are asked to provide electronic copies of their presentations for a CD or web site. Here, again, extensive, clear notes can serve as a surrogate for your actual presentation.

Step 1: Use the slide organizer to the left (Figure P-35) or press the **Page Up** key to find the slide titled "Increase in Robberies."

Figure P-35: the slide organizer helps you quickly find the slide you want

Step 2: Add this note to the "Notes" box below the slide:

As this graph shows, robberies were actually average or low until August of this year, when they began to climb. September, October, November, and December were all significantly higher than average. Part of this increase is explained by the prolific downtown purse snatching pattern that affected holiday shoppers.

Feel free to add notes to other slides for later printing.

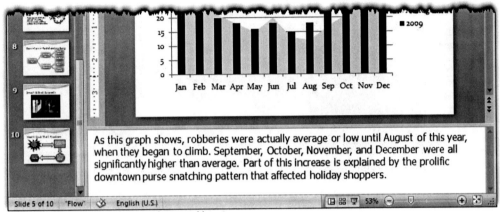

Figure P-36: a note of explanation for our robbery increase

Extensive notes can stop an otherwise well-intentioned speaker from trying to cram too much information on a slide. By reminding yourself of key points, anecdotes, and emphasis in the notes, rather than on the slide, you keep your slides sparse and clean.

Notes can also be added in the "Notes Page" view , which we cover in the next section.

Views

So far, we have been working in PowerPoint in the "Normal" view, which shows the slide organizer, the slide, and the notes, unless you have chosen to close these items. If you have, you can restore them by choosing **View | Presentation Views | Normal**.

There are six other views: three presentation views and three "master" views. The masters allow you to set the default fonts and styles for the slides in the presentation, and we cover those below. The "Slide Show" view actually stars the slide show, and we'll cover that in a few sections. It's worth briefly exploring the other two.

"Slide Sorter" (Figure P-38) shows you a snapshot of all the slides in your presentation. In this view, you can easily re-arrange your slides by dragging them around, or by cutting or copying and pasting them. This view makes it simple to copy and paste slides among two or more presentations. Here, you can also easily delete slides with the **Delete** key, **Home | Slides | New Slide** in between existing ones, and set slide transition schemes.

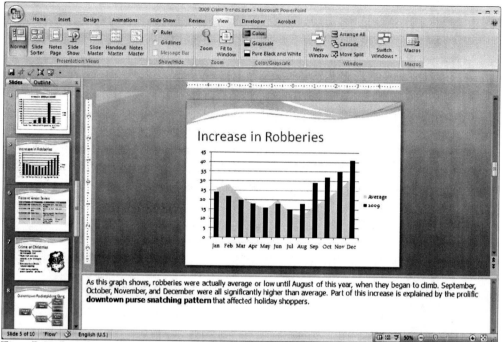

Figure P-37: PowerPoint's "Normal" view, with the slide organizer, slide, and notes

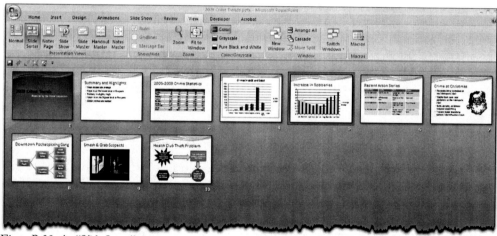

Figure P-38: the "Slide Sorter" view

Double-clicking on a slide in the slide sorter brings you to the slide in its "Normal" view.

Viewing the "Notes Page" (Figure P-39) allows for more extensive editing of notes. You have a larger, sizable box, to which you can modify the text formatting at **Home | Font**. Printing the notes pages also produces reasonably good handouts if your notes are extensive enough.

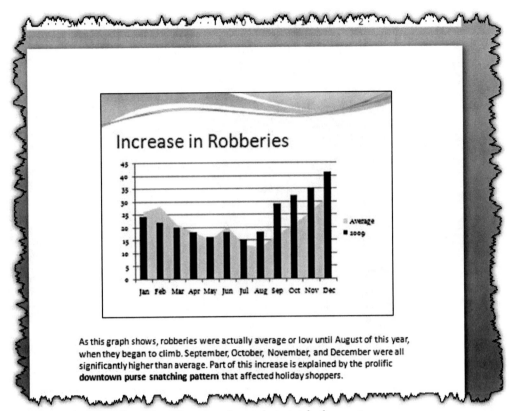

Figure P-39: the "Notes Page" view allows you to format the text style of your notes

The Masters

As you added each text box and title to the presentation, you found that these fonts and styles were already chosen for you. With the "Flow" theme, the default title font is Calibri, 50-point, dark teal; the default text font is Constantia, 26-point black. Of course, you can use the **Home | Font** to change this font, but it only applies to the current slide. What if you want to change this formatting for all your slides?

Also available from **View | Presentation Views** is the ability to change the "master" style for your slides, handouts, and notes pages. By choosing **View | Presentation Views | Slide Master**, for instance, you see the underlying template used for each slide layout. Here you can change the fonts, add background images that you want to appear on each slide, and so on. Have you ever seen a presentation in which the presenter seems to have created the slide design himself? This is where he did it.

Note that changes that you make to the "master" apply only to this presentation, not to the design template it based itself on. To change the template permanently, you would have to open it in PowerPoint from **Office Button | Open**.

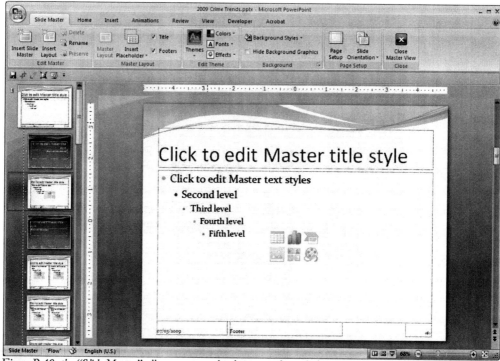

Figure P-40: the "Slide Master" allows you to make changes to the underlying design template

The "Handout Master" and "Notes Master" options allow you to make changes, albeit more limited, to the appearance of handouts and notes.

Animation

PowerPoint offers an enormous range of options for animating text, images, charts, and other elements in your slides. Most of it is wholly unnecessary for the average presentation. In the early days of PowerPoint, it was not uncommon to attend a conference and see slide shows given by presenters intoxicated with the novelty of PowerPoint animation. Text would appear one letter at a time, flying in from all corners of the screen, accompanied by sounds of lasers or typewriter clacks. Photographs flew in and out to the harsh nose of screeching tires. For emphasis, certain words twirled around, got bigger, got bolder, and so on. This all got old very fast.

The best animation is subtle, and it happens for a reason, not for its own sake. The most valid reason is to bring in elements one at a time so that the presenter can explain them in the order that he or she prefers, with the appropriate emphasis.

Step 1: Use the slide organizer or the **Page Up/Page Down** keys to return to the slide titled "Summary and Highlights."

Here is a slide that does not require, but would not suffer from, some basic animation. There are four bullet points. To keep the audience members thinking about the current point, the presenter does not want to display them all at once, but rather one at a time, as he's ready to talk about them.

Step 2: Choose **Animations | Animations | Custom Animation**. The "Custom Animation" box (Figure P-41) pane appears to the right.

Step 3: Select the text box containing the four bullet points. The "Add Effect" button becomes available. Click it and choose "Entrance" and then "Appear"

At this point a couple things happen. First, an animation appears in the animation list in the "Custom Animation" task pane (as in Figure P-41). Second, the numbers 1 through 5 appear next to the bullet points in your text box, indicating the order in which the four paragraphs will "Appear."

Figure P-41: the Custom Animation pane

A host of options are now available involving the animation we just added. Let's cover them briefly.

Step 4: Select the animation #1 listed in the "Custom Animation" box ("Content Placeholder").

The "Add Effect" button will change to "Change," indicating that we can choose a different effect. There are also a few options in the "Start" field, and more available in the drop-down box next to the animation itself.

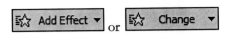

Effects describe the way in which the text, picture, or other element is introduced onto the screen. "Appear," the one we chose, means simply that: the text simply appears. Other options include "blinds," "box," "checkerboard," "fly in," and "wipe." The "More Effects" option gives you the entire range (Figure P-42). It is difficult to illustrate each of these in a printed text, so we encourage that you test them out. Just select them and watch what happens. If you need to see the animation again, click the "Play" button at the bottom of the "Custom Animation" box.

In addition to "Entrance" effects, you can choose "Emphasis" effects that change the style of the text, and "Exit" effects that remove the text from the screen.

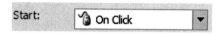

The "Start" box allows you to specify what *causes* the animation to happen. The default is "on click"—it happens when you click the mouse button or hit **Page Down**. The other options are "With Previous"—two objects animated at the same time—and "After Previous"—animation at a specific time after the previous animation (if it is the first animation, it is a specific time after the slide appears).

There are final options under the "drop-down" menu to the right of the animation (Figure P-43). The most important of these is the "Effect Options" selection, which brings up the dialog box shown in Figure P-47. Here, you can set additional options, such as sound and "dimming" (which hides or diminishes each text item after the animation), and whether the text animation applies to the entire text box, or each paragraph, word, or letter at a time.

Multiple Animations per Slide

You can run multiple animations in succession.

> **Step 1:** Return to the last slide ("Health Club Theft Problem"), shown in Figure P-33.

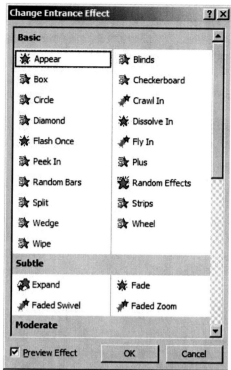

Figure P-42: the full selection of animation options available

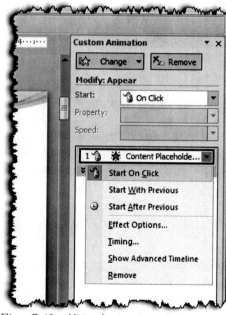

Figure P-43: additional animation options

This slide has a natural flow, which makes it perfect for a custom animation.

Step 2: Click on each object in the order of the "flow," starting with "Thief breaks into car…" Click on "Add Effect" for each one, choosing effects natural to the shapes. For the explosion, square, circle, and hexagon, "box," "checkerboard," "diamond" work well. For the arrows, use a "wipe." This option brings up two supplemental options— "Direction" and "Speed" (Figure P-48). Choose a "Direction" suitable to the arrow.

Figure P-44: the "wipe" effect has two additional options

Step 3: Now select each object that occurs *after* an arrow, click the "Start" box, and change it from "On Click" to "After Previous." You'll see the numbers change to reflect the fewer clicks necessary to run the animations. When you're finished, your screen should resemble Figure P-45.

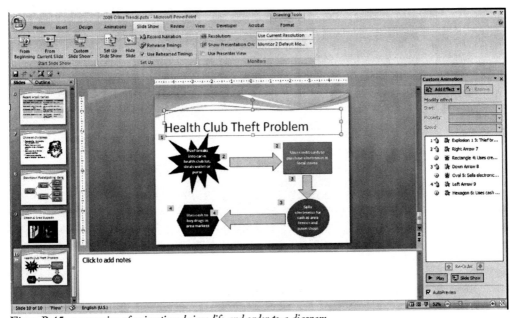

Figure P-45: a succession of animations brings life and order to a diagram

Step 4: Click Slide **Show | Start Slide Show | From Current Slide** (or **SHIFT-F5**) to give it a try. Click through your animations. When finished, press the **ESC** key.

Slide Transition

Not only can you animate objects on slides, you can also animate the transition between slides. Slide transition isn't terribly *necessary*, but it can provide an interesting visual effect when there is a true natural transition between slides (e.g., when a map of a large area gives way to a focused map of a highlighted section). We caution against using it for all your slides, but if you do, it's best to stick with a single transition style rather than experimenting with all of them in a single presentation.

Figure P-46: slide transition options

> **Step 1:** Choose **View | Presentation Views | Slide Sorter**.
>
> **Step 2:** Select the second slide. **Choose Animations | Transition to This Slide** and click the drop-down button to the right of the different transition themes.
>
> **Step 3:** The available slide transitions appear in your task pane. Click through them to see a preview of what they do. Select one and use **SHIFT-F5** to see it in action.

Animating Charts

A final type of animation allows you to add effects to charts. This is actually a very useful type of animation: many viewers will be puzzled by a complex chart simply thrown on the screen: while you're trying to explain what it depicts, they're staring at it with a furrowed brow. But if you introduce the chart elements one at a time, the chart becomes easier to understand.

> **Step 1:** Return to the "Increase in Robberies" slide (Figure P-21), either by double-clicking on it in Slide Sorter view or by paging to it if already in Normal view.
>
> **Step 2:** Choose **Animations | Animations | Custom Animation** and select the chart. Click the "Add Effect" button. For the "Entrance," choose a "Wipe" effect, and in the "Direction" box, choose "From Left."

At this point, you will have an animation that applies to the entire chart, but we're going to change it to apply to one data series at a time.

Step 3: Click on the drop-down menu next to the "Content Placeholder" animation in the list. Select "Effect Options" (Figure P-47). Click the "Chart Animation" tab and change the "Group chart" box from "As one object" to "By series" and then "OK."

Step 4: An arrow appears beneath the "Content Placeholder" ⚡. Click the arrow to reveal the second data series. Click the second and third entries, one at a time, and change the "Speed" from "Very Fast" to "Slow" (Figure P-49). Now run the "Slide Show" to see the result.

This animation allows you to explain what the "average" number of robberies per month means, before you introduce the 2009 data.

Action Settings

Sometimes while giving a presentation, you may want to open another file, run a program, play a sound, or hyperlink to a web site. One way to accomplish this is to simply interrupt the presentation with the **ESC** key and open the appropriate file. But a more professional way is to link to the needed file from within the PowerPoint presentation.

Enter Action Settings. With action settings, you can tell PowerPoint to...

- Hyperlink to a web site, a file, or another slide in the presentation
- Run a program

Figure P-47: changing the effect options for the chart.

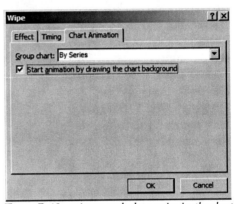

Figure P-48: animate each data series in the chart separately

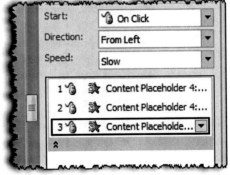

Figure P-49: now you can set separate animations for the "area" section and the "column" section

- Run a macro
- Edit or open the object (suitable for embedded charts, Word documents, Excel spreadsheets, and so on)
- Play a sound

...either when you click on the object, or when you move your mouse over the object.

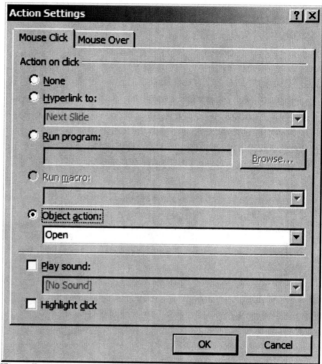

Often, objects or text in your slides will present themselves as obvious places to insert an action setting. If you have a URL for a web site, for instance, it makes sense to tell PowerPoint to link to the site when you click on it. But in case you don't have a ready-made object, you can insert one of PowerPoint's "Action Buttons" from **Insert | Illustrations | Shapes**, and set the animation to run when it is clicked.

Figure P-50: setting an action setting

We'll chose a simple action for our "Crimes in 2008 and 2009" chart (the fourth slide in the presentation).

> **Step 1:** Find the slide with the "Crimes in 2008 and 2009" chart. Select the chart and choose **Insert | Links | Action**. Select "Object" action and choose "Open" (Figure P-50). Then click "OK."

> **Step 2:** Run the slide show by choosing **SHIFT-F5**. Click forward to the Chart, and then click *on* the chart (your cursor will change to an index finger). Excel should launch, allowing you to show the underlying statistics. When you're ready to go back to your slide show, simply exit the spreadsheet.

There is an alternate, and faster, way to establish a simple hyperlink within a presentation: select the object or text and choose **Insert | Links | Hyperlink**. You can hyperlink to a web page, a file on your computer, another slide, or even (somewhat absurdly) an e-mail address.

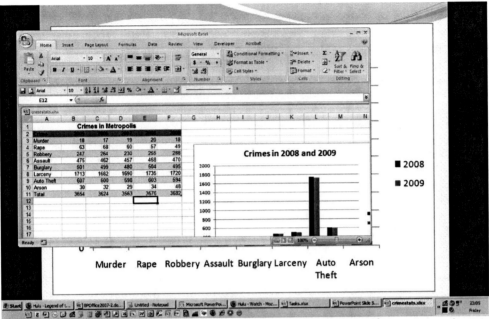

Figure P-51: with action settings, you can, among other things, open a program from within your presentation

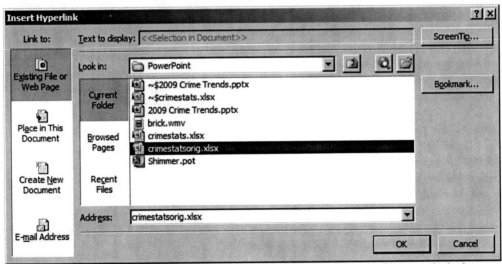

Figure P-52: an alternate way to insert a hyperlink. Note the "E-mail address" option. If you can think of a reason to e-mail someone while giving a PowerPoint presentation, please let us know.

Giving the Presentation

After you've finished designing all the slides, animating what you want to animate, setting your slide transitions, and including action settings, you're ready to give the presentation. We've already done a few lessons where we've switched to the actual "Slide Show" view, which is accomplished by choosing **Slide Show | Start Slide Show** or typing **F5**.

When you switch to Slide Show view, the slides fill your screen and block out all other windows, the system tray, the taskbar, the shortcut bar, the "Start" menu, and so on. You navigate through the slides with your keyboard and mouse buttons:

Left mouse button, **Page Down**, **Enter**, left arrow, down arrow, space bar, "N" key	Advance to the next animation or, if no animations (or no more animations), the next slide
Page Up, **Backspace**, "P" key, left arrow, up arrow	Returns to the previous animation or, if no previous animation, the previous slide
Home key	Jumps to the first slide. Nervous (or clumsy) presenters sometimes hit it while going for "Page Up."
End key	Jumps to the last slide. See above.
Typed number (will now show on screen) followed by **Enter**	Jumps to that specific slide
"W" key or comma	Whites/unwhites the screen
"B" key or period	Blacks/unblacks the screen
Esc	Cancels the slide show
F1	Shows these and other keyboard options

Right-clicking or clicking on the presentation options button (Figure P-53) in the lower left corner (very faint) will bring up a menu of different presentation options. These include viewing the speaker notes (keeping in mind that unless you can first "freeze" the projector screen, your audience will see your notes with you) and changing the pointer options.

One of the pointer options, a pen, allows you to draw on your presentation (the "Slide Show" version only; the drawing disappears when you exit the presentation), which is a nice idea, but often difficult to control with the mouse (Figure P-54). If you know ahead of time that you'll want to call attention to part of a slide, a better solution is to add and animate a oval drawing object.

Previous versions of PowerPoint unceremoniously dumped you back to your desktop when your presentation was done, but the current version includes a black "End of slide show" slide. It's still better to design your own final slide with parting words and your contact information.

Figure P-53: the presentation options button and menu

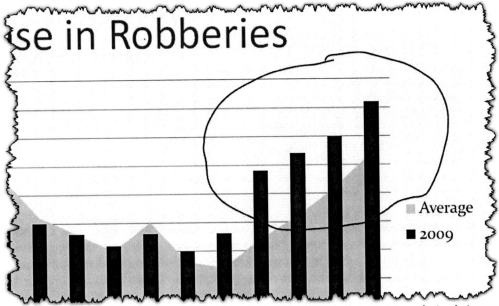

Figure P-54: the on-screen pen allows you to circle…well, kind of…items that you want to emphasize during your presentation

There are other options you can set for giving your presentation by choosing **Slide Show | Set Up | Set Up Slide Show**. We will cover some of them under "Automating Presentations" below, but one vital one for this section is the "Display slide show on" option, where you can choose to display the show on a secondary monitor. This option allows you to see the slide show in Normal view, including any notes, on your own computer while the audience sees the presentation in Slide Show view.

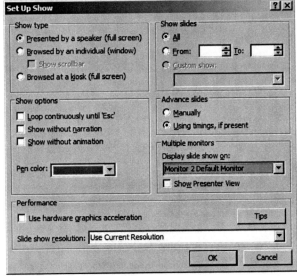

Figure P-55: show set-up options

Automating Presentations

You can automate a presentation for someone to view at his or her own computer, for web sites, for public terminals, and for when you decide to play golf instead of attending your own conference session.

Automation can come in two forms: with narration and without. To record without narration, choose **Slide Show | Set Up | Rehearse Timings**. The slide show will begin, and you can pause as long as you think is desirable between animations and slides.

Figure P-56: the Rehearsal toolbar

(This option is helpful not only to automate the presentation but also for you to time it for an in-person presentation.) As you rehearse, a Rehearsal toolbar appears, showing both the amount of time you have spent on the current slide, and the total time of the presentation. When you finish the presentation, PowerPoint will ask you if you want to save the timings. If you say "Yes," you will be able to see the per-slide time in the Slide Sorter view, and when you run the presentation again, it will advance according to the timing that you already recorded.

Narration works similarly. You begin by choosing **Slide Show | Set Up | Record Narration** (you must have a microphone installed). After setting the technical settings, "OK" begins the show. Speak in a normal tone of voice and advanced naturally through the slides. When you are finished, PowerPoint will save both your narration and the slide timings.

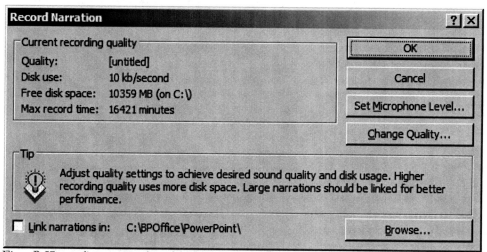

Figure P-57: recording narration for a slide show

You can also set timings manually by switching to Slide Sorter, selecting the slide, and setting the "Advance Slide…automatically After:" setting at **Animations | Transition to This Slide**.

To finish automating both narrated and non-narrated shows, choose **Slide Show | Set Up | Set Up Show** (Figure P-55), where you can indicate how the presentation will be delivered, whether to automatically loop it back to the beginning when done, whether to include the animation and narration, and other various settings.

Printing and Handouts

If a PowerPoint presentation is designed properly, someone simply looking at the slides should not be able to understand it—a human presenter (or recorded narration) should have to be present. For this reason, we are often reluctant to hand out copies of the presentation by itself. Better to create a separate outline, article, or other document designed specifically to *be* a handout. Nevertheless, audiences seem to want copies of presentations, and sometimes it's best to accommodate them.

PowerPoint offers several options for printing slides and handouts, found under **Office Button | Print** (Figure P-58). Here you have four main options, under "Print what":

- **Slides:** prints the slides, one per page, just as they are

- **Handouts:** prints multiple slides per page, between 1 and 9. If you choose 3, the most popular option, PowerPoint will insert some lines next to each slide, allowing audience members to jot their own notes next to the applicable slides

- **Notes Pages:** prints one slide per page, along with any speaker notes written

- **Outline View**: prints a basic outline of the presentation. This only works if you designed each slide carefully, with the appropriate headers and bullet points.

For each selection, you have the option to print in "Color" or "Grayscale"—the latter is recommended when printing on a black & white printer—or "Pure Black & White," which will change the look of your slides considerably.

A good option to create a true "handout" is to use the "notes" box on each slide not to write speaker's notes, but to write an explanation for a reader. Then print and hand outs the "Notes Pages." In **View | Presentation Views | Notes Master**, you can lay out these handout pages exactly how you want, including some space for audience members to write their own notes.

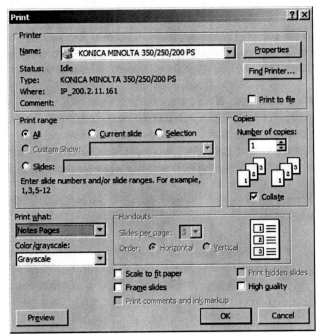

Figure P-58: choosing what to print

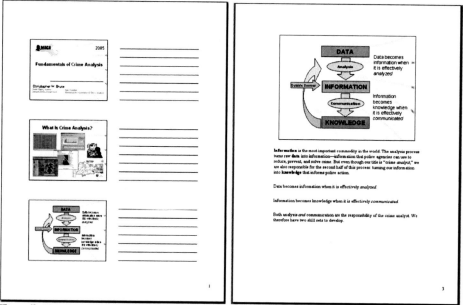

Figure P-59: printing a three-slide-per-page handout (left) and a notes page (right)

Taking It to the Next Level: Good Presentations

With the exception of Slide Libraries (be sure to explore them if you give a lot of presentations), there are few features of PowerPoint that we did not cover in this chapter. Therefore, we will use this section to offer tips on better presentation design and delivery.

Microsoft PowerPoint may be both the best and worst thing to happen to professional presentations. When used effectively, it brings clarity, attractiveness, and excitement to presentations, and it remains the best way to show visual aids. On the other hand, audience after audience has been subjected to "PowerPoint poisoning" in which dozens of slides of too much text and too many animations have been displayed.

These tips should better enable you to use PowerPoint to create truly effective presentations: *

- Consider carefully whether you truly need to use PowerPoint for a particular presentation. Some material is better delivered with standard speeches, hands-on workshops, physical exhibits, and in other formats.

---

* For more information on effective PowerPoint presentations, and effective presentations in general, we highly recommend two brief and entertaining articles by Dr. Jerry Ratcliffe, available at www.jratcliffe.net/papers/ index.htm. These are "Jerry's Top Ten PowerPoint Tips" and "Jerry's Top Ten Presentation Tips." We are indebted to these articles for some of the tips that follow.

- If you do use PowerPoint, consider that you do not need a slide for every point that you want to make in your presentation. Use anecdotes, exhibits, hands-on lessons, group projects, skits, web sites, and other media to best convey your point.

- When you do use a slide to illustrate a point, you do not have to include all the words you want to say on the slide. Remember, slides are there to provide visual aids and to assist in note-taking, not to serve as a substitute for an actual presentation. If a member of your audience needs only to view your PowerPoint to understand your key points, you are including too much in your presentation.

- To better make use of the tips above, consider designing your entire presentation, including all points you want to make and all media that you want to use, *before* you even open PowerPoint.

- Avoid bright colors for your slide backgrounds. Your audience will have to stare at your presentation for a while. Use a darker color background (with light-colored text) to better soothe their eyes.

- Stick with sans serif fonts. If a projector has a bad or failing bulb, it may have trouble displaying the serifs.

- If you do use PowerPoint for a presentation, try to drive all of your other audio/visual media from within the presentation. Embed videos and sounds. If you need to open a web site or other files, hyperlink to them from within the PowerPoint slides. Constantly shifting in and out of PowerPoint in the middle of your presentation is distracting.

- Generally do not go below a 24-point text size. The specific limit will depend on the size of the projection screen and the distance from the screen to the audience. Try to get a look at the room where you will be giving the presentation ahead of time and make adjustments accordingly.

- Similarly, do not use images or charts that your audience will not be able to see. If you have to say, "I know you can't really read this, but this chart shows…" (something we have heard in dozens of presentations), there's no point inserting the chart.

- Maintain continuity in fonts, colors, and styles throughout your presentation.

- Avoid complexity in your animation unless you have a specific reason for it. Use animation when necessary, and use subtle effects.

- Have the presentation running and the title slide on screen before the audience enters the room.

- Even if you are giving a stock presentation that you have given before, give the audience the illusion that you created the presentation uniquely for them. Design your title slide to include the logo of the organization that you're presenting to, and consider including the date. Avoid words like, "When I gave this same presentation last month…" during your presentation.

- Do not use a PowerPoint presentation as a handout. Design something specifically as a handout. One halfway-in-between option is to type lecture notes in the "Notes" section and print the notes pages as a handout.

- When giving the presentation, make the PowerPoint support you, not the other way around. Start making the point on each slide before switching to the slide. Avoid the pause-advance-look-speak process that makes many presentations look amateur. (This is when the speaker finishes a point, pauses, advances to the next slide, turns and looks at the slide, and then starts speaking about the point made by that slide.)

- Avoid looking at the screen during your presentation. Position the computer running the presentation between you and the audience, and look at that instead. Use the options under **Slide Show | <u>Set Up</u> | Set Up Slide Show** to see your notes on the screen if you want; otherwise, use index cards to make sure you cover your key points.

- Invest in a presentation remote so you can leave the immediate area of your computer. Avoid overuse of the laser pointer, though.

In short, use PowerPoint to enhance your presentation, not to control it. With these rules in mind, you and PowerPoint are an excellent presentation team.

CONCLUSION

The Capabilities You Now Have

Whether you began this book with a beginning or intermediate knowledge of Microsoft Office 2007, we expect that you now know more than you did at the start. Now it's time to apply that knowledge. As much as we've covered in these hundreds of pages, there are thousands of pages that we could have written but did not. The capabilities of Microsoft Office's applications are vast. Troll through the aisles of your local bookstore and you'll find 1000-page books about Access or Excel alone!

Your skill with computer applications, much like your skill with any other tool, will be honed by *doing*. The best a book can do is help lay a foundation. It's up to you, now, to build on that foundation. Use these techniques until they become routine. Explore ribbon tabs and "Help" files. See what happens when you double-click on something. Try a new formula or function. Most important, share your discoveries with your colleagues.

Microsoft Office applications help businesses analyze data, communicate information, and save time. To a private company, these results are vital to its "bottom line." The same is true in policing, but our "bottom line" is better public safety. Effective use of these products means better policing, and better policing means improved public safety. We wish you the best in your efforts.

Index

About the Authors

Christopher W. Bruce started his crime analysis career at the Cambridge (MA) Police Department Crime Analysis Unit in 1994, and moved to the Danvers (MA) Police Department in 2001. He became President of the International Association of Crime Analysts (IACA) in 2007 after serving six years as Vice President of Administration. He was also President of the Massachusetts Association of Crime Analysts (MACA) between 2000 and 2004 He served as the senior editor for the IACA's 2004 publication, *Exploring Crime Analysis*.

Bruce frequently teaches Microsoft Office (and Access in particular), as well as other crime analysis topics, at various venues in the U.S. and other countries. He has lectured at ten IACA conferences, twelve MACA conferences, and many other regional crime analysis conferences. He has taught crime mapping and analysis for the Crime Mapping and Analysis Program (CMAP) at the National Law Enforcement and Corrections Technology Center (NLECTC), and he is a lecturer for Suffolk University, Tiffin University, the University of Massachusetts at Lowell, and Westfield State College.

Mark Stallo joined the Dallas Police Department in October 1979. In August of 1985, he was promoted to sergeant and assigned to work three different patrol stations on the night shift. In November of 1988, he transferred to the planning division where he was responsible for the Crime Analysis Team until September 2004. Today he serves as the supervisor for the Identity Theft Squad. In 1990, he worked with a group of individuals to create the International Association of Crime Analysis (IACA). He was Vice-President of Membership of IACA from 1991–1994 and was President of the organization from 1994 to October 2000. Mark has been involved in a number of projects including technical assistance, teaching, and steering committees, including the National Institute of Justice, the Police Executive Research Forum (PERF), the SEARCH group, the National Law Enforcement and Corrections Technology Center (NLECTC), the FBI National Academy and the Southwest Law Enforcement Institute. Mark has consulted for the Government of Argentina on developing a crime analysis program for six of the largest provinces. He has also conducted training for the University of Bucharest and the University of the West in Romania. Mark has also had the pleasure of teaching a number of crime analysts in Trinidad and Tobago. He has authored or co-authored a number of articles and two anthologies "Contemporary Issues, Applications and Techniques in Crime Analysis" and "Texas Crime and Texas Justice." He has authored or co-authored the following books: "Better Policing with Microsoft Office," "Using Microsoft Office to Improve Law Enforcement Operations" and "Using Geographic Information Systems in Law Enforcement." Mark holds a B. S. in Criminal Justice from the University of Cincinnati, a M.S. in Management and Administrative Science, a Master of Public Affairs and a PhD from The University of Texas at Dallas.